The Habsburg Monarchy, 1815–1918

This clear and compelling account of the Habsburg Monarchy in its last century explains why, a century after its disappearance, it has never been more relevant. With extensive discussion of recent historiographic controversies about the Monarchy's character and viability, Steven Beller presents a detailed account of the main strands of the Monarchy's political history and how its economic, social and cultural development interacted with this main narrative. While recognising the importance of these larger trends, readers will learn how the historical accident of personality and the complexities of high politics and diplomacy still had a central impact on the Monarchy's fate.

Although some would see the Monarchy as an atavistic irrelevance in the modern age, its multicultural, multinational experience and inclusive 'logic' were in many ways more relevant to our modernity than the nationalism that did so much to bring about its demise.

Steven Beller is an independent scholar, having studied history at the University of Cambridge, and been a Research Fellow at Peterhouse, Cambridge. He has been a Member of the Institute for Advanced Study in Princeton, and a Fellow of the Institute for the Human Sciences (IWM), Vienna, as well as the International Research Centre for Cultural Studies (IFK), also in Vienna. He has written extensively on subjects in modern Central European and modern Jewish history and was awarded the Austrian State History Prize for the German translation of his first book *Vienna and the Jews, 1867–1938: A Cultural History* (Cambridge, 1989) in 1995. Other books include *Herzl* (1991); *Francis Joseph* (1996); *A Concise History of Austria* (Cambridge, 2006); *Antisemitism: A Very Short Introduction* (2007, 2015); and *Democracy* (2013). He is a member of the European Academy of Sciences and Arts and has taught modern European and modern Jewish history.

New Approaches to European History

Series editors

T.C.W. Blanning, *Sidney Sussex College, Cambridge*
Brendan Simms, *Peterhouse, Cambridge*

New Approaches to European History is an important textbook series, which provides concise but authoritative surveys of major themes and problems in European history since the Renaissance. Written at a level and length accessible to advanced school students and undergraduates, each book in the series addresses topics or themes that students of European history encounter daily: the series embraces both some of the more 'traditional' subjects of study and those cultural and social issues to which increasing numbers of school and college courses are devoted. A particular effort is made to consider the wider international implications of the subject under scrutiny.

To aid the student reader, scholarly apparatus and annotation is light, but each work has full supplementary bibliographies and notes for further reading: where appropriate, chronologies, maps, diagrams and other illustrative material are also provided.

For a complete list of titles published in the series, please see:
www.cambridge.org/newapproaches.

The Habsburg Monarchy, 1815–1918

Steven Beller

Independent Scholar

CAMBRIDGE
UNIVERSITY PRESS

CAMBRIDGE
UNIVERSITY PRESS

University Printing House, Cambridge CB2 8BS, United Kingdom

One Liberty Plaza, 20th Floor, New York, NY 10006, USA

477 Williamstown Road, Port Melbourne, VIC 3207, Australia

314–321, 3rd Floor, Plot 3, Splendor Forum, Jasola District Centre, New Delhi – 110025, India

79 Anson Road, #06–04/06, Singapore 079906

Cambridge University Press is part of the University of Cambridge.

It furthers the University's mission by disseminating knowledge in the pursuit of education, learning, and research at the highest international levels of excellence.

www.cambridge.org
Information on this title: www.cambridge.org/9781107091894
DOI: 10.1017/9781316135679

First published 2018

Printed in the United Kingdom by TJ International Ltd. Padstow Cornwall

A catalogue record for this publication is available from the British Library.

Library of Congress Cataloging-in-Publication Data
Names: Beller, Steven, 1958– author.
Title: The Habsburg Monarchy 1815–1918 / Steven Beller, independent scholar.
Description: Cambridge ; New York, NY : Cambridge University Press, 2018. |
Series: New approaches to European history | Includes bibliographical references and index.
Identifiers: LCCN 2017055415 | ISBN 9781107091894 (hardback) | ISBN 9781107464742 (paperback)
Subjects: LCSH: Austria – History – 1789–1900. | Austria – History – 1867–1918. | Habsburg, House of.
Classification: LCC DB80 .B435 2018 | DDC 943.6/04–dc23
LC record available at https://lccn.loc.gov/2017055415

ISBN 978-1-107-09189-4 Hardback
ISBN 978-1-107-46474-2 Paperback

Contents

Figures

Maps

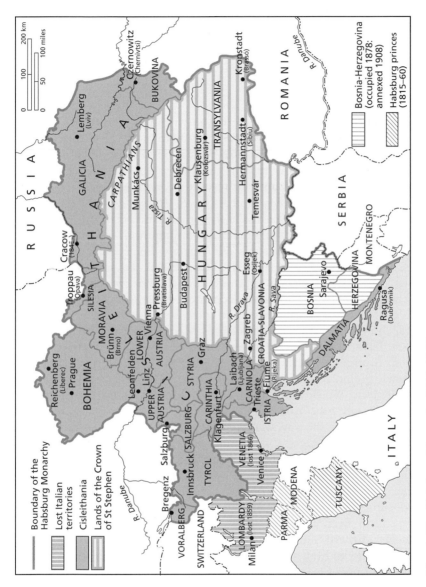

Map 1: The Habsburg Monarchy 1815–1918.

Boundary of the Habsburg Monarchy

Lost Italian territories

Cisleithania

Lands of the Crown of St Stephen

Bosnia-Herzegovina (occupied 1878; annexed 1908)

Habsburg princes (1815–60)

R. Danube

SWITZERLAND

VORALBERG

Bregenz

Innsbruck

TYRCL

Salzburg

SALZBURG

Leonfelden

Linz

UPPER AUSTRIA

LOWER AUSTRIA

Vienna

Brünn (Brno)

MORAVIA

SILESIA

Troppau (Opava)

Reichenberg (Liberec)

Prague

BOHEMIA

Cracow (Kraków)

Lemberg (Lviv)

GALICIA

RUSSIA

Czernowitz (Chernivtsi)

BUKOVINA

CARPATHIANS

LITHANIA

Munkács

Debrecen

Klausenburg (Kolozsvár)

TRANSYLVANIA

Kronstadt (Brasó)

Hermannstadt (Sibiu)

Temesvár

R. Tisza

HUNGARY

Budapest

Pressburg (Bratislava)

Graz

STYRIA

CARINTHIA

Klagenfurt

Laibach (Ljubljana)

CARNIOLA

Trieste

ISTRIA

Fiume (Rijeka)

Zagreb

CROATIA-SLAVONIA

Esseg (Osijek)

R. Drava

R. Sava

BOSNIA

Sarajevo

HERZEGOVINA

DALMATIA

Ragusa (Dubrovnik)

SERBIA

MONTENEGRO

ROMANIA

R. Danube

VENETIA (lost 1866)

Venice

LOMBARDY (lost 1859)

Milan

PARMA

MODENA

TUSCANY

ITALY

200 km

100

0

100 miles

50

0

Acknowledgements

I thank Tim Blanning for inviting me to write this 'sequel' to Charles W. Ingrao's *The Habsburg Monarchy 1618–1815* in the New Approaches to European History series. Ingrao's book is one I have much admired, and I regard it is an honour to write the 'follow-up'. I initially had some doubts about how *new* my approach would be, and readers of two of my previous books, *Francis Joseph* and *A Concise History of Austria*, will find many reminders of those here. On the other hand, Habsburg historiography has recently seen the publication of important, revisionist interpretations such as Pieter Judson's *The Habsburg Empire*, and other, older texts have rewarded closer study. This has all led me to some reevaluation, and hence a new approach after all. The format of this book does not facilitate detailed acknowledgement of the sources used, but this book could well be characterised as a conversation between my previous views, and those of revisionists such as Alan Sked, John Deak, Lothar Höbelt, István Deák, Gary Cohen and Judson, with Helmut Rumpler, Gerald Stourzh, Moritz Csaky, Heidemarie Uhl, Ernst Hanisch, Waltraud Heindl, Manfred Rauchensteiner, Claudio Magris, Jonathan Sperber, John W. Boyer, R.J.W. Evans, C.A. Macartney, Roy Bridge, Mark Cornwall and Norman Stone, offering their own points of order and information along the way, with comments by many, many others added into the mix. I only regret that I cannot acknowledge all more fully.

I am most grateful to Nancy M. Wingfield, Raoul Kneucker and Aviel Roshwald for reading this book in manuscript and offering their sound advice (whether I followed it or not). I would also like to thank the many interlocutors I have had, including Allan Janik, Fritz Stadler, Erhard Busek, Emil Brix, Edmund Leites, Ian Reifowitz, Erik Willenz, Susi Schneider, Erhard Stackl, Brigitte Fuchs, Elisabeth de Gelsey, Gertraud Auer d'Olmio and Jan and Herta Palme – as well as the members of the Wednesday and Friday *Stammtische*. I am further grateful to Eva and Thomas Nowotny, Andrea Schrammel, Andreas Pawlitschek, Harald Günther, Peter Mikl, Andreas Stadler and Christine Moser, who have offered such generous, diplomatic advice and encouragement in recent years.

I thank Günter Bischof for inviting me to the 'Vienna 1900' Workshop at Center Austria, University of New Orleans, in 2016. Regarding recent visits to the region of study itself, I am particularly grateful to Piero Budinich for bringing me to fabulous Trieste and to Helmut Konrad for a visit to Graz. Radmila Schweitzer and the Wittgenstein Initiative have generously invited me to Vienna, as has Christian Glanz, and I am most thankful to Michael Haas for helping out with accommodation there. Klaus Nellen's invitation to speak at the IWM was also most appreciated, and I am very grateful to Oliver Rathkolb for arranging a research visit to Vienna.

Oliver Rathkolb further provided one of the key images for the book, the map of the 1907 election. Ingrid Kastel at the Albertina provided the beautiful image from the Austrian Lloyd. All other illustrations were provided by Hans Petschar and his team at the remarkably comprehensive Picture Archive of the Austrian National Library, for which I am most appreciative.

Michael Watson, Elizabeth Friend-Smith, Abigail Walkington, Ruth Boyes, Sunantha Ramamoorthy and the other members of the editorial team also have my gratitude, as do the anonymous readers of the proposal and the first draft.

It remains to thank the extended Haiböck family for their remarkable generosity and hospitality all these years. I shall always be deeply grateful to my beloved, now departed, parents, as well as my splendid parents-in-law, Doris Brimmer and the much missed Andrew F. Brimmer. I owe my wife, the remarkable Esther Brimmer, more than I can say. I would also like to thank my son, Nathaniel, for his insistence on my writing another book – whether he meant this one or not.

The book itself is as much a warning as a recommendation: about what happens when decisions are made with unforeseen consequences, or misfortune upends a promising future, and something or someone ends before their proper time. In that spirit, I dedicate this book to the memory of my dear, much mourned, cousin, Francis Davin.

STEVEN BELLER, WASHINGTON, DC, 23 OCTOBER 2017.

Introduction: Austria and Modernity

The Habsburg Monarchy in its last century was one of the largest European polities by area and population, and was, as we shall see, a major player, a 'great power', at least in theory, until its demise in 1918. Yet it is not often studied at the forefront of nineteenth- and early twentieth-century European History.

There are several reasons for this. It was not a successful nation-state, unlike France, Germany or Britain, or, in various forms, Russia. In its nineteenth-century manifestation the 'Monarchy' was the archetypal Central European state, so it did not fare well as a subject during the Cold War, when there was no Central Europe, only binary 'Western' and 'Eastern' halves. There is also the consideration that after 1918 it no longer existed, and it is always an extra reach to study something that has no obvious and significant successor, as is the case with the Habsburg Monarchy. There is even some reason to think that neither students nor professors are particularly attracted to study a subject with such an atavistic, 'feudal' moniker. In a world where democracies and republics are the norm (even when the most successful democracies tend to be constitutional monarchies), and empires, such as the Habsburg Monarchy was, are frowned upon, getting anyone to pay attention to a Monarchy named after an aged, and by now rather obscure, dynasty is always going to be a hard sell.

The fact that the very identity of the subject is the cause of all sorts of confusion cannot help either. The history of the lands ruled by the Habsburg dynasty (from 1780, Habsburg-Lorraine) is such a long and convoluted one that it is best to call them by its ruling agent, hence the rather anodyne title of 'the Habsburg Monarchy' used by both Charles W. Ingrao, the author of the first volume, covering the early modern period of 1618–1815, and by myself in the sequel for the more 'modern' period of 1815–1918. Yet that territory and that history are also often named 'Austria' and 'Austrian', partly because the Habsburg dynasty had adopted the name of the House of Austria centuries before, when its main territory had indeed been in what is now part of the Austrian Republic, and partly because that is what contemporaries called this political entity for most of its premodern and modern career. So both Ingrao and I often use such 'Austrian' terminology to describe what was, more accurately, 'the Habsburg Monarchy' and 'Habsburg': that is, such things pertaining to the Habsburg Monarchy.

The 'Monarchy', moreover, should not be thought of merely as the hierarchical and dynastic political authority of the Habsburg family and its servants, but rather the whole political, social, economic and cultural nexus of a vast territory and populace in the middle of the European continent. One could call it 'Habsburgia', or more scatologically but with fine literary precedent, 'Kakania',[1] to get away from overemphasising the 'monarchical' aspect, or one could call it, somewhat inaccurately, the 'Habsburg Empire', because it was after all the empire ruled by the Habsburgs, except for the fact that the political leadership in parts of the Habsburg realm came to resent and deny that they were part of an 'empire', or at least the Habsburg one. Indeed, up until 1806 there had been a crucial ambivalence in the imperial status of the Habsburg lands, because their imperial title had not derived from the Habsburgs' territorial possessions, but rather from their having effectively made the office of emperor of the Holy Roman Empire (which extended over what is now largely Germany) hereditary in the House of Habsburg/Austria (-Lorraine). So perhaps it is just all too confusing to take the Habsburg Monarchy seriously.

In the first half of the period covered by this book, the irony was that there was really no such problem. From 1804 (which did admittedly overlap for a couple of fraught years with the Holy Roman imperial title), the polity and territories under study were known simply as the Austrian Empire, or 'Austria'. Yet it is a central event in the history of the Habsburg Monarchy that the crisis of the 1860s led, from 1867, to 'Austria' being renamed as 'Austria-Hungary', or, informally, the Dual Monarchy, and the official appellation of 'Austria' ceased as a formal name for any territory in the Monarchy, let alone the whole empire, to the extent that it still was one. It became the informal name of the 'Austrian' half of the Dual Monarchy, but even then disputes over the nature of the new political establishment meant that the 'Austrian' half was known officially but informally as 'Cisleithania' (the lands this side of the Leitha River), but formally, and tautologically, as 'the lands represented in the *Reichsrat*'. It was only during the First World War that the Austrian

---

[1] Robert Musil's witty, if scatological, nickname for the Monarchy based on the acronym 'k.k.', 'kaiserlich-königlich', imperial-royal. For further explanation, see the section Squaring the Circle II in Chapter 3.

Figure 1. Poster advertising service by the Austrian State Railways to Ragusa (Dubrovnik). Note the map showing how to get there from as far away as London, and showing routes either by sea via Trieste or overland by railway, with connection through Bosnia, via Sarajevo. (Published with permission of the Austrian National Library.)

half was once more formally called 'Austria', as a concession to Hungary, but this 'Austria' included parts of what is now southern Poland and Ukraine, and much of the eastern Adriatic coast. Beautiful Dubrovnik (Ragusa), in southern Dalmatia, was in 'Austria'.

Such confusions and indeterminacies should not perhaps take such a prominent place in the introduction to a book which is intended to provide a straightforward (if stimulating) history of its subject. The more one investigates just how confusing the very name of the subject is, perhaps the more one realises why it is not such a popular topic of academic teaching and research. It is easy to be scared away. Yet that is not the intention, and in many ways this meandering excursus into the subject's very name is an appropriate introduction to the topic, for it gives a taste of what is to come, the history of one of the most complex, and complicated, but also diverse, pluralistic and indeed significant polities in European history. It is the history of how a polyglot and supranational polity faced up to the challenges of a modernity where such polyglot, supranational entities were regarded as premodern holdovers from a feudal *ancien régime*, which had no place in the modern age of nation-states and representative, even democratic, governments. It is also the history of a region which produced – because of, or in spite of, its polyglot, supranational, premodern characteristics? – a remarkable amount of the culture and thought that has shaped our modern world.

Whether it be Vienna 1900, Budapest 1900, Kafka's Prague or even James Joyce's Trieste, the old, fusty, dynastic 'Habsburg Monarchy' was also home to much of what made up global modern culture, and hence modernity, into our own age. It was also the birthplace of the worst aspects of modernity, of the racist nationalism that led to Nazism and political antisemitism. Ludwig Wittgenstein was one of the greatest thinkers of the twentieth century; as a teenager he attended the same school in Linz, for a brief period, as Adolf Hitler. Both were born and grew up subjects of the Habsburg Monarchy. Nor should it be forgotten that it was the Habsburg monarch himself, Franz Joseph, who officially started the First World War that was to bring about not only the collapse of the Monarchy, but also the self-destruction of much of European civilisation for the next three decades or more. Yet the same polity also presaged much of the antidote to this, in the form of the rationale and logic of the European Union, which, at writing, was still a large part of our current diverse, pluralistic and multinational, multicultural modernity (or post-modernity).

Finding out how this area of the world, how its political and social structures, its economic and cultural development, rose to the challenges of modernity, or not, and how it in turn shaped that modernity, is something that should be central to understanding modern European history, and modern Europe, indeed the modern world, in a way in which current academic syllabi normally do not acknowledge. The claim of this book is that the Central Europe of the Habsburg Monarchy was indeed not something to be ignored in a rush to divide between West and East or categorise in terms of discrete national histories, but rather was, as the name suggests, *central* to modern history, and hence to our modernity.

The Habsburg Paradox: The Relevance of an Irrelevant Empire

So much about what made the Habsburg Monarchy distinctive resides in its paradoxical contrariness. The norms of modern European history point westward, towards the Atlantic, but, as Claudio Magris so poetically described, the greatest geographic symbol of Habsburg Central Europe, the River Danube, starts in the Black Forest, far to the west of the source of the Rhine, yet ends up thousands of miles to the east, flowing into the Black Sea. The river, and the Monarchy it once flowed through, go against the current, if you will, of modern European history.[2] Studying Habsburg Central Europe is studying the 'other' Europe that did not quite follow the narrative of modernisation through the nation-state that was the norm all around it (and that includes the Russian Empire and the Balkans).

Yet this eastward-looking contrariness should not be regarded as the whole story. As it happens, there were other rivers in the Monarchy that led elsewhere and had their own symbolic power. The Moldau (Vltava), the Czech national river, flows north from the southern Bohemian border with Upper Austria, into the Elbe, and thence the Atlantic at Hamburg. The Vistula, the Polish national river, has its source in the mountains that were the border between Silesia, a Bohemian crownland, western Galicia (now both in Poland), and Hungary (now Slovakia). As fate would have it, the river flows through Auschwitz, then the Polish capitals of Cracow and Warsaw, before entering the Baltic at Danzig. There are yet more riverine fates for the Monarchy. The Rhine itself touched Habsburg territory at Lake Constance, and until 1866 the Po, the great river of northern Italy, flowing through Lombardy and Venetia, was largely a Habsburg river. Even after that date, rivers such as the Adige and the Isonzo flowed from Habsburg territory into the Mediterranean, where the Monarchy had its major ports: Trieste – for Austria – and Fiume (now

---

[2] Claudio Magris, *Danube: A Sentimental Journey from the Source to the Black Sea* (London, 1989).

Rijeka) – for Hungary. The whole east coast of the Adriatic was Habsburg territory.

The Monarchy was not just one going against the stream of history, but at the same time was open to influences from the Atlantic west, Baltic north and Mediterranean south. It was in many aspects a quite modern state, and saw itself as such, as a modernising force in Central and Eastern Europe. It was both inward and outward looking. Again, geography, while not necessarily fate, was symbolic of the Monarchy's complexity. At the Monarchy's core was the Danubian Plain nestling in the protective embrace of the Alps and their Carpathian extension. Yet the Monarchy's industrial centre was to the north of this range, in the Bohemian crown-lands, as was agriculturally important Galicia, and, until the engineering masterpiece of the Southern Railway, the southern extension of the Alps blocked easy communication with the Monarchy's main port at Trieste. Mountains might protect the Monarchy, strategically, but they also got in the way of making it cohere. This might explain why it remained such a diverse region, economically, culturally and also in terms of its ethnic composition. It faced not two ways but four, and was never able to impose a real uniformity on its lands and population for long enough.

This led to some strange paradoxes. For much of its existence the Habsburg Monarchy had been the imperial power in Germany, and had gained much of its prestige and (soft) power from this role, and even up until 1866 it was the premier, presiding power within the German political world. The executive centre of both the Holy Roman Empire and the German Confederation had been Vienna, not Frankfurt-am-Main, let alone Berlin. And yet Germans comprised only about a quarter of the Monarchy's population in the nineteenth century, with the rest of the population being comprised of a most diverse group of ethnicities, or 'nationalities' as they came to be called. The Monarchy was hence the great polyglot, supranational/multinational polity of Europe.

At the same time, the geographically most coherent part of the Monarchy, the Kingdom of Hungary, was regarded throughout our period as a Hungarian nation-state by the Hungarian political nation. This was so even when, as late as the 1860s, only 39 per cent of the population spoke the national Hungarian language (Magyar). The supranational Monarchy thus contained within it one of the most aggressively nationalising (and successfully so) nation-states in nineteenth-century Europe. Yet overall the Monarchy never seemed able to gain a coherent *national* identity, so that what was 'Austrian' or 'Austro-Hungarian' was always rather ambivalent, as we have discussed. That was what made it appear a dynastic, supranational holdover in an era of national integration, and hence an irrelevant relic; yet that is also what ended up making it so relevant from the perspective of today's complex, multinational, globa-lised modern world.

The strangest paradox of all, however, is how a polity that is increas-ingly seen by its historians as so successful in encouraging pluralist cul-tural innovation formally started the war that destroyed that same pluralist culture.

To understand how this distinctively 'Austrian' situation had arisen by 1815 requires a recap of the (inevitably) complex and spectacular history of the Monarchy and its dynasty, the Habsburgs, up until that point.[3]

The Indispensable Power?

The Habsburg dynasty was one of the most powerful and prestigious powers in Europe in the late medieval and early modern periods, and even in the nineteenth century the Habsburg Monarchy still held a special status close to being the sort of 'indispensable power' that Madeline Albright once described the United States as in world affairs. The Habsburgs began as a rather minor ruling family in southern Swabia, what is now part of Switzerland. The family got its big break when Rudolf Habsburg was elected German king in the late thirteenth century and proceeded to defeat Otakar of Bohemia. As a consequence, the lands of the extinct Babenberg dynasty, centred on the duchy of Austria, came under the rule of the Habsburgs. Over the course of the fourteenth century, the Habsburgs shifted their power base (or it was shifted for them) from what is now Alsace and northern Switzerland to their Austrian lands, and they adopted the title of the House of Austria. Up until the early fifteenth century they were junior partners to the Luxemburg dynasty, but through dynastic accident and canny exploita-tion thereof, the Habsburgs (re-)gained the imperial office in 1452 with Friedrich III and then acquired a massive and wealthy territorial empire through a series of famous dynastic marriage alliances centred on Maximilian I.

By the early sixteenth century Maximilian's grandson, Charles V, was Holy Roman Emperor, and ruler of the wealthy Burgundian lands, including the Netherlands, and the Kingdom of Spain, including Spain's new conquests in the New World, as well as much of Italy. It was an immense empire, so immense (and unwieldy) that he soon gave the less significant part, the Austrian lands, to his younger brother

---

[3] The following section goes over ground already covered well, and in more detail, by the book of which this one is the sequel, Charles W. Ingrao, *The Habsburg Monarchy 1618–1815,* and readers are urged to read that for a fuller understanding of what preceded the nineteenth-century developments outlined in this book.

Ferdinand. So powerful did the Habsburg position appear, that Charles was urged to become a 'universal monarch' of Christendom, but this proved to be hubris, largely because of the adverse effect on Habsburg authority of the Reformation (as well as resistance from France and the challenge of the Ottomans), and the sheer, unmanageable extent of his lands.

After Charles, the House of Austria (Habsburg) was split into two, the *senior* Spanish line, and the *junior* Austrian one. The Spanish branch, with gold and silver flowing in from South America, was the leading power of Europe, casting the Austrian cousins in the shade for many decades. Nonetheless, the Austrian line – partly because it was not as powerful, and hence less of a threat to the prince electors of the Holy Roman Empire, retained the imperial title. In addition, yet another dynastic marriage alliance meant that the death of the Jagellon king, Louis II, at the Battle of Mohacs in 1526, resulted in the Austrian branch acquiring a sizeable Central European domain. The trio of Austria, Bohemia and Hungary was to prove the core of the future Central European Habsburg Monarchy of the eighteenth and nineteenth centuries. Yet there were several chapters of hubris and disaster still to go before then.

The later sixteenth century saw the Spanish Habsburgs as the leading power of the Catholic Counter Reformation, most famous in English history for the Armada of 1588. Their Austrian cousins, beset by the threat of the Ottoman Turks, struggling to maintain a hold of 'royal Hungary' – the part of its newly acquired kingdom not in either Turkish hands or in autonomous Transylvania – and having to deal with the religious divisions in the Empire, and in its Austrian and Bohemian lands, initially took a more conciliatory course. Yet with the succession of Ferdinand II, who had grown up under Spanish tutelage, the Austrian branch also pursued a hard line in returning its subjects to the Catholic faith. The resultant Thirty Years War (1618–1648) was a catastrophic turning point for both Central Europe and the Habsburgs. Initial political and military success led Ferdinand II to overreach, with drastic conse-quences. A limited conflict became a European-wide war, with the Spanish attempting to regain their Dutch territories, Sweden intervening as the champion of the Protestant cause, and the French, guided by Cardinal Richelieu, choosing raison d'état over religious loyalties to help the anti-Habsburg, Protestant party, and supplant Spain as Europe's leading power. Meanwhile large tranches of German Central Europe, including parts of the Habsburg lands, were ransacked, pillaged and laid waste by the roaming, largely mercenary armies, of both sides. The Peace of Westphalia that ended the war was an acceptance by the (Austrian) Habsburg imperial house of a severe diminution and contraction of the powers of the imperial office, and the beginnings of a new international system based not on imperial suzerainty but rather state sovereignty, which was soon to be presided over by Louis XIV's France.

Within the Austrian and Bohemian lands, however, the conflict had the reverse effect, leading to a huge gain in the power of the Habsburg dynasty and their political, military and religious allies. The large part of the nobility that had been Protestant was either executed, expelled, dispossessed or forced to convert, and there developed a distinctly Habsburg system of rule by the Baroque trinity of dynasty, aristocracy and (Counter-Reformation) Church. The Habsburgs also regained their footing as a major European power by the late seventeenth century. While the Spanish branch faded, the Austrian Habsburgs eventually found a new role in allying with the other European powers to their west, even Protestant ones such as the Dutch United Provinces and England, to counter a now dominant France. To their east, the military threat from the Ottoman Empire reached a critical level in 1683, with the siege of Vienna, but this perceived threat to Western Christendom resulted in a rallying of Christendom's forces against the infidel, and a major victory for the Habsburg dynasty, with their eventually reclaiming the entire Hungarian kingdom and more from the Ottomans.

When the Spanish line ended in 1700, the Austrian Habsburgs attempted to bring their cousins' entire heritage back under their, Habsburg control in the War of the Spanish Succession (1700–1714), but they were unsuccessful. Spain and the Spanish overseas empire went to a junior branch of the French Bourbon dynasty. Nonetheless, the Austrian Habsburgs gained potentially valuable territories in the Netherlands and Italy, and by the early eighteenth century, with their imperial title and their now greatly expanded territories in Central and Southeastern Europe, were again one of the great powers in Europe – a vital player in the balance of power and an arbiter of relations within the Empire. It is at this point that the Habsburgs were first and foremost a Central European power, based preeminently on the resources of the territories within the Central European bloc that came to be known as the Habsburg Monarchy.

A House that had so often been favoured by dynastic accident now struck very bad dynastic luck, in the form of not producing any direct male heirs. The Pragmatic Sanction of 1713, a modest document declaring the 'inseparable and indivisible' nature of the Habsburgs' territorial possessions, had been published by Charles (Karl) VI before it was clear that he would have no male heir, simply to establish the legal basis of Habsburg rule, but that legal document needed to be recognised and accepted by all the relevant interests and powers, foreign and domestic, to gain legitimacy and validity. Once it did become clear, after the death of Charles's son in 1716, it became much harder to gain this recognition for Charles's preferred heir, his daughter Maria Theresa. Charles was able to gain such recognition and assent from most powers, at considerable cost to Habsburg power and finances, but when he died unexpectedly in 1740, many of the promises and agreements made proved of little or no value. Maria Theresa's claim was challenged, and in a particularly cynical manoeuvre Friedrich II of Prussia seized the crownland of Silesia while claiming to be protecting Maria Theresa's right of inheritance. There followed two major conflicts, the War of the Austrian Succession (1740–1748) and the Seven Years War (1756–1763), which saw Maria Theresa survive as Habsburg ruler, and become empress in 1745 with the election of her husband, Francis Stephen of Lorraine, as Holy Roman Emperor. She never regained Silesia, however, and had to suffer the severe loss of prestige (humiliation) of accepting upstart Prussia as a serious counterpart within the German, and European, states system.

The onset of the 'struggle for supremacy in Germany' was to have immense consequences in European history, but the immediate effects on Habsburg foreign and domestic policy were significant enough. Maria Theresa began a transformation of the Monarchy from an agglomeration of provinces and lands, where the monarch ruled largely indirectly through the landed aristocracy and the Church, towards a centralised state. Initially this amounted to little more than closer supervision of the provincial estates, to gain greater revenue for the military force needed to maintain the Monarchy's status as a great power. This did involve the creation of a much larger bureaucracy centred on Vienna, however, and it was accompanied by the beginning of a complete overhaul of the education system and the status of religious institutions within the Monarchy. Maria Theresa's reforms were relatively circumspect, and did not extend, for instance, to Hungary or the Austrian Netherlands, but they did transform the government of the core Austrian and Bohemian lands. Moreover, the logic of 'Enlightened Absolutism' that was behind this reform campaign was fully implemented when Maria Theresa's son, Joseph II became Habsburg ruler in 1780.

An idealist (or ideologue) without his mother's sense of political practicalities, Joseph II set out to expand and perfect her reforms. Much as Ferdinand II had tried to impose the true faith in the seventeenth century, now Joseph II attempted to bring about the rule of Reason. As in the first case of hubris, the second also led to crisis for the Monarchy. Acting as a 'philosopher-king', in imitation of his role model, ironically Friedrich II of Prussia, Joseph took what was still a fairly ramshackle set of territories and tried to make it a uniform, united state centred on his person, as 'first servant of the state'. The intent was to do away with all the mediatory interests, such as the privileges and institutions of the nobility and any sets of particular provincial legal rights (constitutions), that got between ruler and citizen, state and society. He did this in order to increase the power of the Habsburg state, but simultaneously – and he thought inevitably linked – to increase the prosperity and freedom of his subjects, so that they indeed became citizens. As he told the leaders of the estates of Brabant and Hainault in 1789: 'I do not need your consent to do good.' He was tragically wrong, because his reforms, though meeting initially with much acceptance, were eventually rejected by the previous ruling interests in many of the provinces, most vehemently in those lands, the Austrian Netherlands and Hungary, where Maria Theresa had seen it as better to let be. By 1790, Joseph II, beset by revolution in the Austrian Netherlands (Belgium) and rebellion in Hungary and elsewhere, was forced to retract many of his most radical measures, including the state-wide land survey that would have been the basis for the emancipation of the Monarchy's peasants. Nonetheless, many of Joseph's reforms were not repealed, and in greatly expanding the Habsburg bureaucracy, and putting that bureaucracy at the centre of his plans for a centrally governed state of legally equal citizens, putting religion under state supervision, decreeing tolerance for minority religious groups (including Jews and Protestants) and emphasising the need for education and rational enlightenment over religious faith and authority, Joseph II created a template for an alternative version of the Habsburg Monarchy that was to be highly influential in the coming century.

There was also a dramatic change in the Monarchy's foreign policy after 1740. In order to counter the new threat of Prussia, Austria made peace with its old threat, France, in the 'diplomatic revolution' of the 1750s. This revolution did not bring back Silesia, but it did usher in a new diplomatic game which was even more cynically based on *Realpolitik* than before. Maria Theresa and Joseph II were not the most effective players, but they did gain some territory: Galicia as part of the first Partition of Poland in 1772, and the Bukovina from the Ottomans in 1775. The latter acquisition was a move to integrate Galicia with another Habsburg territory, Transylvania, and this was evidence of the new preference of rulers for having territorially integrated states. As emperor, Joseph II attempted (but failed) at least twice to swap the potentially wealthy Austrian Netherlands for Bavaria, largely in the interest of the Habsburg Monarchy's territorial integrity.

Secular reason of state trumped any sense of inherited right or tradition. This was not exactly new: the House of Lorraine (of Joseph's own father) had ended up rulers of Tuscany for the convenience of the great powers, but there was a new spirit abroad, where ancient conventions and rules were seen as opportunities of 'state-rational' exploitation rather than something to uphold as such. Joseph II was quite ready to play this game, and became notorious as emperor for exploiting (abusing) his imperial rights and position for Austrian interests and not those of the Holy Roman Empire as a whole. Yet he might have paid heed in 1766 when Johann Count Pergen warned him, indirectly and subtly, of the consequences of being seen to abuse the traditional rules and privileges for rational state ends, in the loss of what we would call 'soft power' within the Empire and states system. This was because much of Habsburg status and power still rested, whether Joseph II recognised it or not, on its claim to imperial authority and legitimacy, as a leading power of the *ancien régime*. The Habsburg Monarchy was a major player by 1790, but its position still relied on its place within the traditional rules and conventions of the states system – just as it still relied as much on its legitimacy and the traditional rules and conventions *within* the Habsburg 'state', as on the brute power of its military and control of its bureaucracy.

This position was to be severely tested in the coming decades. After Joseph II's death in 1790, his younger brother, Leopold II, was able to keep the Monarchy together and safe from its external enemies by retrenchment and adept diplomacy. Any further progress along the lines of the enlightened state both Joseph and Leopold envisioned (albeit in different versions) was made null by two events: Leopold II's death in 1792, when he was succeeded by his son, Franz II; and the cataclysm of the French Revolution. Franz II might well have been more conservative than his father and uncle to begin with, but it was the experience of the French Revolution and the quarter of a century of war (and Habsburg humiliation) that followed that turned him definitely into a reactionary.

Joseph II had actually greeted the initial revolution in France in the summer of 1789 as a form of confirmation, as essentially the implementation of his reform programme. In many ways he was correct, except for the representative aspects, but as with the initial, relatively moderate revolutionaries in France, the Habsburgs got much more than they bargained for: a nationalist type of radical reform that culminated in the hypertrophic form of Enlightened Absolutism of Napoleonic imperialism. In some ways the radical Josephist reform programme inoculated the Monarchy domestically from much of the French Revolution's ideological impact; conversely, the Revolution was a disaster for any continuation of the Josephist reforms. Revolutionary France, as the model of a rationally organised nation-state based on the sovereignty of the people, became the ideological nemesis of all that the multi-ethnic and supranational Habsburg Monarchy, still set within the tradition-laden imperial context, stood for. Yet for two decades, from 1792 to 1812, revolutionary France swept all before it, including Austria. Austria became the defender of legitimacy and monarchy, and it was symbolic that one of the great martyrs of the revolution was Marie Antoinette, Franz II's aunt. While other powers, such as Prussia and Russia, took time off from resisting the French to complete the cynical, state-rational partition of Poland in 1793 and 1795, Austria remained the leading continental opponent of the revolutionaries. (Austria did go along with the third partition, seeing the Polish rebellion of 1794 as an outlier of the Revolution.) And she kept losing. In 1797 Austria briefly gained the territory of the defunct Venetian Republic (including Istria and Dalmatia), but as compensation for much greater losses elsewhere; and in any case lost it again in 1805, along with such traditionally Habsburg territories as Tyrol. After yet more military and diplomatic disaster, Austria was reduced by 1810 to a truncated satellite of the now French Empire of Napoleon Bonaparte, forced to enter yet another, humiliating, dynastic marriage alliance, this time of Napoleon with Marie Louise, Marie Antoinette's grand-niece.

The Habsburgs had also lost one of the mainstays of their legitimacy and authority, the office of Holy Roman Emperor. Napoleon's radical reorganisation of German Central Europe had made it clear by 1804 that the ancient, traditional institution of the Empire was living on borrowed time, and Franz II declared himself Franz I, Emperor of Austria that year, in essence so that he could still call himself emperor. (It was stressed that the declaration of there being an Austrian Empire changed no legal relations in any Habsburg territories. The 'empire' was an empty legal shell.) In 1806 Franz II/I wound up the effectively defunct Holy Roman Empire, and from now on the Habsburgs were emperors of 'Austria' alone, but it was not all that clear what 'Austria' was. After the crushing defeat of 1805, the new foreign minister, Count Johann Philipp Stadion, attempted to recast Austrian identity in the new national terms that had inspired the French and now also some of their opponents, such as the Spanish, and by 1809 he confidently claimed – in French: 'We have constituted ourselves into a nation.' Yet it remained quite unclear at this point whether this was primarily referring to the *German* nation of which the Habsburgs continued to claim leadership (as former Holy Roman Emperors), or to the diverse populace of the 'Austrian Empire', the lands ruled by the Habsburgs. The onset of yet another crushing defeat in 1809 made this question moot, and all such talk of nationalism was dismissed under the new, diplomatic regime of Prince Clemens Metternich, but it shows the difficult situation for Habsburg legitimacy and authority. In an age where popular sovereignty and national solidarity appeared to be the new foundations of loyalty and obedience, it was a problem when you were not even sure of which nation you were.

The stunning failure of Napoleon Bonaparte's invasion of Russia in 1812, and the subsequent retreat and then rout of the French forces in the following two years, meant that by the autumn of 1814 Austria's fortunes had reversed once again. It had miraculously become the diplomatic doyen of Europe, and host to the Congress of Vienna, at which Europe was 'restored' to a condition similar (although hardly the same) to that before the French Revolution of 1789. The details of this settlement, and Austria's role in it, are discussed in Chapter 1, but what is significant here is the way in which the remarkable, phoenix-like reappearance of the Habsburg Monarchy as Europe's 'indispensable power' at the Congress in 1814–15 both continued a long tradition of the Habsburgs being central to the European states system, and also set the Monarchy's course for the next century. It had not only been Napoleonic hubris that rescued Austria, but also Metternich's brilliantly astute and skilled diplomacy, along with the military success of first the Russians and Prussians, and British, and only then the Austrians, that had eventually won the day for the Allies, and particularly Austria. This lesson was not lost on Metternich or his monarch, Franz, and Austria's role in European power politics became central to its purpose. It was, indeed, the Monarchy's fate to be always as much tied to its diplomatic position and foreign policy for its raison d'être as it was to sorting out its domestic affairs.

As we shall see, the Monarchy functioned in the three decades from 1815 up to 1848 as the 'coachman of Europe', but this pride of place did not last. In the crisis decades of the 1850s and 1860s, Austria was to lose its central regulatory role in European diplomacy, largely as a result of being unable to navigate the fine line between commitment to the established order and playing the renewed game of *Realpolitik* as an independent state actor. It is ironically fitting that its main diplomatic error was to take a position of armed neutrality in the Crimean War, the very position that had secured great success in 1813–14, but was disastrous forty years later, and one of the main reasons why Austria lost its status as a first-rank great power in the 1860s. Even as a second-rank great power, however, what was now Austria-Hungary found an 'indispensable' niche in the states system. Allied after 1878 with Germany, the Monarchy had a certain room for diplomatic manoeuvre, and it used this in its remaining sphere of interest, in the Balkans.

More importantly, its existence was seen by all major powers, its ally Germany, but also Britain, Russia and France, as necessary to prevent a power vacuum taking its place, for no other arrangement in the region was seen as being able to replicate the Monarchy's balancing role so effectively, or deal with the complicated set of competing national interests within, and across the border of, the Monarchy. The same reason was behind the preservation of the Ottoman Empire for a remarkably longer time than many had thought possible, and it is often thought that it is no coincidence that the demise of the Ottoman Empire in Europe in the Balkan Wars of 1912–1913 was so shortly followed by the other multinational empire, the Monarchy starting a world war that was to end in its own destruction. Nonetheless, the Habsburg Monarchy remained an 'indispensable' power in the minds and plans of European diplomats, even those in the Western Alliance, right up until its complete subordination to Germany at Spa in 1918. At this point, it ceased to have that indispensable character, but by then it had also ceased to be a truly independent power, and hence had lost that vital balancing and mediating role which the Habsburg dynasty had normally possessed, going all the way back to Rudolf I. Once it had become dispensable, the Monarchy's days also were numbered, as proved the case.

Black Legend, Habsburg Myth, Austrian Idea

A similar tale could be told of the domestic rationale of the Monarchy, which until its last few months was seen as 'indispensable', or at least not likely to collapse any time soon, a durable, reliable political framework, by the vast bulk of its populace, and most of their political leaders, in all nationalities and classes. This has not always been acknowledged in the historiographical record, where for a long time after 1918 the nineteenth-century Monarchy was predominantly seen as a 'prison of the nations', a quite unnecessary supranational monstrosity that got in the way of the healthy development of its various component national groups, who only achieved freedom when the Monarchy inevitably collapsed. Even then, however, there was a minority, revisionist opinion, now become in recent decades the predominant understanding, that the Monarchy had actually been a relatively benign political entity that had somehow or other created a situation where the region's immense diversity and multiple linguistic and ethnic groupings were able to live together in relative peace and prosperity, and security, right up until the fatal and fateful shots rang out in Sarajevo in 1914. It is, on the face of it, quite a stark contrast of interpretations.

There was a long tradition of such a divergence in interpreting the Habsburg tradition. For centuries the 'black legend' cast the Habsburgs as papist suppressors of freedom of thought and religion, just as the Monarchy later became a 'prison of the nations'. The black legend had its origins in the stories spread abroad by the Protestant opponents of the Habsburg-supported Counter Reformation, and it is quite true that the Habsburg dynasty, initially Philip II of Spain and his heirs, but subsequently also his Austrian cousins, were militant in restoring Catholicism in their lands (and in attempting to re-conquer those of their lands, such as the Netherlands, that had gone over to Protestantism). There was an almost natural transition from this Protestant animus against the Habsburgs to the nationalist call for 'freedom' that was behind the negative image of the Monarchy in nineteenth and twentieth accounts and historiography. There were actually direct links: the Hungarian nationalist movement had at its core the Calvinist tradition of many in the nobility, and also the historic example of the success of Transylvania in retaining its autonomy and its Protestantism against Habsburg attempts at restoring their rule in the sixteenth and seventeenth centuries. Czech nationalism was often associated with the proto-Protestant Hussite tradition, and the national 'disaster' of the Battle of the White Mountain of 1620 was seen as both a national and religious (Protestant) tragedy. There were times, therefore, when it was difficult to distinguish between the religiously based 'black legend' and the secular notion of the Monarchy as the 'prison of the nations'. Negative accounts of Metternich's Austria in the English-speaking world played off this anti-Catholic sense of Habsburg repression of freedom of thought and belief.

The obverse view of the Monarchy, as a relatively tolerant, accommodating polity, that did its best to make its peoples happy and prosperous, also had its roots in an old tradition, *pietas Austriaca.* It was almost like a photographic negative of the black legend. It saw the Habsburgs as a lenient, generous, high-minded dynasty, dedicated to ruling their God-given lands with grace and mercy. Indeed in the sixteenth century the stress on the Habsburgs as the imperial dynasty having a special responsibility to maintain Christendom's unity had had some inclusive and mitigating effects on the impact of the Counter-Reformation, before Ferdinand II had resorted to the harder, Spanish form of inducing religious conformity. Nonetheless, *pietas Austriaca*'s sense of a gentle, God-fearing Habsburg power, intent on defending the authority of the established order and the true faith – against infidels and heretics – was also transmuted into its more modern counterpart of the 'Habsburg myth'. One of the classical literary expressions of the Habsburg myth, Franz Werfel's *The Pure in Heart*, directly took over the admiration of Catholic piety, as its original German title illustrates: *Barbara oder die Frömmigkeit* (Barbara, or Piety) The sense of the dynasty being at the top of a Catholic spiritual order of grace, albeit a complex one, was a central characteristic of the Habsburg myth, even when, after 1918, its most famous exponents were Jewish writers such as Werfel, Joseph Roth and Stefan Zweig.

A central feature of Zweig's version of the Habsburg myth, his memoir, *The World of Yesterday*, was the evoking of a 'world of security' which had existed under the Habsburgs and definitely did not after 1918. The Monarchy thus became an orderly, spiritually settled, safe world, where people knew their place and also could trust in the loyalty and faith of the whole Habsburg community, where everyone, as Roth once put it, could find a home. The Habsburg myth was redolent with the yearning for a lost home, nostalgia in its proper sense, and it centred on the sense of safety, being able to count on others. One of the most poignant of all renderings of the sentiment behind it is in the form of a parody, in Gregor von Rezzori's *Memoirs of an Antisemite*, when the concept of 'Loyalty/ Faithfulness' (*Treue*) is shown to be a chimera, a myth, only practised by the Jewish character who then is destroyed by the betrayal of the character to whom she had originally been loyal. One of the more contemporary emanations of the myth has been the remarkable film, *The Grand Budapest Hotel*, which is a superb, slightly surreal confection of the romanticised Central Europe described in the work of Stefan Zweig. The lead character, Ralph Fiennes's Monsieur Gustave, in his elegance, immense skill and ingenuity, imaginative flexibility, and loyalty above all else, is the Habsburg myth personified.

Perhaps the most moving non-fictional account in the Habsburg myth tradition is François Fejtö's *Requiem pour un empire défunt* (Requiem for a Defunct Empire), but much of the historiography of recent decades, from such historians as Péter Hanák, and the current doyen of East Central European History in America, István Deák, has been tinged with a wistful regret for a purer, more ordered Central Europe, before civilisation collapsed. A large number of the current generation of revisionist historians are indeed Deák's pupils, and they share this sense of almost spiritual loss.

Most of them, and indeed most revisionist historians of the Monarchy, do not subscribe, as such, to the romanticised Habsburg myth, which they clearly understand as a myth and a literary construct. They are, however, within a variant tradition of this myth, the 'Austrian idea'. This also has origins in Austrian self-understandings, but those of a less spiritual and more intellectual, rationalist and pragmatic character. These go back to Philipp von Hörnigk's cameralism, and Joseph von Sonnenfels and the Austrian Enlightenment, and indeed to Joseph II and the tradition of Josephism he inspired in the Austrian state bureaucracy and educated elite.

The 'Austrian idea' views the uniting of the three core territories, Austria, Bohemia, and Hungary in the sixteenth century as a fortunate event that produced immense practical benefits for the inhabitants of the resultant Habsburg Monarchy. Whatever the exact origins of the territorial bloc in Central Europe, whether it was a voluntary union or a more typically imperial result of conquest, it was having one state, one polity governing this immense and diverse region that was such a positive factor. Viewing 'Austria' as more than just the dynasty's possessions, but rather an entity unto itself, was implicit in the Pragmatic Sanction, but really came into its own with Joseph II's concept of service to the state being the prime good. The creation of the 'Austrian Empire' in 1804 and Stadion's attempts to create an Austrian sense of national identity from 1805 to 1809, empty and confused though they might appear, furthered the Austrian idea. As Stadion's example suggests, 'Austrian' national identity could easily get confused and conflated with an Austrian identification with the German national cause, but it was there nonetheless. Archduke Johann, for instance, was a strong advocate of the German national cause, but he was also 'Austrian' enough to be the proud patron of efforts to encourage the development of a Slovene literature and press.

Given subsequent history it is ironic that some of the most fervent advocates of this pragmatic understanding of the Monarchy's raison d'être were Slav nationalists, advocates of what came to be known as Austroslavism. Most famously František Palacký claimed in 1848, in refusing to attend the creation of a German nation-state at Frankfurt, that Austria was a far better solution for the variety of peoples in Danubian Central Europe, who needed unity against the threat of Russia to their east. Hence, 'if the Austrian Empire did not already exist, one would have to hurry to create it, in the interests of Europe, in the interests of humanity'. Until the last year of the Monarchy, most Czech national leaders, and the leaders of most other Slav nationalities, shared this basic assumption that it was better for the small Slav nationalities to be within the larger, Austrian whole or Austro-Hungarian duality, than left on their own to defend themselves against the predations of great powers such as Russia and Prussia/Germany. The Polish example was still fresh in their memory.

The sense of Austria having a special character, and indeed mission, of containing great diversity within unity was one shared by Crown Prince Rudolf, and the *Crown Prince Project*, officially titled *The Austro-Hungarian Monarchy in Word and Picture*, a multi-volume, encyclopaedic account of many aspects of the variegated Monarchy, was perhaps one of the most prominent contemporary expressions of this liberal, inclusive sense of Austrianness. Emperor Franz Joseph at times also saw the importance of the Monarchy's function as a shared home for so many disparate ethnic and religious groups, but unfortunately he did not act on this insight consequentially enough. Additional, perhaps surprising, advocates of the Monarchy's pluralistic role, were the Austromarxists. Austrian socialist intellectuals such as Karl Renner and Otto Bauer saw the Monarchy's multi-nationality more as an opportunity than a threat in the realising of the socialist future, seeing 'cultural autonomy' within a multi-national state as a solution to the problem of nationalism. It is also fairly predictable that many advocates of the Austrian Idea would be Jewish, given the problematic nature of Jewish identity within a nationalist framework. One of the most cogent theories of the meaning of Austria was thus formulated by a rabbi, Joseph S. Bloch, who saw how the nationally neutral Austrian state could allow all the various national groups to enjoy equality and autonomy within the larger, united whole, while Jews, a religious and not a national group in his view, remained 'Austrians *sans phrase*' – Austrians without qualification or exception.

There were many other advocates of the advantages of having a large united polity in Central Europe. The central bureaucracy came to see itself as having a positive role not only in arbitrating between the nationalities, but also in encouraging the cultural flowering of each national group. Economists emphasised the huge benefits of the empire as a free trade zone, and even after 1914, during the war, writers such as Hugo von Hofmannsthal were elaborating a combination of Austria as both a spreader of German culture to the East and a home for national diversity. As this suggests, there could be much ambivalence about this 'Austrian Idea' and perhaps its most successful formulation was from 1929, by the Hungarian Jewish writer, Oszkár Jászi. His advocacy of a Danubian Federation to replace the Monarchy after 1918 failed miserably, but his account of *The Dissolution of the Habsburg Monarchy* was seminal and remains brilliant, also in its ambivalence. It revolved around the idea that there were both 'centrifugal' and 'centripetal' factors tearing the Monarchy apart but also keeping it together, some at one and the same time. Jászi's 'centripetal factors' are still one of the best summaries of the components of the Austrian idea.

Winston Churchill also came to rue the destruction of the Monarchy, much for the reasons given by Palacký, and recent revisionist historiography picks up on many of the ideas outlined above. David Good's history of the Habsburg economy showed the great advantages that the large free trade zone had offered; in the shadow of the Cold War (as it was thawing), the merits of having a cohering Central Europe not reliant on either Western or Eastern great powers could be appreciated in works such as Emil Brix and Erhard Busek's *Projekt Mitteleuropa*, and the work of historians such as Alan Sked and Pieter Judson has both negated claims about some of the worst characteristics of the Monarchy and highlighted many of its advantages that were overlooked when nationalist historiographies were more in vogue. One of the most characteristic titles of this latest trend in Habsburg historiography (and one of the best introductions, albeit in German) is Helmut Rumpler's *Eine Chance für Mitteleuropa*, a chance for Central Europe.

One of the things that makes this title so poignant for Central Europe's history in the nineteenth century is that, if there was a chance, it was not taken. If one surveys how the various historiographic traditions reflect the actual historical record, it is not too difficult to see that all three of them have something to contribute, even the idea of the 'black legend' of Austria as a prison of the nations. As we shall see, the Habsburg Monarchy was not always the happy collection of co-operating nationalities under a benign and wise emperor. Especially in the first half of the period, in the wake of the trauma of the Revolution, Habsburg rule could be oppressive and reactionary, with little or no willingness to adapt the political system to the needs of a modernising economy and hence society. Yet there were other traditions, and other approaches, even from within the dynasty itself, not to mention the larger society, that did indeed lead to a successful meeting with and mediating of modernity.

Absolutism and traditionalist hierarchy were shaken by the revolutionary crisis of 1848, which in turn led to a renewed attempt from the Habsburg authorities to mediate modernity – by combining absolutism with modern, rational legal and administrative systems, and a modern, liberal economy, in the 'neo-absolutism' of the 1850s. When that failed to provide the Habsburg dynasty with the power that it required to maintain its status, the monarch decided to bow to the inevitable and accept the liberal system of constitutionalism. When that proved only half-effective, neither solving the Hungarian problem nor preventing Austria's humiliation at the hands of Prussia, Franz Joseph opted for a compromise with both liberalism and the strongest national groups, German and Magyar, within his empire. This resulted in the Dual Monarchy. The splitting of the Monarchy in two produced two very diverging approaches to dealing with the consequences of modernisation: on one side of the Leitha, a multinational approach where the hegemonic nation was forced to give (some) ground to the other national groups by the dynastic ruler, realising many aspects of the Austrian idea of diversity in union; and on the other, far side of the Leitha, an approach where the hegemonic nation was given full rein to dominate the other national groups by the dynastic ruler – with the dynastic rulers of both sides being the one and the same, Franz Joseph.

Despite this strange dichotomy, both sides of the Monarchy actually dealt surprisingly well with the challenges, and opportunities, of modernity in its last couple of decades, were economically on the rise, indeed began to be at the vanguard of many cultural and intellectual movements. This was because beneath, or beside, the political conundrum of the Monarchy, there were institutions – of government and of society – as well as key social groups, common to both sides of the Leitha, that responded well to the changing, modernising world, and developed regardless (almost) of the Monarchy's other travails. Yet there were other aspects of the Monarchy, other social groups, and other institutions, not least in the governing circles, and in the dynasty, and tragically that included Franz Joseph, whose attitudes and interests, try as the individuals involved might, never did quite make the adjustment necessary to function well in the modern age, or realise the chance that the Monarchy offered to the people of Central Europe. That is why it ultimately fell, because of the failure to adjust – Habsburg myth, or Austrian idea notwithstanding.

Land of Possibilities

It is as well to remember one thing in the following narrative about the Monarchy's career in its last century: Things could always have been different.

One of Franz's other brothers could have been emperor. The young Franz Joseph could have chosen to be a constitutional monarch from the beginning, despite his upbringing. The Austrians could have been luckier at Solferino, Magenta or Königgrätz. The Hungarian leadership might *not* have proven amenable to compromise in 1867. Rudolf might not have despaired and committed suicide. Georg von Schönerer might not have attacked the editorial offices of the *Neues Wiener Tagblatt*. Sigmund Freud might have decided to continue his career as a biomedical researcher. The young Ludwig Wittgenstein might have, like at least two of his brothers, committed suicide. Otto Weininger might have decided not to. The young Adolf Hitler might have been accepted by the Academy of Arts. The Czech and German politicians in Bohemia might have reached a compromise. The Hungarian leadership might have decided not to back down in the crisis over the Chłopy Order of 1903, and universal male suffrage might have been introduced by force in Hungary as well as Austria. Gavrilo Princip's bullets might have missed in Sarajevo in July 1914; the old Franz Joseph might have decided at the last moment that humiliation was preferable to war. Karl might have proven a wilier ruler; the Allies might have been more circumspect about the Monarchy's survival; the Hungarian leadership might have decided in October 1918, as before, that compromise was better than abolishing the union of Austria-Hungary. All sorts of counter-factuals are possible, good and bad, and the Monarchy's alternative fates are open to endless speculation.

That is a very Austrian approach to take, and in a sense a nonsensical one. History has already happened, by definition, inevitably (until they invent time travel), so could never have been different from what it was. And yet, in the Austrian context, so complex and with so many different, apparently conflicting trends and parts, it does seem to make some cultural sense. Indeed it was a mark of turn-of-the-century Austrian culture to deal not in certainties or decisive events, but rather in possibilities, probabilities and what might have been. Robert Musil's great novel about the last years of the Monarchy, *The Man without Qualities*, saw Austria as the land of possibilities, the place where people were often paralysed into inaction by contemplating not only what would happen, but what could happen, all the other possibilities available. Admittedly this was a novel written well into the interwar period, and as much about Weimar Berlin as prewar Vienna, but the indefiniteness it describes, the conditionality, is something that was present in prewar Vienna and the Monarchy. One can see it in the way that Austrian German, then as well as now, always seemed to be in the conditional and the subjunctive tense. It is perhaps no coincidence that one of the great philosophical works by an Austrian (albeit working in Cambridge), Ludwig Wittgenstein's *Tractatus Logico-Philosophicus*, had as a central concept a mapping of language according to possibilities within truth-tables.

Central European culture was not one which encouraged certainties. Perhaps this was due to the historical experience, where the Monarchy had so often seemed so solid and permanent, only to be wracked by revolution and military defeat, and yet re-emerged in yet another, indispensable form – which nonetheless was more conditional than it perhaps might appear. (The conditionality of the Compromise of 1867 was perhaps the embodiment of this ambivalent state.) Then again, the very constitution of the Monarchy, with its ethnic and religious diversity, its various stages of economic, social and cultural development, its political complexities and crosswinds and contradictions, its nationalisms and its cosmopolitan, supranationalist elements, its hierarchies and its equalities, its 'marginocentricity' and its, often subterranean and masked, connections and interlinkings, did not make for a straightforward, simple approach to modernity, or to the world at large.

No wonder it did not fit that well into a world of binary logic, where nation-states were supposed to be defined clearly by their borders and their decisively different national characters, so that you were either 'French' or 'German' but never both (as the bowdlerised version of the rule in classical logic of the 'law of the excluded middle' that is behind nationalism insisted). Habsburg – Austrian – language, and logic, tended rather to the 'law of the included middle', not to be decisive, to see all sides of an argument, to see both one side and the other, to *be* often one side and the other (to the extent that many Central Europeans had multi-ethnic backgrounds and spoke several languages). It was a culture fated, almost, to see ironies rather than coming to definite conclusions, not definite theories but rather the penumbra of possible alternative inter-pretations that connected, one to the other. Individuals raised in this world, especially if they were raised in its interstices, between the national groups rather than at their centres, on the cusp of integration rather than in the middle of the compact majority (or majorities), never knew the exact, whole, picture or answer for any question – or rather they knew, instinctively, that there was not one.

As we shall see, this lack of a decisive approach, a lack of a definite national identity, or of a unified national culture, or even of an obvious, straightforward political purpose, was a large part of what brought the Monarchy down, repeatedly, during the course of the nineteenth century, a century of modernisation on national, decisive lines. Yet it was the same logic that created this indefiniteness, this conditionality of existence and this appreciation for the complexity of sustainable solutions in a pluralist world, that was also its greatest value, and its greatest legacy. Learning about the Habsburg Monarchy in its last century is also to discover many of the most valuable lessons and legacies for today's Europe, and indeed for today's world. Never has an irrelevant empire been more relevant.

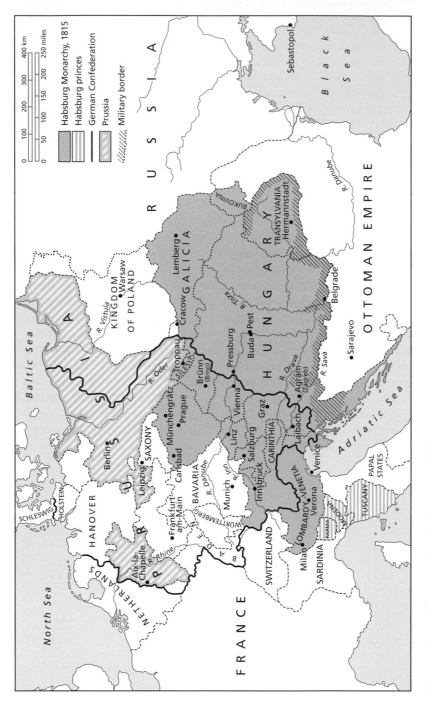

Map 2: Central Europe after the Congress of Vienna in 1815.

1   1815–1835: Restoration and Procrastination

On 18 June 1815, the Allied forces defeated Napoleon's French forces at the Battle of Waterloo. This finally brought an end to the extended nightmare that the French Revolutionary and Napoleonic Wars had represented for the Habsburg Monarchy. The Monarchy had embodied for much of that period the staunchest counterpart to France's revolutionary modernity, and it is perhaps fitting that the territory on which the battle was fought had been Austrian before those wars, part of the Austrian Netherlands. But no longer. Nor were the troops that finally defeated Napoleon Austrian, but British and Prussian. There were good reasons for this. The Habsburgs had already ceded their territories in the Netherlands to the Dutch, and the Austrian forces were not in the immediate theatre of combat when Napoleon's final campaign commenced, nor were the Russian forces. As it turned out, neither were required to bolster the victorious British and Prussians. It is still ironic that the battle that secured Europe and the Monarchy against further French depredations took place on formerly Austrian ground, but with no Austrian troops present.

The Habsburg Monarchy was in many ways still the indispensable power it had been before 1789, and the first couple of decades after Waterloo were to prove a highpoint in Austria's role in European affairs, as the 'coachman of Europe'. Yet the quarter-century of war had unleashed a whole set of dynamic forces that brought immense change, not only in the geographic composition of the Monarchy and its place in the European states system but also within Austria's society and economy, and this was both ongoing and deeply threatening to the powers that be, or at least it was seen that way. How the Monarchy's ruler, Franz I, and his main advisor, Prince Clemens Metternich, responded – or not – to the new developments, was to shape decisively the whole of the Monarchy's subsequent career.

A World Restored?

From an Austrian perspective, 1815 was not so much about Waterloo as about the Congress of Vienna. The war had appeared to be over in the spring of 1814, with the Treaty of Paris of 30 May. It was at that point that Austria had already swapped its territories in the Netherlands for a dominant position in Northern Italy. Under Metternich's initiative, the combatants were invited to the Habsburg capital to negotiate a settlement of all the outstanding issues that the wars had produced. The Congress of Vienna met in September of 1814, and the Final Act was signed on 9 June 1815, before Waterloo. Napoleon's Hundred Days adventure required a second, more punitive Treaty of Paris, signed on 20 November, and on the same day a Quadruple Alliance of Britain, Austria, Prussia and Russia was signed, with the express purpose of never allowing a revolution in France again. This collection of treaties and agreements formed the core of the Vienna settlement that provided the continent with a general peace for forty years, and avoided a continent-wide war until 1914.

The main gainers from the peace in terms of land and population were Prussia and Russia, which was only to be expected, as they had been the main powers in the march across Europe in 1813 and 1814 that had resulted in France's defeat, while Austria had played a diplomatic waiting game as an armed neutral until almost the last moment. Russia's main gain was enough of central Polish territory to form a Kingdom of Poland, with the tsar as king. Both Prussia and Austria ceded Polish territory they had once possessed after the partitions of Poland in the 1790s, but Prussia was more than compensated by a large chunk of Saxony, Westphalia and most of the German Rhineland, which was to prove a vital acquisition when that area became the heart of German industrialisation in the next decades. The negotiations over the fate of Poland and Saxony had been one of the most contentious points of the Vienna Congress, and the result was evidence of Russia's new power. Austria remained ruler of Galicia, with the free city of Cracow as an awkward vestige of Polish independence.

Austria was only a marginal beneficiary in terms of territory. It gave up its ancient territories in southwest Germany ('Further Austria'), and gave its Netherlands territories to the Dutch king, to form a United Netherlands, as a bulwark against French aggression. This was also the ostensible reason why Prussia was given the German Rhineland, and Piedmont-Savoy was handed Genoa. In return, however, Austria regained Lombardy and also acquired the lands of the former Venetian Republic, including its Dalmatian littoral. Moreover, junior members of the Habsburg dynasty were installed as monarchs of Parma, Modena and Tuscany, so that the Monarchy dominated Northern Italy, again with the ostensible rationale of providing a (secondary) bulwark against French aggression. To the north, Austria also regained, on paper at least, a predominant role, as president, in what was now the German Confederation, a semi-rationalised version of the defunct Holy Roman Empire. As further compensation and integration of her territories, the Monarchy also gained the formally clerical territories of Trent, Brixen and Salzburg. The latter was ceded by Bavaria in 1816, and so was a relatively late addition to Austria proper.

Having survived the near-death experience of the revolutionary wars, this was quite a good outcome for the Monarchy, as it returned it to the centre of the diplomatic world. The Vienna settlement was a triumph for Metternich, who was able to play off the various powers against each other brilliantly, and persuade the really powerful of the need to follow his lead. In shaping the peace, Metternich was able to forge a strong alliance with the British representative, Viscount Castlereagh, on the basis of the need for a balance of power on the European continent. At the same time, he parried the more idealistic notions of the Russian tsar, Alexander I, surrounded by many quite liberal advisors, such as Count Ioannis Capodistrias, in favour of Austria's much more reactionary position.

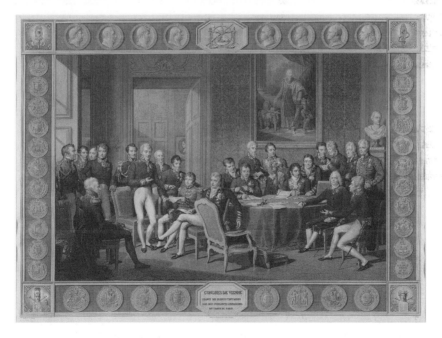

Figure 2. *The Congress of Vienna, 1815*, after a painting by Jean Baptiste Isabey. Metternich stands front left, with a gesture towards Castlereagh, sitting relaxed in a chair, front centre.
(Published with permission of the Austrian National Library.)

This saw any constitutionalism, as Capodistrias proposed, or talk of nations or peoples, as on the slippery slope to 'revolution'. What was needed to combat this threat was instead to preserve legitimacy and the monarchic principle above all else.

Initially the Congress of Vienna was seen by many to be a chance for all the various states and powers in Europe to come together as one to form a new consensus combining a restoration of the best of the old, with monarchies, principalities and states of all sorts abiding by law – international and domestic – with an embrace of the modern forces unleashed by the revolutionary wars, such as constitutionalism and nationalism. Yet Metternich, as host and hence organiser, ensured that all major decisions were taken by the four main allies, plus France when necessary, in private among themselves, with little decisive input from outside groups or powers. The negotiations resembled a card game, with the stakes being souls and territories, and the goal satisfaction of great power interests, often with little reference to traditional rights let alone national or linguistic coherence – and this suited Metternich's pragmatic, dynastically oriented approach well. It was thus that he was able to make Austria, or himself as its representative, the co-ordinator of the new, anti-revolutionary, European states system.

An indication of his intent and skills in diplomacy and persuasion is given by his transforming Alexander I's 'Holy Alliance' of September 1815 from a potentially liberal to a reactionary document. Initially inspired by his Romantic Christian religiosity, Alexander's original version was a declaration for a religious fraternity of all subjects and soldiers, as 'fellow countrymen', in other words a fraternity of peoples; but Metternich, by a few astute edits, accepted by Alexander to gain Austrian support, changed this into a unity of thrones, not peoples, a call to monarchical paternalism, not popular solidarity. This was a typical way in which Metternich, the 'Don Quixote of legitimacy' as Grillparzer was to name him, deflected and subdued the more positive aspirations that had come with the opportunities of restoration and renewal offered by 1815. Austria thus began this new era as the representative of the reactionary adherence to an only quasi-restored legitimacy, and the leader of the old-new order, which became known as Metternich's 'System'.

Metternich's System – Abroad

Subsequent to the Vienna settlement, the allies had arranged to meet when required to confer on how to manage the European states system, and how to protect it from what was seen as the ever-present threat of revolution emanating from France. Hence was created the Congress

System, which established the principle of the Concert of Europe, whereby conflicts and problems were to be solved by negotiations and diplomacy, coordinated by the main powers. Metternich, as 'coachman of Europe', was the leading spirit of this system, which in many ways was a positive precursor of later attempts at institutionalising international co-operation. Metternich, however, was intent on using it for his own, Austrian ends, to preserve the balance of power when possible, but above all to prevent any change to the monarchic, conservative status quo achieved in the Vienna settlement. Metternich's System became a byword for the collaboration of reactionary monarchs to intervene to suppress not only revolution but any moderate constitutionalism or reform.

The first Congress, at Aix-la-Chapelle (Aachen), went quite well, and saw the rehabilitation of France, now as a member of the Quintuple Alliance, but already in 1818 the powers were faced with the problems of revolution and demands for constitutional rule, specifically in the rebellion of Spain's South American colonies. This was initially resolved by an agreement to call for mediation, but subsequent revolts, coups and revolutions in the Iberian and Italian peninsulas revealed unbridgeable gaps between the balance-of-power interests of Austria and Britain on the one hand, and the more reactionary call for intervention to defend legit-imate rule, by Russia, France and Austria on the other. The fact that Austria found itself on both sides of this scale suggests both the complex-ities of Metternich's management of what was now seen as his System, but also, eventually, its unworkable character.

Already, at Troppau in 1820, Britain's co-operation in the system appeared in jeopardy as Castlereagh could not officially agree to the policy of intervention in Naples proposed by Metternich, even if he privately sympathised. In contrast, it was at Troppau that Metternich was able finally to convince Alexander I to follow his reactionary course of repres-sion of 'revolution' wherever it occurred, and give up the moderate constitutionalism suggested by his more liberal advisers such as Capodistrias. The next Congress, at Laibach (Ljubljana) in 1821, saw the approval of Austrian intervention, in both Naples and Piedmont, with Britain remaining an estranged neutral. At this point, the System seemed to be working well. Italy was entirely under Allied-approved Austrian tutelage.

The German Confederation, similarly, had bowed to Metternich's reactionary influence. The immediate post-war period had been marked by a surge of nationalism among students, not surprising given the extent to which German nationalism had been whipped up to counter the French occupiers during the war. The celebrations at the Wartburg in

1817 by student duelling fraternities, the *Burschenschaften*, had alarmed not only Metternich but many conservatives in the various German states. The assassination of the writer August von Kotzebue (in Russian pay) at Jena by a radical nationalist student in March 1819 gave Metternich the opportunity to pressure the German states to clamp down not only on the liberal student nationalists, but also on the nascent, constitutionalist reform movements in many of those states, including Prussia. The Carlsbad Decrees were agreed upon by the Federal Diet of the Confederation in September 1819, and in November Metternich initiated a process whereby the constitutional language in the Vienna settlement concerning the German states was finalised in the most conservative version possible. A distinction was made between estates-based constitutions which respected the monarchic principle, and new-fangled representative constitutions which implied ministerial responsibility and hence the anathema of popular sovereignty. The former and not the latter were agreed upon in the final, 1820 version of the Vienna Final Act. Metternich was also able to induce the Prussian king, Friedrich Wilhelm III, effectively to shut down the movement for a representative constitution in Prussia that he had promised in 1813, and the main advocates of reform, Wilhelm von Humboldt and Hermann von Boyen, were dismissed at the end of 1819.

At the Congress of Verona in the autumn of 1822, called to discuss the Allied response to another crisis in Spain, Metternich's System appeared never to have been stronger. Yet this was deceptive. Metternich's longtime, if increasingly sceptical, ally, Castlereagh committed suicide just before the Congress met, and in any case the British position had become increasingly hostile to the reactionary interventionist policies to which Metternich had directed the Alliance. Britain officially protested the Alliance's decision to sanction a French intervention in Spain, and although the Congress handed Metternich yet another diplomatic triumph by acceding to his proposals, when the French intervention actually occurred it ignored the Congress's conditions, undercutting the Congress's (and Metternich's) authority. This eventually led the new British government, under George Canning, to abandon the Congress system entirely and recognise the rebel Spanish colonies in South America, famously 'calling the New World into existence to redress the balance of the Old'. Verona marked the end of the Congress System and the high tide of Metternich's influence.

The loss of Britain as a diplomatic partner meant Metternich came to rely, and hence be dependent on, Russia as his main support. As long as Russian goals coincided with his, this was supportable, hence the significance of his having persuaded Alexander I of the threat of any form of liberal reform or constitution anywhere in Europe as being part of a vast conspiratorial network emanating secretly from the revolution's heart in Paris. If, however, Russian goals came to differ, then the loss of the British counterpart meant Metternich was boxed in with no alternatives, and this is in effect what happened after Verona with the Greek question.

Already at Laibach, the Greek revolt of 1821 had been a cause for great concern for Metternich, not because of the horrendous massacres associated with it, but because it threatened his hold over Alexander I. As the most powerful leader in the Orthodox world, Alexander felt a great responsibility for the Orthodox Greek population in the Ottoman realm, quite apart from the territorial designs Russia had on the Ottomans' Balkan lands, and so it was all that Metternich could do, with Castlereagh's help, to restrain Alexander at Laibach from invading Turkey.

The brutal nature of the revolt, especially the methods used by the Turkish authorities to suppress it, produced a wave of support for the Greek cause not only in Russia but also Britain and France. Philhellenism was stoked by the death of the great Romantic idol, Lord George Byron, at Missolonghi in 1824, and a public campaign, including politically inspired canvasses such as Eugène Delacroix's *Massacre at Chios*, from the same year, put immense pressure on Western governments to help the Greeks; meanwhile Alexander reconsidered his position in 1824 and prepared to go to war against the Turks. Metternich could do little by this stage but, officially, go along with the principle of a truly independent Greece, even while using conference discussions in Moscow to delay Russian action. The invasion of Greece by a large Egyptian army under Ibrahim Pasha at the invitation of the Turks, with its threat of a massacre of the Christian population, heightened the crisis. The death of Alexander I in late 1825 had little effect on Russia's trajectory, and Britain and Russia now took the lead in helping the Greek rebels, joined in 1827 by France. The Battle of Navarino in September 1827 saw a joint British-French-Russian fleet destroy the Turkish-Egyptian navy. Navarino sealed the fate of the Egyptian expeditionary force, and by 1830 Greece was effectively an independent state, a status recognised officially in 1832. Neither Prussia nor Austria was much involved in the intervention by the great powers after 1825, even though Austria's possession of Dalmatia made it one of the nearer powers (and the Habsburg province of Transylvania bordered the Romanian Principalities, where much of the conflict between Russia and Turkey took place). Greek independence showed the hollowness of Austria's position, and Metternich's System, when Russia was not on board.

By 1832, however, this had long been clear, because of dramatic changes in Western Europe. The liberal July Revolution in Paris in 1830 and the coming to power in Britain of the Whigs, with Viscount Palmerston as foreign secretary, saw a large part of Metternich's System come undone. Soon after the revolution in Paris, there was a revolt in the southern (formerly Austrian) Netherlands against Dutch rule, and the crisis was solved by a conference in London, hosted by Palmerston, which resulted in Belgium becoming an independent country in 1831. Despite historic links, Austria did not play a central role in negotiations, and even Metternich accepted that London was a more appropriate venue for negotiations, as Vienna was too far away. In Poland, on the other hand, the 1830 revolt in the Kingdom of Poland was easily crushed by Russian forces, with the moral support of both Prussia and Austria. Similarly, in Italy Metternich was able to prevail against French threats and crush nascent nationalist revolutions in various parts of central Italy by 1831. In Germany too, any resistance to the status quo was soon suppressed, and in 1832 Metternich had the Confederation pass the Six Acts, confirming the reactionary settlement of 1820.

By 1833, there was no longer a unified allied approach as there had been during the Congress period. In the west, liberal regimes in Britain and France supported liberal, constitutional regimes in both Portugal and Spain, forming the Quadruple Alliance in 1834 (not to be confused with that of 1815). In the east, in September 1833, Russia, Prussia and Austria met at Münchengrätz to reaffirm their alliance against liberal reform, and to back the reactionary counter-claimants to the thrones in Spain and Portugal. Russia and Austria also concluded a secret treaty to maintain the Ottoman Empire against threats, primarily from Mehemet Ali of Egypt. By this time, however, Austria was simply accepting the fact of Russian predominance, as signified by the Treaty of Unkiar-Skelessi between Russia and Turkey. No matter how much Tsar Nicholas might flatter Metternich as 'my chief' in the art of diplomacy, Austria was following rather than leading. As great-power attention shifted to the Eastern Question (of what to do with the ailing Ottoman Empire), Austria's role became less central, Metternich's advice more frequently ignored.

By 1835 Metternich might still have maintained control in Austria's spheres of interest in Italy and Germany, but the days when he shaped European diplomacy were fading. Even in Germany, the creation in 1834 of a Prussian-led German *Zollverein* (customs union) demonstrated the weakening of the Austrian position. Austria had gained the reputation abroad of being the champion of reaction, and the enemy of national self-determination (in Germany and Italy) and of liberal constitutionalism everywhere. On 5 May 1835, the first railway line in continental Europe opened in Belgium. At a time when the wonder of the steam-powered railway engine was spreading from Britain to the Continent, it was no longer so flattering to be seen as the 'coachman of Europe'.

Metternich's System – at Home

It is no accident that a history of the Habsburg Monarchy after 1815 starts with foreign policy, as there was in the history of the Monarchy, by its very nature – dynastic and agglomerative – a 'primacy of foreign policy'. This was particularly so in the period at hand, however, as the chief political figure in the Monarchy, Metternich, put priority on foreign as opposed to domestic policy. When he came to power in 1809, it was as Franz I's foreign minister. Although the immense confidence Franz I put in him meant that he was also de facto the Monarchy's chief minister for domestic affairs by 1815, he was only officially given the office of chancellor in 1821 (hence covering both foreign and domestic competencies). His predisposition was to see domestic affairs as a means of enabling and supporting what was important, which was the assertion of Habsburg power on the European stage, a typically Habsburg approach.

Nonetheless, the internal condition of the Monarchy was of vital concern, if only for this reason of enabling Habsburg power, and Metternich's System also extended to domestic affairs. His responsibility for domestic policy was not as clear-cut as in foreign policy, and Metternich once said: 'I may have governed Europe occasionally but Austria never.' In certain respects he was even telling the truth. Domestic policy only officially came under his aegis when he became chancellor in 1821, and from 1826 there was already a strong rival on the domestic policy front in the form of Count Franz Anton Kolowrat-Liebsteinsky, as member of the State Council and soon head of the political and financial sections, and from 1829 head of the budget commission. The battle between Metternich and Kolowrat for control of the domestic policy agenda would continue all the way up to 1848, so Metternich did not have the unrivalled freedom of action that he had in Austrian foreign policy. Even more significant, however, was the fact that he relied entirely for his power and position on the good graces of Emperor Franz I – and the ultimate decider of policy, domestic *and* foreign, was the emperor. It was only because Metternich knew so well how to manage the emperor, and anticipate his wishes, that he remained his chief advisor and chancellor. Metternich's System was as much Franz's System – or rather it was designed to achieve the goals that Franz set it.

What this meant in practice was that as much as possible was done to prevent political change of any kind, and to snuff out 'revolution' wherever it might appear. The trauma of the years of revolution and war before 1815 scarred Franz deeply, and this was reflected in Austrian domestic policy in the post-war period. Franz, and hence Metternich, came to rely on legitimacy as the basis of Habsburg authority, rather than the rationalist concept of state-service followed by Joseph II and the subsequent tradition of Josephism in the state bureaucracy. This meant a return to older forms of loyalty, and Franz was intent on changing the ethic of the officialdom from loyalty to the state to personal loyalty to himself and the House of Habsburg-Lorraine. The curriculum of the university law degree necessary to enter higher echelons of the officialdom was changed specifically to encourage this change of sentiment. When informed by an advisor that a petitioner for an audience was a patriot, Franz I, so legend has it, asked: 'But is he a patriot for me?' Whether this ever happened or not, it was true to the spirit of Franz's government after 1815.

Franz, suspicious of others, and jealous of his power, also turned executive decision-making into a personal function. As absolute monarch, he could ask whomever he liked for advice, and was not confined to what the State Council said. Decisions were thus made, or not made, at his desk, in what was euphemistically called the *Kabinettsweg* (study-way) of governing. His natural procrastination meant that many government decisions and processes were stalled. Metternich tried in 1811 and again in 1817 to get Franz to accept a stronger, more formalised form of government, including a new, quasi-legislative Imperial Council, which included delegates from the various provinces. This has been misinterpreted as an outline for a federalised empire, but was in fact just an attempt to provide some order to the methods of the executive (Franz). It was never acted on, as with so many of the official initiatives that ended up at the back of Franz's desk – hence Metternich's complaint that the Monarchy was never 'governed', just 'administered'. Meanwhile, to bolster the sense of legitimacy, traditional sources of authority were maintained, and indeed some revived, such as the Galician Diet in 1817. Yet this was, outside of the Hungarian lands, merely window dressing, with the various 'deliberative bodies' of the provincial diets largely there not to participate in policy but for show, to disguise the fact that it was the central government that controlled the Monarchy.

This meant that Austria relied on Joseph II's bureaucracy to run the government, but instead of being a force for expanding the progressive state, it became an instrument to maintain the status quo, and to suppress all political discussion that called for change, for any such discourse was seen by Franz and Metternich as incipient 'revolution'. Thus arose a new version of the 'Black Legend' as Metternich used the bureaucratic apparatus to crack down on dissent wherever it appeared in the Monarchy. This involved the expansion of the police force, and the secret police, creating a network of spies and informers, and secret interception of the mail. This was all to sniff out the secret revolutionary societies that Metternich was convinced were behind the liberal and nationalist revolts all over Europe in the early 1820s and then again the early 1830s. It also meant imposing a heavy regime of censorship and the threat of imprisonment against journalists and writers who challenged Habsburg authority. Not surprisingly, all this drove dissent underground, and in a form of self-fulfilling prophecy many radicals, and not a few liberals and nationalists, then found solidarity in secret societies such as the Italian nationalist Carbonari, which then provoked Metternich's paranoia about 'revolution' yet further. After 1820, membership in the Carbonari became high treason, and so activists who, in a more open society, would have been political opponents then became traitors instead, as in the case of Silvio Pellico, and were sentenced to death. Though his sentence was commuted to life imprisonment, Pellico ended up in Spielberg prison, in Brünn (Brno), Moravia, and his memoirs of his time there (he was released in 1830) became one of the many sources that critics used to paint Metternich's Austria as a cruel, oppressive, police state.

This is a little unfair. While Metternich's Austria did indeed pioneer many of the methods of what was to become the 'security state' so familiar to us today, the security apparatus was, as Sked points out, simply not large enough or comprehensive enough to create a truly effective police state. Censorship was spotty and often lax, many banned titles were smuggled in and read by the educated classes, most intercepted mail was from diplomats, not the public at large, and harsh sentences were often mitigated, as in the case of Pellico. The extent to which there were such arbitrary mitigations of legal decisions could be seen as countering the claim that the authorities were strict upholders of the rule of law, but this would disregard the fact that most of the time the legal system was respected by the authorities, and too much clemency would be a strange charge against a supposedly oppressive government. This does not mean that Austria was not a police state, just that it was a relatively mild and inefficient one. Moreover, it did achieve its main purpose, which was to dampen and indeed extinguish most political (and intellectual) life in the Monarchy, especially at its centre in Vienna.

The suppression of an active political scene meant that the emerging German-speaking middle class and intelligentsia in the Monarchy never gained the practical experience in representative politics that their equivalents elsewhere in northwestern Europe did at this stage of social and economic development. This was not only a deficit for the Monarchy's political development, but also for the sense of its coherence as a polity. Had there been more of an active forum for political debate in these crucial post-war decades, a more Viennocentric, albeit German-speaking, but *Austrian* political consensus might have been able to mitigate, or even co-opt the centrifugal forces of nationalism that were to dominate politics later in the century. The fact that Franz was never under physical threat, that he was indeed a popular figure in Vienna and much of the Monarchy, has been cited as evidence that this lack of a political opening was not something that was missed by the Austrian public, and hence not necessary. The question should be, however, whether this placidity of the populace was not an ideal situation in which the opening to representative, constitutional government could be introduced? This had been what Franz's father, Leopold II, had once envisaged, and it was seen at the time as the political form of the future by many, including his brother, Johann. That Franz and Metternich refused, and went backward, was one of those great missed opportunities of Habsburg history.

The place where a stronger Austrian identity did develop, almost despite Franz and Metternich, was *within* the bureaucracy. While maintaining the status quo was their main mission under Metternich, the Josephist tradition meant that officials did preserve progressive goals and the sense of the primacy of the state. The state's control over religious life continued even with the Romantic fervour associated with the circle around Clemens Maria Hofbauer, and even though Metternich was interested in improving relations with the papacy, he did so largely because he saw the usefulness of religion as a support for authority, and as such wanted to retain control of it. Thus religious fervour among the populace and lower clergy was something of which he was deeply suspicious, as for most of his life, as a product of the late eighteenth century, he shared the rationalist scepticism of many Josephist officials and higher clergymen.

The state also expanded the primary education system, to include girls as well as boys, and in the vernacular language of the local population, although here as well there was a certain ambivalence. The need for educating the populace in the basics was something the practical Franz could appreciate, but he was wary of anything more than that. In 1821 he remarked to a teacher: 'There are new ideas around that I cannot, and shall never, approve of. Stay away from these and keep to what you know, for I do not need scholars, but rather honest citizens. Your duty is to educate youth to be such. Whoever serves me must teach as I order;

anyone who cannot do this, or who comes with new ideas, can leave, or I will arrange it for him.' Enrolments in secondary and higher education actually fell off after 1815, due largely to government parsimony, but also to this sort of discouragement from the apex of society. There was also a certain rigidity in the Josephist approach itself. The emphasis on uniformity and administrative centralisation meant that good intentions often were defeated by local conditions, as was the case when attempts to introduce primary education in Dalmatia foundered on the imposition of pay scales and teaching credentials that were quite unrealistic given Dalmatian traditions.

In the financial and fiscal realm, there was some reform, such as the establishment of the National Bank in 1816, which remedied to some extent the state bankruptcy of 1811. Yet the reforms that were implemented under the aegis of Kolowrat, such as that of consumer goods taxes in 1829, were neither very effective nor uniformly applied, belying the centralist ethic of the bureaucracy, and did not produce the required revenues. For an absolute monarch, Franz was quite reluctant to impose his power on the established interests in his lands, and even if nobles in the core Austro-Bohemian lands paid some taxes, they were minimal, and because collection of major taxes such as the land tax was left to the provincial estates, revenue always seemed to come up short of expectations. The officialdom's function of imposing state control over local nobilities and, if necessary, defending the peasantry against their masters, was often neglected, and there was little pressure to extend bureaucratic control downward.

'Bureaucratic absolutism' was resented by both noble and peasant, by the former for threatening to exert too much control, and the latter for exerting too little. Local jurisdiction was left largely to the noble landlords, as before, and there was no significant land reform, with compulsory *robot* (labour service) still a feature of the agricultural system in much of the Monarchy. In the west, *robot* had largely been commuted into money rents, but in the east it was still common, even if the slow rendition of it by the peasants often made it quite uneconomical for landlords. A new land survey might have produced a large increase in revenues from the land tax, but it faced opposition from noble interests at Court, and was only partially complete by 1834. State monopolies on salt and tobacco similarly disappointed, although the tobacco monopoly did start to show a profit for the state after reform in 1834. Hungary, which was always a separate fiscal entity in this period, with its own tariff barrier to the rest of the Habsburg lands, produced only a tiny proportion of total revenue for the state, and much less than it should have done relative to the other provinces.

The result of Kolowrat's inability to expand revenues sufficiently, or overcome local exceptions and particularisms, combined with Metternich's initially frequent use of Austrian troops to carry through his interventionist diplomacy, meant that there was never enough money to pay for anything but the basic state functions. The sluggishness of revenue growth meant the underfunding of the army, and eventually a curtailing of Metternich's use thereof in foreign adventures: Austria was 'armed for eternal peace', Kolowrat remarked in 1827. Under his control, the fiscal situation did improve somewhat, which is why he remained in charge of Austrian finances, but the persistence of a fiscal deficit led not only to penny-pinching in the state apparatus, but also to a chronic problem of how to finance the immense state debt it still owed from the war, the interest payments of which accounted for almost 30 per cent of the budget. The solution used was to resort to loans from private banks to finance the debt it still owed from the war, and this had an adverse effect on the capitalisation of the private sector, and hence on growth.

All of Europe experienced a post-war depression from the war's economic dislocations, but Austria's economy suffered more than most, and was slower to recover. From the late 1820s, the economy grew at a respectable rate, keeping up with the *Zollverein* territories, but not as fast as in the industrialising West. Growth was patchy, concentrated initially in the northwest quadrant, nearest the German and Atlantic markets, with Bohemia's textile industry being an economic driver, while Hungarian growth was low, and industrialisation there nearly non-existent. The System might not have been as harsh or as absolute as advertised, due to its inefficiencies and the fact that it was spread so thinly and unevenly over the Monarchy's society. Yet its combination of holding back political development while not exerting sufficient power over the vested interests in society to produce a healthy fiscal and financial position meant that it was a drag on the Monarchy's political *and* economic development, but with very different effects and consequences regionally. Metternich's System was intent on stasis and keeping control at the centre, but it could only delay change, and the way it did so was, eventually, to empower not the centre, but the periphery.

Culture without Politics: Biedermeier

The political quietism and initially sluggish economic growth resulting from Metternich's System had as its corollary (and consequence) what is now known as the culture of Biedermeier. 'Biedermeier' was not a contemporary word. It first arose in 1854 as a composite satirical moniker for a fictitious writer of stodgy, conventional poetry, and only around 1900 did it start being used to describe Central European culture and style of the period from 1815 to 1848. That said, 'Biedermeier' has come to stand for the modest, resigned, private and domestic approach prevailing in the culture of the era. In furniture design, this meant a simplified, more utilitarian version of French Empire styles; in music it came to connote the private, sensitive, domestic art of a composer such as Franz Schubert; in painting, as in the work of someone like Ferdinand Georg Waldmüller, it signified a culture that also emphasised the private life, middle-class domesticity, set in an idealised, natural, often Alpine landscape; in literature, in the plays of authors such as Ferdinand Raimund and Franz Grillparzer, it spoke a language of fatalism and resignation, and acceptance of one's lot – a culture without politics.

This was very understandable in some respects. The relief of war's end meant concerns naturally turned from the political to the more domestic, and it is notable that the emphasis on domesticity was one encouraged by the example of the emperor himself, who usually wore civilian attire, not military uniform. The imperial family consciously chose to create an image of familial respectability and domesticity, which was quite at odds with the more 'aristocratic' lifestyle of Metternich, with his various mistresses. The emperor's personal modesty, and approachability (he held frequent sessions where subjects could have an audience with him) meant that he was quite popular with the general public, at least in the Vienna area. The connection of the Habsburgs to the people was greatly enhanced, at least in the popular imagination, by the legendary romance between Archduke Johann and the 'postmaster's daughter', Anna Plochl, which resulted in their morganatic marriage in 1829. Franz I might have stood in the way of the marriage for a decade, but his and the dynasty's image still profited from it with the public.

Instead of worrying about politics, writers and artists, along with 'bürgerlich' (civil)[1] society, could, according to the authorities' version of Biedermeier life, devote themselves to their art and their craft, and provide enjoyment and pleasure. In some ways, it is ironic that one of the greatest musical works in Western civilisation, and one of the great hymns to human solidarity, Ludwig van Beethoven's Ninth Symphony, should have been written and had its premiere in Metternich's Vienna, in 1824. On the other hand, Beethoven had lived in Vienna most of his life, despite his antagonisms to it, and the symphony does end with a setting of

---

[1] The word 'Bürger' (with its correlates 'bürgerlich' and 'Bürgertum') is often translated as 'citizen', but just as often has the meaning of 'civilian', 'bourgeois' or 'member of the middle class', and can mean all of these at once. Its meaning and hence translation depends on its functional context, how it is being used, and will be translated as such.

Friedrich Schiller's 'Ode to Joy', which in some sense was precisely what the authorities saw themselves as enabling. Schiller himself had likened the Viennese to the hedonistic Phaeacians of Greek myth, and in Austrian lore the Biedermeier period is often nostalgically called the *Backhendlzeit* (time of fried chicken) to denote it as a time of peace, prosperity and enjoyment. In that (rather blinkered) sense, Beethoven's Ninth fitted right in.

One of the most famous works of the period from a modern Austrian perspective was Grillparzer's *King Ottokar's Fortune and End*, which is most renowned for its paean of praise to the glories and fruitfulness of the land of Austria, and the confident modesty of the Austrian. This was a most Biedermeier-like sentiment, yet the play at the time, in the mid-1820s, took Grillparzer two years to get permission to perform, due to the suspicions of the censors. This sort of pressure on writers is perhaps one reason why music was so much stronger as an artistic tradition in the

Figure 3. *'The Grand Gallop', by Johann Strauss Sr.*, etching by Andreas Geiger and Johann Christian Schoeller, from *Bäuerles' Theaterzeitung*, 1839.
(Published with permission of the Austrian National Library.)

Biedermeier era, because its 'message' was not so prone to political interpretation. The *Gesellschaft der Musikfreunde*, soon to be known as the *Musikverein*, had been founded by members of the public, including, famously, Fanny von Arnstein, in 1812 and became a major sponsor of music performances, including that premiere of Beethoven's Ninth. It is also fitting that this was the era in which the Viennese waltz became established, with Johann Strauss the Elder starting his own orchestra in the 1820s.

The compensations of living in Vienna, then as now, were many, with the coffeehouse already a major institution of sociability. By the 1820s, life was quite pleasant for many in a growing middle class, and the same could be said for many of the other cities and towns in the provinces. As long as one did not cause too much of a ruckus, things were, within limits, fine. Step out of the comfort zone, however, and things could get difficult fast. The young writer, Moritz Saphir, came to Vienna to make his name in 1822, and was employed as a theatre critic for the *Wiener Theaterzeitung*. By 1825, his biting reviews had caused such a ruckus that he had to leave town. Vienna was not a good place for too much critical writing, or overtly critical art of any kind, in this period.

One musical work of the Biedermeier era in Austria perfectly reflected the desired sweetness and harmless, homespun domesticity of the culture. In 1818, in the newly Austrian province of Salzburg, a young Catholic priest, Joseph Mohr, and a village schoolmaster, Franz Xaver Gruber, created the carol, 'Stille Nacht', and performed it at the Christmas Eve service in Oberndorf, on the Salzach, just a few miles upstream from where the river meets the Inn at Braunau.

Culture *as* Politics: Nationalism

The placid calm of Biedermeier culture was deceptive: political and critical art might have been largely muffled by the System at the centre, in Vienna and its environs, and in those parts of the Monarchy to which the German-speaking culture of the middle classes and officialdom extended, but elsewhere all was far from still – largely because of one major development: nationalism.

Metternich, a diplomat, aristocrat, top servant of the Habsburg dynasty, and head of an extensive state bureaucracy, had little time for questions of nationality or national identity, and was often dismissive of their significance. As someone who came from a Rhenish family, what national perspective he had was German, and he just assumed that the Monarchy was primarily a German state, as the leading power within the

German Confederation, and that the central bureaucracy's main language should be German, even if the latter was largely for functional, as opposed to nationalistic reasons. Nor did there initially appear to be much reason to question this. German was increasing in use as the *lingua franca* of educated circles and commercial centres in early nineteenth-century Central Europe, not only in Vienna but also Prague and Pest. German appeared to be the predominant language of the entire region, just as Metternich's System dominated (and suppressed) political life. Yet even during the heyday of the System, there was subtle, and not so subtle, resistance from the peripheries to the apolitical, Biedermeier centre, in various nationalistic forms.

One quite traditional form of resistance was provincial particularism, and provincial rivalry. Even provinces, such as Bohemia, that had been integrated into the central government structure might wish to claim their own cultural space and identity, as made evident by the establishment (by, among others, Kolowrat) of a Patriotic (National) Museum, funded by the Diet, in 1818. At the same time, the fact that Bohemia and its nobility were so integrated into the Habsburg government meant they were in positions of power, and Hungarian leaders, such as István Széchenyi, could view them jealously as superior rivals.

By the early nineteenth century, such provincial or regional pride and identity often took a national form, at least rhetorically. In theory, at least, this provincialism transformed into political nationalism could apply to the entire population in the 'patria' (hence the Prague museum's title), and so there was the possibility of a civic nationalism without ethnic or cultural markers; but this is not how most nationalisms developed in the Monarchy, even those based on political units such as crownlands (Bohemia) or kingdoms (Hungary).

Part of the reason was that, initially, the 'nation' involved was normally the 'political nation' of the regional nobility in its various rankings and privileges, as represented in the vestigial remnants of provincial power, the estates in the provincial diet. Previous historical developments often meant, however, that this 'political nation' was far from representative of the population as a whole, and as literacy and political and cultural consciousness increased, this became both a problem and an opportunity. In order to be more convincing as a representative of 'the nation', and to be seen to be more responsive to the *modern* Romantic notion, elaborated most famously by Johann Gottfried von Herder, of nations as the product of organic cultural development, the leadership of the political nation often led or encouraged the movement to define the 'nation' not politically but culturally. In this way, the power of the 'people' as a whole, the ethnocultural '*Volk*', could be summoned to the national (political) cause. Political nationalism tended in these circumstances to take on the forms of cultural nationalism.

Cultural and social realities often got in the way of this ideal vision, with ironic effects. The political nation could end up appealing to a popular national culture whose language most of the political nation could not speak, even if they were, by descent, members of that linguistic culture. This applied to the 'political nation' in both Bohemia and Hungary.

Then again, the national culture and language to which the political nation appealed might cover only a minority of the population of the province or kingdom. Such difficulties of distinction are one of the reasons why, in traditional historiography, the political identity of the Kingdom of Hungary is 'Hungarian', while the culture and language of the dominant national group is 'Magyar' – although Magyar is just an anglicised version of the Magyar (Hungarian language) word for Hungarian. It is nonetheless useful to explain a situation in which a member of the Hungarian political nation could support cultural Magyar nationalism without speaking Magyar, and claim Magyar as the national language of Hungary, even though for a large majority of the Hungarian population (including himself) Magyar was not their primary language, if they spoke it at all.

In yet another, crucial category, were nationalisms that had no political nation to act as matrix, but rather were based on cultural and linguistic affinities among often peasant communities. These so-called nations without history often had almost nothing but their linguistic affinity as the basis for national identity, and hence were the purest form of 'cultural nationalism', as their national identity and culture was constructed, sometimes even invented, for them by historians, writers, academics, journalists and orthographers, almost from the logic that, following Romantic thought, they *must*, as with all peoples, have their own, inherent culture and hence 'national' identity.

All variants – provincial particularism, political nation/noble nationalism, political nationalism and cultural nationalism – could intertwine and play off against each other, creating complicated, often even strange, combinations, especially when challenged by the very involved, complex ethnolinguistic distributions within the Habsburg lands.

Metternich was wont to call the Monarchy an 'agglomeration', and this does capture the fact that it was composed of provinces, territories and kingdoms of various forms and stages of development, and also with various stages of national identity and consciousness. If a province contained more than one ethnocultural or ethnolinguistic group, as almost all of them did, there was also the possibility of a range of national consciousness within the province. How the relevant educated classes (sometimes just a small band of dedicated intellectuals and scholars) responded to the challenge of 'reviving' or 'restoring' (sometimes constructing or inventing) national culture and identity could determine the relative balance between 'nationalities' (the word usually used in Habsburg historiography for these ethnocultural and linguistic groups); and how the Habsburg authorities approached the various claims to identity of the 'national' or proto-national groups also could have a large impact.

The most contentious and strongest nationalist movement in this period was in Hungary. Most of the Monarchy – the Austrian hereditary lands, the Bohemian crownlands, Galicia, Lombardy-Venetia and Dalmatia – was governed through the United Court Chancellery by the central Habsburg bureaucracy as an absolute monarchy. In addition, the Military Frontier along the Monarchy's southern border with the Ottoman Empire was directly ruled by the Court War Council (the military). Hungary and its partner, Transylvania, however, had a quite different status. They had shaken off Joseph II's attempts at uniform centralisation in 1790, and were still governed separately, through their respective Court Chancelleries – albeit these were located in Vienna – and their political nations still claimed special rights according to their supposedly ancient constitutions, making both Hungary and Transylvania in legal terms limited, not absolute, monarchies. They also had a quite different form of administration. In Hungary, a relatively small royal bureaucracy (Franz was king, not emperor, in Hungary), with roughly 1,000 officials in central offices in the Chancellery in Vienna and the Court of the Palatine in Buda, and another 3,300 in the countryside, relied on a noble-led system of local administration in Hungary's counties (*comitati*). The royal bureaucracy was constantly battling with the local noble assemblies that ran the counties over the provision of recruits for the army and increased revenue (taxation), and had periodically after 1790 attempted to obtain changes from the Hungarian Diet, where the noble estates were represented, but without much success.

From 1811, Metternich and Franz, who disputed the validity of constitutional claims, had attempted to rule Hungary entirely through the bureaucracy, without calling the Diet, but dogged resistance from the counties, combined with the chronic fiscal and financial problems of the Monarchy, caused them to recall the Diet in 1825, in the hope of obtaining more revenue. (The Transylvanian Diet had also last met in 1811 and was not recalled until 1834!) Their requests for more revenue were met with resistance, and instead came a storm of demands, especially concerning the rights of the 'nation'. By this point, due to the development of a strong *cultural* nationalism from the 1790s on, this increasingly revolved around the replacement of the traditional language of administration in Hungary, Latin, by the 'national' Magyar language, despite this being the spoken language of only a minority of the Hungarian populace (roughly 40 per cent in 1846). In Hungary, Metternich's System ended up having to deal with politics after all, and in a very aggressive, nationalist form. The aggression was partly due to fear of Magyar being swamped, due to the rise of German and the renaissance in Slavic languages. This combination of pride and fear caused Széchenyi in 1825 to donate his annual income to promote the formation of a National Academy to 'propagate the national idiom'. In 1827, Széchenyi also founded a National Casino (a type of gentlemen's club) in Pest to encourage the liberal nationalist opponents to the royal government. In 1830, the Diet passed a law making knowledge of Magyar compulsory for public office, and it had already become a compulsory subject in schools, even in Croatia.

The Magyar national revival also took the form of a social and economic reform movement, again inspired by Széchenyi, one of the great liberal figures in Central European history. His series of books, *Credit* (1830), *Light* (1831) and *Stages* (1833) discussed the problems of the still feudal Hungarian economy, and the reform programme of liberalisation and general economic modernisation that would solve it, in his view. One reason for this was that the existing divide between lord and peasant vitiated the very possibility of a united *nation*, so there needed to be a dissolution of social divisions. Ironically, many peasants spoke (a form of) Magyar while many of the higher Hungarian nobility, though Magyar in background, spoke mainly German, French or anything but Magyar, but were still Hungarian nationalists. Széchenyi also thought that the best way to strengthen the Magyar element in society – Magyarisation – was for Magyars to set such a good example politically and socially that Slavs and Germans would adopt Magyar culture voluntarily, but he was just one voice, and even at this point in the early 1830s there was already a coercive side to cultural Magyar nationalism.

The aggressive 'propagation of the national idiom' by the Magyar political nation in turn antagonised the defenders of other national/linguistic groups. In Croatia, while the scholarly revival of the 'South Slav', 'Illyrian' language had been going on since the turn of the nineteenth century, it was only after experiencing the aggressive tactics of Magyar cultural nationalism that a strong Croatian cultural nationalist movement took shape.

It says something about the power of linguistic scholars in this period, such as Ljudevit Gaj, that they effectively created modern Croatian (and for many decades Serbo-Croatian) out of the profusion of different dialects, and across significant political borders. The Croatian 'nation' was split between several provinces: Croatia-Slavonia, since the twelfth century part of the Hungarian lands; Dalmatia and Istria, once Venetian now part of Austria; the 'Hungarian littoral', since 1822 jointly ruled by Vienna and Hungary; and much of the Military Frontier. If the language and nation was defined as 'Illyrian', then the 'nation' could extend to the Austrian provinces of Styria, Gorizia and Carniola (now territories partly or mostly in modern Slovenia) and Trieste, because the 'Alpine-Slavic' or 'Carniolan' language spoken there was close enough to one of the dialects of Croatian to be included. Indeed from 1808 to 1813 the French had included this region in the 'Illyrian Provinces', with a capital in Ljubljana, but with a Croatian dialect as administrative language that was not the local one. That 'Alpine-Slavic' came to be regarded as a distinct language of 'Slovenian' was as much due to the choices of language scholars as it was to the cultural reality. Instead of Croatian joining up with Slovenian, the choice of the što dialect as the basis for modern Croatian pushed the language in a more southeasterly direction.

The publication of Gaj's new 'Croatian-Slavic orthography' in 1830 was a crucial breakthrough in establishing a modern cultural Croatian national consciousness, and as such it was a political act. In 1832, the Croatian Diet, the *Sabor*, heard a speech in Croatian for the first time. Gaj and his allies meanwhile, with some support from the Habsburg authorities (as a counter to Magyar pressure), had larger ambitions, seeing Croatian as really the language of a much larger, 'Illyrian' nation including all South Slavs (except perhaps Bulgarians). Nationalism could never, it seems, be anything but expansionist. Slovaks, Romanians and Serbs also had their cultural nationalist champions attempting to assert their identity against increasingly repressive Magyar nationalism, but with far less political success.

In the rest of the Monarchy, where the System was in full control and politics as such not allowed, nationalism nonetheless was a rising factor, and a political one, even when it was cultural. There were also distinctly 'historic' nations, with a strong national consciousness, even if that national consciousness was not necessarily being acted upon, yet. Lombardy-Venetia had already been part of the Napoleonic Kingdom of Italy from 1806 to 1814, and there was a legacy of both radical liberalism and liberal Italian nationalism, among Milanese and Venetian intellectuals and members of the nobility. Some of the political prisoners in the Spielberg mentioned earlier got there for sympathising with revolts in other parts of Italy – Naples and Piedmont, in 1820–1821 – joining the secret society of the Carbonari as a patriotic response. The advent of Giuseppe Mazzini's Young Italy in 1831, in the wake of the failed revolts of 1830 in central Italy, marked a further stage in the movement of Italian unification that came to be known as the Risorgimento.

There were, however, no revolts in Lombardy-Venetia in this period. Initially, Habsburg rule in its Italian provinces went quite well: the administration was probably better than anywhere else on the peninsula, including Piedmont; and the northern Italian economy prospered under Austrian rule. Indeed the Italian provinces were the wealthiest in the Monarchy, and revenues from them were vital for maintaining what financial health Austria possessed. Metternich dismissed the threat of Italian nationalism, notoriously declaring that Italy was merely a 'geographical expression'. He pointed to the 'municipal spirit' whereby competition between city-state loyalties always came before Italian unity. Italian was used as the language of administration in the lower levels of the bureaucracy, and Metternich sought to emphasise the local power of the Austrian viceroy, Archduke Rainer, even when he actually kept strict control of policy. Yet the clumsy and arrogant handling by the Austrian authorities of the native political nations, the Lombard and Venetian nobilities, caused considerable alienation, with many of their members looking to the neighbouring, independent Italian state of Piedmont as an alternative base of validation, with implicit nationalist implications. A relatively new addition, Lombardy-Venetia was never culturally or socially much integrated into the Monarchy, and possessed strong, Italian cultural traditions quite distinct from those north of the Alps.

At the other, northeastern extremity of the centrally ruled area of the Monarchy, Galicia, a similar story played out. Initially, after the restoration of the Galician Diet in 1817, the Austrian authorities gave the local 'historic' political nation, the Polish nobility, considerable 'national' space, and *cultural* nationalism was encouraged. In 1817, the University of Lemberg (Lviv/Lwów) was reopened, and in 1827 a chair of Polish language founded there. Count Joseph Ossilinski was a major contributor to the Polish cultural renaissance as prefect of the Vienna Court Library from 1809 to 1817; returning to Lemberg in 1817, he founded the Ossilineum in 1827, which was to become a major centre of Polish learning. Ruthenes (Ukrainians today) were 44 per cent of the Galician population, but were one of the 'nations without history' of the Monarchy. The Habsburg authorities allowed Ruthenian cultural nationalism too, and there was a Ruthenian seminar at the university in Lemberg, but the main national power in the province was the Polish nobility.

The relatively good relations between the authorities and Poles soured with the Polish revolt against the tsar in Congress Poland in 1830. The suppression of the revolt by Russia was, given Metternich's

System, naturally supported by Austria, which nonetheless admitted a large number of Polish émigrés into Galicia. In the 1830s, many Polish nobles were tried in Galicia for high treason because of their conspiring to overturn Russian rule in Congress Poland (only eight were eventually executed). Cracow, the independent Polish city-state, was occupied by the Austrians from 1836 to 1841 to stamp out Polish resistance to Russia. At the same time, the authorities funded a Polish grammar book for use in elementary schools, allowed the use of Polish in patrimonial courts and required knowledge of Polish for the local Austrian bureaucracy. Cultural nationalism was encouraged, on the assumption that political nationalism could be suppressed.

The problem was there was not ultimately much of a difference in the context of the Monarchy. The final group to be discussed was also the crucial example of how provincial patriotism, cultural nationalism and political nationalism could all combine in a potent mix. The Czechs were not regarded by contemporaries as a 'historic nation'. Instead the Czech language was looked down upon by most in the educated classes as a peasant tongue, and the main language of education and commerce in the Bohemian crownlands (Bohemia, Moravia and Silesia) at this time was German. These provinces were an integral part of the centrally ruled part of the Monarchy, indeed its economic centre, even if ruled from Vienna. As such provincial pride dictated that the Bohemian *patria* be celebrated, hence the founding of the Bohemian Patriotic Museum in 1818. At the same time, in the Romantic spirit of a search for roots, and even in conscious imitation of the example of German scholarship, the 'native' language had been revived by scholars and its ancient literature rediscovered, as part of the Slavic renaissance, associated with scholars such as Pavel Šafařík and Josef Dobrovský. In his zeal to prove the antiquity of the Czech tongue, a scholar like Václav Hanka could even forge documents in Old Czech so that he could 'discover' them in 1817 and 1818.

Provincial patriotism and cultural nationalism then combined when a pupil of both Šafařík and Dobrovský, František Palacký, was appointed as archivist of the Bohemian Museum in 1823. Palacký began the *Journal of the Bohemian Museum* in 1825, originally in Czech and German, but soon enough he dropped the German edition, because in his words Czech was the 'historic national language' of Bohemia. An organ of a patriotic provincial museum thus became the home for language-based Czech nationalism. He then set about writing his hugely influential *History of the Czech Nation in Bohemia and Moravia*. The first volume was published originally in German, and only subsequently in Czech, but as the title suggests, Czech nationalism and not Bohemian patriotism was now the focus. In 1830 the *Matice Česká* (Foundation for Czech) was founded as an association to fund the journal. Originally a largely aristocratic group of patrons, it soon became an organisation of middle-class Czech nationalists – whose primary language, however, was often still German.

By 1835, under the noses, and often with the approval, of Metternich and the Habsburg authorities, cultural nationalism had made large inroads in almost all corners of the Monarchy, but the consequences of this regional definition of identity, of the advance of the periphery over the apolitical centre – that the regime had aided in engineering the ethnicisation of Austrian politics against the interests of the state as a whole – were not yet clear.

The Age of Improvement

Then again, the political quietism at the apolitical centre was as deceptive as the supposed non-political nature of cultural nationalism. Even if Metternich's System appeared to have made things stand still politically, this did not mean that Austrian society or the economy stood still as well. Far from it: if members of the nobility and middle classes could not associate politically as citizens, they could do so as music lovers, patrons of town museums, businessmen encouraging development or academics rediscovering the past. Civil society might be hamstrung, but civic society was not. Indeed, the parsimonious nature of Habsburg finances meant that there were opportunities for civic endeavours that might otherwise have been funded by the state. The rise of an economic middle class with the renewed growth of the 1820s meant many of these opportunities were grasped. As in much of the rest of Western and Central Europe, this era, despite the System, was an Age of Improvement.

Biedermeier might have been modest and domestic, but it was also a bourgeois, self-sufficient culture that projected middle-class, *bürgerlich* values. The hero in Raimund's play *Der Verschwender* was not the noble wastrel, but rather Valentin, the servant-cum-carpenter. The domestic scenes in Waldmüller's paintings are of bourgeois families. If the state would not finance higher forms of education for the public, private citizens would step in, as they did in Troppau in 1814 to form a museum and educational institution. The initiative might come from aristocrats originally (as in Prague with the Sternbergs and the Patriotic Museum), but the associations which funded these civic institutions soon enough became predominantly middle class in membership. Societies and associations were formed (always having to gain official permission, of course) to encourage economic development, or further the improvement of farming techniques, and in the discussions that occurred at their meetings members practised the arts of speaking, debate and consensus-building, so that these apolitical associations were a training ground for later politicians. In cities and towns, gentlemen's clubs, or 'casinos', open not only to the nobility but to the educated and propertied middle class too, provided another setting for civic sociability. And then there were always the public coffeehouses where the local and national events could be read about in an increasing assortment of newspapers, and discussed.

The emerging urban civic culture arose along with the growth of industrial and commercial towns. In the 1820s and early 1830s, economic growth could be patchy, but those patches could also be great success stories, such as the textile centre of Brünn, with a population of 30,000 by 1830, or Hungary's commercial centre, Pest, with 44,000 by the same year. Trieste had become a major port, with 43,000 inhabitants by 1820, and 80,000 by 1840. Economic success bred civic pride, and a sense of self-validation for the bourgeois values of industriousness and thrift of the entrepreneurs and merchants who led the economic achievement, in contrast to more aristocratic, 'feudal' values. On the other hand, many of the initiators of this new culture of material progress, and the patrons of the associations which encouraged it, were aristocrats, who took pride not only in the success of cities, but also of their provinces.

We have already seen how liberal noblemen such as Széchenyi expressed their *national* pride in funding national institutions of learning, but this was just a variant of the noble funding of provincial and civic museums, and educational institutions all over the Monarchy, whether they had a nationalist purpose or not. The Bohemian example in Prague was deeply ambivalent in this regard, but the same phenomenon occurred in primarily German-speaking provinces as well. The pioneering effort in creating a sense of provincial cultural identity in an enlightened, progressive manner had taken place in Graz in 1811, with the founding of the Monarchy's first educational museum, the Joanneum, and its initiator had been none other than the youngest brother of the emperor, Archduke Johann.

Johann's career is one of the great 'might-have-beens' of the Monarchy's history. He was much more liberal than Franz, much more a disciple of his father, Leopold II, and uncle Joseph II, a convinced Josephist in many respects. Johann had been deeply involved in the Tyrolean rebellion in 1809, eventually against his imperial brother's wishes, and had been banished from that province in 1813. From 1807 residing in southern Lower Austria, he devoted himself to 'improving' the neighbouring, relatively backward province of Styria, starting with the founding of the Joanneum.

Figure 4. *Archduke Johann and Anna Plochl*, after a painting by Matthäus Loder (1781–1828).
(Published with permission of the Austrian National Library.)

He did so as an advocate of practical enlightenment, and of the urban and rural middle classes, not the nobility, which he held in low esteem. (This was the same Habsburg who fell in love with a *bürgerlich* commoner in 1819 and married her in 1829.) He undertook a trip to Britain in 1815, at war's end, where, among other things, he met James Watt and received an honorary degree from the University of Edinburgh. Impressed, positively and negatively, by industrialising British society, he applied the experience he had gained there, his Josephist principles and his commitment to improvement, to Styria's economy and society. In 1819, he founded the Styrian Agricultural Society, which he explicitly opened up to non-noble members, with many local branches. (This was allowed despite the suspicions of such a decentralised network from the Viennese officialdom.) In 1828, he instituted a fire insurance company for Styria, with a remarkably democratic governing structure.

He also purchased an iron works near the Erzberg and became an advocate of modernisation of Styria's iron industry. He was instrumental in introducing the pyramidal opencast mining still seen there today. In 1832 and 1833, he arranged for industrial exhibitions in Graz, and in

1837 he helped establish the Styrian Association for Encouragement and Support of Industry and Trades. He was even patron of the 'Carniolan' (Slovene) newspaper, *Novice*, which he championed as a means of bringing the new agricultural methods to the Carniolan peasantry. He was also one of the strongest advocates of the railway in the Monarchy, offering a detailed proposal for a railway from Budweis (České Budějovice) to Trieste, over the Semmering, as early as 1825. These are just highlights of a remarkable career of constant advocacy of improvement, whether as farmer, industrialist, scientist or citizen. It was not that the Habsburgs were a hopelessly reactionary dynasty – it was just that the Habsburg who was emperor until 1835 was.

Nonetheless, as will be clear by now, not all of the positive, Josephist side of the Habsburg legacy was prevented by the refusal of Franz and Metternich to admit change. One aspect of Josephism that survived quite well was in the government's industrial and commercial policy. Newfangled ideas such as Kantian philosophy might be prohibited in higher education as dangerous to religious belief and hence authority, but technical knowledge and education were of practical benefit, and hence encouraged. The Viennese *Polytechnikum* was opened in 1815, and Austria imported many of the new, industrial techniques from the West, especially Britain. It also welcomed large capital investment from foreign financiers, notably (but not only) from Jewish banking families such as the Rothschilds, Arnsteins and Pereiras. The Rothschilds especially came to take up a central role in Austrian finance, both of the state and of industrial projects. The massive Vitkovice iron works, based on the latest English technology, was built with Rothschild money in the 1830s, and was soon to be connected with Vienna and other industrial centres by the Northern Railway: the *Kaiser Ferdinand Nordbahn* (the first segment opened in 1838), also financed by the Rothschilds. At a time when most of the Jewish populace in the Monarchy were still oppressed by humiliating restrictions – on marriage and residency, for instance – a Jewish financial and industrial elite emerged that was to have a profound effect on Austrian history.

There were also other signs by the 1830s that Austria was doing better economically, benefiting as did the rest of Western and Central Europe, from the new steam-engine driven technologies (which Johann had been among the first Austrians to see up close). The Danube Steamship Company was founded in 1831; in Trieste, the Austrian Lloyd, founded in 1833 as an insurance company, quickly became a shipping company, its steamships plying their trade in the eastern Mediterranean and elsewhere; and steam engines drove the burgeoning growth of the textile industry, especially cotton. Austria's first railway started operating between Budweis (on the Moldau) and Linz (on the Danube). Perhaps characteristically, it operated with horse-drawn moving stock and was not much of a success. The real future lay with the steam railway of the Rothschilds' *Nordbahn*. The partners behind that project had sought the concession for it quite early, in 1829, but Franz, ever suspicious of change, had refused to grant it, and it was his son, Ferdinand, who gave the go-ahead over five years later. Even when the economy did quite well, there were certain aspects of Metternich's System that served as a drag on it.

2   1835–1851: Revolution and Reaction

Franz I died on 2 March 1835, after an eventful four decades as Habsburg ruler. His successor, as one would have expected according to the dictates of legitimacy, was his eldest son, Ferdinand. Franz left his heir a testament (composed largely by Metternich) whose central advice was, predictably, 'to rule and not to alter', but one might have expected that the relatively young new emperor (Ferdinand had been born in 1793) would nevertheless be a force for change, as relatively young rulers often are. This was not the case. Ferdinand would, it is true, preside over a revolution during his reign, but it would not be of his bidding; the real agent of change would be another, much younger Habsburg, his nephew, Franz Joseph. Over the next fifteen or so years, Austria would stagnate under an only slightly amended version of Metternich's System, its government trying more to hold back change than to take advantage of the many opportunities opened up by mid-nineteenth-century technological advances and the growth of a new economy and society. The paralysis of the centre would encourage ever more pressure from the increasingly nationalist peripheries, which came to full flood in the revolutions of 1848. Yet the very contradictions of multiple nationalisms in one polity, the lack of political experience of the populace and the strength of traditional values of loyalty and faith in the existing, monarchical order would redound to the benefit, and survival, of the Monarchy, giving it and its new emperor one more chance to adjust to the new, modern world. The response was to go back to a new version of the old, absolutist ways.

The System Seizes Up

The main reason why Ferdinand was not an agent of change was also a major problem for a government that ruled according to the principle of dynastic legitimacy: Ferdinand was mentally incompetent. This had been clear for many years, and had not legitimacy played such a role in Habsburg thinking, another of the somewhat more intelligent brothers, Ludwig probably, would have succeeded, but Ferdinand was intent on being emperor, as was his right, and so he was. The need for a form of regency was evident from the start, and initially Metternich tried to take advantage of the situation to take over power – as had been outlined in the testament he had written for Franz. The Habsburg family members, including Franz's two brothers, Karl and Johann, resisted this outcome, as did Kolowrat, who was by now in charge of finance and most domestic matters. After considerable and lengthy Court politicking, a truce was called between the factions, and in December 1836 (approaching two years after Franz's death), a new State Conference was established, with Metternich, Kolowrat and Archduke Franz Karl as permanent members, other officers being called on as needed, and with Archduke Ludwig as presiding member.

Metternich tried to get the Conference to discuss and decide policy decisions orally, hence speeding up government, but soon enough government reverted to the *Kabinettsweg*, with this time Ludwig being the obstacle to any decisive policy-making. There was now a stand-off between Metternich, in charge of foreign affairs, and Kolowrat, in charge again of finance and most domestic matters, although Metternich continued to play a large role concerning the police, Hungary and the Italian provinces. The deadlock between Metternich and Kolowrat was not so much a battle of ideology. Kolowrat was not really the liberal contemporaries thought he was – he was just not quite as ruthless in his attempts to stop any form of political opposition as Metternich was, on occasion taking the side of the diets against the centre, or protecting writers critical of Metternich from the censors, and thought Metternich's intolerant approach counter-productive. The deadlock did have a paralyzing effect on the government, though: the System's immobility now became stagnation. The problem of fiscal, and hence financial, weakness, the result of Kolowrat's unwillingness or inability to press harder against the vested interests in the provinces (primarily his fellow high nobles) continued to hobble Austrian policy at home – and also abroad, because, as we saw, Austria was 'armed for eternal peace', lacking the funds to launch any more major foreign interventions, without risking the creditworthiness of the state.

In foreign policy, it was clear that Austria was no longer a truly leading power. When the Eastern Question was revived in 1839 by another conflict between the Ottoman Empire and its supposed vassal, Mehemet Ali, Britain and Russia took the leading role against Ali's backer, France, while Austria was just in the supporting cast. Two events associated with this crisis in 1840 illustrate the ambivalences of the diplomatic and political situation.

The first was the Damascus Affair, one of the most infamous cases in the nineteenth century of blood libel, in which several members of the Jewish community of Damascus were accused of the ritual murder of a Christian monk. The case was taken up by the French consul, Ulysse Ratti-Menton, and to curry favour with the French backers of Mehemet Ali, Ali's governor of Syria, Sherif Pasha, launched an investigation that 'proved' that the Jews had committed ritual murder. At this point, two Austrian officials made a decisive intervention. The consul, Casper Merlato, who had originally accepted the ritual murder accusation, changed his mind when an Austrian citizen and Jewish merchant, Isaac Picciotto (nephew of the Austrian consul in Aleppo, who was Jewish) got caught up in the investigation. Over the next weeks, Merlato and his superior, the Austrian consul-general in Alexandria, Anton von Laurin, showed conclusively the falseness of the claims against the accused Jews, setting off a famous affair which saw the great names of European Jewry, Moses Montefiore and Adolphe Crémieux among them, rallying to the cause of proving Jewish innocence and the complicity of the French diplomat and the Mehemet Ali regime in blood libel. The affair was resolved in the late summer of 1840, when the threat of defeat at the hands of the European powers (primarily British naval forces in the Mediterranean) led Ali to order the release of the Jewish prisoners in Damascus. Without the diplomatic context in which it happened, the Damascus Affair not only would be incomprehensible, but also would likely not have had as happy an ending as it did. The fact that Austrian diplomats played such a central role, when Austria was still regarded as reactionary in the West because of its denial of Jewish emancipation, suggests the complexities of the era.

The second was the French response to their effective defeat in this round of the Eastern Question, when France threatened to go to war to support Mehemet Ali, and the French premier, Adolphe Thiers spoke of the need to restore France's natural border on the Rhine. The response to this hostility from one of the leading liberal powers was in many respects edifying for Metternich, showing as it did not only the end of the liberal entente between Britain and France, but also the solidarity of the other German states with Austria as the presiding member of the German Confederation. There was, however, also the fact that this crisis of 1840 became one of the great rallying points of German nationalism in the German states, and marked the debut of one of the great anthems of the German national cause, *Die Wacht am Rhein* (The Watch on the Rhine). This resurgence of German nationalism was something that Metternich had long feared, but now appeared powerless to prevent. Meanwhile, an attempt in 1841 to deal with the Prussian-led *Zollverein*, either by joining it or forming a rival trade group, failed due to a lack of consensus within the State Conference, caused by the opposition of protectionist Bohemian industrialists, and the problem of how to include Hungary in such an agreement.

If Germany looked to be slipping out of Austrian control, the position in its other main sphere of interest, Italy, where Austria had been the dominant power, also began to look fragile. The Italian nationalist movement led by Mazzini was gaining momentum by the late 1830s in Italy's intellectual class, and also increasing support from other powers, especially Britain. While Metternich stood by his policy of reactionary absolutism, Palmerston urged the other Italian states to introduce liberal constitutions to ward off revolution, and began to see a united, Italian nation-state as a better guarantee against French aggression than Austrian predominance of the peninsula. The election of the 'liberal pope', Pius IX, in 1846 then produced a qualitative increase in the threat of Italian nationalism to Austria's position. Palmerston's suggestion, that perhaps it would be better for Austria to give up Lombardy-Venetia to Piedmont to concentrate on her other sphere of interest in the Balkans, was hard to accept when Lombardy-Venetia was Austria's richest province and its revenues a major reason why Austrian finances did not entirely collapse.

Metternich had also lost out in his support of the Dutch king against the creation of independent Belgium, which the Dutch were eventually forced to recognise in the Treaty of London of 1839. His support of the reactionary candidates to the Spanish and Portuguese thrones also was unsuccessful, given the dominance of British naval power and 'gunboat diplomacy'. Austria was now seen in European public opinion as the hive of reaction. The occupation of Cracow from 1836 to 1841 to put down Polish nationalist unrest also did nothing to lessen the perception that Austria was now the Russian tsar's police agent, and this view was shared by the more liberal parts of the Austrian intellectual class as well.

In the Swiss Sonderbund War of November 1847, when the more liberal cantons defeated an attempt by conservative cantons to split away, Metternich was unable to do anything to prevent this success of the 'party of movement' against the 'party of order', and the outcome of the war was seen across Europe as a sign of imminent (progressive) change. Metternich, in his own terms, had already sensed this in March of that year: 'The world is very sick, and every day the gangrene spreads.'

There was little improvement on the home front either. The new sales tax of 1829 did not solve the revenue problems of the state, and various tax privileges of provinces such as Tyrol and Galicia were not abolished. So the state remained impecunious, set on a policy of parsimony, unable fully to close the budget gap and still paying almost a third of the budget to interest on the state debt. The underpaid, but obedient, relatively efficient and honest officialdom kept things ticking over, but the state was unable to launch any major initiatives when it came to such policies as expansion of educational opportunities, or the state financing of peasant buy-outs of their *robot* liabilities. The one area where the state did launch a major initiative was also crippling to finances, and this was the expansion of the railway system.

On the face of it, this was a story of success: the *Nordbahn* continued to be expanded: in 1839 service from Vienna to Brünn began; by 1846 Vienna was connected to Prague, Brünn and Cracow. By 1848, Vienna was connected by rail to Hamburg. Hungary was linked into the growing network by 1849. To the south, the Southern Railway (*Südbahn*), which was to connect Vienna to Trieste and northern Italy, had reached Graz by 1844, and work continued on this line and a link between Venice and Milan, to create an internal network between the Monarchy's main economic centres, to encourage commerce and industry, while at the same time affording the Austrian military much greater ease of transportation of troops to potential hot spots. The strategic implications of the railway network had been behind the assertion of state power in 1841 to determine the shape of the rail network, and to nationalise the railway system in wartime. This intervention in the railway building program ended up being extremely expensive for the state. There was little immediate impact of the decision in 1841, but in 1847 the financiers of the railway network, the Rothschilds, Arnstein and Eskeles, and Sina, got out of financing the network, because of the low rate of return, and left the state to take up financing the completion of the line to Laibach (reached in 1849) and Trieste (1857), and the Lombardy-Venetia and Hungarian lines, with loans from the same set of bankers, at higher, more profitable interest rates for those bankers. This put yet more strain on Habsburg finances, especially given the difficult economic crisis that had started in 1846 (as we shall see). By early 1848, the Habsburg Monarchy was not in a good position, financially and hence politically, to weather either a financial or political crisis – and yet, by then, it was clear that there were many on the horizon.

Vormärz: Anticipating Change

While the government of the Monarchy had changed little since 1815, with Metternich still the leading figure, its economy and society had changed significantly. Peacetime had seen a constant increase in the population, of about 1 per cent per annum, so that by 1843 the

Monarchy's population stood at 37.5 million (including 4.8 million in Lombardy-Venetia). This rise in population had been accompanied by a rise in agricultural productivity which more or less kept up, so that before the harvest failures of the mid-1840s there was no Malthusian subsistence crisis, generally speaking (although enserfed peasants in parts of Galicia and Hungary might have disagreed). There had also been demographic and economic shifts within this increased population, with some shift from countryside to cities, although in 1845 80 per cent of the population was still living in villages, and about three-quarters of the workforce was still in agriculture, forestry or fisheries. Attitudes on the land also were changing, as cash crops for the market came to replace subsistence ones in many areas, and as economic differentiation also led to social differentiation, with the emergence of a large class of agricultural labourers. The largest change in Habsburg society was the emergence of large and growing towns. Vienna had increased from 250,000 in 1817 to 357,000 in 1848; Prague from 65,000 to 115,000. Commercial and industrial centres continued expansion: Brünn from 30,000 in 1830 to 45,000 in 1840; Pest from 36,000 in 1810, 44,000 in 1830 to 100,000 by 1848. Trieste, at 80,000 by 1840, continued to expand as a major commercial link to the Eastern Mediterranean and beyond.

The main significance of this growth in towns was the concomitant emergence of urban classes, of nascent industrial proletariats and of much larger semi-industrialised, artisanal classes, as well as an educated and propertied middle class (the basis of Biedermeier culture already discussed) which greatly expanded in the 1830s and early 1840s. It was this growing middle class, the *Bürgertum*, that was particularly attracted to the newfangled ways of thinking: progress, liberalism and nationalism. Alongside the urban middle classes, however, were also many within the nobility who accepted the assumptions of such 'bourgeois' ideologies, and, in the case of Hungary and Galicia, it was the nobility, especially the lower nobility or gentry, that led the supposedly 'bourgeois' call for liberal reform, partly because they had to adapt to more bourgeois livelihoods as the traditional agrarian economy transformed.

As anticipated in the previous chapter, calls for reform at the regional periphery almost inevitably took nationalist forms. In Lombardy-Venetia, Austrian rule remained for much of the period largely unchallenged, as the economy prospered. Nonetheless those who were dissatisfied with Habsburg rule looked to a nationalist solution, either through neighbouring Piedmont-Savoy or through the papacy in Rome, the latter option enjoying a massive boost with the election of Pope Pius IX, the 'liberal pope', in 1846. Culture and scholarship also played a part in the growth of an assertion of the need for national unity, and animosity in Lombardy-

Venetia towards Habsburg rule: Giuseppe Verdi's *Nabucco*, with its thinly veiled critique of absolute rule, and its praise of popular liberation, received its premiere at La Scala in Milan in 1842; the Congress of Italian Scientists met in (Austrian) Venice in 1847.

The main centre of oppositional – and nationalist – politics in the Monarchy was, as before, Hungary. In Hungarian historiography, the 1830s and 1840s are seen as the 'reform era', although in the series of reform diets, 1832–1836, 1839, 1843–1844 and 1847 (which met at Pressburg, in Magyar Pozsony, modern-day Bratislava) not many major reforms actually were put into law. Many of the reforms concerned the use of the national, Magyar language, which became Hungary's official language in 1844. There was a partial emancipation for Jews in 1840, and a liberalisation of laws for business. The main reform proposals concerning the end to noble tax privileges and the emancipation of the peasantry were never passed, because the conservative majority in the Diet were reluctant to part with their noble privileges. The era nevertheless saw a renaissance of Magyar literary culture, and a vibrant debate *about* reform. That debate saw an intrinsic connection between the national and the social questions, and a radicalisation of the reformist-nationalist cause.

Széchenyi had been the great nationalist reformer of the 1820s and early 1830s, and his policy of improvement continued through the later period as well, most dramatically in the building on his initiative of the Chain Bridge (designed by British engineers) from 1842 (completed 1849), that for the first time connected the two parts of what would be the national capital: Buda and Pest. Yet his combination of evolutionary, moderate reform, compromising with the Habsburg authorities, and a permissive approach to the assimilation of the other nationalities to the national Magyar culture, was overtaken by more extreme versions of essentially the same combination. The trade-off was now one of full, compulsory emancipation of the peasantry and the abolition of noble tax privileges, with independence for Hungary as a constitutional monarchy (with a Habsburg still as monarch) and full, almost compulsory, Magyarisation of the other nationalities by all – mostly legal – means available. There were various politicians who led Hungarian politics in this more confrontational direction, including Baron Miklós Wesselényi, and even, at this time, Baron József Eötvös (despite his insights into the destructive and selfish nature of nationalism), but the person who became the leader of liberal reform in Hungary was Lajos Kossuth, editor after 1841 of the newspaper *Pesti Hírlap*, who took radical positions on both the social and national issues. The rivalry between Széchenyi and Kossuth, more personal than ideological in truth, is a staple of Hungarian historiography of this era, but it needs to be reiterated that most of the reform programme was never passed before 1848. The nobility, while attracted to the national cause, were wary of committing to the other side of the ledger, which was the repeal of their privileges, and Metternich was wont to use the threat of this 'reform' as a weapon against the nationalist reformers. Hungarian politics were thus also at a deadlock in late 1847, and the conservative government, under Count György Apponyi, appeared to be gaining some control over the counties, and hence the government in general, before other forces intervened in early 1848.

In Galicia, the relatively good relations between the government and the Polish nobility suffered mightily from the consequences of the failed rebellion in the Russian-controlled Kingdom of Poland in 1830. Although the government still did its best to improve education and the economic situation in the province, it also attempted to repress anti-Russian efforts by Polish nobles, leading to the occupation of Cracow 1836–1841 and the condemnation to death of fifty-one nobles for high treason (for anti-Russian plots). As a result, the Polish political nation in Galicia had become alienated from Habsburg rule by 1846, and quite nationalist in outlook.

In both the Hungarian and Polish cases, however, there were other nationalist notes, from other nationalities that had developed their cultures and identities, and hence their presence and power, to much higher levels than before 1835, even if that national identity was still largely confined to a small group of academics and intellectuals. In Galicia, the main 'minority' nationality involved was the Ruthenes, at 44 per cent of the population, largely in the eastern half of the province. In the provincial capital, Lemberg, Ruthene scholars in the Uniate (Greek-Catholic) theology department of the university, had developed a national culture, with Metternich's encouragement (to Polish distaste), and this took shape in the 1830s, with a grammar (1834), and an anthology of Ruthenian literature (1837), albeit with a distinct gravitating towards (non-Austrian) Kiev.

In Hungary and Transylvania, there was a whole panoply of 'nationalities' with scholars intent on developing their innate culture (as they saw it). Slovak nationalism was represented by two scholars, Pavel Šafařík and Ján Kollár, who pursued the idea of Panslavism. Kollár's *Slavic Ethnography* (1842) included an ethnographic map showing, notoriously, the isolation, and hence doom, of the Magyars surrounded by a 'Slavic sea'. However, the Panslavism of these scholars had little practical result, and their efforts for Slovak little resonance with the mass of Slovaks (who were largely peasants), for the Slovak they constructed was largely incomprehensible to the dialect-speaking peasants.

The Romanians in Transylvania faced a similar situation, of a national culture still being developed, by a small group of intellectuals. In 1834 students at the Uniate seminary in Blaj were astonished when their professor, Simon Bărnuţiu, gave his lecture not in Latin, as was traditional, but, for the first time, in Romanian. This was a sign of a growing determination to establish a national literary culture by scholars, but it was still a small concern in the 1830s: the *Gazeta de Transilvania* of Blaj, founded in 1838, had only some 250 subscribers, a possible readership, perhaps, of 2,500, in a Transylvanian Romanian population of 2 million. Then again, most Transylvanian Romanians were illiterate, and those who could read were far likelier to know the Cyrillic alphabet of the Eastern Orthodox Church than the Latin one in which *Gazeta* was published, for strong ideological reasons concerning the Roman origins of Romanians. There was thus a certain gap between the nationalist world view and reality.

On the other hand, the effort by Magyar nationalists to make Transylvania a Magyar-speaking state had the effect of sparking Romanian national solidarity, much as the similar attempt in Croatia had sparked Gaj's Illyrianism (Croatian nationalism). Despite Romanian-speakers comprising a majority of the population, Transylvania's Diet had representation for only three official constitutional nations: Magyars, Saxons and Seklers (a group closely related to Magyars), and none for Romanians. When the Diet was recalled for the first time in twenty-three years in 1834, the Uniate and Orthodox bishops, traditional leaders of the Romanian community(ies), petitioned for recognition of the Romanians as a fourth nation, but it was rejected, and again in 1837 and 1841. Instead, in January 1842, the Diet passed a language law making Magyar the official language of the land, including provisions to make it, eventually, the language of instruction in the Uniate and Orthodox seminaries. This provided a rallying cause for the nationalists, including Bărnuţiu, who wrote of 'a law of absorption which destroys nationality'. Partly as a result of the threat of Romanian unrest, the emperor (in effect Metternich) never gave the law sanction, but the net effect was to boost antagonism between the Magyar elite and a newly conscious Romanian nationality.

Croatian nationalism also continued to develop in opposition to Magyar assertions of supremacy. Initially, Gaj's Illyrianism was tolerated by the authorities (Metternich) as a useful balance to Magyar ambitions, and from 1835 his *Morning Star* – from 1836 *Illyrian Morning Star* – became the organ of an expansive Croatian nationalism, which soon developed various economic and cultural national associations. Eventually, in 1843, Metternich acceded to Magyar concerns about Gaj scheming to form a unified South Slav state by cracking down on the whole concept of 'Illyrianism', and banning the word 'Illyrian' itself. Interestingly, Metternich made it clear that this did not mean the Monarchy was favouring Magyar over Illyrian (Croatian). The decree of 1843 banning use of the word Illyrian stated: 'there will be no contest between Illyrianism and Magyarism. Croatia has rights. I will know how to protect them'. The Hungarian Court Chancellery was ordered to rein in Magyar nationalist efforts 'to spread the Magyar language at the cost of other nationalities'. Metternich did not accept the supremacy of Magyar as the national language of the Hungarian nation-state. Illyrianism might be too much, but the Croatian language should be protected from Magyar nationalists. Gaj himself lost influence in the Croatian nationalist movement, but the movement continued. In 1847, the *Sabor* made Croatian the official language of Croatia-Slavonia, instead of Latin.

In the Monarchy's most advanced territories, the Bohemian crownlands, Czech nationalism built on its earlier encouragement by Bohemian patriotism and German Romantic theories of the organic nation. Palacký continued his work at the Patriotic Museum and spreading his Czech-nationalist message through the Museum's Czech language quarterly. The *Matice Česká* increased its publication of Czech literature, and in 1845 another stalwart of Czech nationalism, Karel Havlíček took over the editorship of the *Pražské noviny* (Prague News) giving educated Czechs a Czech-language quality newspaper for the first time.

Metternich and the Habsburg authorities appear to have been unconcerned at this development, seeing it only as a controllable source of local pride, and perhaps a balance to potential German liberal ambitions. The head of the police (and censorship), Count Joseph von Sedlnitzky, is reputed to have told Palacký 'that the government is glad that the Czechs wish to remain Czechs', and this generally permissive approach was also recognised in an editorial of the *Augsburger Allgemeine Zeitung* on 12 December 1838: 'one of the most fortunate fundamental ideas of the Austrian state which has long served as a principle is complete respect for nationality, which forms an integrating force in the Monarchy. This generous and liberal outlook has solved a difficult task, that of forming the heterogeneous parts into a whole, one which other states with the system of centralisation could not accomplish. The government allows Germans to be German, Bohemians to be Bohemian [Czech], Italians to be Italian'. One can question whether this was in turn too rosy a view of Metternich's *politically* oppressive System; nonetheless, the Czech historiographical claims of an Austrian crackdown on Czech nationalism before 1848 do appear to be a 'black legend'.

Indeed there was really little reason why the Habsburg authorities should suppress Czech nationalism, because the movement's leaders tended at this point to be supporters of the Monarchy, as a way out of having to choose between Germany and Russia. It was, after all, Palacký who gave the most famous formulation of Austroslavism, as the way in which the smaller Slav nations could, through being a majority in the Monarchy, be the predominant power in their own state. Havlíček too, after a sojourn in Russia before 1845, was no fan of the idea of Panslavism, and very much an advocate of Czech nationalism, for Czechs alone. It is also the case that Czech nationalism, though growing, was still a rather small and poorly funded movement in the 1840s. It would have been difficult to see it as the major threat to the Monarchy's existence that some later saw it as. On the other hand, the antagonism to the idea of Vienna as the German overlord was already present, and as Havlíček discussed the British oppression of the Irish, and meant the German-speaking Austrian oppression of the Czechs, the political intent, and the political consequences, should have been clear at the time, were the Czech national cause really to take off.

Nationalism was not the only way in which Habsburg society structured itself in *Vormärz*. There were also socio-economic, class divisions which also were in a process of change, and often interacted with nationalism in explosive ways. The most significant class division remained that between noble landowners and the peasants who, under whatever coercive or voluntary arrangement, worked the land. In times of crisis, the resentments and hatreds that underlay the relationship, as in the performance of compulsory labour, the *robot*, could overcome the usual hierarchical and deferential norms of feudal society. Hence in 1831, in northern Hungary, a cholera outbreak, combined with rumours of nobles poisoning wells, led to 40,000 peasants sacking their lords' properties and killing many of them, and was only put down with difficulty by the Habsburg authorities. Something similar happened in western Galicia in February 1846, when a revolt by Polish nationalist nobles in the free city state of Cracow (only recently occupied by the Austrian military) spread to the neighbouring Austrian territory. Instead of the revolt being supported by the Polish peasantry, however, the peasants turned on their noble superiors, proclaiming themselves loyal subjects of the Austrian emperor, and massacred the noble rebels and their own lords. The violence against the Polish nationalist (noble) rebels was only stopped by the intervention of the Austrian military. This was a vivid illustration of the fact that the relationship between 'political nation' (nobility), Habsburg state and the 'people' (largely peasantry) was a triangular one, with the peasants often regarding the Habsburg state as their protector against their noble lords, even if they were of the same 'nation'. There was, in other words, whether through competing nation-alisms, or class conflicts, much room for manoeuvre for the Habsburg government in this multi-national, polyglot and socially still premodern world.

That said, within the educated classes and the 'political nations' there was increasingly an overall feeling of a need for change, of a need to break out of the situation of 'martial law in peacetime' of the System. The relative prosperity of the 1830s and growth of the urban educated class led to frustration and even contempt for the censorship still being imposed, albeit less effectively, after 1835. There was a change in tone: at the *Theater an der Wien* Raimund's fables were replaced by Johann Nestroy's farces (*Possen*). Reliant on the local dialect, word play, and with frequent ad-libbing, Nestroy's comedies were excellent vehicles for both parody and social and (well-disguised) political criticism, which often got past the censors. Moritz Saphir returned to Vienna in 1834, eventually gaining permission in 1837 to found his own journal, *Der Humorist*, which also acquired a reputation of sly satire of Austrian society (and government). Grillparzer attested to an easing off of censorship, in practice at least. He himself withdrew from public life after the discoura-ging failure in 1838 of *Weh, dem der lügt!*, but he was one of the signatories of a protest letter against the arbitrary nature of censorship in 1845. Other writers, such as Eduard von Bauernfeld, became bolder in their critique of the System. His *Grossjährig* (Of Age), performed in 1846, was a veiled, but unsubtle attack on the persistence of Metternich and the government in treating Austrian society like children instead of adults. That the premiere was at the *Burgtheater* suggests a certain relaxation of the once quite strict enforcement of the ban against criticism of the government.

Austrian writers also got around the censors by having their criticism of the System published abroad and then smuggled into the country. In 1828, Carl Postl published his broadside against the System, *Austria as It Is*, under the name Charles Sealsfield, in London. In 1841 Victor Andrian-Werburg published in Hamburg his critique of Austrian bureau-cratic centralism, *Austria and Its Future* (the second part published in 1847, also in Hamburg). 1841 was also the year in which Ignaz Kuranda, a Jewish liberal journalist originally from Prague, started pub-lishing *Die Grenzbote* in Brussels, and having it smuggled into Austria for his German liberal readership. Many of them would have been members of the Legal-Political Reading Association, founded in 1841 in Vienna, which became a forum in which academics, businessmen, lawyers, but also a number of aristocrats, and students as associate members, could discuss the topics of the day, and, informally, their political aspects. Such associations, which saw aristocrats and the middle classes intermingle to discuss cultural, economic, social and implicitly political affairs, were proliferating in cities and towns across the Monarchy. Austrian civic society was outpacing a stagnating government system.

Up until 1846, there was no real sign that any of this was an immediate threat to the System, but the deterioration of the economic situation from the mid-1840s on started to change that. The longer-term background to 1848 might well have been a gradual decrease in peasants' and workers' living standards since the 1820s, as technological changes disrupted traditional labour patterns, but it is unclear whether data for France and Germany are applicable to the Habsburg Monarchy. Much clearer is the fact that the harvest failures of 1846, following on the potato blight of 1845 in more northern sectors, created a potential for famine, with many dying of starvation in Galicia. While government measures were able to avoid massive starvation (unlike in Ireland), the agrarian crisis led to food price inflation in the towns, and then, even though the 1847 harvest was good, a major economic depression due to lack of demand, which severely affected the urban lower classes as factories and artisans dismissed workers and journeymen – and this then led to a general credit crisis, which partly explains the withdrawal of financiers from direct funding of railway construction in 1847. And, as we saw, this put extra pressure on Habsburg finances, and hence on creditworthiness.

Meanwhile, in Italy, there was a combination of the usual, chronic insurgency with more specific and threatening developments for Austrian hegemony. A typical conspiratorial revolt in Palermo in January succeeded this time in toppling the government in Naples. In Rome, the 'liberal pope', Pius IX had called a consultative assembly for the Papal States in 1847, and, inadvertently or not, raised the ambitions of Italian nationalists, also in Lombardy-Venetia. In December 1847, a tobacco boycott was launched in Milan, which led in January to the 'tobacco riots'. And then news came through about the revolution in Paris on 22 February and the fall of the regime of Louis-Philippe, which set off crises in many German states and encouraged the 'party of movement' throughout Europe. In turn, on 5 March, a report from the National Bank in Vienna meant to reassure creditors led to a run on the banks, the 'bank hullabaloo', as investors lost confidence in the government's ability to pay to send troops to suppress the riots, and continue to pay its creditors. Liberals in Vienna called for the constitutional control of state finances, following the example of Kossuth's call for an Austrian constitution (to safeguard Hungary's) on 3 March before the Diet in Pressburg (just down river). On 11 March, a comprehensive petition demanding moderate liberal reform, written by Bauernfeld (the playwright) and Alexander Bach (a founding member of the Legal-Political Reading Association), was handed in to the Lower Austrian Estates, which was to consider it on 13 March.

In the crisis, financial, diplomatic and political, the government was prostrate and Metternich pessimistic. He once likened Austria to an old pair of shoes. Well-worn in, they were extremely comfortable, but beware anyone who wore them in the rain! The Austrian shoes were about to get soaking wet.

The Springtime of the Peoples

When 13 March came, radical students and sympathetic workers marched to the *Landhaus* to present their own (more radical) petition to the Estates. Adolf Fischhof, a Jewish physician, gave an impassioned speech in front of the assembly's building, and in the crowded area the Estates received a committee of the protesters and then, feeling threatened by the large crowd that had gathered, sent their own deputation to the *Hofburg* with a reform petition. The tense situation then became a revolutionary one when troops fired on the demonstrators, killing five. Unrest and rioting spread, and in a state of panic the government first acceded to requests from Vienna's mayor to arm a new Civic Guard of propertied citizens to keep order; as things continued to get out of hand, leading members of the Habsburg family, with Archduke Johann reportedly in a leading role, induced Archduke Ludwig to sack Metternich, who was replaced by Kolowrat, and then the next day, 14 March, got him to promise to grant a constitution. The very next day, 15 March, Lajos Kossuth arrived in Vienna to present the demands for major reform from the Pressburg Diet, and in Budapest, his supporters led a revolutionary crowd that forced the royal government to accede to its liberal-nationalist demands.

The Viennese revolution was only one in a cascade of events that had received its initial impetus from the February revolution in Paris: German nationalists had already, on 5 March, sent out invitations to the Frankfurt *Vorparlament* (preliminary parliament), with the aim of creating a German nation-state. Yet the fall of Vienna and Metternich's System was almost as significant a catalyst: 17 March saw revolutions in Venice and Cracow; 18 March, Berlin and Milan, where the one attempt to counter the revolution by the use of troops failed, with the Austrian general, Josef Radetzky, withdrawing his troops after five days. In other cities in the Monarchy, there was a more measured, usually positive response to the revolutionary events in Vienna and Budapest, with no revolution as such, and a welcoming of the new, constitutional empire. In Trieste, the attempt at an Italian nationalist revolt was quickly put down by the port's pro-Habsburg merchant patricians who saw the Monarchy (correctly) as the main source of its prosperity. In Zagreb, the meeting of a 'national assembly' on 25 March was another (nationalist but pro-Habsburg) response that was to provide a key model. Over the next days and months, the plurality of revolutions, a product of the Monarchy's polycentricity, as well as the breadth of its spheres of interest (in Italy and Germany), created a most complicated set of parallel narratives, but with crucial interactions, usually with Vienna at the centre but not always, that makes any account of 1848 almost as hard to follow for historians as it was for contemporaries.

In addition, each revolution was composed of multiple revolutions, often at cross-purposes to the others. There were at least three major different forms of revolution involved: often there was a regional political nation, a noble elite, attempting to gain, or regain, control over its traditional territories, as was the case in Hungary, northern Italy, and Cracow (as well as Lemberg, but less convincingly); in the cities and towns liberals attempted to bring the imperial bureaucracy under constitutional control; in the countryside the peasantry sought to free itself from the vestiges of the feudal agricultural system with its dues and *robot*. Other revolutions could be added: the demands from urban workers and the poor for better conditions; and especially the efforts of nationalities that were not yet represented by 'political nations' to gain a say in how they were governed. These structurally differentiated revolutions not only interacted with each other, but also across the geographic plane, so that the support of journeymen and students for radical social policies in Vienna also involved support for German nationalist goals in Frankfurt. Another instance of structural and geographic complexity: Romanian peasants in Transylvania greeted the abolition of serfdom, but also became strong supporters of the Romanian nationalist cause, primarily to oppose the Magyar masters whom they blamed for their – economic – oppression, and this led them to oppose the Hungarian government in Budapest, who had promised the abolition of serfdom.

One way of gaining some clarity to the situation is viewing it through the lens of foreign policy, for the revolutions became caught up in at least three wars: a war of national unification in Italy; a war of national expansion/defence in Schleswig-Holstein; and a war of national independence in Hungary (if you were Magyar). The first began almost immediately after the March revolutions, when Carlo Alberto of Piedmont-Savoy declared war on Austria on 23 March explicitly to create a new Italian nation-state; the second similarly was sparked as early as 21 March, when Denmark annexed Schleswig, provoking a revolt on 24 March, and a Prussian invasion on 11 April, commissioned by the German

Confederation. The Hungarian war took a little longer to get going, but the potential was already there when the new Hungarian government in Budapest took power after 15 March, and the imperial government in Vienna appointed Josip Jelačić *ban* of Croatia on 23 March. All of the great powers were involved at one point or another. Britain intervened diplomatically in Schleswig-Holstein, and verbally in Italy. France, crucially, did not intervene seriously in Germany or Italy in 1848, partly out of a wish to avoid repeating the history of 1792, and when she did intervene in 1849 it was against the revolution in Rome. Russia was in some ways a marginal factor in 1848 – unaffected by any substantial internal unrest – but in others was central – for its threatened intervention in Schleswig-Holstein, and its actual intervention in Hungary in 1849. Prussia was clearly central to the German Question. Austria was centrally involved in all theatres: Germany, Italy and of course Hungary and the rest of the Habsburg Monarchy – in such a way that it is difficult to distinguish foreign from domestic policy, so intertwined were the two.

The very complexity of the revolutions, of their motivations and social causes and bases, as well as their involvement in international conflicts, had its own, very negative impact, on the outcome of 1848, but this was far from evident when the 'springtime of the peoples' began. Initially power seemed to fall almost effortlessly into the laps of the revolutionaries, as though it was just meant to be. It looked like the idealism of the French Revolution of 1789 was going to work out this time, that its message of rational progress, popular sovereignty and individual liberty had been right all along; indeed one of the main reasons why the regimes folded so easily, like a house of cards, was not only that they were by then ideologically and financially bankrupt, but also because they wished to avoid the equivalent of the Terror of 1793 at all cost, and perhaps the liberals were right to predict the inevitable victory of constitutional, representative government? As we know in hindsight, this was not how things turned out, just as we know the Arab Spring (or even 1989?) did not work out as hoped, but to understand events, we need to remember that this was not how contemporaries saw things. Florian Ziemialkowski later recalled participating in Vienna in April in a celebration of the nations, with the Polish flag placed next to the black-red-gold German flag, and the 'blue-white-green' Hungarian one: 'we all lived as if in a beautiful dream'. For revolutionaries like him, in March and April 1848, a new world of constitutionalism, individual liberty and national unity appeared ready for the taking – it just needed to be implemented correctly.

From the perspective of the imperial government in Vienna, it was clear from the first that this was easier said than done. The post-Metternich regime of a 'responsible ministry' headed by Kolowrat and mostly staffed by bureaucratic officials of the old regime only lasted a couple of weeks before there was a reshuffle, and Count Karl Ludwig Ficquelmont, another holdover, became prime minister on 4 April. The same day, the State Conference was abolished and Archduke Ludwig was replaced by his brother Franz Karl as the main, unofficial, representative for the incapacitated Ferdinand. It is as well to note, though, that at no point did the imperial family officially give up power, and the 'responsible ministry' was still composed of old-regime bureaucrats. There might have been a revolution, and Vienna after 15 March was for some weeks calm, but the government in Vienna was just a milder form of its predecessor, intent on keeping the Monarchy together as much as possible.

This looked like a tall order in the post-March world. Northern Italy was in a state of war, mostly in the hands of either nationalist revolutionaries in Milan and Venice or the Piedmontese Army, with Radetzky's forces hunkered down in the fortresses of the Quadrilateral: Verona, Mantua, Peschiera and Legnago. Meanwhile, the liberal nationalists in Hungary were able to use the perilous situation in which the Habsburg interest found itself after 13 March to exact huge concessions from the government and imperial family. Eventually Ferdinand, along with Franz Karl and his son (and the prospective heir) Franz Joseph, journeyed to Pressburg to sanction the April Laws, which consisted of the entire reform programme of the Kossuthian liberals, making Hungary virtually an independent nation-state, with Ferdinand as king, but with a constitution, and a 'responsible ministry' under a minister president, for the time being Count Lajos Batthyány. The emancipation of the peasantry and the creation of a parliament with an extended (but not universal) male franchise was also enacted. The imperial government in Vienna also accepted the request from Frankfurt for elections to the German National Assembly to be held in May. On the imperial plane, it looked as though the Monarchy was on the verge of dissolving.

In Vienna itself, arguments between moderates and radicals about the government's proposed constitution, drawn up by Minister of the Interior Baron Franz von Pillersdorf and published on 25 April, resulted in a radical revolt of students and their lower-middle- and working-class supporters on 15 May. The unrest prompted the imperial family, sensing again French precedent, to flee to Innsbruck on the 17th. In the reaction, there was another radical revolt on 26 May, and a Security Committee took control of the city, headed by none other than Adolf Fischhof. The situation was made worse by an economic and financial crisis and an ill-conceived public works programme that caused more worker unrest. Nonetheless Fischhof proved a responsible leader, the imperial government continued to function, now led by Pillersdorf, and by June things had calmed down again. Elections for the new, unicameral constituent assembly, the *Reichstag* (imperial parliament), were held in late June and early July, in Vienna and throughout the Monarchy – excluding Hungary and Lombardy-Venetia that is. The franchise gave all Austrian 'independent' male citizens over 24 the vote, which was very broad for the time, about 50 per cent of Austrian men above 24, and 10–15 per cent of the total population. The actual election of deputies was indirect, in order to compensate, it was hoped, for the voters' lack of political education. The actual participation was well below 50 per cent, as many were unused or actively hostile to voting, especially a considerable number of Galician peasants who saw it as a noble plot. Others took the opportunity to vote in fellow peasants as deputies, so that a quite large number of *Reichstag* members were illiterate. Nonetheless, the elections were generally peaceful, and were the one occasion in the nineteenth century when many in the lower classes, especially the peasantry, had the opportunity to vote.

Archduke Johann arrived in Vienna on 24 June, sent by the imperial family as mediator, and negotiated with the Security Committee a new government. This was headed from 18 July by the foreign minister, Johann von Wessenberg, a retired diplomat, with Alexander Bach at Justice and another moderate liberal, Josephist centralist, Anton von Doblhoff, at Interior, and this moderate liberal government was accepted by Fischhof's Security Committee without protest. Archduke Johann, the *Bürgerfürst* (citizen-prince) trusted both as sympathetic to *bürgerlich* interests as well as for his history as a supporter of the German national cause during the Napoleonic Wars, was now, ironically, the main representative of the Habsburgs – on two fronts. On 12 July, he had taken the oath in Frankfurt as *Reichsverweser* (imperial regent) of the nascent German Empire; on 22 July, as representative of his nephew Emperor Ferdinand (still in Innsbruck) he opened the new *Reichstag* of the *Austrian* Empire. Of the assembly's 383 deputies, 190 were Slav, and one-quarter were peasants. Despite problems with translation, and the illiteracy of a considerable number of deputies, the *Reichstag* got down to its discussion of the new constitutional and legal framework of the empire. On both fronts, Frankfurt and Vienna, the opportunities for real progress seemed just starting.

On 12 August, the imperial family returned to Vienna from Innsbruck, apparently as confirmation of a political stability in which the revolution's moderate achievements could now be put in concrete constitutional and legislative form. The most substantial evidence of that occurred only a few

Figure 5. Opening of the *Reichstag* by Archduke Johann, in the Winter
Riding School of the *Hofburg*, 22 July 1848.
(Published with permission of the Austrian National Library.)

weeks later, when the *Reichstag* passed the key legislation of the revolution: the full emancipation of the peasantry, on 7 September. In reality,
the tide had already begun to turn against the revolution, even in its
moderate form. The emancipation of the peasants in any case gave to
the largest and most potent block of change-seekers what they had sought,

so that the revolutionaries, whether liberal or radical, were now on their own when facing the monarchical forces of 'order'. Moreover, those monarchical forces had already experienced a striking change in their fate.

In mid-June Prince Alfred Windischgrätz had provoked and then subdued a radical revolt in Prague, and then chosen to impose martial law and suppress the entire revolutionary movement in the city. He had ordered the Prague National Committee dissolved, and had sent home the delegates of the Slavic Congress that Palacký and his Czech nationalist allies had summoned as an Austroslavist, pro -Habsburg Monarchy answer to the German National Assembly in Frankfurt. Instead of seeing this all as an attack on constitutionalism, German liberals and radicals in Vienna and elsewhere applauded the bombardment of Prague as a blow against Panslavism, and a step towards the realisation of a German nation-state, which was quite to misconstrue the goals of the conservative absolutist Windischgrätz. For him what was important was that the Austrian military had proven once again that it could restore 'order'.

In mid-July had come the next stage in the resurgence of the imperial party. In Lombardy-Venetia, Piedmontese rule had not proven all that effective, alienating the rural lower classes and radicals, while Radetzky's remaining forces terrorised the countryside, as at the atrocity at Montebello, deterring opposition. The Piedmontese also delayed any direct engagement with the Austrian forces, allowing them to be reorganised and reinforced from Tyrol. When the armies finally did meet, at Custozza on 23 July, Piedmontese incompetence handed Radetzky an unlikely but decisive victory, so that Lombardy and most of the territory of Venetia were soon back in Austrian hands, and only Venice held out. Lombardy-Venetia was now treated as a conquered territory, and muchneeded revenues once more were exacted to balance Vienna's books, at the cost of deep alienation of the populace. Yet in Vienna, and north of the Alps generally, except for a few hard-bitten and insightful democrats, the defeat of Italian nationalism was seen as a victory for Austrian constitutional monarchism and the German nation. Johann Strauss the Elder wrote the *Radetzky March* to celebrate, and Grillparzer wrote a poem praising the general for saving the Monarchy through his military feats: 'In deinem Lager ist Österreich', he wrote, 'In your army camp is Austria', without irony.

Meanwhile the situation in Hungary had developed in ways fatal to the success of the revolution in the Monarchy overall. The achievement of a 'lawful revolution' through the April Laws had left two major questions still in some dispute: just how independent was Hungary when it came to foreign policy and military affairs; and just how extensive was the reach of Hungarian power? Did the national government have control over where

Hungarian troops in the Habsburg army were deployed? Did the writ of the national government in Budapest extend to the whole of the lands of the Crown of St Stephen, including Croatia-Slavonia, Transylvania and the Military Frontier, and did Hungarian (Magyar) national interest have absolute priority over that of the other nationalities in the land?

Nationalism had been the force that achieved Hungarian power, but it was also nationalism, of the smaller nationalities, that was to contribute to its undoing. In Galicia, the efforts by Polish nobles in Cracow to claim 1848 as a Polish national uprising had been checked (with encouragement from the Habsburg governor, Count Franz Stadion) by the appearance in Lemberg, the provincial capital in eastern Galicia, of a Supreme Ruthenian Council, representing the large numbers of Ruthenians in the province, even if the vast bulk of them were illiterate peasants. Stadion had then cemented his advantage in the province by declaring the emancipation of the peasantry from *robot* and all feudal obligations on 22 April, the day before the Polish nationalist Central National Council had planned to do so. Something very similar happened in Hungary, at least in the peripheral lands. 'National assemblies' – in effect mass meetings – were held by Croats in Zagreb as early as 25 March, by Slovaks in Liptovský Svätý Mikuláš a little later, on 10–11 May, by the Serbs in the Military Frontier in Karlovci on 13 May and by the Romanians in Transylvania in Blaj on 15–17 May, where a crowd of approaching 40,000 is reputed to have gathered. Despite the fact that the actual nationalist movements before 1848 had been the concern of only a tiny minority in these groups, and largely cultural at that, in the existential crisis of the revolution nationalism provided the collective factor that allowed other interests and goals to be expressed, and realised.

The key interests that were combined were the peasants' goal of emancipation, and freedom from the central control of the Magyar-speaking government in Budapest. That government had also proclaimed the emancipation of the peasantry, as did almost every assembly and government in 1848, but the Magyar nobility in Transylvania, for instance, had been resistant to this step, and continued to be. It should also be considered that even when nobles accepted the need to end feudal obligations the question remained as to who should pay for this, how much they should be compensated for the loss of their rights and 'property', and who would gain what portion of the lands to be divided up as a result. After decades, centuries of oppression, Romanian peasants in Transylvania had only mistrust for their Magyar noble lords, and preferred to seek a solution through their own national state, under the rule of their (Habsburg) monarch. A delegation was thus sent by the Blaj assembly to the emperor (soon to be in Innsbruck) to plead their case, while the

Hungarian government in Budapest asserted its power to punish these 'traitors' to the national (Hungarian) cause. The result was to be a savage civil war in Transylvania between Hungarian forces and peasants orga- nised by Romanian nationalists. An uprising against the Budapest gov- ernment in the Banat by Serbs had a similar origin.

The crucial case was, however, Croatia. Here the combination of local Croatian nationalist resistance to overweening Magyar rule (already evi- dent before 1848) combined with the Habsburg-loyalism of the new *ban*, Jelačić, who had also become a senior figure in the Austrian military, as commanding officer of the *Grenzer*, the border troops of the Military Frontier. From the start of his appointment in late March, Jelačić refused to accept the Hungarian government's authority in Croatia-Slavonia, even when the government was given that authority by the Hungarian king. He claimed authority instead from the Austrian emperor, who was in reality the same person as the Hungarian king, Ferdinand. Over the next few months the stand-off between Budapest and Jelačić was the object of extensive, and often duplicitous negotiations and communica- tions between the Imperial Court (after mid-May in Innsbruck) and the constitutional 'responsible ministry' in Vienna. In June Jelačić was offi- cially relieved of his position by the emperor, but he stayed in power in Zagreb, and as the Habsburg position improved, the Imperial Court's approach to Jelačić did as well, so that in late August, he was reinstated as *ban* and commander of the *Grenzer*. On 11 September, Jelačić, with a nod from the Imperial Court, crossed the Drava and invaded Inner Hungary.

The response in Budapest was a radicalising of the revolution, as the parliament and indeed the royal government of Batthyány acceded to radical nationalist demands to prepare for war against the invading imperial forces. The final break came when Count Franz Lamberg was sent by the imperial government to Budapest as a special commissioner and commander-in-chief of all Habsburg forces in Hungary to negotiate with the Budapest government, and on arrival on 28 September was set upon by a radicalised mob and lynched. Vienna appointed Jelačić to replace him and declared the Hungarian parliament and government dissolved, effectively declaring war against Budapest. On 2 October Batthyány's government resigned and Kossuth was made head of state ('regent-president'), and as head of the National Defense Committee virtual dictator of Hungary.

Meanwhile, Jelačić's invading forces proved less effective than expected, losing several battles against Hungarian forces, and being forced to retreat by early October towards Vienna. It was at this point that the final crisis in Vienna's revolution occurred. On 6 October, the imperial government ordered the Viennese garrison to march to support the retreating Jelačić.

Under the pressure of a large crowd organised and incited by Vienna's radicals, the troops mutinied and in the ensuing unrest Count Theodor Baillet von Latour, war minister, was lynched. The Imperial Court immediately fled, this time to Olmütz (Olomouc) in Moravia, along with most of the government ministers and many members of the *Reichstag*, who reassembled in Brünn. Vienna, still hosting a majority of the *Reichstag* membership, returned to the control of the Security Committee, but now under more radical leadership, and with far less prospect of a peaceful outcome than in May. The Imperial Court directed Jelačić's forces and troops from Windischgrätz's Prague garrison to besiege and then retake the city. A last gasp attempt by Hungarian forces to relieve their radical (largely German nationalist) allies in Vienna was beaten back at Schwechat on 30 October, and on 31 October the second, more radical 'October revolution' was crushed by the combined forces of Windischgrätz and Jelačić, with German reports decrying the barbarity of the Slav troops. Several of the revolutionary leaders, including Wenzel Messenhauser and Hermann Jellinek, were summarily executed, along with a visiting member of the Frankfurt Parliament, Robert Blum.

The Vienna revolution was effectively over. In the safety of Olmütz the imperial 'camarilla' planned a new strategy for the Monarchy. On 21 November Wessenberg was replaced as prime minister by Prince Felix zu Schwarzenberg, Windischgrätz's brother-in-law. Initially there were some reassuring signs for those intent on preserving the constitutional and legal achievements of the revolution. The *Reichstag* reassembled at Kremsier (Kroměříž), Moravia – far from the radical dangers of Vienna – on 22 November and was encouraged to continue its discussions about a new constitution. Schwarzenberg appeared to want to work with the assembly and the popular forces unleashed by the revolution. It was clear, though, that power no longer lay with the assembly. On 2 December, without any input from the *Reichstag*, Ferdinand was coerced by the Imperial Court members into abdication, and was replaced by his eighteen-year-old nephew, Franz, with his full name of Franz Joseph. The young man would offer a different, more vigorous image of the dynasty, and he had not been forced to agree to the demands of Hungarians, or anyone else, yet. For the moment the main goal of the dynasty was to reassert complete power over its realms, and so a force of 70,000 under Windischgrätz was dispatched to reconquer Hungary. By December, the Hungarian government had been forced to evacuate Budapest. Having looked to be in a state of dissolution, the Habsburg Monarchy now seemed stronger than ever, thanks to the discord among its many opponents and the brute force of its obedient military forces. Reaction appeared to be back in charge.

Figure 6. *Empress Maria Anna and Archduchess Sophie escort Franz Joseph I to the throne*, by Leopold Kupelwieser. This is an allegorical interpretation of Franz Joseph's ascension on 2 December 1848. His mother leads him, and the throne and crown are surrounded by three generals: Windischgrätz, Radetzky and Jellačić. The old emperor, Ferdinand, and Franz Joseph's father, Franz Karl, are very much in the background.
(Published with permission of the Austrian National Library.)

Squaring the Circle I: Austria and Germany

While the revolution proceeded in tandem in Vienna and Budapest, a parallel, if interlinked, process occurred in Frankfurt-am-Main. The attempt there to establish a German national government was of major concern to Austria, and the failure to square the circle of how to integrate Austria with the German national state was to have far-reaching consequences for the Habsburg Monarchy.

The relationship between Germany and the Habsburg Monarchy is one of those complex relationships which modernity, in the form of nationalism, deeply unsettled and eventually broke. Austria had been the leading power within the German political system since the fifteenth century. As Holy Roman Emperors, and then as presiding power of the German Confederation, the Habsburg dynasty had been the premier

German power, even if (as with Prussia) a significant part of its territory lay outside the bounds of the Empire/Confederation. In the *ancien régime* before 1789, and even in the restored version of the Confederation, the political relationships had been either loose enough, or subtle and multi-layered enough, for this ambiguous situation not to matter too much. However, the attempt at a national 'closer union', as represented by Frankfurt, was bound to raise questions about the Austrian-German relationship: was Central Europe to be organised according to the 'modern' logic of the nation-state, or was it to remain in some form of multi-state, and multi-national federation, as presently with the overlapping combination of the German Confederation with the Habsburg Monarchy?

Initially, as we have seen, the answer appeared definitely to lie in the direction of nation-states. The 'springtime of the peoples' was as easily understood as the 'springtime of the nations' and even the nation-states. In Germany, dissatisfaction with the current arrangement of the Confederation had been building already in 1847, and a group of fifty-one self-selected leaders had called at Heidelberg on 5 March – *before* 13 March – for a 'preliminary parliament' to meet in Frankfurt to discuss how to create a more effective national government. When the revolution occurred in Vienna, the immediate response of many revolutionaries, especially the more radical and democratic ones, was to see it as a German *national* revolution. On 1 April the German black-red-gold tricolour flew from St Stephen's steeple; on the 2nd, it flew above the *Hofburg*. Many liberals and Josephist officials also had sympathies with the German national cause, and the post-March ministry readily agreed, as did all the other German states in the Confederation, to hold elections for the prospective national parliament, which took place with a generally broad franchise, in a two-stage process in late April and early May.

One might ask how a multi-national empire like the Habsburg Monarchy could ever take part in the election for one national constituent assembly, but at the time this did not appear as unrealistic as it might. When the elections to Frankfurt were held, it appeared as though most of the parts of the Monarchy outside the 'German' core: Hungary, Lombardy-Venetia and even the Poles in Galicia, were participating in forming their own nation-states. Had the Monarchy fallen apart, as seemed probable, the remaining part of the Monarchy, which was indeed that within the Confederation, and which was the only part in which elections were held for Frankfurt, might have been able to be integrated. Admittedly, those provinces included the Bohemian crownlands, Carniola, the Adriatic Littoral and Trieste, so a large number of Czechs, Slovenes and Italians and other non-German-speakers, but then, as Hungarian and German nationalists argued at the time, the nation-state of France included Breton-speakers in Brittany, and Provençal-speakers in Provence, so why could not a German nation-state include Czechs and Slovenes? The Czech nationalist leadership, as we saw, objected to this approach, boycotted the Frankfurt elections and organised the Slavic Congress in Prague to promote an Austroslavist alternative vision. Nonetheless, Austrians went to the polls to vote for *two* constituent assemblies in 1848 – in April/May for the German National Assembly in Frankfurt; and in June for the Austrian constituent assembly, the *Reichstag*. Moreover, the purview of the elections was quite similar in principle, given the exclusion of Hungary and Lombardy-Venetia from the *Reichstag* election, with only Galicia and Dalmatia the additions for the Austrian electoral area.

Moreover, it did not seem entirely unreasonable, given the historical background, that the German and the Austrian states should be so inter-linked. As we saw, Archduke Johann was able to play a leading role in both governments in the summer of 1848, taking the oath of imperial regent in Frankfurt only a few days before opening the *Reichstag* on 22 July. The very fact that he had been elected imperial regent in Frankfurt on 29 June by a huge majority of deputies suggested the attraction to them of the 'greater German' (*grossdeutsch*) approach, of including (German) Austria in the new Germany, especially for those from the Catholic and South German areas. It was always going to be an issue of how to effect the integration, however, given that the Monarchy was still, for all said above, a multi-national, supra-national empire, with whole provinces, such as Galicia, that German politicians would prefer not to be included in the German nation-state – that is why the assembly's president, Heinrich von Gagern, put the discussion of the German nation-state's borders on the back burner.

The September crisis over Schleswig-Holstein (also a question concerning the half-in, half-out status of territories) delegitimised the Frankfurt government, including Johann, which was shown to be a toothless, paper tiger, entirely reliant on the military power of still independent states, in this case Prussia, and unable to defend the national interest (against Britain and Russia as well as Denmark). The parliament and Johann were saved from radical, nationalist protesters by Austrian and Prussian troops, but the failure in the Schleswig-Holstein case hardened nationalist positions, and turned attention to finding a decisive leader with power, who could defend national interests in ways the imperial regent could not – and in practice this meant either being Prussian-led – 'little German' (*kleindeutsch*) – or Austrian-led 'greater German'. At the same time, in the autumn, the Habsburg government was reasserting its power over *non*-German parts of its empire: Italy and Hungary – precisely when the Frankfurt parliament was turning to the question of borders.

The upshot of those discussions was that Frankfurt decided in a vote on 27 October, by 340 to 76 (with revolutionary Vienna still besieged), that the new German nation-state could only be comprised of German states. German princes who ruled non-German lands could not rule them as part of their German state, but only through a form of personal union.

This was potentially still a form of 'greater German' policy, as it was believed by many deputies that it enabled the parts of Austria within the Confederation to be still part of Germany, but required relations with those outside its boundaries to be reconstituted, so that Vienna would still be an extra-territorial capital to its former non-German lands. Had the conditions of the summer prevailed, with a virtually independent Hungary, and Lombardy-Venetia only tenuously still Austrian, the prevailing, generous interpretation of what were 'German lands' could have included the 'Brittany and Provence' of Germany: the Bohemian crownlands and the southern, mainly Slovenian provinces, as well as Trieste. They were ancient Habsburg, hence German, territories, with German-speaking educated and economic elites, and within the old German sphere of the Holy Roman Empire, after all. Italian-speaking Trieste would easily be accepted as vital to German interests in the Mediterranean. This would have meant only a rearrangement of relations, along Hungarian lines perhaps, with Dalmatia and Galicia, not an impossible task, as these provinces were quite peripheral to the Monarchy. Yet conditions were not the same as in the summer. Lombardy-Venetia had been reconquered, and the Hungarian (and Croatian) situation was radically different. Many Austrians saw the Frankfurt vote as an attack on the integrity of the Monarchy, forcing Austria to be effectively broken up for the sake of German unity. Moreover, once the October revolution in Vienna was crushed – only a few days later – it became clear that the new government of Schwarzenberg would make no concession to German national unity that impinged on *Austrian* political unity. One sign of the degree to which the new Austrian approach rejected Frankfurt's approach, and its legitimacy, was the summary trial and execution of Robert Blum, a Frankfurt parliamentary deputy, on 9 November, for his participation in the October Viennese revolution.

The refusal to negotiate at all on Austria's political unity meant that any possible 'greater German' compromise was effectively impossible. Johann's prime minister, Anton von Schmerling, a 'great German' Austrian, resigned on 12 December. On 28 December, Schwarzenberg rejected any exclusion of Austria, and insisted on its membership – and leading role – in the German Confederation; on 4 February he demanded that the whole of the Austrian Empire be included in the German nation-state, which was unacceptable not only to 'little German' supporters, but also to many 'greater German' ones, as it would effectively mean the end of the German character of the German nation-state. On 7 March, when he ended the Kremsier *Reichstag*, he had issued a 'decreed constitution' that proclaimed the indivisibility of the Austrian Empire, and its absolute legal sovereignty, so that Frankfurt's laws were no longer valid. Austrian unity prevailed over any interest in Austrian integration into a German nation-state.

There had been this tension in the Austrian-German question all along, going back to the arguments between Bauernfeld and Bach about what to include in the petition of 11 March. Bauernfeld had wanted to include the possibility of giving up territories in order to effect the integration of German Austria into a German nation-state; Bach had refused any such concession of the integrity of the Habsburg Monarchy for the sake of national goals. Yet it was still viewed as a tragic outcome by many that the 'greater German' option was thus set aside, leaving the way clear for the 'little German' alternative of excluding Austria and going with Prussian leadership. When the Frankfurt parliament voted at the end of March to invite the Prussian king, Friedrich Wilhelm IV, to be the 'people's emperor', Johann, still the imperial regent, wrote that he was 'at his wit's end' ('am Ende des Lateins'), an expression that would be repeated in even more tragic circumstances almost seventy years later.

Friedrich Wilhelm IV refused the imperial title on 3 April, precisely because of its 'popular', constitutional origins. This marked the culmination and failure of Frankfurt – soon thereafter most deputies were recalled or left, leaving a radical core which moved to Stuttgart and was eventually dispersed by troops in June. Johann continued as imperial regent, ordered to stay on by Schwarzenberg, until he resigned the office in late December 1849. He left Frankfurt on New Year's Day, 1850. Meanwhile, Friedrich Wilhelm IV attempted to obtain the German imperial title by the agreement of his fellow German monarchs, forming the Erfurt Union of late March, but by then Schwarzenberg, with Russian backing, was in position to check any such ambitions, and at the Punctation of Olmütz of 29 November (known as the 'humiliation of Olmütz' in Prussian historiography), did so. There were more negotiations, the Dresden Conference, to create a German union including Austria based on monarchs, not the people. Schwarzenberg again proposed a version of his 'empire of seventy million', but this was rejected. The conference broke down in May 1851, and Germany returned to the regime of the German Confederation, as before March 1848. The circle had not been squared; Habsburg power had, it is true, been reasserted, but at the cost of showing how difficult integration of Austria would be into a *national* German state, and how relatively easy, and acceptable to the German political nation outside of Austria, a Prussian-led solution might be. For the moment, though, the attempt to solve the relationship between Austria and Germany on a national plane was back to square one.

Reaction

By 1851 Schwarzenberg's government had been able to turn back the clock on many of the changes effected by the revolution, at least on the surface.

The main problem at the beginning of 1849 remained Hungary, and this turned out to be much more difficult to defeat than it first appeared. Budapest might have been seized by Austrian troops in January, but the Hungarian government continued to have widespread popular support and was now aided also by liberals, democrats and radicals from other national conflicts, who saw Hungary as the last hope for the revolution. In Transylvania, one of these foreign supporters, the Polish revolutionary émigré general, Józef Bem, led Hungarian forces in early 1849 to a successful campaign against a combination of Romanian-nationalist-led peasant guerrillas and Austrian forces from the Military Frontier. By early April, Bem had even seen off a small Russian intervention force, and began negotiations with the leader of the one remaining major opposing force, Avram Iancu.

In Inner Hungary, the Austrian advances were also reversed in the spring of 1849 by the Hungarian forces under Arthur Görgey, and renewed war in northern Italy in March meant that Austrian forces could not easily be reinforced. Politically, as well, the conflict was made even sharper by the March constitution decreed by Schwarzenberg's imperial government, which made clear in its claim to political unity of all Habsburg lands that there would be no return to the particularist days of the Hungarian Diet. In response, Kossuth declared in Debrecen on 13–14 April the dethronement of the Habsburg dynasty and Hungary's independence. With the Austrian forces in humiliating retreat, Budapest was retaken in May. Austrian finances were once again strained, and there was resistance to conscription in Carinthia and Bohemia. The Austrian situation was so dire that in April the new emperor, Franz Joseph, had felt forced to sack Windischgrätz, the hero of the Reaction who had been so instrumental in his ascending the throne. His eventual replacement, Julius von Haynau, was able to turn the situation around quite quickly, especially as, after Radetzky's victory at Novara on 23 March, Austrian reinforcements could be sent from Italy. Before the improvement was evident, however, Franz Joseph had undergone the humiliation of having to ask for major Russian intervention from Tsar Nicholas I. The Austrian forces would probably have won in any case, but the prospect of Russian intervention put the verdict of Hungarian defeat in little doubt. On 18 July Budapest was recaptured; on 13 August Görgey surrendered at Világos to the Russian forces, effectively ending the war.

The Russians handed the Hungarian troops over to the Austrian plenipotentiary, Haynau. Already with a reputation for brutality as the 'Hyena of Brescia', Haynau now exacted revenge on the Hungarian rebel forces for their rebellion, but also for the humiliation that their heroic resistance had caused the Habsburg emperor, in having to ask his Russian counterpart for help. Schwarzenberg is reputed to have suggested to Franz Joseph a policy of 'a little hanging first', and the young emperor did not intervene to stop the policy until Haynau had already carried it out. At Arad on 6 October, thirteen Hungarian rebel generals were executed, and in Budapest on the same day, Batthyány was executed by firing squad. In all, 114 'rebels' were executed. Several who had fled into exile, including Count Gyula Andrássy, were executed in effigy. This cast a pall on subsequent Austro-Hungarian relations.

By October the Italian situation had also been fully resolved. Carlo Alberto's renewal of war on 20 March (he refused to renew the armistice) led to almost immediate defeat of the Piedmontese forces by Radetzky at Novara on 23 March, and Carlo Alberto's abdication. The revolutionary regime in Florence surrendered in April. In June the new French president, Louis Napoleon, intervened in Rome – against the revolutionary regime – to restore the pope. Finally, on 28 August, the last remaining revolutionary hold-out in the Habsburg Monarchy, the island city of Venice, surrendered. 'Order' had been fully restored.

So had, effectively, the absolute power of the Habsburg emperor. Schwarzenberg, who was the real power at this point, with the young, inexperienced emperor following his mentor diligently, had initially shown a readiness to work with the Kremsier *Reichstag*, or at least allow it to work on its proposed constitution, which it industriously proceeded to do. The deputies came up with a constitution that many subsequent historians have viewed as a workable and sophisticated solution to both the nationality problem of the Monarchy and the tension between centralised government and local, provincial autonomy. The two problems were linked, to the extent that most advocates of a strong central government were German-speaking (officials, urban elites, the educated middle classes), while those who wanted more power at the local, provincial level tended to be non-German-speakers, mainly Slav, although there was a large contingent of the nobility, who, for historic and political reasons, advocated 'federalism' and provincial power. The compromise reached at Kremsier was for domestic power to be divided between three levels of representative government: a central parliament, parliaments for the historic provinces and assemblies in *Kreise* ('circles' or counties), which would be divided along ethnic lines, within those provinces. This was a model for accommodating national concerns about education and culture, and other matters, while at the same time allowing international co-operation on more general political issues at a provincial and imperial level. There were frequent attempts later in the Monarchy's history to introduce just such a redrawing of political boundaries to ease national tensions, and the fact that Kremsier was not realised is seen as another of those tragically missed chances in Habsburg historiography. Although recent revisionist interpretations have cast doubt on how effective it could have been, it was agreed on by a freely elected constituent assembly, and so, as Robert Kann has said, it 'represented the will of the people'; it could have been the basis for a workable solution, had it been tried.

The constitution that the *Reichstag* hashed out also included a guarantee of the equal rights of every nationality in the empire, and the usual liberal rights of the citizen. The Catholic Church was disestablished, and the legal equality of all citizens proclaimed. It was in many respects a moderate, liberal document. In one aspect, its assertion of popular sovereignty, the draft constitution was quite radical, especially in a Monarchy in which 'legitimacy' had been such a strong concept for so long, and indeed Franz Joseph, tutored by Metternich in political theory and a strong believer in the doctrine of Divine Right, whose office had been given him 'by grace of God', regarded this as blasphemous, but then the *Reichstag* agreed to remove the relevant clause. (Franz Joseph never accepted the concept of popular sovereignty, even in 1867.)

There were other aspects, objectionable to Franz Joseph and his ministers, which remained, that were restrictive to monarchical power. Ministers would be responsible to the parliament, not the monarch; there was to be only a suspensive veto, and the powers of proroguement and dissolution were weak. The emperor would have large powers over foreign policy, but otherwise this was a constitutional, parliamentary regime, with power more in the representative legislature than in the imperial executive. The draft constitution also excluded the rebel provinces of Lombardy-Venetia and Hungary from its purview, at a time when the emperor and Schwarzenberg were intent on restoring, in one sense at least *establishing*, imperial unity to all Habsburg territories.

The new emperor's motto, after all, was 'Viribus unitis' – with *united* powers. It is not, therefore, that surprising that Franz Joseph and Schwarzenberg decided early in 1849 to end the Kremsier experiment. On 4 March, the *Reichstag*'s constitutional committee had finished its work, and it was planned for the full *Reichstag* to promulgate the new constitution on 15 March, the anniversary of the day in 1848 on which Ferdinand had made his promise of such a constitution. This never occurred, because on 6 March, the deputies were informed by the interior minister, Count Franz Stadion, of the *Reichstag*'s dissolution, and the next day the assembly was dispersed, some of its members arrested.

The same day, 7 March, the government issued a 'decreed' constitution, written by Stadion. The interior minister was actually a convinced liberal constitutionalist, and his constitution followed many of Kremsier's points, but more in favour of imperial power. Its most significant point was the insistence on the unity of the Habsburg state, which, as we have seen, had a major impact both on the German question, and the Hungarian conflict. It proclaimed ministerial responsibility to the *Reichstag*, and it also outlined a whole interlocking hierarchy of administrative and legislative levels, introducing the level of *Bezirk* (district) below that of county, and at the lowest level that of the *Gemeinde* (commune), which was to be an autonomous body whose competences were to be administered by elected councils. This final point of communal autonomy was to be one of the most fruitful products of Stadion's constitution, and the law that he drafted shortly thereafter, on 17 March, the 'Law on Communal Autonomy' was to prove seminal. Yet the constitution never went into effect. It was immediately suspended on the grounds of the emergency situation facing the Monarchy in March 1849.

'Provisional' laws were passed by the government, including the Commune Law, and some of these, such as Bach's creation of district courts to replace manorial courts, and Schmerling's set of judicial reforms, which introduced trial by jury, were quite liberal, in the spirit of Stadion's constitution. However, liberal, constitutionalist hopes were to prove misplaced. Stadion himself suffered a nervous breakdown shortly after drafting the Commune Law, and his successor as interior minister, Bach, soon suspended that law in October 1849, and annulled it in March 1850, virtually eliminating communal autonomy. Schwarzenberg and his ministers continued to operate under the principle of ministerial responsibility to the *Reichstag*, based on the constitution some day coming into force. The set of communal elections held in the autumn of 1850 seemed to suggest some acceptance of the forms of representative self-government envisaged in the Stadion constitution. Schwarzenberg himself also saw advantages of the constitution's formal governing structures, which allowed him, among other things, to plead 'ministerial responsibility' to dissuade the young emperor from unwise decisions. Unfortunately, it did not prove strong enough for Schwarzenberg to prevent the young emperor from making one of those unwise decisions.

Franz Joseph, brought up in the traditions of Habsburg absolutism to despise anything constitutional, decided that even acting under a suspended constitution was too much of a limit on his power. In the same autumn of 1850 as the communal elections were taking place, Franz Joseph asked an old, Metternichian and Josephist official, Karl Kübeck, to explore the setting up of the *Reichsrat* (imperial council) outlined in the constitution. Kübeck took this opportunity to argue against the principle of ministerial responsibility, hence against Schwarzenberg's constitution-based government. Instead a system reminiscent of the constitution-free pre-1848 system should be substituted, where ministers reported directly to a *Reichsrat* of elder statesmen who then advised the monarch, who would then rule.

This *Reichsrat* was instituted in March 1851, and by August Franz Joseph was confident enough to make explicit his wish to do away with the constitution, asserting the 'inapplicability of the English-French constitutional principle to the Austrian imperial state'. In September, Metternich returned to Vienna; preparations for a renunciation of the March Constitution gathered pace, despite Schwarzenberg and Interior Minister Bach's circumspect resistance. On New Year's Eve 1851, 'Sylvester' in German, the *Sylvesterpatent* overthrew the constitution and returned Austria to absolutist rule. It was in reality three edicts. The first cancelled the March constitution, except provisions of legal equality and the emancipation of the peasantry. The second annulled all fundamental rights guaranteed to Austrian citizens, except for the freedom of worship of members of Austria's 'recognised' religions. The third abolished all other laws that had arisen because of the revolution. This included the principle of equality of language and nationalities, and all the representative bodies in Stadion's scheme, except the communal councils, whose autonomy was nevertheless severely circumscribed. Absolutism had been entirely restored, the reaction entirely successful.

Except it did not restore the absolutist system of before 1848; indeed in its radical nature it did away with large chunks of what Franz I had insisted on maintaining. The reaction, as interpreted by Kübeck and Franz Joseph, had opened up a very authoritarian, top-down path to the very modernity that Franz I, and in his own way Metternich, had always warned against. Even if it was from above, what was to happen next was, nonetheless, revolution.

3   1852–1867: Transformation

At the beginning of 1852, the Habsburg Monarchy appeared to have wholly withstood the dramatic challenge afforded by the revolution of 1848. In many ways, it was in better shape. Instead of a mentally incompetent invalid as emperor, there was a dashing, virile, and quite well-educated, and well-trained young man in total control of government. The military had proven ultimately strong enough, and loyal enough, to put down a series of revolutions; the many nationalisms that had been unleashed by the 'springtime of the peoples' had proven an advantage to the Habsburg government, as they had cancelled each other out. The Monarchy's alliances had stood the test as well: Russia had come to its rescue, not only against the Hungarian insurgency in 1849, but also when support was needed to deter Prussia in 1850 from going it alone with the other German states in the crisis that led up to the Punctation of Olmütz. Prussia, meanwhile, largely due to the character of its king, Friedrich Wilhelm IV, had ultimately not been able to overcome its habit of deferring to Austria. In that sense, as Alan Sked has argued, Metternich's System had not been defeated; in 1852 it appeared vindicated. Austrian prospects looked good.

Fifteen years later, the Austrian Empire no longer existed as such, was now clearly a second-rate power, with Russia its deadly enemy, and Prussia its successful usurper of supremacy over the German states. The young emperor who had once so self-confidently regained absolute power had now had to allow his power to be fettered by not one but two, even three, constitutional systems: in Hungary, Cisleithania (Austria) and in Austria-Hungary. This radical transformation had many causes. It turned out that the changes set in train by 1848 could not be so easily reined in, more because of the revolution's consequences outside the Monarchy's borders than within them. Once again, foreign policy was to show its primacy in Habsburg history. As important, though, was to be the *manner* in which the Monarchy's leadership responded to the challenges of post-1848 modernity. At the centre of that leadership was the new, young emperor himself, Franz Joseph.

Franz Joseph: The Ultimate Habsburg

Franz Joseph had become emperor on 2 December 1848, as an eighteen-year-old. At the time it appeared that he had been put there largely as a cypher, as someone whose youth and vigour would energise the supporters of the Monarchy – and the monarchy – and who had not been forced to make all the promises about constitutions and respecting rights that Ferdinand had. Governing was supposed at the outset to be done by Schwarzenberg, and for the first couple of years it was. As we saw, however, Franz Joseph had gone against Schwarzenberg's advice, thrown off the constitution in the *Sylvesterpatent*, and by the beginning of 1852 had asserted his power as absolute ruler of the empire. This had not necessarily been foreseen in 1848; also not foreseen, because not foreseeable, was the remarkable fact that Franz Joseph was to remain emperor until his death on 21 November 1916, almost a full sixty-eight years, in other words for almost the entirety of the Monarchy's remaining career. It is true that there was one last emperor after Franz Joseph, Karl, so officially Franz Joseph was only the penultimate Habsburg emperor. Nonetheless, Franz Joseph had become so identified with *his* empire that his very death, during the Monarchy's worst-ever crisis, is seen as having presaged the Monarchy's death as well. From now on, whether he or his subjects wished it, Franz Joseph was going to be at the centre of his Monarchy's history. In that sense, Karl was only a slight punctuation – Franz Joseph was the ultimate Habsburg.

From his birth on 18 August 1830, Franz Joseph had appeared destined to be emperor; especially after it became clear in 1831 that Ferdinand's marriage would never produce children. He was certainly brought up to fulfil that role. His mother, Sophie of Bavaria, married to Ferdinand's next eldest brother, Franz Karl, did all she could to ensure that 'Franzi' would become successor to Ferdinand, and that he was properly prepared for his imperial office. (Before his becoming emperor he was known as 'Franz' alone.) The regimen of Franz's instruction and training was so taxing that he had a stress-induced breakdown at thirteen. The education he received had a distinctly conservative, reactionary slant: Joseph Fielo taught him history in such a way as to impress on him that no Habsburg should ever get near to either liberalism or constitutions. Perhaps more surprising was that Franz's religious education was also extremely conservative, so that his views on the status of the Roman Catholic Church in the Monarchy were more reactionary than those of the Habsburg religious establishment. This was due to his mother's strong Catholic piety and conservatively Romantic religious sentiments, and to the influence of Abbot Othmar von Rauscher, who taught Franz philosophy from 1844.

His mother, particularly, was to have a very strong, heavily reactionary influence on her son until her death in 1872. Franz von Hauslab was his military instructor. The finishing touches to Franz's upbringing as emperor were administered by none other than Metternich himself, who from November 1847 would meet with the Habsburg heir to impart the art of statesmanship, and to stress the primacy of foreign over domestic policy for a Habsburg emperor.

The young man that emerged from this upbringing was punctilious and hard-working; he had some gifts as a draughtsman as shown by sketches preserved in the archive, but was intellectually not particularly curious or bright – his younger brother Ferdinand Max (Maximilian) was much smarter. Franz was responsible and earnest, if sometimes rather obstinate. He was also quite brave, physically. Indeed Franz really shone when it came to military matters, which he loved. At age five he proclaimed: 'What is military is what I like best.' He never really changed his opinion; throughout his life he showed a strong preference for wearing uniform (just like Joseph II, and unlike Franz I or Ferdinand). Military life, its regimentation and order, appealed to his character, as did the tendency in (Habsburg) military circles to go for practical, expedient solutions, rather than anything too highly theoretical. Franz Joseph was never a great thinker. The military also was an opportunity for Franz to prove his manhood, which he did by participating in a couple of battles in the Italian campaign in 1848, and then again, as emperor, in the capture of Raab (Györ) in Hungary in the spring of 1849, before discretion got the better part of valour and on Schwarzenberg's advice he withdrew. He was thus predisposed to attribute the survival of the Monarchy, and his chance to be its ruler, to his generals and troops, and he drew the conclusion, as Joseph Redlich puts it: 'that material might, physical force, in the shape of the standing army and military police, constituted the kernel of the state, at any rate under a monarchy'.

By 1852 Franz Joseph had become a dashing, vigorous and very self-confident monarch. When he married Elisabeth of Bavaria (his first cousin) in 1854, after a whirlwind and quite romantic courtship, he looked the part, in his red and white uniform, as the husband of Europe's 'most beautiful princess'. His decision to abandon the fig leaf of constitutionalism was strong evidence that he felt himself, as destined ruler of the Habsburg realm, quite capable of ruling in practice as well as on paper. In any case, he had a very capable minister president in Schwarzenberg, to advise him, at the beginning of 1852. One should add, however, that Franz Joseph was from the very beginning an extremely conscientious ruler, that the image of his working for hours at his desk dealing with the details of administering a whole empire, like some bureaucrat-in-chief, was mostly accurate. Indeed, from his own perspective, the main purpose of abandoning constitutionalism was that ruling as a constitutional monarch was immoral. After Louis Napoleon's coup d'état in Paris in December 1851, Franz Joseph commented: 'He is perfectly right. The man who holds the reins of government in his hands must also be able to take responsibility. Irresponsible sovereignty are, for me, words without meaning; such a thing is a mere printing machine for signatures.' Only a properly absolute ruler could take full responsibility for his actions and decisions, and so it should be in Austria, from Franz Joseph's perspective.

This moralising about the monarch's responsibility was associated in the emperor's mind with the need to exercise his most sacred responsibility of preserving the status of the one, true religion, Roman Catholicism, in the Monarchy. Against the later characterisations of Franz Joseph as a benign defender of religious toleration, it is as well to remember that it was Franz Joseph who, when the *Sylvesterpatent* was being signed, refused to sign the decree enacting Jewish emancipation. The emperor's quite pronounced religious conservatism, the product of his mother's influence and his education, was to have a large impact on Austrian politics in the ensuing years.

How the monarch was to exercise his responsibility was also a matter in which Franz Joseph's attitude and character were to have a profound influence on subsequent events. Brave, but not very imaginative; conservative, even reactionary, but also practical and empirical in his approach, prepared, ultimately, to let the ends justify the means; another aspect of Franz Joseph's approval of Louis Napoleon's actions was that it showed his respect for someone who was ready to do almost anything to get the job done. In Franz Joseph's case, this meant that nothing, not even centuries of tradition and established practice, or even, at times, his own values and preferences, should get in the way of realising the power of the Habsburg monarch (himself), as that was identical with the power, prestige and status of the Habsburg Monarchy itself.

When Franz became emperor on 2 December 1848, he had ascended the throne not as 'Franz', but with two of his names, as 'Franz Joseph'. This had been a nineteenth-century form of publicity stunt: a conscious appeal by the Imperial Court, in a time which had witnessed a surge of support for modern, progressive and 'liberal' ideas, and demands for the state to intervene in the peasant-lord nexus, but now wanted 'order' to believe that the Habsburg dynasty could provide the answer to all of this. 'Franz' recalled the emphasis on legitimacy and order of Franz Joseph's grandfather, Franz I, and in other times would have been adequate. Now, though, the added 'Joseph' played to the memory of the 'liberal' emperor, famous for being the plough-following friend to the peasants, Joseph II (the new emperor's great-grand-uncle). It turned out, in many ways a most apt appellation, more apt than its instigators probably imagined, for Franz Joseph did indeed represent two of the most prevalent sides of Habsburg tradition. On the one hand, he had strong, very conservative convictions on the role of the monarch, and on the place of religion in society and the state, much as his grandfather had; but on the other, his practical, empirical approach, and his willingness to do away with obstacles to the realisation of Habsburg power, constitutional or otherwise, marked him out as a true heir to his 'enlightened absolutist' ancestor and namesake, Joseph II. In that way as well, Franz Joseph proved the 'ultimate Habsburg', combining the conservative absolutism of Franz, with the much more radical approach, even more absolutist, of Joseph. The other, minor key of Habsburg tradition, of looking to the participation, in some form, of the citizens in imperial affairs, represented by Leopold II and Johann, was not so evident. The Habsburg Monarchy which Franz Joseph now led had been saved from a revolution from below, but it was clear that many of the issues that had caused that revolution needed to be dealt with. What Franz Joseph embarked on in his first decade as emperor was nothing less than a revolution from above.

Revolution from above: Neo-Absolutism

In January 1852, Schwarzenberg was still minister president, and the government did not initially change much from what it had been since November 1848, a champion of the reassertion of Habsburg power, and at the same time a force for radical, often progressive, reform. Its radical nature arose primarily from Schwarzenberg. Despite being a scion of Austria's high aristocracy, Schwarzenberg held his fellow aristocrats in contempt as politically and administratively incompetent. Instead the ministers that he had chosen in 1848 had been almost all 'new men', talented officials, but also former revolutionaries, and prominent liberals, such as Alexander Bach and Karl von Bruck. Had Franz Joseph chosen his ministers back in 1848 the number of 'new men' might have been much less. The emperor, unlike Schwarzenberg, valued the high aristocracy, as having been, next to the military, the most loyal sector of Habsburg society during the revolution. He preferred the society of the high nobility, and suspected the middle classes, and even ennobled officials, of being 'concealed democrats'. Under the emperor's influence, the Imperial Court became *more* exclusive, and the military became staffed by many officers from the high nobility. When it came to domestic policy, however, he relied on Schwarzenberg, who was effectively the emperor's political mentor in the early months of his reign, and had come to appreciate the competence of his ministers: when Schwarzenberg unexpectedly died in April 1852, Franz Joseph appointed the person Schwarzenberg had recommended to replace him as foreign minister, Count Karl Buol-Schauenstein, but he did not appoint another minister president, and abolished the Ministerial Council, for an absolute monarch should rule alone. His interests were primarily in the military, and, as Metternich had instructed, in foreign policy. Therefore he left domestic policy largely in the hands of the officials chosen by Schwarzenberg, the most influential of which was the interior minister, Bach.

This was the same Bach who had co-written the petition of 11 March with Bauernfeld, and it might at first seem strange that a prominent liberal revolutionary of 1848 should become best known for giving his name to the 'Bach era' of neo-absolutism; many contemporaries criticised him for betraying the liberal cause. On the other hand, neo-absolutism, the imposition of modernity through the absolute power of the state, was, in its way, imposing the sort of world that liberals had wanted in March 1848. It was federalist conservatives such as Count Egbert Belcredi who were especially put out by the neo-absolutist programme, because it was erasing the rights of particularist interests such as the provincial nobility: 'What conservative institutions the revolution from below left intact, the revolution from above has continued to destroy.' Liberals had, in contrast, wanted an end to noble privileges, and the establishment of a uniform state and society that treated citizens equally, but also enhanced their opportunity for individual betterment, intellectually but also materially. Bach had always been on the Josephist wing of the liberal movement, more intent on reforming the state and preserving the unity of the Monarchy than on integration of Austrian Germans into Germany. Many liberals had been disappointed, and frightened, at the chaos and social insurgency summoned up by the revolution, especially in October. When it came to deciding the franchise of Vienna's communal (city council) elections in 1850, an initial acceptance of a broad franchise had turned into that of a quite narrow one, to ensure against the wrong people (the less well off) having a vote, with a three-level curial system added on to diminish the influence of even those less wealthy who did still qualify. It made some sense, in the circumstances of the Habsburg resurgence of 1848–49, to compromise with those in power, to try and shape the emerging, new state and society in a progressive, rationalist, market-oriented and egalitarian – liberal – manner, and who knew what the resulting *political* changes would be to keep abreast of the new dispensation?

That there was a new dispensation was clear from the start, because before all else the government had to put into effect the emancipation of the peasantry, which no one, certainly not Schwarzenberg, Bach or even Franz Joseph, was prepared to stop. This was the one great achievement of the 1848 revolution, and it did change Habsburg society and government definitively. Given the overwhelmingly agricultural character of the Habsburg economy, the radical change in relationship between peasant and lord meant change in almost all other aspects of life, and it was the foundation stone on which all other aspects of neo-absolutism arose. The diversity of agricultural relationships across the Monarchy was a challenge in itself, and the agricultural system in Lombardy-Venetia and Dalmatia was so different that the law did not apply. Where it did, the actual process of emancipation, involving as it did detailed knowledge of land and usage values and calculations of the proper compensation levels, for the landlord of each individual estate, was complex and lengthy. Just providing the legal basis for the emancipation took until 1853 for Hungary, 1854 for Transylvania; the ministerial commissions who decided compensation issues only finished their work in Bohemia in 1854, in Galicia and Hungary in 1857. The process by which peasants and the state paid the required compensation also required quite complex financial arrangements, generating huge amounts of debt and credit to manage. In a situation where there was such diversity of size and character of landholdings, it was, and still is, hard to determine who exactly benefited and who did not. Some large landowners were able to use their promised compensation as capital to develop their remaining lands and new industries, and their enterprises were often staffed by peasants made effectively landless by the settlement. On the other hand, peasants with large holdings in Bohemia did well out of the settlement and the good market for their goods, so paid off their fiscal obligation ahead of time, while nobles with small-to-middling property were ruined by the loss of *robot*. Overall, what was clear was that Austrian agriculture was now much more modern, freed from feudal restrictions and hence much more reliant on the market. The peasants who remained on the land were now free and equal with their former noble masters, no longer under their patrimonial administration or courts, in a new, modern world.

The most obvious impact on government was the need to replace those patrimonial administrations and courts with state equivalents. This had been a primary reason for Stadion's Communal Autonomy Law, to fill the vacuum left by the loss of nobles' control over 'their' peasants. Yet leaving the local communes full control over their lives was not an option for the Habsburg officialdom, and one of the central purposes of neo-absolutism was to rejuvenate and expand the Habsburg bureaucracy to meet the new challenge of extending the state's direct presence to this lower level. Bach devised a new hierarchy of governmental institutions, starting with the central government in Vienna, the province, and then *Kreis* (county), and introduced at the lowest level, just above the commune, the *Bezirk* (district). Moreover, with Hungary regarded as a conquered rebel territory, Bach broke up Inner Hungary into five provinces and introduced the standard, Austrian bureaucratic system, entirely doing away with traditional Hungarian forms. He did almost exactly the same for loyal Croatia as well, which was the occasion for a famously ironic comment on the similarity of punishment and reward in the Habsburg universe, but the intent was clear: the Habsburg Monarchy was a unified state, and it should have a unified, uniform, and centralised administration – and an extensive one. Due to the combination in the *Sylvesterpatent* of administrative and judicial functions at the district level, Bach decided to create district offices at all the district courts in the Monarchy. This meant establishing 1,463 new district offices, and in addition 80 district offices in cities, and new buildings for all of them. This was an immense increase in the purview of the Habsburg state (as well as a very large burden on expenditures).

There were some variations in the bureaucratic systems in each province, and one of the more notorious of these was a gesture Bach made to Hungarian national sensibilities, by ordering that district officials there, known as *Stuhlrichter* (in Magyar *szolgabiró*), wear a specially designed, supposedly 'Hungarian' uniform. This caused the officials to be ridiculed by Magyar nationalists as 'Bach's hussars', and it was to an extent merited, because the intent of this expansion of the bureaucracy was to exert central control, to realise the ideal of a unified Habsburg state, and break the power of nationalist particularism. There was also a higher purpose for the new officialdom. In his *Rundschreiben* (circular) of 15 August 1849 to all of his officials, Bach set out a veritable 'moral code', much like Joseph II's 'Pastoral Letter' of 1783. The official was not simply to shuffle paper, but rather to get to know the citizens whom he served, gain their trust and confidence, instruct and lead them for their own betterment, with spotless integrity, responsibility, and fairness. He was to respect the 'equality of all nations', and, it was assumed, speak the languages of the province. And he was to be entirely obedient to the central government (not the local powers). The official, in other words, was to be a paragon of good government – and an agent of the tutelary state, imparting civilisation as defined in Vienna.

The official was also required to speak German. This was, from Bach's perspective, not so much a furthering of German nationalist goals, as an attempt to establish an all-*Austrian* bureaucratic language that allowed communication across the whole government. German was to be the 'internal language' of the bureaucracy, but the 'external language', with which the official communicated with citizens, was either German or the local vernacular. Bach's Circular assumed that the officials would also speak, if necessary learn, the language of the citizens under their purview. German thus was to function as the mediating *lingua franca* of Austrian modernity, allowing the many nationalities to live alongside each other; and if a district official was posted to a Slovak-speaking part of Hungary, it made sense that speaking Slovak was prioritised, although knowing Magyar would also be useful. The new officialdom reflected the multi-nationality of the Monarchy. They were far from being only Germans. Considerable numbers of German-speaking Czechs gained employment in Galicia and Hungary, even if they were dismissively characterised as 'Germans' by the locals. And most of the new officials in Hungary were still Magyars, despite what nationalists might later claim. The new administrative system in Hungary worked well, so that when Hungary later gained autonomy most of it was retained, along with a large portion of the personnel.

The education system received a similarly centralist and modernising overhaul, even though the minister responsible, Count Leo Thun-Hohenstein, was a conservative, strongly Catholic nobleman with Bohemian 'patriotic' loyalties. When he became minister for religion and education in July 1849, there were already well-developed plans for educational reform, and Thun was open-minded enough to let them proceed, largely under the guidance of Franz Exner, with Hermann Bonitz the main influence on secondary education, and Karl Ernst Jarcke on university matters. A provisional law was passed in September 1849, but the definitive new educational system was only finalised in 1854. Primary education was, as before, to be given in the vernacular language of the majority of the pupils in the locality. It was in secondary and higher education that there was a major change, a radical effort both to bring Austria up to modern standards and also to provide a uniform, empire-wide system. Both goals resulted in promoting a German liberal agenda.

The reform programme was modelled on Prussia's education system, and as there was, almost by definition, a dearth of suitably educated Austrian teachers, the deficit was made up by importing a large number of Reich Germans, who, even though most were Catholic, had German national loyalties and liberal political views. Jarcke's advice to Thun on the personnel choices for university posts also led to many appointments from the Germany beyond the black-yellow frontier. The subsequent German liberal hegemony within the Austrian higher education system was thus a product of the policies of Thun, the Catholic conservative.

When it came to providing a uniform education system, the German liberal cause also benefited, for one of the principal ways in which this was realised was by making German the dominant language of instruction (Lombardy-Venetia excepted).

There were some bilingual, or even trilingual schools where German shared the function of language of instruction with others, but even here the last years of *Gymnasium* (grammar-school) education were normally in German alone. As with the bureaucracy, the leading reason for making German the almost exclusive language of instruction was its status as the Monarchy's *lingua franca*. At universities where there was a highly diverse mix of nationalities among the students, it made a certain functional sense to have lectures and instruction in one language. Similarly, many *Gymnasien* drew pupils from large areas, and hence many nationalities, and as secondary schools were supposed to be a source for the educated officials of the new, German-speaking bureaucracy, it made eminent sense that instruction should be in German. This did not placate non-German nationalists, and the overtone that the civilisation spread by Austria's civilising mission would be one in German is unmistakable, but even Thun and his deputy, Alexander von Helfert, both of whom were sympathetic to the Czech cause, were convinced that the Bachian centralism that demanded German as a the language of instruction was 'the necessary restraint against the ruthless power ambitions of the historic nations'.

In the Bach/Thun concept of Austria in the 1850s German was seen as providing the administrative frame in which the other nationalities could thrive and develop. In a speech in 1853, the orientalist scholar, Joseph Hammer-Purgstall, praised Austrian law for treating its citizens equally, while recognising and respecting their linguistic diversity, and that German was simply the utility language beside which Austrian multilingualism would flourish: 'the more languages of the Monarchy one learns, the more one becomes a true Austrian'. There was a sense in which Austrian identity came to be a combination of supra-nationality and national diversity. Helfert was behind an effort to create an Austrian state consciousness based on the study of the historical origins of the Austrian state; the historian Joseph Chmel saw Austria as a state in which 'quite different nationalities' could 'strive together as brothers in one family for a common goal'. In 1857 he saw the aim of Austrian history was to 'show that humanity is greater than nationality'. The Bach era saw a great deal of research into the history of the many nationalities, and if the political realm was a no-go area, *cultural* nationalism blossomed as never before. Looking back in 1862, Palacký saw the time of neo-absolutism as a period of great growth for Czech culture. But one could go only so far.

Peter Kozler, a Slovene nationalist, found himself accused of high treason when he tried to publish a map that showed the Slovenian language borders – *without* showing the borders of the respective provinces. He was found innocent, but his map had to wait until 1861 for publication.

The Kozler case indicates that neo-absolutism was still absolutism, that a strict control was kept over Habsburg society. There was a new, somewhat more effective, version of the pre-1848 police state. One of Bach's first acts as interior minister in 1849 had been to create a gendarmerie as the enforcement arm of his bureaucracy. This body not only served to ensure public safety and that the officials' orders be obeyed, but also spied on the officialdom itself, as well as the rest of society, with a sliding scale of monetary incentives for successful denunciations from informers. The gendarmerie was transferred in January 1852 to the chief of police, Baron Johann von Kempen, who ran an efficient and quite stringent department, including heavy censorship of the press. Kempen was one of the set of conservatives, such as Count Karl Grünne and, until his death in 1855, the president of the *Reichsrat*, Kübeck, who were constantly pressing Franz Joseph to crackdown against the 'liberalisation' of Bach and the other ministers. Franz Joseph had the secret police spy on some of his ministers, just to make sure of their loyalty. It should also be remembered that martial law was only lifted in Vienna and Prague in September 1853, and in most of the rest of the Monarchy in 1854, in Transylvania only in 1855. The revolutionary unrest occasionally kicked up long after the surrenders of 1849: in February 1853 there was a Mazzinist uprising in Milan; on 18 February 1853 a Hungarian tailor attempted to assassinate Franz Joseph. Although this attack actually helped revive the emperor's popularity somewhat (a collection to show gratitude for the emperor's survival was started by his brother Ferdinand Max and resulted in the *Votivkirche*, finished in 1879), it was also seen by conservatives as signalling a need for caution. The Bach era was politically, and also socially and culturally, quite oppressive. It is perhaps fitting that one of the great classics of Austrian literature published in this era, in 1857, was Adalbert Stifter's *Der Nachsommer*, a tale of resignation and retreat into a carefully controlled private world.

There were two areas where the regime did give up a large amount of control: religion and the economy. The decision to give up control over the Catholic Church in the Monarchy was a sign of just how much Franz Joseph was *not* entirely a Josephist, inasmuch as state control over the Catholic Church was one of that political tradition's main planks, but it was an indication of his deeply held, and very conservative Catholic convictions, which he shared with his minister for religion and education, Thun. The resultant Concordat of 1855, a birthday present for the emperor, returned control over Church affairs to the papacy, along with the management of most primary education in the Monarchy, and the regulation of marriage. One of the consequences of Church control over primary schools was to change the balance between German and other languages in favour of the latter, going against Bachian centralism. The Church was otherwise quite a strong supporter of the monarch, but the loss of control over the message from church pulpits in an age of mass illiteracy was still a major cession of power.

In economic affairs, there was also a concerted effort to reduce government control, following the predominant, *laissez faire* economic theory of the time. The main problem for the state was the usual, chronic one: the budget deficit, and the inability of the government to gain credit on favourable terms. The disruptions in revenue collection caused by the emancipation of the peasantry, and the large expenditures needed for the expansion of the bureaucracy, compensation of landowners, investment in the railway infrastructure, as well as the high cost of the military and also the servicing of state debt, meant that deficits continued to be the norm for the budget. The National Bank was taken up almost entirely with securing loans for the state. Over the course of the 1850s, however, the economy grew at a pace comparable to the rest of Europe, and there were several reforms which helped that growth, as well as the financial situation, both for the state and private investment. By 1859, the Austrian economy, and even Austria's fragile finances, looked to be doing reasonably well.

In November 1851, the tariff barrier between Austria and Hungary was abolished and replaced by a customs union for the empire. In 1852 there was a large reduction in tariffs, and in 1853 a commercial treaty with Prussia meant a de facto integration with the *Zollverein*. The problem with state finances spiked with the military expenditures necessitated by the Crimean War (see below) from the autumn of 1853, and attempts by the finance minister at the time, Andreas von Baumgartner, to solve this by raising a patriotic 'national bond' proved inadequate.

Baumgartner was the model for the figure of Baron Reisach in Stifter's *Nachsommer*, and one of Austria's leading (liberal) academics, but he was not a good finance minister, and his solution to the credit crisis, the sale of the state-owned railways in 1854, to a French-led syndicate, was ill-considered on many levels, not least that the sum eventually paid was only about half of the massive investment that the state had made in the network. The situation was rescued by the return of Bruck, commerce minister until April 1851, and from March 1855 finance minister. He raised taxes, reduced military expenditure and continued the sale of the railways; one of his major initiatives was to collaborate with Anselm

Rothschild to set up what became the biggest banking institution in the Monarchy, the *Credit-Anstalt*, in October 1855. For the first time, private Austrian capital, from Jewish financiers and also the landed high nobility, was able to be invested in large-scale capital projects. Eventually, Rothschild and his investors in the *Credit-Anstalt* were able to displace the French-led syndicate in ownership of the railway network, and the new bank proved a major source of funding for industry.

In 1856 Bruck greatly reduced import tariffs; in 1857 the Southern Railway was finally completed, so that Trieste was now fully linked up with its Habsburg hinterland. The year 1857 saw a crash on the Vienna Stock Exchange, but by 1858 Bruck was able, finally, to solve the Austrian currency crisis. In 1859 a very liberal *Gewerbeordnung* (Industrial Code) was passed that effectively abolished guild restrictions on industry and trade. Many more railways were in the process of being built or planned. It appeared that Austria's economy was on the verge of radical modernisation and high growth.

Meanwhile, the monarch was also attempting to improve the image of the Monarchy, and the levels of his own popularity. His marriage to the beautiful Elisabeth in 1854 had helped, and she was to prove an asset, at least in the early years, especially with the Magyars. On a visit to Budapest in 1857, Franz Joseph might have alienated sympathisers by avoiding receiving a high-profile petition, but Elisabeth's wearing of the national colours, now red, white and green, was noticed and popular. Another attempt to gain popularity and the prestige of modernity was the decision in 1857 to raze Vienna's city walls, and, as with Haussmann's Paris, drag the imperial capital into the nineteenth century. The set of boulevards and prestigious, imperial buildings that would result, known collectively as the *Ringstrasse*, were meant to showcase the new, modern Austria. At either end of the development, however, were large barracks, and in between large open spaces for troops to be mustered: the *Ringstrasse* was also at its inception (as with Hauptmann's Paris no less) a counter-revolutionary measure to stop the threat of barricades ever again bringing down the government. The need for force to maintain the neo-absolutist regime was still clear.

By 1859, the revolution from above had been remarkably effective in modernising many aspects of Austrian life, but that did not mean it had succeeded. In many ways, it had fostered the very forces that were to bring it down. The logic of *Vormärz* returned, where economic prosperity in the propertied and educated middle classes increased their social self-confidence, and their political frustration with not being treated as adults by the authoritarian regime. The Chambers of Commerce set up by Bruck back in 1850 were the one institution that continued to hold elections, and they provided a forum for economic – and implicitly other – criticism of the government. The opening up of sources of private capital for state funds, as represented by the *Credit-Anstalt* and Bruck's financial arrangements, led again to increased calls for some constitutional (investor) control over state finances. Events such as the Schiller Centennial celebration of 1859, with its praise of Schiller as the poet of freedom, had an obvious message of dissent from the neo-absolutist regime. Meanwhile, the erasure of traditional rights and noble privileges at the periphery meant that even conservative 'federalists' were prepared to combine with liberal nationalists, still sullen and unaccepting of the modern, centralised administration, whether it be in Lombardy-Venetia, Hungary, Croatia, Galicia or elsewhere.

None of this might have counted had it not been for another aspect of the regime. For all the cavilling, the regime had achieved control, and there was still no prospect of large-scale resistance to it. The wish for peace might have allowed this imposed, absolutist modernity to remain in place long enough to generate sufficient stability and prosperity to gain acceptance. Yet the regime's support was superficial, and hence its position was fragile, with little or no margin for error. And there was another aspect to the regime: it was said that Franz Joseph's neo-absolutist regime ruled with four armies: one that marched (the military) one that sat (the bureaucracy) one that knelt (the clergy) and one that crawled (informers). Of these, three proved quite effective: the bureaucracy, the Church and the police state. What was to let the whole system down was the one that had saved it in the first place: the military. The reason for this was that in the areas where Franz Joseph had reserved to himself the most influence, in foreign policy and the military, Austria's performance was to prove calamitous.

The Sorcerer's Apprentice

When Franz Joseph took absolute power on New Year's Eve 1851/2, he thought he could still rely on the sage advice of Schwarzenberg, and the latter's death so soon afterwards left the emperor fully responsible but without a trusted mentor. In domestic policy, this was not so problematic, as Bach could be relied on. In foreign policy, however, the loss of Schwarzenberg's diplomatic skill and cunning proved disastrous, and Franz Joseph's conduct of foreign and military policy over the next several years too closely recalls the tale of the 'sorcerer's apprentice'. It is unclear, given Austria's situation after 1848, whether neo-absolutist Austria could have survived intact, given the emergence of *Realpolitiker* such as Napoleon III, Count Camillo Cavour and Otto von Bismarck, but what is clear is that under Franz Joseph's clumsy and inexperienced hand, Austria never stood a chance.

The problems started with his choice of personnel. On military policy, there was a war minister, Anton von Csorich, but when he resigned in 1853 the post was left unfilled, so that Franz Joseph was in immediate control of his army. In any case, von Csorich had been largely bypassed by the emperor, who relied much more on Quartermaster-General Heinrich von Hess, and, his aide-de-camp and closest, most influential advisor, Grünne. The emperor appointed Grünne head of the Military Chancellery and then adjutant general, in charge of all military questions. In this position, Grünne indulged his ultra-conservative attitudes, to most deleterious effect. Unlike the bureaucracy or the education system, there was no serious overhaul of the military. It had, it is true, beaten back the revolution, and defeated a rebel army in Hungary and the Piedmontese army in Italy, so perhaps some complacency was understandable, but it was misplaced. The Piedmontese army was not a serious fighting force, and the difficulties against the Hungarians should have been a clue for the need for reform. Yet none was forthcoming.

Grünne used his great influence over Franz Joseph to get members of the high nobility, and his protégés, such as Count Ferenc Gyulai, appointed to the commanding positions in the army, despite little evidence of military skill, thinking that rank was more important than competence. This was a waste of scarce resources; Grünne spent much of the military budget making sure that the troops were well turned out and good at parade drill. However, there were very few manoeuvres, and so no real practice, and the army was terribly organised and trained as an actual fighting force. Apart from the favoured high-noble few at the top, officers and troops were poorly paid and supplied, with substantial corruption in the commissioning of supplies. The equipment was also out of date. In 1851 the military leadership was introduced to the new, rapid-fire, breech-loading rifle, but Franz Joseph was advised by General Vinzenz von Augustin, that these new-fangled weapons were unreliable and hard to incorporate in Austrian infantry training, given the poorly educated, ill-disciplined, polyglot nature of the army's conscript troops. So the emperor stuck with the much slower but well-known front loader – a decision that was to doom the Austrian military fifteen years later. Many of the logistical and organisational problems in the military were known to Grünne, but he kept the bad news from the emperor, whose great self-confidence, and confidence in Grünne, meant that he never condescended to question him.

The military's main purpose for most of the neo-absolutist era was to look good at parades and be an agent of domestic political control, and in this it was quite good at being a deterrent to internal revolt. Yet this came at a steep, and in purely military terms very wasteful, price. It has been calculated that only roughly half the huge military budget went to actual military purposes, the other half being swallowed up by the highly inefficient military bureaucracy and the army's domestic role. An army of 800,000, the largest in Europe, thus cost even more than it should, certainly more than the state, given all its other expensive outlays, could really afford. This was before any mobilisation took place, and so the Finance Ministry was constantly attempting to prevent the army actually being employed in warfare, because of the cost. This was, admittedly, partly due to the fact that the imposed nature of the state meant that it was reluctant to test loyalty too much by over-taxing the populace (when that populace was the one being controlled by the domestic use of the military). Yet it is also true that the army, if mobilised, was very expensive indeed: in 1854, at the beginning of the Crimean crisis, the army's whole annual budget had been spent in the first three months, and there was not the confidence in the state's financial instruments to maintain these sorts of expenditures for long. The need to extend mobilisation well into 1855 was a major reason for the financial crisis of 1855, and Bruck's retrenchment to solve this led to cuts in the military budget, and a demobilisation of most of the army well before the end of the Crimean War. It was clear even then that an overuse of the military could bust the budget, cause a crisis of financial confidence and destroy the state itself.

Expensive, inefficient and hamstrung by financial constraints, the military was a very dubious instrument of Habsburg power, that needed to be used very carefully, if at all, as an extension of foreign policy. Here again, in the Habsburg priority of the conduct of foreign policy, personal choices by Franz Joseph proved ill-judged. Admittedly, he chose Buol as his foreign minister on the dying Schwarzenberg's recommendation, but the general historical verdict is that it was nonetheless a poor choice. Metternich, now back in Vienna, said of Buol 'since he has no conception of the need of keeping a plan of action before his mind, he conducts his politics like a forester who has no idea of orderly tree-cutting. One way or the other, wood is felled – but what about the forest?' The problem was that this could as easily be said of the emperor, who claimed full control of foreign policy, and so must be held responsible for its dire results.

It is true that developments on the international scene would have taxed even Metternich. The first major crisis of the period, the Crimean War, had its origins in a dispute between France and Russia over the Holy Places in Jerusalem. Yet this was only a proxy for a contest between Napoleon III, an adventurist trying to reassert French power and undo the Viennese settlement, and Nicholas I, a Russian reactionary intent on letting none of that happen, while asserting Russian power at the same time. This developed, through an intricate tangle of failed diplomatic initiatives and subterfuges, into a stand-off between Russia on the one hand, and Turkey and her two Western backers, France and Britain, on the other, with Austria caught somewhere in the middle. In theory this was not necessarily a bad place to be. Metternich himself opined: 'The state of the middle cannot let herself be tugged either in the eastward or westward direction ... and must never allow itself to be misused as the vanguard of the East against the West, or the West against the East.' In practice, however, in the way Buol (and Franz Joseph) managed Austrian participation in the diplomatic and military encounters, the position of armed neutrality ended up alienating both sides in the conflict.

The worst consequence was undoubtedly the loss of the Russian alliance. Back in 1849, Russia had come to Austria's aid in Hungary, but even then it had been clear to Schwarzenberg that any debt felt towards Russia could not be a decisive factor in policy. Hence his reported remark, which he probably did make: 'We shall astound the world with our ingratitude.' Russia might be ideologically on the same page, and the tsar and young emperor great friends, but Russia had interests which were not the same as Austria's, especially when it came to Turkey and the Turkish-occupied Balkans. One side of Franz Joseph, and many of his military advisers, felt that a pro-Russian approach was still preferable, and were prepared to consider the Russian proposal of an Austrian hegemony in Serbia and the western Balkans, in return for Russian dominance in the Danubian Principalities of Moldavia and Wallachia (most of modern-day Romania); but the other side, along with Buol and many of the domestic ministers, saw that this undermined the integrity of Turkey, and hence the Viennese settlement, and would alienate the Western powers, and so was not at all in Austria's interest: ideology and friendship should not come before the interests of the Monarchy, of the Austrian state. Hence Franz Joseph's justification of the eventual break with Russia: 'One must above all be an Austrian.'

Franz Joseph tried very hard to avoid this break with his former saviour and ideological ally by persuading him to stop the march to war, but Nicholas I would not be deterred from his aggressive policy, and in July 1853 Russian troops occupied the Danubian Principalities, starting a war with Turkey. Almost a year of negotiations then took place, along with partial mobilisation along the border, before Austria on 3 June 1854 sent an ultimatum to Russia to evacuate the Danubian Principalities, and then, on 8 August joined with the Western Powers in signing a note in Vienna setting out to Russia their joint conditions of peace. The sense of betrayal on Russia's part was then completed when Austria, after Russia agreed to allow an Austrian occupation of Moldavia and Wallachia to replace theirs, then entered into an alliance with France and Britain on 2 December. Nicholas and his successor, Alexander II, were from this moment irreconcilable enemies of Austria.

The second-worst consequence of Austrian diplomacy was the alienation of the Western Powers. Despite on paper now being an ally of Britain and France, Austria managed to wriggle out of any commitment actually to use force against Russia. Theoretically allied to the Western Powers, in practice Austria never conducted hostilities against Russia, and played instead the peacemaker. The unpredictability and half-heartedness of the Austrian position deeply antagonised both Britain and Napoleon III, and led to the Monarchy being seen by them as unreliable. Buol was instrumental in getting the parties eventually to the peace table, and the Peace of Paris, signed on 30 May 1856, but the harsh concessions demanded from Russia, the cession of Southern Bessarabia to the Danubian Principalities and the demilitarisation of the Black Sea, were blamed by Russia on Buol, and so increased Russian enmity. Britain and France, on other hand, felt little amity for a state that had, from their point of view, not fulfilled its side of the bargain in the alliance.

From a short-term perspective, Austria came out well from the Crimean War: without going to war, as such, the Russian threat in the Balkans had been repelled. Yet the cost was Austrian alienation of both sides in the conflict. Two other states, however, Piedmont and Prussia, had profited immensely from the conflict. Unlike Austria, Piedmont contributed some troops to the Western war effort, quite consciously to curry favour with Napoleon III in the Italian Question – where Austria was the main enemy of Italian national unity – and the policy worked brilliantly. At the Paris Peace Conference in 1856 Cavour, Piedmont's prime minister, had written a memorandum about reform in the Italian states to Napoleon III, and the response, ominous for Austria, had been: 'What can I do for Italy?' Prussia, meanwhile, even while in alliance with Austria, had taken umbrage at Austria's aggressive stance against Russia, had remained neutral, and thus gained favour in Russia, as well as in the other German states, which did not want German interests risked for Austrian gain. This was potentially dangerous, given the unresolved relationship of the Monarchy with the rest of Germany. The upshot of this was that an apparently triumphant Austria was in a very weak position, without its old standby of the Russian alliance, or any others to replace it. In January 1857, the British ambassador to Vienna, George Hamilton Seymour, saw clearly how Austria was completely isolated, in huge danger should a new crisis arise.

The need to make new friends, or patch up relations with old ones, was not clear to either Buol or Franz Joseph. When Prussia requested aid over its dispute with Neufchâtel over Hohenzollern hereditary rights in 1856–1857, Buol preferred to refuse help to keep Prussia down, rather than seeing this as an opportunity to defend legitimacy and invoke (hence validate) the German Confederation's article 47 that obliged members to mutual aid in case of a defensive war. This was an unwise precedent to set, given Austria's position. That position became much worse when Napoleon III and Cavour renewed their conversation about what could be done for Italy. Both had revisionist ambitions concerning the 1815 settlement, and Austria's northern Italian territories were the obvious target, as they had been for Piedmont back in 1848. At Plombières in the summer of 1858, Napoleon III and Cavour hatched a plot: if Austria could be made to start a war against Piedmont, then this would mean that the defensive alliance of Prussia and the German Confederation members would not be operative. France could then come to Piedmont's aid, defeat the Austrian army and gain large tranches of northern Italy for Piedmont. In return, Piedmont would cede to France parts of Savoy that had once been French, such as Nizza (Nice), achieving a cherished nationalist goal of restoring territory, and pride, to France. A few months later, almost to the letter, this is what happened when Austria fell into the trap in April 1859.

Napoleon III did his part. At the 1859 New Year's Day reception for diplomats in Paris he addressed the Austrian ambassador, Count Alexander von Hübner, with an expression of regret at the deterioration of relations between Austria and France. In the spring, Cavour's government began to make provocative claims against Austria and mobilise its forces, knowing full well that this would injure Franz Joseph's sense of honour and dynastic prestige. It worked. On 27 April, he stated in the Ministerial Conference that war against Piedmont was 'a commandment of honour and duty'. There were other, more rational reasons for Austria starting the war, which showed the problems of neo-absolutism. For a start, it had been obvious to the Austrians from January that something was afoot, and so plans had been made for the army in Italy to be reinforced, and martial law proclaimed in Lombardy-Venetia, because the population could not really be trusted. But then, if the army was mobilised, state finances could not cope with a lengthy mobilisation. In fact, Franz Joseph had initially resisted expansion of the military in early 1859 on precisely those grounds, and when the ultimatum was sent to Piedmont on 23 April, the army was not yet fully mobilised. Buol, meanwhile, hoped that the ultimatum, would itself cause Piedmont to climb down in the face of Austrian overwhelming force. Even at this late point, they could not really see the trap. Cavour rejected the ultimatum, Austria declared war on 29 April, and France declared war in defence of Piedmont.

As soon as it started, even before any fighting, the war was a disaster for Austria. A run on the banks began the destruction of all of Bruck's carefully constructed financial arrangements and prompted him to say that even victory would result in financial crisis. He need not have worried: all of the unaddressed problems of the Austrian military united to assure Austrian defeat. The reluctant Austrian commander, Gyulai, Grünne's man and unsuited for the job, held back, allowing the French and Piedmontese armies to unite. At the Battle of Magenta on 4 June, the Austrians suffered a narrow defeat and retreated, leaving Milan free to be entered by Napoleon III and Vittore Emmanuele in triumph. Gyulai was 'retired'. Buol had already been sacked in May, and replaced by Count Johann Bernhard Rechberg, but it was too late for effective diplomacy. Franz Joseph now took command of the army himself, and led it into a second major engagement, at Solferino on 24 June. This was also lost, though narrowly. Some claim that the battle would have been won had Franz Joseph not ordered a premature retreat, but he did. He was driven to tears by the shocking casualties of the battle. Magenta and Solferino were such bloody battles that they inspired the founding of the Red Cross, and the naming of a new, fresh-blood-coloured dye: magenta.

With the home front collapsing in financial chaos, and news of the French trying to foment an uprising in Hungary with General György Klapka's Hungarian Legion, the situation appeared dire. Attempts to gain Prussian help, against the national enemy of the German nation, were met by Prussian demands for Austrian concessions within the German Confederation that Franz Joseph's sense of Habsburg prestige would not brook, even at this point. Instead, Franz Joseph decided to respond to an offer from Napoleon III for a quick armistice that the French emperor was prepared to make on relatively agreeable terms for reasons of his own. The resulting preliminary peace was signed on 12 July at Villafranca. Austria gave up only Lombardy, retaining Venetia and the Quadrilateral. Venetia would be part of an Italian federation of states. The rights of the Habsburg rulers in Central Italy were hypothetically kept, if they could confirm them. Lombardy was ceded to Napoleon, who then was to cede it to Piedmont, in return for Nizza and its hinterland. By the time the final peace treaty was signed in Zürich on 10 November, the central states were well on the way to being annexed by Piedmont, and there was no federation. By early 1860, Piedmont had become the core of a nascent Italian nation-state. By early 1860, neo-absolutism was dead. After Villafranca, Franz Joseph had taken the train directly back to Lower

Austria, and on 15 July had issued the 'Laxenburg Manifesto', promising some amendment in the way the Monarchy was governed. A prolonged crisis ensued in which the whole Bach system crashed. In the autumn, the emperor attended a performance at the Viennese Opera, and he was not noticed – the worst social disgrace polite society could deliver. By then Hungary was in turmoil, the state's finances in ruins, the economy in deep depression, the emperor's and the monarchy's legitimacy and authority in deep crisis. Absolutist modernity was finished – but what would follow it?

Eight Years of Crisis

When Franz Joseph returned home after Villafranca, he had been emperor of Austria for just over a decade, and fully absolute monarch for only just over seven. It was to take longer, at least another eight years, and many would say with some justification, twelve, for the crisis caused by defeat in the Franco-Austrian War to work itself out. The emperor and his advisors were faced with two pressing necessities: to keep the state going, in the most basic terms of having enough money or credit to pay the bills; and where possible to preserve the position of the Monarchy, externally and internally. The Monarchy survived, in partly recognizable form, but Franz Joseph was unable to restore Habsburg power, either that of the Monarchy as a great power, or that of himself as Habsburg emperor within the power structures of his empire, to what it had been in 1859, let alone 1848. By the end of the crisis, there had been a huge diminution of the Monarchy's position externally as regards Germany and internally regarding Hungary; and his own power within the empire was no longer absolute, but limited by exactly the kind of constitutionalism his upbringing had taught him to despise. The result of the crisis for the populace of the Monarchy, on the other hand, was quite positive: a degree of stability by 1867 (definitely by 1871), and a platform for peaceful development that was to prove surprisingly productive until the very last years of the Monarchy.

There were many stages to the restructuring of the Monarchy to achieve the necessary basis of political and financial support. There were many different interests involved, but they can be grouped into two main parties. On one side was a conservative-federalist bloc that was represented in the government in 1859 by individuals such as Thun, and came to include not only the provincial high nobilities, but also, increasingly, nationalists from all nationalities apart from the Germans. On the other side, were liberal-centralists, who were represented in the government in 1859 by individuals such as Bruck, and came to include most of the Monarchy's propertied and educated middle classes, as well as the critical bloc of financiers, many of whom were Jewish. It was Anselm Rothschild who is said to have summed up this party's central message in 1860: 'No constitution; no money'. Somewhere along this spectrum could be found the emperor, acting as indecisive mediator-cum-arbitrator between the parties, frequently changing his mind, agonisingly trying to decide how much to lean either way, and, moreover, along a different axis, reluctantly coming to terms with how much of his own power as emperor he was prepared to give up, to keep his subjects – and especially his creditors – satisfied, or at least co-operative.

The debate whether to make of the Monarchy a heavily decentralised, conservatively ruled and noble-dominated collection of loosely connected provinces, or a centralised, constitutional state with 'far-reaching liberal-isation' in all aspects of public life, along modern, progressive lines, began immediately after the defeat, with discussions within the government, led by the new foreign minister, and also now prime minister, Rechberg. On 21 August, Bach and Kempen were dismissed as scapegoats for the catastrophe (Grünne was let go by a reluctant Franz Joseph in October). Bruck gained portfolios, and at this point was one of the most influential ministers; on the other hand, the new interior minister was Count Agenor Goluchowski, a conservative promoter of provincial autonomy, and the programme that the government proclaimed on 23 August was vague, with some liberalisation measures promised, but the word 'constitution' studiously avoided, and only the creation of 'bodies representing the estates' promised.

The pressing question of reform of the state's finances was addressed by the establishment of a budget commission in November, but it was only on 5 March 1860 that the first solution for the governmental crisis was attempted, with the summoning of a Reinforced *Reichsrat*. This took Kübeck's *Reichsrat*, an advisory executive body, and added to it considerably more members, including 38 to be elected, in theory, from provincial assemblies, *Landtage* in German, also called diets[1] (which themselves still had to be set up), making it into a quasi-legislative/representative body. Moreover, the mechanism of how to select members from Hungary led to the abandonment of Hungary's division into five provinces, indicating a readiness to reinstate the traditional structures there, of diet and counties. When the now Reinforced *Reichsrat* met on 31 May, the provincial assemblies did not yet exist, so their 'representatives' were selected by the

---

[1] The provincial assemblies were new bodies, but they have come to be known in English, somewhat confusingly, as 'diets', even though this is the term for the old meetings of provincial estates.

emperor's advisors, with a strong preference for conservative high nobles – so that all six Hungarian 'representatives' were from the 'Old Conservative' faction – and the middle classes and financial sector relatively under-represented, given their importance in financial matters.

The 'liberal' side had also been severely affected by the loss of Bruck, who had been (unjustifiably) sacked on 22 April and had committed suicide the next evening. This tragic event had further unsettled financial markets, leading the new finance minister, Ignaz von Plener, to an even more deflationary cutting of the budget. A period which was one of strong economic growth elsewhere in Europe was thus one of severe depression in Austria.

This financial instability gave the *Reichsrat* great power over the emperor, and it was able to get Franz Joseph to agree to its having supervisory control over state finances. It then turned itself into a form of Constituent Assembly, with the conservative, high-noble, federalist majority proposing in a 'report' (draft constitution) a highly decentralised system with the provincial assemblies having most power. The liberal members proposed their own, minority report, of a strong central assembly, but it was a version of the decentralised, federalist plan that Franz Joseph chose to promulgate on 20 October, largely on the promise from the conservative Hungarian members of the *Reichsrat*, led by Count Antal Szécsen, that acceptance of their plan would lead to Hungarian cooperation, its rejection to Hungarian revolt.

The resulting 'permanent and irrevocable instrument', known as the October Diploma, was the second attempt at recasting the government. It promised to garner support from the high nobility that Franz Joseph trusted and respected, and solve the problem of Hungary, without having to give up all that much executive power. Hence he reported to his reactionary mother quite optimistically: 'Now we are going to have a little parliamentarism, but all power stays in my hands, and the general effect will suit Austrian circumstances very well indeed.' This proved wildly over-optimistic. For a start, the emperor, as head of the central bureaucratic state, did give up a lot of power. It is true that the emperor's prerogative in foreign policy and the military was left alone. Also, the *Reichsrat*, now at 100 members, was ostensibly to have the power of consent over taxation, and was to have a say in imperial matters such as economic policy, in cooperation with the provincial assemblies, but this was open to be interpreted as an advisory rather than legislative power.

However, most power was reserved to the provincial assemblies, which themselves were to be versions of the Hungarian Diet. A major concession of *imperial* power from the emperor was the restitution of Hungarian rights, effectively to pre-1848 conditions, with the restoration of a separate Hungarian Court Chancellery and, of course, the Hungarian Diet. The Hungarian chancellor was to have a seat in the central government, with another Hungarian minister without portfolio. There was something similar for Transylvania, and partially for Croatia. The result for central government was that the imperial ministries of the interior, justice, and religion and education were abolished, with a new minister of justice for the non-Hungarian part of the Monarchy (what would later be called Cisleithania), and the old interior minister, Goluchowski, now occupying the new position of 'minister of state'. The emperor still had a great deal of power, over the weak central assembly, but at the expense of a huge loss of undivided central power. The formal unified state of the Habsburg Monarchy ceased in 1860, not 1867.

This was not entirely clear in 1860, because the October Diploma never went into effect as initially envisaged, rejected by almost all sides of the Monarchy's political kaleidoscope. It turned out that the Hungarian Old Conservatives represented only themselves, that Hungarian public opinion, now led by the wily Ferenc Deák, would not accept any settlement simply imposed on them, with some sort of imperial body with tax-wielding power, that did not recognise the independence enacted by the April Laws. Meanwhile, Polish and Czech nationalists demanded a similar deal to that of the Magyars, and the liberal leadership of the German middle classes decried the lack of real taxpayer control over expenditure and taxation. Furthermore, their fear of being shut out of influence in favour of the old ruling class of the nobility appeared confirmed by the publication of statutes for the new provincial assemblies in December, which made the new assemblies much like the old, noble-dominated provincial estates of before 1848. Added to the ongoing fiscal and financial crisis was what amounted to a funding strike by investors, a lack literally of creditors, financiers confident enough to lend any more to the impecunious state, without adequate control by creditors and taxpayers. This paralyzed Franz Joseph's ability to respond to foreign policy crises such as the continuing amalgamation of the Italian nation-state, because that required money he no longer had or could borrow.

So Franz Joseph switched tactics again, and on 13 December replaced Goluchowski by Anton von Schmerling (Johann's prime minister at Frankfurt) as minister of state. Schmerling was a 'great-German' liberal constitutionalist and supporter of bureaucratic centralism, but was prepared to work around two key, mutually reinforcing obstacles: recognition of the special status of the Lands of the Crown of St Stephen, i.e., Hungary; and Franz Joseph's continuing refusal of recognition of the need for an explicitly constitutional system. When the emperor appointed the new Schmerling-led government, he demanded from the new ministers that they sign a document promising that they would defend the throne from the need for any more concessions of his imperial powers, the outer limits of which had already been reached; in other words that they would not make him agree to a constitution formally limiting his power.

What Schmerling came up with on 26 February 1861, however, did precisely that, informally. The February Patent, written with the help of Hans Perthaler, was on the face of it only 'enabling legislation' for the October Diploma, but it completely changed the power-balance within the new political arrangements. What had been a strongly decentralised system with few real checks on monarchic power changed into one that restored a strong central government with real power for the representative assembly at its centre, and strong *practical* limits to the emperor's power. This new parliamentary body was ostensibly still Kübeck's *Reichsrat* of 1851, and officially still only 'consultative', but it now amounted to an imperial parliament: a bicameral legislature, with an Upper House of notables, and a Lower House of 343 members sent to it from the provincial assemblies. The formula for how many members were sent from each respective province was complex; as was the composition of each provincial assembly, which usually had four electoral 'curia': great landowners, Chambers of Commerce, urban communes and rural communes. The provincial representation to the *Reichsrat* of each provincial assembly was then apportioned according to the relative strengths of the curia within that assembly.

The central parliament thus remained an indirectly elected body composed of members sent from the provincial assemblies (similar to the United States Senate until 1913), but the balance of legislative competence now shifted powerfully in favour of the central parliament, as German liberal centralists (and the financial sector) had wished, and those legislative competences in areas of taxation, the budget and finance, for instance, threatened to produce what were effectively constitutional controls over the executive. The new system was formally still one granted by Franz Joseph, who retained power in foreign policy and the military, but he was right to be concerned that his ministers were pushing him beyond the 'outermost limits' of acceptable reductions to his still supposedly absolute power.

Another special feature of the new *Reichsrat* was that there were, as there had been in the October Diploma, two versions of the *Reichsrat*: questions that concerned the whole Monarchy would be discussed by the full assembly, including the 120 members from the Hungarian lands and the 20 from Venetia; but questions that only concerned the hereditary lands, Bohemian lands, Dalmatia, Galicia and Bukovina could be discussed by the members from those (core) provinces in a 'narrower'

Reichsrat. This in effect provided recognition of Hungarian special status, but what if the Hungarians refused to send members? Then, as was to be interpreted by Schmerling, parliament could effectively ignore Hungary, discussing general, imperial matters, even if its membership was only that of the 'narrower' *Reichsrat*, a form of centralism by default. Moreover, the 'genius' of the February Patent from a German liberal viewpoint lay in the way in which the complex structure of the curias, and the formula for the relative representation of provinces, was manipulated in an extraordinary 'electoral geometry' (akin to American gerrymandering) that assured a German dominance within the parliament. When the de facto 'narrower' *Reichsrat* eventually met, in the summer of 1861, 119 of its 203 members were in the German liberal, 'bürgerlich' camp, broadly defined.

The result of all this was that the February Patent was embraced by the German liberal middle classes and the financial sector, but vehemently rejected by almost everyone else. The Venetians boycotted the whole process entirely, but provincial assemblies did meet throughout the rest of the Monarchy on 6 April, as prescribed, including the Hungarian Diet. Most provincial assemblies also sent their representatives to the *Reichsrat*. However, the Croat *Sabor* did not send members, nor, crucially, did the Hungarian assembly in Budapest, viewing the *Reichsrat* as an illegitimate body not recognised in the April Laws. There was a stand-off with the central government, which resulted on 21 August 1861 in Schmerling reimposing absolutist rule in Hungary, and the Hungarians, including the restored county administrations, part of the government, instituting passive resistance, mainly in the form of a tax strike (which had in any case been growing since the mid-1850s). Schmerling's response was: 'We can wait', and to conduct government as though the 'narrower' *Reichsrat* was the full version. Yet most groups apart from the German liberal bloc had turned up only to demand their own provincial autonomy, and after a period in which the disproportionate German dominance of proceedings became clear – a majority of 130 (including Ruthene allies) out of 203 – various groups walked out, the Galician Poles, then the Bohemian Czech members in 1863, Moravian Czech members in 1864, even the German Conservative Tyroleans. The *Reichsrat*, 'Schmerling's Theatre', thus became virtually a German liberal debating club, in which liberals such as Karl Giskra could push their constitutionalist agenda, acting as though they had rights even when they formally did not, for instance demanding ministerial responsibility – and partially getting it; and in which a state debt control commission was set up to supervise state finances, all much to Franz Joseph's discomfort.

Schmerling's strategy was now that laid out by Bruck in his political testament in 1860, *Die Aufgaben Österreichs* (The Duties of Austria), whereby Austria needed both to become a liberal, constitutional state and also to remain a part of Germany; and Germans should remain the hegemonic group in Austria, for the sake of the economic prosperity and political and cultural progress of all groups. This was the basis of what now became the central plank of Austrian foreign policy, the reassertion of Austrian influence and power in the German Confederation, or, in Schmerling's terms, the 'moral conquest' of Germany.

Re-establishing Habsburg hegemony in Germany was something Franz Joseph very much supported, especially as a compensation for the loss of Austrian influence and power in Italy (apart from Venetia). On 22 May 1860 the monument to Archduke Karl had been unveiled in the *Heldenplatz* (Heroes' Square), with one of the dedications to 'the persevering fighter for Germany's honour', and a sense of Austria's continuing mission as an integral part of Germany was something that the emperor and Schmerling shared. This inevitably meant rekindling the rivalry with Prussia, but from 1862 the chancellorship of Otto von Bismarck and the ensuing Army Bill Crisis had put in question Prussia's liberal constitutional character and hence its qualification in the eyes of other, by now, fairly liberal German states, to be the prospective leader of a united Germany. Austria, in contrast, with its German-dominated, liberalising *Reichsrat*, looked relatively benevolent as a hegemon. So Schmerling, once Johann's minister, now attempted to make another Habsburg, Franz Joseph, the leader once more of a German government. The Austrians came surprisingly close: at the *Fürstentag* (Princes' Assembly) at Frankfurt in August 1863, Franz Joseph managed to persuade the great majority of German princes to back Austrian plans for a reform of the Confederation that would have effectively created a nascent German government – under the Austrian emperor's presidency. The problem was that Bismarck's Prussia was not to be pressured into agreeing to such a thing, and there was no one on the Austrian side with the ruthless diplomatic skill to put Prussia in a position not to refuse.

Franz Joseph himself did not help by his resistance to constitutionalism at home, despite the fact that Austrian constitutionalism was one of the main attractions to the other German states. Similarly, his resistance to showing any flexibility or accommodation of Prussia as the other German great power within the Confederation allowed Prussia to argue that the Austrians would not be inclusive leaders of Germany, so why should they co-operate? Therefore, King Wilhelm I of Prussia was able not to attend, and his absence meant that the lavish celebrations of Franz Joseph's birthday under a black-red-gold canopy were pointless from a political perspective. To Franz Joseph and Foreign Minister Rechberg, Schmerling's liberal strategy appeared to have only shown that nothing could be achieved against Prussian conservative resistance, and so they backed away from the idea of a liberal reform of Germany, and adopted a policy of conciliation and co-operation towards Prussia – which was to prove even more disastrous.

The situation in late 1863 was diplomatically in flux. Napoleon III, for instance, demonstrated a wish to conciliate the Habsburgs by offering Franz Joseph's brother, Ferdinand Max, the opportunity to be Emperor Maximilian I of Mexico, and he and his wife Charlotte left Miramare, their dreamlike, neo-Gothic castle on the shores of the Adriatic north of Trieste, in April 1864. This was soon revealed as an unrealistic piece of Napoleonic imperialist adventurism that was to end tragically in Maximilian's execution on 19 June 1867, and Charlotte's madness, but in 1863–64 it looked like an attempt at reconciliation. There were still immense possibilities in a complex world that was still not sorted out. In Miramare itself, the 'Throne Room' is ringed by portraits of the major monarchs of Europe, several of which are monarchs of the various German states, along with Napoleon III, all players in the complex game of diplomacy – but Franz Joseph was not the one who mastered the game, nor was Napoleon III; Bismarck was.

The instrument by which Bismarck trapped Austria into an impossible situation was the return of the Schleswig-Holstein Question in late 1863. To German public opinion, it was clear that German interests against Denmark had to be protected, but the question was how? Franz Joseph and Rechberg decided that Austria should choose the conservative option, by allying in January 1864 with Prussia, rather than supporting the liberal-backed claimant, the Duke of Augustenburg, thus undermining any standing of Austria as a liberal alternative to the militaristic Prussia. Through the first half of 1864 Prussian and Austrian armies secured victories against the Danish army, the Austrians doing better than the Prussians, but the end result of the peace in August was that Prussia and Austria occupied the two duchies far distant from Austria, and adjacent to Prussia. It was clear by the autumn that Rechberg's pro-Prussian policy had left Austria with the burden of yet another military campaign that it could not afford to no real end except improving Prussia's position. Franz Joseph replaced Rechberg on 27 October with Count Alexander Mensdorff-Pouilly, in order to come up with a better policy to handle Bismarck's Prussia, but none was produced. The joint occupation of Schleswig-Holstein left Bismarck with the option to trigger conflict at any point he chose.

If Schmerling's forward policy in Germany appeared to have led only to failure by late 1864, Franz Joseph had come to the conclusion that 'Schmerling's Theatre' was not working for his interests at home either.

The membership of the *Reichsrat* might be dwindling in numbers, representing less and less of the Monarchy's provinces and peoples, but its German Liberal majority kept trying to chip away at the emperor's prerogatives, most notably when it came to control of the military. Franz Joseph refused such demands, and in early 1864 had furiously dressed down Schmerling for having the temerity to praise Austrian constitutionalism, for Franz Joseph still wanted to consider himself an absolute monarch. Allowing parliamentary meddling in the army, his area of prerogative, was thus anathema to him, and he gave no ground on the issue; in return the *Reichsrat* repeatedly denied requests for further funds for the army, and actually reduced military expenditures. There were sound reasons for this: given the poor shape of the economy, and Hungary's tax strike, revenues kept disappointing, deficits persisting, and by this point servicing the state's debt had ballooned to 40 per cent of the budget, so making economies in the administration and military made a certain sense, from a German liberal perspective, but it still impinged mightily on Franz Joseph's ability to conduct an active foreign policy. Moreover, it was in stark contrast to Prussia, where the military was expanded in complete defiance of any parliamentary restraints.

So Franz Joseph changed tack yet again. As early as December 1864, he began secret negotiations with the Hungarians' leader, Deák, and this time there was progress towards a position that was between centralism and federalism: dualism, whereby the Monarchy would be governed in two parts: Hungary (including all lands of the Crown of St Stephen) on the one side, and all the other provinces of Austria on the other. In return for recognition of the April Laws, in other words Hungarian quasi-independence, Hungary would accept some common institutions, arrange for Croatia to have autonomy, and generally return to being a loyal supporter of the king, Franz Joseph. This was the import of Deák's famous Easter Article of the spring of 1865, and Franz Joseph now responded positively, appearing in Budapest in June promising 'to do everything possible to satisfy the peoples of my Hungarian Crown'. On 27 July, on the closing of the *Reichsrat*, Franz Joseph fired Schmerling and most ministers, except Mensdorff and the two Hungarians, Chancellor György Majláth and Count Moritz Esterházy. The new minister of state was Count Richard Belcredi, a federalist, which was to complicate matters, but it was clear that Franz Joseph was now intent on a dualist solution. On 20 September, Franz Joseph suspended the February Patent, but not the October Diploma as such. Then he summoned the provincial assemblies and the Hungarian Diet, which met in December. Things did not go as smoothly as planned in gaining

Hungarian agreement, but negotiations for yet another new settlement did continue into the spring and summer of 1866.

Then the German Question struck Austria across the bows. Ever since the occupation of Schleswig-Holstein in 1864, Bismarck had been playing the Austrians along, stoking conflict between the occupation forces, waiting for the ripe moment to strike. The Convention of Gastein of 14 August 1865 had avoided war by splitting the administration of the duchies into Prussian-ruled Schleswig and Austrian-ruled Holstein, but this was just a temporary arrangement. By 26 January, Bismarck was ready to start the process leading to war. Meanwhile Austrian German policy continued to chop and change, and the suspension of the liberal 'constitution' of the February Patent in September 1865, as well as Austria's continuing internal problems with finances and the nationalities, undermined her image as a reliable ally of the other German states. The Bavarian prime minister, Ludwig von Pfordten wrote in October 1865: 'Austria, financially bankrupt, in a state of political anarchy, is at the moment incapable of action. We cannot now nor for a long time count on Austria.' Yet it was not the German states that were the main problem. When it came to the decisive moment in 1866, they sided (many lukewarmly) with Austria.

The problem regarding Prussia was Austria's isolation, yet again, on the international, great power level. Russia was still irreconcilable, but Napoleon III had shown himself ready to deal, as in the Mexican adventure, and intimated the possibility of alliance, if Austria would just make some concessions to Italy. There was even a proposal for the new Italian state to buy Venetia for a considerable sum, that would have helped solve Austria's financial plight. Yet Franz Joseph refused to contemplate this, not only on the basis of his imperial honour, but also because he still held out hope of restoring Austria's position on the peninsula against the 'illegitimate' Kingdom of Italy. This allowed Bismarck to step in and arrange an alliance with Italy on 8 April, which meant Austria would have to fight in the now very foreseeable war on two fronts. Napoleon III took the opportunity to threaten to intervene on the side of Austria's enemies, if Austria did not cede Venetia. Eventually, on 12 June, with hostilities already under way, Austria had to agree to the cession of Venetia simply to gain French neutrality. On 2 July, the eve of the Battle of Königgrätz, Franz Joseph offered to cede Venetia in return for French intercession, but by then it was too late. Refusal to give up its position in Italy meant that Austria lost its position in Germany as well.

The Austro-Prussian 'Seven Weeks' War was ostensibly caused by the Schleswig-Holstein dispute which came to a head in the German Confederation's Assembly in June 1866, but this was really just window dressing: the real purpose was the Prussian takeover of northern Germany and the expulsion of Austria from German affairs – plus the annexation of Venetia by Italy. Italy and Austria had already mobilised in the southern theatre in late April, and Prussia had decided on war as early as February. The war officially started on 16 June with the Prussian invasion of Hanover, Saxony and Hesse-Kassel. On 20 June Italy declared war against Austria. On 22 June, Prussian armies invaded Bohemia. On the Italian front, the Austrian forces did excellently, with a dramatic victory at Custozza (again) on 24 June, and a crushing naval triumph at Lissa on 20 July. By then, however, the war had already been hideously lost in the northern theatre.

On paper, the Austrian forces should have been victorious, with superior numbers and with the advantage of interior lines as the defending force. They also had superior artillery, as had been demonstrated in the Schleswig-Holstein campaign. It was not even a case of the military being underfunded, despite what the *Reichsrat* had done with the budget. What turned the northern campaign into total defeat were the superior tactics and training of the Prussian forces, especially the ultra-effective use of breech-loading rifles by the infantry, combined with all those flaws and weaknesses of the Austrian military described above for the 1859 fiasco that had really not changed much seven years later. In the aftermath, many, including Franz Joseph, made a scapegoat of the commanding general, Ludwig August von Benedek, for the catastrophe. Much of this criticism has been shown to be valid. Certainly making a stand at Königgrätz (also known by its Czech name of Sadowa) on 3 July, in *front* of the Elbe, thus cutting off any Austrian means of retreat, was unwise to say the least. On the other hand, it had been Franz Joseph who had appointed the unwilling Benedek, along with the rest of the incompetent high military leadership, and it was under the emperor's jealously guarded prerogative of control of the military that the necessary reforms had failed to occur.

Even had the military performed better, Bismarck's box of diplomatic tricks, with potential internal revolts against the Habsburg authorities, would have done for the Austrians. As it was, Königgrätz effectively marked the end of Austrian involvement in Germany. The eventual Peace of Prague, of 23 August 1866, was actually quite a mild result, given the depth of the Austrian defeat. Austria had to accept the formation of a Prussian-dominated North German Confederation, and a South German Union, linked militarily and commercially to the northern colossus, and not linked to Austria, but consisting of sovereign states. A sizeable war indemnity was paid to Prussia, and Austrian rights in Schleswig-Holstein given up, but no territory was handed over.

Figure 7. *A Glorious Chapter for the Austrian Artillery. The Army Artillery Reserve after the Battle of Königgrätz on the 3rd of July 1866*, by Rudolf Otto von Ottenfeld, 1897. Königgrätz was one of the most traumatic events in the Monarchy's history.
(Published with permission of the Austrian National Library.)

The only territory that was ceded by Austria was in the peace treaty of Vienna on 3 October, whereby Venetia was ceded to Napoleon III, who then immediately gave it to Italy. But then Austria had already agreed to give up Venetia before the war even started.

In a way, Austria had come out of this better than expected. The existence of the South German Union meant that Austria was potentially not even fully excluded from German affairs, and much of the next few years of diplomacy revolved around the attempt to rescue the Austrian position, just as Franz Joseph had refused to give up on restoring influence and power in Italy after 1859. This was to prove a pipe dream, because of Bismarck's other massive achievement in bringing France to war in 1870 and delivering an even more crushing defeat to Napoleon III, allowing the unification of the Prusso-German Empire in 1871. 1866 was to prove, in retrospect, the year Austria lost the struggle for the supremacy in Germany. That, however, was in an unforeseeable future. For now, expulsion from Italy did look permanent, and the only possible way back into Germany lay in establishing a workable domestic government system, which could end the long crisis that had been set off in 1859. That meant sorting out, finally, the other major extant problem: how to deal with Hungary.

Squaring the Circle II: Austria and Hungary: Austria-Hungary

It should be clear by now that one of the major political problems in the Monarchy had for decades been how to integrate Hungary and its Magyar leadership more effectively into the Monarchy's affairs. This had become even more urgent after the restitution of the Hungarian Diet in 1861, and the point-blank refusal of the Magyar political nation that it represented to co-operate with what they saw as illegitimate forms of Habsburg rule. The dissolution of the Diet had only led to passive resistance and a tax strike, in effect a national revolt, and Schmerling proved incorrect in thinking that he could wait this out, or rather that Franz Joseph could, because as far back as late 1864 the emperor had decided that he needed to settle with his Hungarian subjects. The process of negotiation took over two years, and was interrupted by the catastrophic war with Prussia, but the *Ausgleich* (Compromise) did eventually happen in early 1867.

Legend, especially Hungarian legend, has it that Empress Elisabeth, 'Sisi', played a central role in reconciling her husband with the Magyar people whose culture (and horses) she so admired, and her affinity to the leadership of the Hungarian nobility might indeed have played a positive role. Yet the main reason for the Compromise was that both Franz Joseph and the Magyar leadership decided that it was in their mutual interest to arrange it. Austrian defeat in the war and provisional expulsion from Germany probably helped to bring about the Compromise. Franz Joseph still thought he could re-enter the German game, as was suggested by his appointment of Baron Friedrich Ferdinand Beust, former prime minister of the Monarchy's defeated ally, Saxony, as foreign minister on 26 October 1866, but he would need to secure his shaken power and prestige to do so. A settlement with the Hungarians would go a long way towards this. He was also in all likelihood favourably impressed, and grateful, when Deák famously assured him that Magyar demands were the same after Königgrätz as they had been before, that there would be no taking advantage of Austria's plight.

Ironically, it was Austria's defeat and exclusion from Germany that encouraged Magyar support for a deal with Franz Joseph even more. As Eötvös was to explain, the exclusion of Austrian Germans from Germany deprived them and the centralist government that they supported from the power and prestige that came with being a 'German state' and part of the Confederation; shorn of that potential support, German power *within* the Monarchy did not have to be feared by Magyars in quite the same way as before, and instead the reduced Monarchy was just the right size to provide Hungary with protection but also virtual independence. The crushing of the Polish Revolt in 1863 by Russia showed what could happen to a medium-size nation without a state to protect it, and the emergence of a strong Prussia would not improve the situation for such nations, so the Hungarians were better off inside a large state such as the Monarchy, especially if they could govern themselves and have a large say in running it. This was the logic of Austroslavism, but for Magyars.

Austria's Germans, obversely, were now no longer sure of their dominance within the Monarchy. Bruck and Schmerling's strategy of being strong as Austrians in Germany and Germans in Austria was dead, and therefore many German liberals, chief among them the Styrian autonomists led by Moritz Kaiserfeld, saw the need to adopt a more defensive posture, and defend German *national* interests in the Monarchy in partnership with the Magyars' defence of theirs – and the Magyar leadership was happy to agree. The most basic rationale for dualism was summed up by Gyula Andrássy when he reputedly said: 'You look after your Slavs and we will look after ours.' Apparently it was Andrássy, possibly with Sisi's help, who persuaded Franz Joseph to opt for dualism and not federalism in 1866. He was also strongly supported in this by Beust, who saw especially the strategic implications of dualism for Habsburg power in Germany.

This did not mean, however, that there was an entirely clear path to a dualist settlement even in late 1866. The minister of state was still Belcredi, who, as a supporter of conservative, noble-led provincial federalism, tried his best to frustrate a dualist outcome. Slav nationalists also asserted a preference for a federalist outcome that would not circumvent their interests in the way dualism threatened to do. The Slav Conference that met in Vienna from 25 July (the day of the Nikolsburg armistice) would have divided the Monarchy up into five nationally oriented blocs of provinces: the German Alpine and Danubian provinces; the lands of the Bohemian Crown; Galicia and Bukovina; Hungary; and a South Slav territory. However, Belcredi could not support this either. Seeing this as a covert form of nationalism, he saw it as a threat to the unity of the supranational Monarchy that he, as a conservative federalist, still believed in. Instead, Belcredi attempted to get support for his conservative federalist agenda by calling on 2 January 1867 for elections to the provincial assemblies on 25 February to send members to the meeting of an extraordinary *Reichsrat* that would debate (and reject, he hoped) whatever settlement Franz Joseph and the Magyar leadership were in the process of finalising. This was opposed by Beust and the dualist negotiators, and the result was a decisive debate in the Ministerial Council on 1 February.

The protocol of the debate is a revealing document on a topic so central to the Monarchy's subsequent history. Beust outlined a starkly 'realist' rationale for dualism: 'I am quite aware that the Slav peoples of the Monarchy will view the new policy with mistrust; but the government cannot always be fair to all the nationalities ... Therefore we have to rely on the support of those with the most vigour (*Lebenskraft*), who are closer to each other in spirit, and whose mutual interests are complementary – and those are the Germans and the Hungarians.' Belcredi responded that the government should not rely on individual nationalities but be above all of them, and that the Slavs could not be so easily ignored, only to be countered in turn by the emperor himself: 'It might be that the way suggested by Count Belcredi is the less objectionable, but that of Baron Beust ought more quickly to lead to the desired goal.' A few days later, Franz Joseph asked Belcredi again if he was still opposed, and he said he was if the 'non-Hungarian' lands were to have no say in the settlement: 'For in these and not in Hungary does the monarchy have its strongest support and it is there that the will to preserve its mighty unity is indubitably still present. To what will a policy lead, which totally spurns the Slav majority of the population of these lands?'

That was an excellent question, anticipating the main problem with the Compromise, but Franz Joseph needed his settlement, and so dualism won the day. On 7 February Belcredi resigned and was replaced by Beust, now prime minister, foreign minister and interior minister in one. It was shortly after this that the final deal was signed between Franz Joseph and the Hungarians, on 15 February; on 17 February Franz Joseph appointed Andrássy, once burnt in effigy as a rebel, as Hungarian prime minister. On 27 February the former Hungarian Diet, now the Hungarian Parliament, was opened, and on 15 March Andrássy and his ministers were sworn in. Meanwhile, elections were called for an ordinary session of the 'narrower' *Reichsrat*, with the goal now to use Schmerling's 'electoral geometry' to secure a large German majority, which was successful: when the assembly met on 22 May, 118 out of 203 deputies were from German parties. To ensure an amenable atmosphere, the Polish contingent from Galicia were bought off with promises of giving the Polish leadership in Galicia a de facto version of the Compromise, with Poles granted autonomy and hegemony in Galicia, and a *Landesminister* (central minister representing a province) in the Viennese central government, which is what eventually occurred. Slovene deputies gave their support for less generous trade-offs. The Czech deputies continued their boycott from 1863. Any federalist threat to dualism was over.

As it turned out, the *Reichsrat* had no say in the Compromise anyway. Franz Joseph went ahead with the Hungarians more or less regardless of the Austrian half of his realm. The Hungarian Parliament passed the Compromise, 'Law XII of 1867' on 29 May, and Franz Joseph submitted himself to the medievalistic ceremony of coronation with the Crown of St Stephen as Hungarian king on 8 June. On 28 July, as king, he then gave sanction to Law XII, the final nail in the coffin of the unitary Habsburg state. Many members of the *Reichsrat* in Vienna protested at being ignored in the agreement to the Compromise, but they were brought around by Beust's promise of the granting of a proper constitution, which was to be eventually achieved in December. Beust still had to overcome Franz Joseph's anti-constitutionalism, but his argument was helped by Law XII, which stipulated that both states in the Dual Monarchy would be 'completely constitutional'. So the *Reichsrat* 'took note' of the fait accompli of the Compromise.

Figure 8. *Emperor Franz Joseph and Empress Elisabeth after Their Coronation as King and Queen of Hungary in 1867*, after the painting by Eduard Engerth. Gyula Andrássy leads the paying of homage to the (imperial-)royal pair.
(Published with permission of the Austrian National Library.)

The Compromise, the document on which the rest of the Monarchy's career was to be based, has been most aptly described as 'both perfect and imperfect'. It transformed the Austrian Empire into the Dual Monarchy of Austria-Hungary. On one side was Hungary, all of Hungary: reunited with Transylvania and the lands of the Military Frontier, as well as with Croatia-Slavonia, for which its own form of Compromise, the *Nagodba*, was to be agreed in 1868. On the other side was everything that was not Hungary: its official title was the tautological 'the lands and provinces represented in the *Reichsrat*', its informal official title was 'Cisleithania', in other words, the lands this side of the River Leitha, which was the traditional border between Austria and Hungary just to the east of Vienna. Hungary is sometimes called 'Transleithania', but this is just another name for Hungary. Cisleithania was unofficially called 'Austria', but this could not be the officially recognised name from the perspective of the Habsburg authorities in Vienna, because to them 'Austria' was still the whole empire, including Hungary.

Hungarians thought differently, seeing Hungary and the rest of the former empire as separate entities, side by side. Austrians tended to see Austria-Hungary's common government as *above* the two halves, Hungarians saw it as *between* them. On 24 December Franz Joseph appointed Beust imperial chancellor, suggesting there was still an imperial government above both halves, and his chancellery continued after his dismissal in 1871 as the 'presidial section' of the Foreign Ministry. The enabling legislation for the Compromise, that was eventually passed *post factum* by the *Reichsrat*, the 'Law of Delegations', also differed from the Hungarian Law XII in claiming competence for 'common affairs for *all* the lands of the Austrian Monarchy', but the Hungarian law was the original one. Even there, however, there were differences between the Magyar version and its German translation, and real, if subtle, linguistic inconsistencies in the meaning of the respective word for 'joint' which created more room for argument.

There were famously tedious and confusing arguments over the initials of the Monarchy: was it 'k.k.' – *kaiserlich-königlich*, imperial-royal, or 'k.u.k.' – *kaiserlich und königlich*, imperial and royal? The former, used more by Austrians, implied there was still an empire, including the kingdom of Hungary; the latter suggested two entities, imperial Austria *and* royal Hungary. The latter, Hungarian preference, increasingly won out, although there was always the possibility of using 'k.k.' in Cisleithania to describe the 'imperial-royal' relationship between imperial Austria and royal Bohemia. The relationship was so complex and controversial that a suitable coat-of-arms for Austria-Hungary only saw the light of day during the First World War. 'Austria' eventually returned as an official appellation for Cisleithania in 1915, but this was a triumph of the Hungarian interpretation of the Compromise. Louis Eisenmann accused Cisleithania of lacking 'national egoism', but that seems the obvious consequence.

The Compromise was officially, as we have seen, not one between Cisleithania and Hungary, but between Emperor Franz Joseph and his Hungarian subjects, or rather between King Franz Joseph and his Hungarian subjects. What this meant in practice was that the Compromise was not a binary relationship but a triangular one, with the emperor-king in the middle, at the apex (depending on your interpretation). What Hungary and Cisleithania shared was a common monarch, who had retained his full prerogatives in foreign policy and military affairs; in addition, what they continued to co-operate on was maintaining a customs union and a common currency, a fairly successful precursor of contemporary 'Euroland'.

These were two different sets of relationships. The first was the strongest and most principled, but because it derived from the 'indivisible and inseparable' principle of the Pragmatic Sanction, this strong, permanent set was called, confusingly, 'pragmatic'. This set included the three common ministries that exercised Franz Joseph's prerogative, all that remained of the imperial state: Foreign Ministry, War Ministry and Finance Ministry, the last to arrange for the funding of the first two. These ministries were under the control of the joint monarch, but had to account annually to an institution called the Delegations. This body consisted of delegations from the Hungarian Parliament and the Cisleithanian *Reichsrat* (the 'narrower *Reichsrat*' of the February Patent) which met annually, alternately in Vienna and Budapest. The Delegations then determined the budget for the common ministries, which were then to be passed by the two parliaments. The two delegations did not, however, do any of this together. Because Franz Joseph was so appreciative of Deák's not increasing demands after Königgrätz the eventual Compromise was no compromise, but rather an acceptance of the full Hungarian demands as of the summer of 1866. One example is that the Compromise ensured that there would never ever again be an imperial parliament. The Delegations met and deliberated separately; provision was made for joint votes if agreement could not be reached, but all negotiations between the two delegations were to be done in writing, and if there was a vote, it was to be held in silence, without any cross-deliberation harming Hungarian sovereignty. What this meant in practice was that the Delegations were inoperative, by Hungarian design, and never properly fulfilled their supposed role of keeping control over the joint government ministries.

There was further the question of the 'Quota', that is to say the relative proportion each state had to provide, in army recruits and funding, for the upkeep of the common ministries, primarily for the imperial armed forces. The negotiations on this were to be held every ten years by Deputations from the two parliaments (which *did* meet and talk together). Initially the Quota was set at a ratio of 70:30 for Cisleithania and Hungary, reflecting the relative poverty and lack of development of the Hungarian lands. As Hungary grew richer, the proportion came to be seen as unfair to Cisleithania, and the Hungarians felt frustrated at not being able to have control over their own national army. Yet Franz Joseph was never going to give up control of his imperial army (or navy), which continued to swear loyalty to him as Habsburg emperor and not to the dualist state, let alone Cisleithania or Hungary. That was the whole point of the Compromise, to retain control of what mattered, the army. There were militias in both halves, the *Landwehr* and the *Honvéd*, but both were deliberately kept at a low level, as auxiliary to the k.u.k. army, so as not to threaten its superior imperial status.

As a result of not having much control over the army, members of both parliaments, the Hungarians in particular, resisted paying for it, returning to the sort of controversies over military budgets of the earlier 1860s; there was ample scope for this because the military contingent and budget, even if they were set every ten years in the quota negotiations, were voted on annually in both parliaments. It was simply assumed that the budgets would be passed, and there was no provision in either parliamentary system for what would happen if they were not. Vienna could fudge the problem with the emergency clause of Article 14, but the Budapest parliament did not have even this. As a result of the chronic stand-off over control of the military, the decennial negotiations over the Quota tended to set the contingents and budget at lower levels than desirable, and were always extremely contentious.

Along with the Quota, the Deputations also negotiated every ten years over the second set of relationships, called 'dualist' (*paktiert* in German). These were not permanent as such and not part of the common government, as such, but rather agreements between the two parliaments (and emperor and king) to be renewed every ten years, and, nonetheless, economically of the greatest significance. They covered issues associated with the customs and commercial union, especially as regards the state debt, currency and tariffs, which were often a bone of contention. Bargaining over the 'pragmatic' question of the Quota and the other 'dualist' matters became so contested and drawn-out that in later rounds there developed an almost constant crisis, giving rise to the expression 'empire on notice', because of the decennial limit on agreements.

Then there was a third part of the Compromise, which was not in the document itself, which was the actual executive body of Austria-Hungary, the Joint Ministerial Council, known also as the Crown Council. This was the informal council that Franz Joseph formed to consult with on his prerogatives: foreign and military affairs. This consisted usually of the emperor, the three joint ministers, and then the prime ministers of Cisleithania and Hungary, sometimes their finance ministers, and the chief of the General Staff, and the heads of the two militias – anyone whom Franz Joseph chose to consult. It was not in the Compromise documents, but the Crown Council became the emperor-king's own organ of executive government, and because of the ineffectiveness of the Delegations and the complexities in the dual budgeting process, left Franz Joseph with what amounted to the absolute power over foreign and military matters that he had most cherished all along.

The great historical expert on the Compromise, Louis Eisenmann, once wrote on its respective benefits and burdens: 'The equation of community and dualism was as follows: equal rights, two thirds expenditure for Austria, three quarters influence for Hungary.' That is about right. The Hungarians never really paid their fair share of the common fiscal burdens, because the Quota was never set high enough for Hungary; on the other hand, the Magyar leadership was able, through its influence over their king, and the very asymmetries of the Compromise, to exercise immense influence over foreign affairs and trade policy, and, as we shall see, the formal structures of Cisleithanian politics. However, they were not the only winners from the Compromise; so too, as designed, were the German Liberals, and Franz Joseph. Austria-Hungary is best described, at the onset at least, as a German-Magyar condominium, as Andrássy had hoped in 1866 it would be. Belcredi had feared exactly the same thing: that dualism would not undo Schmerling's centralism, but rather produce a constitutional-centralist, Magyar-dominated Hungary, and a constitutional-centralist German-dominated Austria, a return to 'a reduced form of Schmerling's ideas'. But this solved only one problem, and not that well, for it left out of consideration, as Belcredi had pointedly referenced with the emperor in February 1867, the concerns of the Slav majority of the population.

The Compromise was far from settling how the Monarchy was governed and for whom. Instead, all the groups that had been left out now tried to emulate it, used it as a model for their own relationship to the state. Galicia's Polish political nation had already been promised a de facto deal of autonomy and hegemony in Galicia, to the detriment of the Ruthenes, and this was arranged in 1868. Slovene politicians were initially satisfied by minor concessions; Romanian efforts to retain some autonomy in Transylvania failed, but were to return. The Croats got their Compromise in 1868, and it worked quite well initially, but its flaws were to allow a later generation of Magyar leaders to return to Magyarisation *in* Croatia. The Czechs also attempted to emulate the Magyars, by trying for their own historical-rights-based deal, which they almost achieved with the Fundamental Articles in 1871. They were stopped, as we shall see, by pressure being put on Franz Joseph by German Liberals in Cisleithania, the new German Empire and Andrássy's Hungarian government, based on stipulations in the Compromise. Yet the Czechs too would get a de facto version of the Compromise's local autonomy and hegemony, and there would be no let-up from now on in the political and nationalist strife surrounding those nationalist, centrifugal efforts.

The centre/periphery dynamic that had, after many decades, led to the Compromise with Hungary was not solved; it was just divided in two, like the division of a cell. The German-Czech conflict in one half, and the South Slav (Serbo-Croat) question in the other, would be the two chronic problems that unsettled the Monarchy until its end. All that was different was the identity and relative strength of the national hegemon and the other groups challenging for their deal. Adolf Fischhof, the 1848 revolutionary and later liberal political theorist, was to warn in 1878 of the threat to the Monarchy's existence, 'so long as our constitution, instead of being the wax which wields our territories into a whole, is the wedge to drive them apart'. The problem with the Austro-Hungarian Compromise was that it was not so much that the circle was squared, as that it was split in two.

4   1867–1879: Liberalisation

The disaster of Königgrätz and Austria's exclusion from Germany had a traumatic effect on Austrian German culture, and a crisis of identity for Austrian Germans that was to have a profound, ongoing impact for the rest of the Monarchy's career. One well known, pithy response was from Franz Grillparzer, Austria's bard, who wrote on a photograph in 1867: 'I was born a German, am I one still?' A more musical response occurred with the 15 February 1867 choral premiere of Johann Strauss the Younger's *By the Beautiful Blue Danube* waltz. Later, this became the informal Austrian national anthem, accompanied by an anodyne, Austria-praising text. The original text by Josef Weyl, however, was performed in Carnival and started with a challenge to its audience: 'Viennese be happy! .... defy the times – O God the times! – of sadness'. The *Blue Danube* waltz began as a carnevalesque effort to escape, for the moment, the nadir in which Vienna and Austria found itself.

By the end of 1867, the situation had changed yet again, and a much more optimistic era opened, with liberal regimes in both halves of the new Dual Monarchy (which had effectively begun three days after the *Blue Danube* premiere on 18 February with the agreement between Franz Joseph and the Hungarian leadership). Liberalism, in the shape of a German government in Vienna and a Magyar government in Buda, appeared triumphant, and set fair for a long rule. This turned out, for Cisleithania at least, to be deceptive, but for over a decade liberalism had an immense impact on all aspects of life in the Monarchy.

The German-Magyar Liberal Condominium

Two constitutional states were established by the end of 1867. In Hungary, the April Laws of 1848 had already become the basis of a constitutional regime in the spring. In Cisleithania, the December Constitution was put into law by imperial sanction on 21 December. It was composed of five 'Basic Laws', one of which was the aforementioned Delegation Law that had codified the Austrian version of dualism.

Neither constitution created a fully 'constitutional state' as that term would be understood today, or even as understood in Britain at the time. The position of Emperor-King Franz Joseph was still far too powerful for that, also in domestic affairs. In Hungary, the Punctation of 17 March, a secret agreement between the king and the Hungarian negotiators, had given Franz Joseph several key powers, most powerful of which was a 'presanction on legislation', effectively a prophylactic veto. He was also given the power of appointment over the top officials in the central bureaucracy, and ministers remained responsible to him and not to parliament, as such. Similarly in Cisleithania, Franz Joseph remained in a powerful formal position. The December Constitution had been officially granted by his grace, so there was never an admission by Franz Joseph to the concept of popular sovereignty. There was also no real ministerial responsibility in the parliamentary sense. Legislation was required to be signed by the relevant minister as well as the emperor, but this only resulted in a narrow, legal version of ministerial responsibility, which in any case was never realised because of the failure to set up the State Court that would have adjudicated such cases. There was no ministerial responsibility in the sense of ministers and governments being voted out by a parliamentary majority. Franz Joseph retained that power to hire and fire: ministers ultimately answered to him and not parliament. The state officialdom remained the same state officialdom of before the Compromise, just with its purview over Hungary removed, and so it remained under the control of the bureaucrat-in-chief, Franz Joseph. The emperor also retained the powers of prorogation and dissolution of the *Reichsrat*, as well as significant emergency powers as listed in the notorious Article 14, which, as we shall see, would prove a very strong handle to counter the powers that the constitution did give to the *Reichsrat* over budgetary matters. The emperor was thus from the beginning in a powerful position to counter liberal policies, had he wished.

For the time being, however, he did not wish to do so. Rather, in order to get his Monarchy back to its position as one of Europe's great powers and restore the status of the Habsburg dynasty, he felt constrained to work with the German Liberals, who, dislike them though he might, did have an apparently unassailable majority in the new *Reichsrat*, especially given the continuation of the Czech deputies' boycott. It was not even a new *Reichsrat*; it was the same *Reichsrat* that had existed, off and on, ever since it was created by the February Patent of 1861. Nothing was changed: it was still a bicameral legislature, with an Upper House, the *Herrenhaus* (House of Lords) composed mainly of the high nobility, and a Lower House, the House of Deputies, where the German Liberals ruled. One of the main reasons why there was only a set of five 'Basic

Laws' rather than a fully new constitution was the desire by the German Liberals to preserve the advantages of Schmerling's 'electoral geometry', and the electoral system, with its curias, remained exactly the same.

The December Constitution was nonetheless a very liberal document in many key respects that gave Austrian political life from this point on a much freer and more progressive framework. There was an enumeration of the basic liberties and norms of a constitutional state, such as freedom of speech, worship, association and also of movement. It guaranteed equality before the law for all individuals, regardless of religious confession, which made this the point at which full Jewish emancipation is seen as first occurring in Austrian history. There were also arrangements outlined for establishing a fully independent judiciary at all levels within the state, making Cisleithania a fully articulated *Rechtsstaat*, with the full rule of law, independent of officialdom or emperor, for the first time. The institutions envisaged in the December Constitution were set up soon after: the *Reichsgericht* (Imperial Supreme Court) in 1869, to protect the constitutional rights of citizens; and the *Verwaltungsgerichtshof* (Administrative Court) in 1875, to offer redress for citizens against the administration. Both courts would fulfil their role as independent judicial voices quite forcefully, with major impact on how Austrian politics and society would develop.

The constitution, although centralist in intent, left considerable powers to the provincial assemblies or diets, including the crucial power of electing the deputies to the *Reichsrat* itself, as the indirect election process of the February Patent had prescribed. (Nothing of the 'electoral geometry' was tampered with.) The constitution also did not make German the official state language of Cisleithania, quite unlike Magyar's status in Hungary. Instead, partly at the suggestion of the Slovenian liberal, Lovro Toman, but with their full agreement, the writers of the constitution included, *verbatim*, the Kremsier *Reichstag*'s generous and idealistic draft of the Law on Nationality Rights, which became the famous Article 19 of the December Constitution. This guaranteed the use of the *landesübliche Sprache* (locally current language) for children in schools and adults in communicating with officials, and so forth, and proclaimed the equal rights of all '*Volksstämme*' (nationalities).

Once both constitutions were in place, the liberal governments could begin a spate of legislation bringing major liberal reform to many areas of life. Andrássy's government had been operating in Hungary since the spring. For all its liberal ideological credentials, it was heavily aristocratic in its composition, befitting the particular character of Hungarian political life, with a very large nobility including the populous, land-based gentry, and with the urban centres, primarily Pest, still largely populated by German-speakers, many of them Jewish, and leaving politics to the Magyar aristocrats and gentry. The new prime minister of the Cisleithanian government of 30 December was also a high aristocrat, Prince Carlos Auersperg, but his cabinet was composed largely of non-aristocrats, or officials with acquired minor noble titles, and so merited the triumphant title of the *Bürgerministerium*, with its connotations not only of the citizenry (as opposed to the nobility) but also of being middle-class, even 'bourgeois' in an almost (French) revolutionary sense. Much was made at the time of the cultural change this involved, with the bearded, ex-revolutionaries such as Karl Giskra, the new interior minister, challenging the norms of the officials (with clean-shaven chins, as prescribed by the anti-revolutionary codes of the bureaucracy) that had previously dominated government. This was an exaggeration, however, as the liberalism of the new ministry showed considerable continuities with the Josephist, centralist and top-down, tradition – from which many ministers still came.

One major piece of legislation that was, perforce, joint was the Army Law of 1868, which had to be passed, as laid down in the Compromise, by both parliaments. This re-established a joint army (the old imperial army that was Franz Joseph's most cherished area of power), set rules and levels of conscription and funding, as agreed; but it was also an attempt at liberal reform. It scaled back the size of the military establishment, and set new, more humane and reasonable rules on conscription and discipline. The joint war ministers that were appointed, General Baron Franz John (1866–68), and General Baron Franz Kuhn von Kuhnenfeld (1868–74) began the modernisation of the armed forces in the law's spirit, even if Archduke Albrecht, Franz Joseph's appointee as inspector general, did his best to keep reform to a minimum.

In Cisleithania, the new liberal government had the advantage that liberalisation had started before the Compromise. The *Reichsrat* had already passed in 1862 the Law on Communes (*Gemeindegesetz*), based on Stadion's statute of 1849, and this law was to prove crucial in providing for far-reaching autonomy for city, town and also village governments. There was to be more legal reform with the new Criminal Law Code of 1873, that introduced limited use of the jury system, another liberal favourite.

In terms of economic policy, the new regime fully embraced the laissez-faire ideology of the time. The constitution had abolished any remaining legal constraints on the peasantry, and land law and company law were liberalised (we would say deregulated). There were also (joint, Austro-Hungarian) free trade treaties passed with the monarchy's main trading partners, which also were negotiated in a liberal spirit. The one exception was in labour law, and the approach to trade unions, which was very oppressive. There were distinct limits to mid-nineteenth-century liberalism when it came to the worker/employer nexus.

The liberal economic policies facilitated, but also were given credence by, the huge boom that followed the end of the eight-year crisis. The 'seven fat years' of the era known as the *Gründerjahre* (founders' years) changed central Europe's economy dramatically. Two bumper harvests in 1867 and 1868, at a time when the rest of Europe was suffering poor harvests, combined with the sense of relief and opportunity provided by the dawn of the dualist liberal era, set off an avalanche of public and private investment, in both Cisleithania and Hungary. There was a new spate of railway construction, and further afield the opening of the Suez Canal on 17 November 1869 (attended by Franz Joseph on his one extensive foreign state trip) provided commercial opportunities that Austrian firms were quick to take up. The Austrian Lloyd shipping line started a Trieste-Bombay service in 1870. It was with immense optimism and confidence in progress and the rectitude of their liberal principles that the two governments undertook their new mission.

Both governments adopted radical reform in two interconnected areas: religion and education, and the connecting theme was anticlericalism. Anticlericalism was a strong feature of nineteenth-century liberalism throughout Catholic Europe, and Austria-Hungary was no exception. One of the first goals of the Auersperg government was to overcome the concessions made to the papacy in the Concordat of 1855. The anticlerical May Laws returned control over education and marriage to the state authorities, and proclaimed the legal equality of religious denominations. This did not happen without resistance from the Catholic hierarchy. Bishop Franz Joseph Rudigier of Linz, Franz Joseph's former religious tutor, issued a Pastoral Letter in September 1868 calling for resistance, and was eventually sentenced to two weeks imprisonment in July 1869. This form of martyrdom was cut short by a pardon from the emperor, but it marked the beginning of political Catholicism in Austria. Such resistance only made liberals more determined. The Primary Education Law of 14 May 1869, seen by many liberals as the summit of their enlightening achievement, provided for a system of universal, free compulsory primary education for a minimum of eight years, paid for by the provincial governments and municipalities, with a state-mandated curriculum. Children were still allowed to attend religious schools, but for no less than the mandatory eight years and with mandated hours of secular education. This was followed the next year, in the summer of 1870, by the formal abrogation of the Concordat following on from the highly controversial

Papal Declaration of Infallibility. Franz Joseph, still a conservative Catholic, allowed all this anticlerical legislation with a heavy heart, not least because his mother, Archduchess Sophie, made her horror of it clear to him; but he was prepared to go along with liberal policy, partly because it did return power in key areas to the Habsburg state, and the Papal Declaration of Infallibility was a direct challenge to his position as the *Habsburg* prince within the power structures of the Church.

In Hungary, there were similar developments. The autonomy of religious organisations was recognised, which particularly helped the Protestant denominations. Obversely, the Concordat was declared invalid in the lands of the Hungarian crown in 1868 (earlier than in Cisleithania), and power over Church-state relations was handed over to the minister for religion and education. The year 1868 also saw an Education Law, mainly the work of József Eötvös, that called for compulsory education from age six to twelve. In the initially liberal spirit of the government, children were to be taught in the local language. Denominational schools were still allowed, but under closer state supervision. The law was more hypothetical than actual, as less than half of Hungarian children were going to school in 1870.

There was another statute designed by Eötvös that also reflected the initial liberalism of the times, the Nationalities Law of December 1868, which was somewhat different in approach from the Cisleithanian Article 19 of the constitution. The Hungarian equivalent proclaimed a unitary Hungarian 'nation', in the concept of a civic nationalism, where the sum of all citizens composed the 'nation', but it also recognised that all individual citizens were equal in their right to *their* personal nationality. There were thus no communal rights for nationalities, but each individual had an equal right to use their language on all levels below the national, state level: that is, at the county level and below, when dealing with officials or in courts, and in education. At the national, state level, however, in the central administration, in the parliament, and also at University, the official language of the state, Magyar, had to be used. After all, the state was a Hungarian (Magyar in Hungarian) nation-state.

In 1868, the liberal Hungarian leadership was also prepared to make a sub-Compromise with the Croatians, the *Nagodba*, that reflected the logic of the Austro-Hungarian Compromise to some extent, and gave Croatia, on the face of it, a considerable amount of autonomy. However, it was much less than the Croatian leadership had wanted, and had to be forced through by a rigged and pressured election, to gain a *Sabor* (Croatian Diet) that was willing to sign up. In 1868 the deal looked fairly acceptable, with Croatian becoming the language of use of the Croatian administration and diet, which had control over domestic, Croatian matters. However, 'common affairs', worth 55 per cent of Croatian revenues, were to be controlled from Buda. The Croatian executive, the *ban*, was to be responsible to the *Sabor*, but he was to be appointed by the Hungarian king, Franz Joseph, on the recommendation of the Hungarian prime minister. There were to be Croatian deputies to the Hungarian Parliament, who could participate when subjects affecting the whole 'State community' were discussed. It looked like autonomy, but was not all that strong, and in many aspects the *Nagodba* left Croatia a part of a Greater Hungary in ways the Austro-Hungarian Compromise did not leave Hungary part of a Greater Austria.

Both the Nationalities Law and the *Nagodba* shared similarities with the anticlerical legislation, particularly in the search for greater power and control for the *national*, central, *Magyar* government. German liberals might be centralists and see themselves as the *Staatsvolk* 'state people', the people whose function was to run the state for the sake of all the rest, but Magyar liberals regarded themselves, Magyar nobles and gentry (comprising most of the 7 per cent or so of the population who could vote), *as* the nation-state. In a positivist era when theories of evolution crossed over into the Social Darwinism of Herbert Spencer, and the 'struggle for existence' was a prevailing concept, the Magyar leadership saw themselves threatened on all sides, by 'Germanisation', Russia, and the advancing 'Slav sea' in which they had once feared to drown. Liberal policy after 1867 was therefore heavily informed by a nationalist-inspired drive to gain control over the Hungarian nation-state. Now that they were in charge, Magyar liberals no longer needed the potential for resistance of the decentralised system of county administration, so, in an ironic twist, the Hungarian Parliament now followed in the footsteps of Bach's hussars. The Law of 10 April on County Administration, and ensuing laws in 1870 and 1872, saw the famed autonomy of the counties make way for central control. Each county *föispán* (governor) was now nominated and appointed by the central government. There was still an *alispán* (deputy-governor), elected by the local county assembly, but with much less power than before. Judges for the local courts were now appointed by central government, and, unlike Cisleithania, there was never a full separation of the judicial and administrative functions at the lowest level. From being a highly decentralised state, Hungary became one of the more centralised ones, with power concentrated in the Magyar-speaking parliament and administration in Buda.

This might explain both why the Magyar political nation thought of Hungary as a Magyar nation-state, even when Magyar-speakers comprised only 40 per cent of the population of the lands of the Hungarian crown, and also why its political life continued to revolve around the question of 'Public Law', in other words the Compromise. Even though the Magyars had effectively won their battle for very strong autonomy, and had many other nationalities within their borders whose leaderships wanted their own national rights to be recognised, Hungarian politicians continued to act as though it was still an oppressed nation yearning to break free. The politics of nationalism in the Hungarian public space were hardly ever about nationalities, almost always about how much Hungary should get yet further away from Austrian oppression – how much of the Compromise to accept or reject. The Hungarian political spectrum went from the government party, the Deákists, who thought the Compromise the best deal available (which it was) all the way to the rejectionist 'Party of '48', which was the successor to the Kossuthists, and who still regarded Kossuth as the legitimate leader of Hungary. For them only independence was an acceptable outcome, along with a more egalitarian, democratic society, in the spirit of Kossuth. Somewhere between these two was the 'Left Centre', led by Kálmán Tisza, whose party programme, the Bihar Points of April 1868, was ostensibly quite radical, demanding a renegotiation of the Compromise to gain much greater freedom for Hungarians, including the abolition of the Delegations. For the first few years, the Deákist Party held a large majority in parliament, but this began to be eroded by the other parties, on the Magyar nationalist argument that the Compromise was bad for Hungary.

Politics in Cisleithania were never this simple, because of the pre-existing presence of nationalities who were either their own political nation, such as the Galician Poles, or who were given a voice by their allies within the political structures, as was the case with the Czechs and the conservative-federalist wing of the Bohemian nobility. The next attempt to square the circle in the Monarchy took place in Bohemia.

Squaring the Circle III.i: Bohemia

In Cisleithania two problems intertwined: how to satisfy the demands of national leaderships for the equal rights of their nationalities to respect and inclusion, and how to satisfy the demands of provincial leaderships for proper levels of autonomy and resources. The German liberals might have wanted to rule their side of the condominium much as the Magyars ruled theirs, as a German centralised state, but they simply could not. Germans comprised only 37 per cent of the population of Cisleithania, not quite the 40 per cent of Magyars in Hungary, but more importantly the political landscape was quite different. There were too many other groups with established power bases to pull off the Magyar trick of a nation-state in a sea of nationalities: everyone wanted their own version of what the Hungarians had gained.

Hungary made a deal with Croatia, and the Vienna government could similarly make a deal with the Galician Poles, which is what they did, despite the fact that Poles were only a minority of the population, with almost as many Ruthenes, about 43 per cent, and a large minority, about 10 per cent, of Jews. This was because the Poles were the 'political nation'. Polish was made the language of the education system above primary level in Galicia in January 1868, and in February German was removed as a language of justice and administration. (One of the reasons for the founding of a German-speaking university in 1875 in Czernowitz in Bukovina was to compensate for the complete Polonisation of Galicia's universities.) In June 1869, Polish became the '*inner* language' of administration in most instances in Galicia. The Polish leadership in Galicia's *Sejm* (Diet) demanded more, amounting to complete Home Rule, as their Resolution of 24 September 1868 made clear, and the German Liberal government was not prepared to go that far, but it was prepared to cede a de facto autonomy to Galicia's political nation; eventually a quid pro quo of Polish support for the government in Vienna and almost complete autonomy in Galicia was going to be the outcome. The problem was there were many other groups seeking something similar.

There were Dalmatian Croats, the large majority of the Adriatic province's population, who wanted more recognition and inclusion, and perhaps to be united with Croatia, and were not happy that Schmerling's electoral geometry produced an Italian majority in the Dalmatian Diet; there were Slovenes in Carniola, whose leadership did achieve a Slovene majority in the Carniolan Diet, for the first time, in the 1867 elections. The Slovene deputies in the *Reichsrat*, including Toman, were relatively co-operative, making quite practical demands for various concessions, such as an expanded use of Slovenian in schools, or the building of a railway line to help the Carniolan economy, but there was also the threat of more radical demands from other Slovene politicians, such as gathering the various Slovenian-speaking areas of several of Austria's provinces into one large, Slovene province.

The main problem in Cisleithanian politics, as it had been since 1863, was the refusal of the Czech political leadership to participate in the proceedings of the *Reichsrat*. They and their allies in the Bohemian high nobility were outraged that the Hungarians had received what, by right, should have been given to the Monarchy's most prosperous and best-educated province, Bohemia. Much as the Hungarians had succeeded in insisting on the historic rights of the Kingdom of St Stephen (which were largely a historical fiction), so too the Czech leadership argued their nationalist case on the basis of the historic rights of a province, 'Bohemian State Right', much as some of their American contemporaries had argued against federal power by invoking 'states' rights'. Bohemia and the other Bohemian crownlands, Moravia and Silesia, had been integrated into the central government of Austria for over a century at this point, unlike Hungary, and Bohemian noblemen had often been in Austria's leadership. This had caused much jealousy among Hungarian aristocrats in the past, but now the demands to restore historic rights to Bohemian self-government were intertwined with Bohemian noblemen's resentment of Hungarian success. Whatever its source, the reaction of Czech politicians and much of the Czech public to the Compromise was quite vociferous, and long-lasting. There were protests in November 1867, then again in May 1868, when Czech deputies boycotted the Bohemian Diet (where they were in a decided minority, because of electoral geometry). By the autumn of that year the situation had become so grave that the government imposed martial law on 10 October.

Prime Minister Auersperg had already resigned on 26 September over attempts by some of his colleagues to have the government make some concessions to the Czechs (as they had done to the Galician Poles). Count Eduard Taaffe, a moderate member of the government as well as a childhood friend of the emperor, was appointed by Franz Joseph to replace Auersperg. While more concessions were made to the Poles in 1869 over Polish language use, concessions to the Czechs suggested by the more conservative members of ministry were rejected by the more liberal, German centralist majority in what was still the *Bürgerministerium*. The crisis, however, continued to simmer over how much compromise with 'the Slavs'. At first, the more conciliatory ministers, Taaffe chief among them, lost out in early 1870, Taaffe being replaced by Leopold von Hasner on 1 February; but then, shortly after, it was the Poles, frustrated by another rejection of their demands, who brought down the German liberal government. When Giskra proposed a reform of election law to provide direct elections to the *Reichsrat*, a measure which was seen as undermining the powers of the provincial assemblies and a bid for more centralisation, the Polish deputies left, followed by the Slovenes, the conservative, Clerical Tyrolean delegation and twelve members of the conservative-federalist bloc. There were no longer enough deputies in the *Reichsrat* to continue business, Franz Joseph refused to call new elections for the provincial assemblies, and so Hasner and the *Bürgerministerium* were forced to resign on 4 April. The emperor replaced them with what would become an oft-repeated phenomenon in Cisleithanian politics, a *Beamtenministerium* (government of non-political officials), headed by a moderately conservative Polish aristocrat, Count Alfred Potocki.

The Potocki government represented an attempt by Franz Joseph, before the summer of 1870, to break with the German Liberals and attempt a federalist solution to how to govern Cisleithania. The plan was to dissolve the *Reichsrat* and provincial assemblies, and call elections for the latter, which would then return a more amenable *Reichsrat* in the autumn. The problem was that Potocki had little idea of how to proceed in coming up with a system to replace the German liberal hegemony.

Then, as it had in 1866, foreign policy rudely intervened in the form of the Franco-Prussian War of July–September 1870. Franz Joseph had attempted to create his own foreign policy by cultivating relations with the South German states and co-operating with France. That was why he had appointed Beust: not so much to wreak revenge on Prussia – the Habsburg army was not at this point capable of mounting yet another costly war – as to stay in the great power game in central Europe. There had been discussions with the French about possible anti-Prussian arrangements, but they came to nought. In any case, the overwhelming victory of Prussia over the French at Sedan on 1 September 1870, followed by the unconditional surrender of France on 2 September and the collapse of Napoleon III's empire, changed everything for Franz Joseph, again.

Having just been forced into the painful task of abrogating the Concordat (at a time when his government was headed by a Catholic Pole), and thus having to concede a religious relationship for a secular one, Franz Joseph must have had many contradictory responses and reactions to this momentous event in German history. Among his subjects, many who considered themselves 'Austrians' were shocked at the rampant chauvinism expressed by a very large number of *Austrian* Germans, glorying in German (Prussian) military success. Grillparzer, in November of that year, pointedly wrote: 'I am no German, I am an Austrian.' There was thus a sense of the Monarchy, if it were to survive, having to create a clearly Austrian counterweight that was no longer so identifiably German. At the same time, there was now no reason, it seemed, to play along with the German Liberals in the idea of being a German power, given that there was now no possibility at all of being a player in German politics, even South German politics. Then again, on a more practical level, the *Reichsrat* elections of the autumn had resulted in the German Liberals retaining a majority, but a much reduced one, so there was an opportunity, perhaps, to rethink Cisleithania one more time. The whole Monarchy could not be rethought, but perhaps the Austrian half could be.

Over the late summer and autumn of 1870, Franz Joseph had secret discussions with an unlikely pair: the conservative-federalist but very 'Austrian' official, Count Karl Hohenwart, and Dr Albert Schäffle, a Protestant sociopolitical thinker from Württemberg, about their plan for a radical federalisation of Cisleithania, centred on the acceptance of Bohemian State Right within a still dualist framework. A Hungarian-style Compromise with the Bohemian crownlands, as a unit, would be accompanied by a similar Compromise with Galicia, leaving only the German lands and Dalmatia to federalise in some form. By October, it appears that Schäffle had become Franz Joseph's main advisor on the new plan for federalisation. On 6 February 1871, Hohenwart was appointed prime minister with a federalist ministry including two Czechs and, as commerce and agriculture minister, Schäffle, its leading light. The ministry's clear mission was to solve the 'Slav' problem of the Poles and Czechs.

Hohenwart first made major concessions to the Poles, appointing Kazimierz Grocholski to the government as minister for Galicia and presenting a bill in May giving Galicia wide-ranging autonomy. Meanwhile, secret negotiations got underway on the Czech issue, including Hohenwart, Schäffle, the leader of the Bohemian conservative-federalist nobility, Count Heinrich Jaroslav Clam-Martinic, the leader of the 'Old Czechs' (more moderate Czech liberals), František Rieger, and the Moravian politician, Alois Pražák. The basis of the agreement was to be that the Bohemian crownlands would receive full autonomy, the German population would have guarantees for their national interests, the Czech deputies would return to the *Reichsrat*, thus acknowledging the validity of the Cisleithanian state, and Franz Joseph would be crowned Bohemian king. Once a deal had been reached, new elections were called for the provincial assemblies and *Reichsrat* on 10 August, and through imperial and state pressure the result was a two-thirds majority for the federalists in the *Reichsrat*. Franz Joseph, as agreed, then sent a rescript (edict) to the Bohemian Diet on 12 September accepting the principle of Bohemian State Right and calling for the Diet to draw up a new set of laws for Bohemia. The answer that the Diet sent back on 10 October was 18 'Fundamental Articles' that had already been agreed upon in negotiations. This was in effect a Bohemian Compromise assuring Bohemia and the other Bohemian crownlands far-reaching autonomy on the basis of Bohemian State Right. An associated, but separate law also dealt with the Czech-German language issue in an imaginative way that was often to be sought for in later negotiations. There was to be language equality, with bilingualism in mixed districts, officials and judges having to speak in both languages. District boundaries, however, were to be redrawn to create monolingual districts where possible. In order to protect Germans from being outvoted on their national issues, the Diet was to be divided into national curias on educational and cultural budget matters, with each curia having a veto in those national concerns.

It was when the Diet's answer, with the Fundamental Articles, reached Franz Joseph that the true crisis erupted. The German Liberals had already been dead set against the proposal, had boycotted the Bohemian Diet, and now protested vehemently at the destruction of their whole political system, and they were able to persuade many other provincial assemblies to object to the proposal, including in the Bohemian crownland of Silesia. Moravia's Diet also was not prepared to accept the proposal without changes. On the other hand, the proposal had got this far without German Liberal objections and protests stopping it, despite the Liberals' continuing influence in the financial world. Even dire warnings from the finance minister, Ludwig von Holzgethan, of the effect on the financial markets did not have a decisive effect. It was the intervention of two of Franz Joseph's other advisors that sank the project: Beust and Andrássy.

In the summer, Beust had reconsidered foreign policy in the light of Prussia's creation of the German Empire, and he had concluded, as elaborated in a memorandum of 18 May 1871, that the best policy was to be a friend of the new Prusso-German Empire, as a way of protecting Austria-Hungary from the threat of Russia. In a new memorandum of 13 October he added another consideration: because of the very success of the new Germany, the enthusiasm for it among Austrian Germans could be so strong as to unleash a dangerous irredentism among them, leading to the German parts of Austria leaving the Monarchy. In any case, if one wanted to have a completely pro-German foreign policy to isolate Russia, one could not at the same time be 'completely un-German' at home. Beust explicitly pointed in the memorandum to the shocking speed with which the Constitutional (German Liberal) Party had transformed itself into a 'German-National Party'. Beust was, moreover, supported in his analysis by the new German government itself. The final blow, however, was delivered by Andrássy, who asserted that, however much effort had been made to ensure that the Fundamental Articles did not impinge on the Compromise, they did change the Cisleithanian constitution, hence infringed the Compromise, and this was unacceptable to Hungary.

It has been claimed that, had the Czechs been more accommodating in the aftermath of this crisis, had they given the Bohemian Germans some assurance by attending the *Reichsrat* and thus acknowledging the larger empire, so that the Germans did not feel completely isolated from the rest of the Monarchy, a deal could still have been struck. This was the accusation Franz Joseph made to Leo Thun some time later, when the emperor asserted that if only the Czechs had come to the *Reichsrat* in 1871 something could have been arranged. As it was, however, when it came to the crucial decision in the Crown Council of 20 October, Franz Joseph took the side of Beust and Andrássy and rejected the draft of the Bohemian Diet containing the Fundamental Articles, asking for revisions. The Czech side had made clear, though, that there was no going back on the deal, and so Hohenwart resigned on 26 October, knowing full well that the Czechs would end negotiations, not return to the *Reichsrat*, and that the Diet would refuse to continue, as occurred on 4 November.

Franz Joseph had been completely unrealistic in thinking that such a plan could work. He should have known that the Magyars would not allow a further formal federalisation of the monarchy. In any case, this attempt to square the circle would not have worked because there were already two different 'circles' in play: nationalism in the Monarchy had *already* become more ethnic and linguistic, more 'cultural', in its character, than merely a question of giving a province more 'national' autonomy. There was now much more a need to placate Czechs and Germans than to mediate between Bohemian and Moravian provincial federalists and Viennocentrists.

Recent studies have called this doom-laden analysis of the ethnicisation of Habsburg politics already by 1871 a false picture of a society in which ethnically based nationalism was not yet that predominant, and as we shall see, there is some truth to this. On the other hand, Palacký was definitely thinking in ethnonationalist terms in 1873 when he predicted the failure of Austria and blamed it on the 'race despotism' (*Racendespotismus*) of the Germans and Magyars. Was federalism a dead end by this point? If this does mark the point where 'the paths of the two nations of the province parted ways', to become dire mutual enemies, perhaps it was.

The Triumph and Trials of Liberalism, 1871–1879

Having crossed his emperor and caused Franz Joseph's federalist plans to collapse, Beust resigned on 6 November, and was replaced by Andrássy as foreign minister. (Beust was not replaced as imperial chancellor, an office that effectively ceased to exist.) Andrássy was replaced as Hungarian prime minister by Count Menyhért Lónyay. Seeing no alternative, Franz Joseph appointed Prince Adolf Auersperg as Cisleithanian prime minister on 25 November at the head of a largely German Liberal set of ministers. The German Liberals in Cisleithania could now resume their dualist condominium with their Hungarian counterparts.

There was another bout of progressive legislation, that is to say anti-clericalism combined with an expansion of secular education. In Cisleithania the *Reichsrat* passed another set of May Laws extending state control over the Church in 1874. Franz Joseph had prevented the enacting of full civil marriage in 1873, and promised the papacy that he would not allow a *Kulturkampf* to occur in Austria as it was in the new German Empire, but if the liberals did not wage a full-out cultural war on the Church as such, their campaign in the press and on the parliamentary stage against the reactionary obscurantism of the Catholic hierarchy amounted to *Kulturkampf*-lite. In Hungary, there was great pride in expanding and upgrading the higher education system, with the Polytechnic becoming Budapest Technical University, and the law school in Kolozsvár becoming Kolozsvár University, both in 1872. The liberal mission was a Rousseauian one, of forcing people to be free – taking them away from the evil influence of the Catholic Church (as they saw it) and compelling them to become enlightened through education. Creating an educated, enlightened populace would ultimately solve all society's problems, they believed, many of them most sincerely.

In Cisleithania the new Liberal government was determined to learn the lessons that had doomed the *Bürgerministerium*. One of its first major policy decisions was to go through with the concessions to the Poles that Hohenwart had proposed in May 1871. Galicia was represented in the ministry in Vienna by its own minister, and there was virtual autonomy for the *Sejm*, as promised. In return, the Polish delegation to the *Reichsrat* promised to support the Cisleithanian government (but not that of any specific party). The government also succeeded this time around in passing a major reform of the *Reichsrat* electoral system on 2 April 1873, whereby elections to the *Reichsrat* were now to be direct. All the electoral geometry of the old, diet-based system was carried over into the new, direct system, with votes allotted to curias according to province. The franchise for the 'popular' urban and rural seats was set at a minimum payment of 10 gulden direct tax, which meant that roughly 6 per cent of the population had the vote (rather low for Europe by 1873). The number of seats was expanded to 353 (similar to the 343 of the imperial *Reichsrat* of before 1865); the high barrier of the franchise, and the machinations of curial and boundary drawing, meant that 219 of the members in the new *Reichsrat* were in the German Liberal camp. Moreover, the new term of the *Reichsrat* session was extended to six years, avoiding the very frequent elections that had marked the system since 1861. It was a transparent attempt to cement German Liberal hegemony in place.

The Hungarian liberal, Deákist government attempted something very similar. While it experienced nothing as existentially threatening as the

Bohemian crisis, political drift and poor management of Hungarian finances meant that Lónyay's government felt itself so threatened politically that in 1872 it also proposed a 'reform' of the franchise that would have reduced the electorate, which was already only 7.1 per cent of the population, as well as an extension to the life of parliament to five years. The reform was rejected by the parliament, but the government party won the elections by forms of rigging and corruption which were not quite as elegant as Schmerling's electoral geometry, but just as effective. Both governments assumed that their liberal politics would be hegemonic for a very long time.

One reason for this was that the economic expansion that had begun in 1867 was still in full force. There was a huge expansion of the financial sector. Until the mid-1860s there had been relatively few sources of public financing outside the National Bank and the *Credit-Anstalt*. In 1863 the *Bodencredit-Anstalt* had been founded with largely French capital; in 1865 the Anglo-Austrian Bank had joined it (as a rival based on English capital). Between 1867 and 1869, thirty-six new banks were founded in Vienna alone, and in both Hungary and Bohemia provincial banking systems emerged, with the 'national' (Czech) bourgeoisie and Bohemian nobility providing capital in the Bohemian system, while the Hungarian financial system continued to rely mostly on capital from the Rothschilds and English and French banks. Much of the money that was thus made available was invested in the ever-expanding railway network. One of the more prestigious lines developed at the end of the 1860s was the Franz-Joseph Railway, connecting Vienna to Prague and the spa towns and cities of southern and western Bohemia. The line was begun in late 1866, and the Vienna-Prague connection was completed by 18 December 1871, just in time for a royal coronation that never happened. Another line, to the fashionable spas of western Bohemia was completed in 1872. The Hungarian railway network was expanding even more quickly. In Trieste, the Suez Canal meant that shipping possibilities to India and beyond had opened up that few had previously contemplated. In 1879 the Austrian Lloyd started a steamship service to Colombo in Sri Lanka, and in 1880 one to Hong Kong.

Huge fortunes were made in the *Gründerjahre*, and a condition of giddy economic optimism set in. In 1872, 1,005 new stock companies were announced on the Vienna Stock Exchange. Two prestigious events reflected and reinforced the optimism. In Hungary, administrative plans were well under way to create an impressive metropolis to suit the new nation-state: Buda, with its royal citadel, was united with Old Buda and the commercial centre across the river, Pest, to create a new city: Budapest. The new, united national capital was officially established on 17 November 1873.

Figure 9. Trieste's harbour in 1905. 'Vienna-by-the-sea', Trieste was
Austria's main port, and as such a thriving commercial centre.
(Published with permission of the Austrian National Library.)

In Vienna, the *Ringstrasse*, the ring of boulevards surrounding the
Hofburg and the inner city that had replaced the old fortifications, had
been officially opened on 1 May 1865. Begun in 1857 as the symbol of
Vienna's function as the centre of a unitary, neo-absolutist empire, by
1865 it had become symbolic of – transition. A decade after the walls had
been razed, it was still very much a work in progress, as only the avenues
themselves, and a very few of the large buildings and parks that were to
grace it, had been completed. By the early 1870s, however, the empty lots
were beginning to be filled in, and the *Ringstrasse* was fast becoming the
representational street of the new liberal era and the booming economy.
What amounted to an immense urban renewal project was both symbol
and part cause of the boom, as the management of the building lots and
the investments in construction helped generate economic growth. Many
of the prestigious private 'palaces' along the chain of avenues had been
built by Jewish financiers and entrepreneurs, such as Palais Ephrussi
(completed 1873), built with proceeds from the wheat trade, or Palais
Epstein (1871) and Palais Todesco (1864), the prestige projects of

banking dynasties. Some of the important representational buildings, especially musical institutions, were completed relatively early, the Opera in 1869, the *Musikverein* in 1870. Others took longer: the Stock Exchange was begun in 1874 and completed in 1877; the great historicist, representational quadrant of liberal ideology: the Parliament (1873–1883); Town Hall (1872–1883); *Burgtheater* (1874–1888); and the University (1877–1884) was only completed after the liberal era was over.

A less permanent celebration of the power of liberalism and economics was nonetheless most impressive. The World Exhibition – at a time when world exhibitions, from London in 1851 on, were matters of great prestige and economic consequence – was to be in Vienna in 1873, and promised to make Vienna the sort of 'world city' it had always claimed to be. Many of the large hotels on the *Ringstrasse* were built to accommodate the thousands of visitors expected to come to the city for the Exhibition over the summer and autumn. A massive, glass and steel rotunda was built in the Prater expressly for the Exhibition, which opened to the public on 1 May. Just short of twenty-five years since Franz Joseph had ascended the imperial throne, the Exhibition was to be a celebration of Austrian success.

It did not work out quite like that. On 9 May there was a steep fall of values at the Vienna Stock Exchange, which soon turned into a devastating crash, a huge financial disaster. It was part of a general global crisis of the new economy and the subsequent period is known in economic history as the 'Great Depression', but it hit Austria-Hungary particularly hard. Part of the immediate catastrophe was due to the Exhibition itself, the preparations and projections for which had caused quite irrational speculation. As a result of the bankruptcies and uncertainties caused by the crash, the Exhibition itself proved a disappointment, and a cholera outbreak that summer depressed visitor figures (and hence business) yet further, heightening the crisis. The more experienced financial players in Vienna had sensed the irrationality of the stock market values nearing the Exhibition's opening, and so had kept their money out; those who suffered worst from the crash were investors on a small to medium level, many of whom were ruined. Vienna's suicide rate shot up.

The economy was severely affected for a considerable time, reaching a nadir in 1876, but growth then resumed, and the economic damage is now seen to have been not as bad as thought at the time. The Austrian economy recovered better than the Hungarian, partly because the retrenchments of the earlier 1860s had left the Vienna government with a better financial balance sheet, and the better banks had not been caught out by the crash. This left the government more capacity to invest, at the urging of its 'interventionist' wing, in large public works such as the regulation of the Danube, and the building of an aqueduct to supply Vienna with fresh Alpine water. The state also lent large sums to the railways and the construction industry. Eventually, the government started renationalising those railways that could not pay back loans, a process begun in 1875, with the first railway renationalised in 1879. Another response to the economic crisis, which was also responding to external events, was the introduction of a protectionist tariff for Austria-Hungary in 1878 (although it was actually relatively mild in its effects).

In Hungary, the government's financial situation had already been rickety before the crash, and so the financial crisis was that much more severe, especially as the Hungarian economy was much more dependent on agricultural commodities, whose price collapse in this period was one of the main causes of the depression. The price of Hungarian wheat halved. Hungary's wine industry was destroyed by phylloxera, potato blight caused near famine conditions in several areas, and there was also a cholera epidemic. The 'seven fat years' were no more. Government bankruptcy was only avoided by a massive 150 million gulden loan from the Rothschild consortium on exceptionally bad terms. Lónyay had already resigned before the crash, but no better leader was found, and the economic emergency was to have major political consequences, eventually.

The most far-reaching consequence of the crash of 1873 was not economic so much as cultural and ideological: the end of the era of liberal economic optimism, of the certain belief in rational progress and liberalism's moral superiority. One reaction, among the urban middle classes themselves, was a certain fatalism. Johann Strauss the Younger's *Die Fledermaus* has a plot that long preceded the 1873 crash, but when it premiered on 5 April 1874 there were unmistakable echoes in its lyrics and plot lines of the impact of the economic and financial crisis, most obviously in the lines: 'Happy is he, who forgets what cannot be changed.' Another reaction, however, was socio-economic rage from those who suffered, and envy against those who had not, and hatred for those who appeared, despite obvious guilt, to evade just retribution. Many of those who had suffered the most were small investors, new to the game, caught up in the frenzy of ever-higher stock market values; the crushing effects of the drop in those values, and the liberal economic regime that provided little, if any, safety net for failure, made liberalism appear as a heartless, ruthless system that had offered false promises. Many of those more experienced financiers who had avoided major losses by not entering the speculative bubble were, inevitably, Jewish, and it was very easy for anti-liberal and clerical critics to identify Jewish bankers and jobbers as the main cause, and beneficiaries, of the catastrophe. A full-scale movement of political antisemitism did not become established until the late 1870s, but already, in 1875, German nationalist students at Vienna University were cheering the remarks of the prominent medical professor, Theodor Billroth, about the need to limit the number of Jewish students coming to the university, because of their supposedly too commercial, money-oriented instincts.

Nor were liberalism's prospects helped by the fact that subsequent trials associated with the many business collapses that elicited claims of fraud revealed a web of close connections between liberal politicians and many entrepreneurs of questionable moral standing. The fraud trial of the (Jewish) railway entrepreneur Victor von Ofenheim implicated among many others the former interior minister and prominent liberal *Reichsrat* deputy, Giskra, who notoriously characterised a payment of 100,000 gulden for services rendered as a 'tip'. Ofenheim himself delivered a famous defence of his behaviour: 'Moral platitudes do not get railways built.'

Despite all of these negative consequences of the crash of 1873, the short-term political effect was not that great, on the surface at least. The first direct elections to the *Reichsrat* took place in the autumn, *after* the crash, and yet returned the 219 German Liberal deputies out of 353 mentioned above. In Hungary, the government party, already fairly rudderless, did suffer politically from the financial fallout of the crash and the resultant depression, but the eventual result of this was that the government party sought a merger in 1875 with the Left Centre Party, led by Tisza. Tisza had by now accustomed himself to the realities of the new Hungarian politics, and being a very canny politician had realised that King Franz Joseph would never appoint as prime minister anyone who did not accept the main tenets of dualism. He therefore dropped all the more extreme parts of his party's programme, the Bihar Points, and entered negotiations with the government party. On 1 March 1875, the new electoral reform act *reduced* the size of the electorate, to only 6 per cent of the population, making it just that bit more manageable; on 20 October the government party merged with the Left Centre to form the Liberal Party, and Franz Joseph appointed Tisza prime minister. This effectively meant a monopoly of power for the new Liberal Party, which became the 'party of clubs', of the National Casino and the Magyar liberal-nationalist-aristocratic establishment. The Liberal government now consolidated power, with more centralisation and more Magyarisation. In 1876 new administrative committees, nominated by the central government, supervised county administration. If in 1872 there were 22,000 officials, by 1875 there were already 32,000.

On nationalities' policy, Tisza was anything but liberal. If Franz Joseph had initially intended to protect non-Magyar nationalities in Hungary, the appointment of Tisza ended that. An increasing intolerance toward the other nationalities led to Slovak schools being closed down in 1875 and 1876. The liberal Education Law of 1868 was amended in 1879 in the direction of Magyarisation, so that lessons in Magyar for six hours a week were made compulsory in all minority nationality schools. This was just the beginning of what would be a long-term campaign of Magyarisation.

There was no effective opposition to this consolidation of power, certainly no real alternative. The parliamentary parties to Tisza's left ruled themselves out because of their anti-dualism, something the king (Franz Joseph) would not consider. On Tisza's right, there appeared in 1878 the United (1881 Moderate) Opposition Party, led by Count Albert Apponyi, but this was just the old feudal conservatives, without much of a programme or backing. The one political party that had a coherent ideology, the 'Party of those excluded from the franchise', formed in 1880, was suppressed by the government as too radical. So 'liberalism' – of a very nationalist sort – did win out in Hungary.

The Austrian case was quite different. Even if the figures for the *Reichsrat* suggest a very solid liberal position, they deceive. First, the German Liberal bloc was already split. There were 219 German Liberal deputies (and another 49 Polish deputies supporting the government), but they were split, primarily between the 'Old' Liberals led by Eduard Herbst, with 88 deputies; the 'Young' Progressive Club, with a more German-nationalist and socially oriented approach, with 58 deputies; the 'Viennese Radicals' with 5 deputies; and 54 deputies from the Left Centre of Large Landholders. Similar to Hungary's government party, the Liberals were dominant numerically, but split and weakened politically.

Since 1871, the 'Young' Liberals had introduced what became known as the 'politics of the new key'. There were several sources to this politics, but one of the more influential was the group of young students around Victor Adler and Engelbert Pernerstorfer, especially their main ideologue, Heinrich Friedjung. They campaigned for a more socially conscientious, but also more emotional, 'organic' and *nationalist* politics. They denied the possibility of an Austrian *national* identity and emphasised the greatness and power of German culture instead. Closely associated with this group were the German nationalist *Burschenschaften* (duelling fraternities), of which many in the Adler group were members. It was leaders of these duelling fraternities who were among the most prominent instigators of the student antisemitic demonstrations sparked in 1875 by

Billroth's speech. This was despite the fact that many in the Adler group were Jewish, including Adler, Friedjung, and for a time Gustav Mahler.

One of the things that bound this amalgam of German nationalism, social conscience, organicist emotionalism and antisemitism together was adoration of Richard Wagner. The conflict between 'Old' 'Austrian' Liberals and 'Young' German nationalist Liberals appears in some sense as a political echo of the 'War of the Romantics' that had been raging in Vienna's musical world ever since the 1850s, with Eduard Hanslick's *On the Beautiful in Music* (1854) as the defender of rationalist 'Austrian' conservatism against the 'irrationalist' 'new German' school of Wagner, Franz Liszt and their allies. As it happened, the main champion of the 'Austrian' school was Johannes Brahms, a North German Protestant. On the other hand, Brahms was eventually to make Vienna his home.

In the context of the later 1870s, what is important to note is that the Liberals were increasingly split: the 'Old' Liberals were still predominant, but were running out of ideas, were morally compromised by their associations with finance and big business, and if they pursued anticlerical policies that made them unpopular with the emperor, at least they were still 'Austrian'; their 'Young' challengers within the party were following a path of German nationalism that would bring them in direct conflict with Franz Joseph.

The emperor's viewpoint was more important than many Liberals yet recognised. They might have thought that the defeat of his federalist plans had shown him impotent in the face of the hegemony of the German-Magyar condominium, and that the 1873 reform of the *Reichsrat* electoral system had greatly strengthened their position. They had 219 out of 353 seats after all. Yet the *Reichsrat*'s composition could be analyzed in a different way. It was still composed of curias. Two of these curias, the Chambers of Commerce, with 51 seats, and the urban constituencies, with 116 seats, were safely Liberal. Yet the rural constituencies, with 131 seats, were liable to clerical and other anti-liberal influence; and then there were the 85 seats in the curia of 'Large Landowners', which meant, effectively, the high nobility. This group already dominated the upper house of the *Reichsrat*, the *Herrenhaus*, but had a quarter of seats in the Lower House as well. Many of the deputies in the 'Large Landowners' curia were pro-centralist, pro-education and pro-German, and so in the Liberal camp, but they and their electors were still Austrian nobility, and hence obedient to their emperor. Also the German hegemony was artificially strong because of the absence of the Czechs; and the Poles would vote for the government, whatever its colour. Hence the German Liberals were in reality much more exposed than they thought, should the electoral geometry be used against them – by an emperor whom they had challenged over an issue not of domestic policy, but over foreign policy, his remaining prerogative. Unluckily for the German Liberals in Cisleithania, it was an issue of foreign policy that was to bring on the next squaring of the circle in the Monarchy.

Squaring the Circle III.ii: Bosnia

By the 1870s, excluded from Italy and Germany, the Habsburg Monarchy had only the area to its southeast, the 'Near East', known somewhat inaccurately as 'the Balkans', as its remaining sphere of interest. This presented Habsburg foreign policy with many difficulties, and also had serious domestic implications. Greece had become independent, but the rest of this region was officially still part of the Ottoman Empire. Most of the region's population was Christian, but Orthodox, which meant that Russia had an inherent advantage over Austria-Hungary as the 'big brother' of the Orthodox Christian community, and as official protector of the Orthodox in Ottoman lands. In addition, several parts of 'Turkish Europe' were in reality already semi-independent, such as Romania, Montenegro and Serbia, and were becoming increasingly assertive towards their Turkish sovereign. One complication for the Monarchy was that at least two of these semi-independent states, Romania and Serbia, had significant numbers of what they considered their national peoples *within* Austria-Hungary's borders, and especially within Hungary's borders.

While he was still Hungarian prime minister, Andrássy had demanded from the Habsburg military authorities that the liquidation of the Military Frontier (as promised in the Compromise) be speeded up, partly in order to damp down South Slav (Serb and Croat) nationalist unrest in the parts of that Military Frontier that bordered the South-Slav-populated regions of the Ottoman Empire: Serbia and Bosnia-Herzegovina. Yet another uprising in the border region in October 1871 persuaded the Habsburg military authorities to do as Andrássy wished, and most of the Military Frontier was reintegrated into civilian Hungary by 1873, and fully so by 1878. The domestic South Slav problem was already a major part of Habsburg foreign policy before the Bosnian crisis.

Andrássy replaced Beust as Austro-Hungarian foreign minister in November 1871. He continued his predecessor's policy, as Beust had laid it out in his 18 May 1871 memorandum, which called for a close and friendly relationship with the new Germany, in order to isolate Russia. This quite suited Andrássy, being a former Hungarian revolutionary and hence with a large animus against the Russians for their anti-Hungarian intervention in 1849, and simply because it was the main Slav power. As a Magyar nationalist aristocrat, Andrássy also did not think much of the peoples of the Balkan states, describing them in 1873 as 'wild Indians who could only be treated like unbroken horses, to whom corn should be offered with one hand while they are threatened with a whip in the other'. He was also, however, the Habsburg foreign minister, and an adept diplomat. He was quite prepared to finesse his position. When Bismarck suggested a détente with Russia in 1873, Andrássy (along with Franz Joseph) was quite prepared to sign on to the Three Emperors League, if this was the way to stay close to Germany, and keep Russia quiet in the Balkans. He was also quite prepared to offer corn where appropriate, as with negotiations with Serbia and Romania over building railways in the region. The southeastern neighbours became more attractive after the crash of 1873 increased the need to find potential new markets for Austro-Hungarian goods.

The Bosnian revolt of 1875 upset these gradualist plans of low-key economic engagement. One look at the map will show how Bosnia would be a good candidate for filling in the Habsburg circle, at least in a geopolitical, strategic sense. There was not much of economic benefit from taking over the Turkish territories of Bosnia-Herzegovina. There was a mixed population: Orthodox Serbs (a plurality, but not a majority), Catholic Croats, 'Bosniak' Muslims and also a small Jewish community. Bosnia's Muslims comprised the ruling class in the region. In a parallel process to what had occurred in the Monarchy, many of them were from Slav families that had converted to the ruling religion, which for centuries had been Islam. The land was economically under-developed with few major assets; the one major value of the territory economically would be to serve as a route for a railway to connect the Monarchy to the rest of Turkey-in-Europe. Strategically, though, Bosnia was very significant for securing the hinterland of the Cisleithanian province of Dalmatia, which was otherwise militarily very exposed. As things stood in 1875, Dalmatia was split in three by two Turkish enclaves on the coast, which meant that much of the province could only be supplied by sea. Were Bosnia to become Habsburg territory, railways through Bosnia could supply this outlying part of the empire. It looked like the missing piece to the geopolitical Austro-Hungarian puzzle.

There were other, Habsburg reasons why Bosnia could be seen as an attractive acquisition. When the revolt started, Franz Joseph was keen to annex the province as compensation for the loss of Lombardy-Venetia, on grounds of prestige. In terms of great power politics there was also the consideration that this would keep Russia out of such a sensitive area on the Monarchy's border. Then there were other concerns, harking back to

Andrássy's demands about the Military Frontier, the fear of irredentism. As Franz Joseph noted to Alexander von Hübner in April 1876: 'If, for instance, there were an independent Bosnia, Croatia and Dalmatia would quickly swim away from us.' Not only was the loss of Lombardy-Venetia to Piedmont a matter for which Bosnia was to be compensation, it was also an example of what had to be avoided this time around: losing territory to an independent power on your border with a national population partly inside your Monarchy.

It so happened that Franz Joseph's one tour of Dalmatia occurred in April 1875, and there were clearly thoughts of occupation. The emperor told the province's governor that Bosnia would need to be occupied if it ever looked like leaving Turkish control. His tour might even have been the spark to revolt, as his interest in the region raised hopes of Habsburg aid in the event of an uprising. What is true is that barely a month after the imperial visit a revolt started in Bosnia that threw the whole region into turmoil. War was sparked all over the Balkans between the semi-independent states wanting to gain full independence and their Turkish suzerain, and then followed intervention by Russia as the Orthodox Christian protector. Initially, relations between the Monarchy and Russia were quite productive. The Reichstadt Agreement of 1876 appeared to assure the avoidance of confrontation between the two powers, and Russia even accepted Austrian annexation of Bosnia-Herzegovina. Crushing Russian victories over the Turks in 1877–78, however, led in March 1878 to the Treaty of San Stefano, which would have left the Balkans a Russian-dominated area. This was quite unacceptable to Franz Joseph; fortunately for the Monarchy it was also unacceptable to the other major great power in the region, Britain, with the new geostrategic concern of the Suez Canal not too distant. The result of the subsequent diplomatic confrontation was the Congress of Berlin, which met in June and July. Britain (Lord Salisbury) and Austria-Hungary (Andrássy) were able to reverse the worst aspects of San Stefano by the reduction and division of the 'big Bulgaria' that had been seen as such an advantage to the Russians, and Austro-Hungarian interests were rewarded by permission to occupy Bosnia-Herzegovina, and to garrison the territory of the Sanjak of Novibazar (which linked Bosnia to the remaining territory of Turkey-in-Europe).

The occupation of Bosnia was a great diplomatic achievement by Andrássy, but it left the emperor unhappy because it fell short of full annexation. Andrássy's ostensible reason for settling for occupation rather than annexation was that this was the best he could achieve without too deeply alienating Turkey and the other great powers. Apart from that, however, there were very good, domestic reasons why occupation was preferable to annexation, and those reasons went to the heart of the Dual Monarchy's larger political and structural problems.

Annexation in many respects would have been preferable (and would have been possible, in all likelihood). It would have satisfied Franz Joseph's wish to gain territorial compensation for Lombardy-Venetia, although occupation did achieve the goal of keeping other powers (Russia or Serbia) out, and preventing Bosnian independence. There was, however, the consideration that without full annexation Bosnia would remain officially part of Turkey and could therefore not be given a constitutional structure, nor be fully integrated into the constitutional structure of the Dual Monarchy. That would usually be seen as a problem, but from Andrássy's perspective this was the main advantage of occupation over annexation: that occupation left Bosnia-Herzegovina in limbo, just where he wanted it. This was because neither the German nor Magyar partners of dualism wanted Bosnia at all.

Neither wanted yet more Slavs, even Catholic ones, in either half of the condominium, because Slavs already outnumbered the German and Magyar 'ruling nations', and inclusion in either side would also affect the delicate balance of the Compromise arrangements. The Magyar leadership did not want more Slavs in Hungary, but they also disliked the prospect of having more Slavs given over to Cisleithania, because that would make the Austrian half an even more populous, dominant half in the partnership (and more liable to be taken over by Slavs). German concerns exactly mirrored Magyar ones. The question of Bosnian annexation/occupation is one of the first major instances where the absorption of a territory was strongly resisted because of the national implications for a representative governmental system. If the territory you are taking over possesses a population that will vote with your national opponents and unseat you thus from power, is it a good idea to take over that territory?

Occupation squared the circle nicely for Andrássy: it left Bosnia out of the objective political domestic calculations in both Cisleithania and Hungary, because Bosnia became a part of neither. Yet even occupation was unacceptable to a very large part of the ruling class in both halves of the Monarchy. There had been official discussion of the question of occupation from as early as 1876, and the prospect had from the start led to heated debates. In Hungary, those against the dualist settlement in the Independence Party made noises about the threat to Magyar national interests, but the Tisza consolidation meant that the debate never got close to going against Andrássy's policy. Among German Liberals the debate was much more dangerous. The 'old', more 'Austrian' Liberals, who were in favour of dualism, were prepared to accommodate imperial foreign policy and support Andrássy. The 'young', more German-nationalist Liberals tended to be against dualism, like the Hungarian Independence Party, and were also more intent on defending German national interests from the inclusion of yet more Slavs. There was a crucial, additional, cross-cutting factor in Cisleithania: Herbst, the leader of the establishment 'old' Liberals, saw an opportunity in the Bosnian question of making a principled stand on a matter of foreign policy, and thereby challenge the emperor's monopoly in his most important remaining prerogative. If Herbst succeeded, he could make the Monarchy into the truly parliamentary, constitutional state that he thought, as a liberal constitutionalist, it ought to be. Herbst, and a majority of the German Liberal contingent in the *Reichsrat* therefore went against the pro-occupation imperial policy, even though their party's government, the Auersperg ministry, supported it.

The botching of the occupation by the military in July 1878 increased opposition to it and the Berlin settlement, and over the next months Herbst led a vituperative opposition that hoped to use the *Reichsrat*'s budgetary powers to withhold credit authorisations for the expenses of imperial foreign policy and occupation, and refuse ratification of the Berlin Treaty, to force concessions on foreign policy from the emperor. Eventually, the parliamentary battle over Bosnia led in March 1879 to a majority in the *Reichsrat* voting for both the Berlin Treaty and the occupation, 154 to 112, but with a majority of the German Liberals voting against.

This was a devastating result – for the Liberals. Franz Joseph saw the opposition to the exercise of his prerogative as an implicit breaking of the bargain with the Liberals, and a direct threat to his power (which it was). Even before the March vote ratifying the Berlin Treaty, he had sacked the Auersperg ministry, on 15 February, and had appointed a new ministry, with a Liberal, Karl von Stremayr as titular prime minister, but with the emperor's close friend and confidant, Interior Minister Taaffe, as the real leader of the government. In Hungary, Tisza had delivered the parliament's support of imperial policy, so the Hungarian Liberal Party was left in power. Not so in the Austrian half. Taaffe now moved against the German Liberals who had defied the emperor, and set about conciliating the federalist, Slav, conservative and Clerical forces who had been kept out of power during the liberal hegemony. Crucially, he was able to persuade the Czech nationalists to return to active parliamentary politics, and agree to return to the *Reichsrat*. The emperor also made it clear to the landed nobility that he would consider it a dereliction of their duty to him if they voted for the defiant German Liberals. Elections were compulsory, as the six years since the 1873 reform were now up, and so new *Reichsrat* elections were held in June and July 1879, which were a disaster for Herbst and the German Liberals. They were undone by their own electoral geometry. They only lost eight seats in the 'urban' curia, but they lost 20 in the 'rural' curia, and 21 in the 'Large Landowners' one. A total loss of 49 left them with only 170 in the 353-seat *Reichsrat*, a large minority, but still a minority.

Franz Joseph moved quickly. Stremayr was replaced as prime minister by Taaffe on 12 August and formed a ministry that included some Liberal holdovers, including, ironically, Stremayr as justice minister and education minister, but also an assortment of federalists, conservatives, Clericals, and Slavs, that was supported in the *Reichsrat* by almost everyone else apart from the German Liberals (and that included the Poles, who had promised to vote for the government, not necessarily the German Liberal government). The German Liberal hegemony had, narrowly, been broken.

Meanwhile, Andrássy was in the process of achieving his ambition of an alliance with Germany. When he offered his resignation on 6 August, drawing the consequences of the controversy that had surrounded his Bosnian policy, his German counterpart, Bismarck, panicked, fearing that the changes in Austria-Hungary might lead to a Slav-led Monarchy forming a 'Kaunitz Coalition' with Russia and France against Germany to reverse the results of 1866 and 1871. So the German chancellor offered Andrássy an alliance on 28 August. Andrássy agreed to begin negotiations, delayed his resignation, and the Dual Alliance between Germany and Austria-Hungary was signed on 7 October. Andrássy resigned the next day, his job done.

It was only a defensive alliance, but it was to be the linchpin of future Habsburg policy from this point on, and it satisfied one of Franz Joseph's most cherished, long-term ambitions, of a conservative alliance of German powers, if initially he had not imagined it to be this way around, with Austria-Hungary the junior partner. In this way, at the very moment that Franz Joseph freed himself from a reliance on Germans *within* the Monarchy, he had tied his and his Monarchy's fate to Germany externally. In the Bosnian crisis, Franz Joseph had successfully squared the circle of adding Bosnia-Herzegovina to his domains, in an approximate way, while at the same time ridding himself of the German Liberals and bringing in the Czechs to the Cisleithanian, and hence dualist, governmental system. One squaring of the circle had thus led to the approximate and belated success of that other squaring of the circle in 1871. The German Liberals thought this would be a temporary setback, as it had been in 1870–71, but they were wrong. They were never to regain their position as the hegemonic political force in Habsburg politics.

The outcome of the Bosnian crisis was to have immense consequences for them, the emperor and the whole character of the Monarchy he ruled.

The Makart Parade of 1879: Liberalism Exits Stage Left, or Right?

On 27 April 1879 a major cultural and social event took place at the heart of the Habsburg Monarchy, on the avenues of Vienna's *Ringstrasse*. The 'Parade of the City of Vienna' had been initially scheduled a couple of days earlier, as it was to be a celebration of the twenty-fifth wedding anniversary of the imperial couple, Franz Joseph and Elisabeth, but weather had delayed it to the 27th. The imperial family stood for hours on a covered podium (designed by a very young Otto Wagner) in front of the *Burgtor*, the ceremonial gate to the *Hofburg*. Across from them, they could see the scaffolding on the only half-built Art-Historical and Natural-Historical Museums. In front of them, for their viewing pleasure, passed parade float after parade float that had been designed by Hans Makart. The favourite artist of *Ringstrasse* society had also designed the costumes of all the participants in this celebration of, well, of the imperial couple, yes, but also of Vienna, its history, and its glorious, imperial and progressive, present, as symbolised by the as yet unfinished but most modern *Ringstrasse* itself. It had been planned for over a year by the city, and many prominent members of the city's leading lights in the 'second society' (the social elite below the first society of the Court and high nobility) took part in their Makart-designed costumes – and made sure that after their participation they got their photograph taken for posterity.

It was also a celebration of German *bürgerlich* culture, in other words the culture and world view of German Liberals. On the face of it, this might appear an odd claim. Everyone was dressed in historical costumes, dating ostensibly to the 'German Renaissance', and the floats that passed by for imperial approval presented awkward allegorical adaptations of modern themes to historicist forms. How do you represent railways and the machine industry in Renaissance forms? Then again, the nobility also participated, riding by on their steeds dressed in Renaissance hunting costumes. The artists had their own special style, in the more Baroque, flamboyant garb of Rubens, also not particularly evocative of 'liberalism'. Nonetheless, this was German Liberals on parade. The nobles all rode together, and apart from the rest of the parade, which was all 'second society'. The historicist style of the '*German* Renaissance' was explicitly chosen because this was seen as the 'full flowering' of '*bürgerlich* culture', and if it was awkward to present railways, mining, international trade, commercial shipping and the machine industry in Renaissance allegory,

Figure 10. The railways float in the Makart parade of 1879, with winged
wheel and traffic signals.
(Published with permission of the Austrian National Library.)

that did not stop Makart from doing so. If the social elite of bourgeois
Vienna, the capital of German Liberals, were celebrating the imperial
couple, they were also demonstrating and affirming their own values and
their own worth, and after all loyalty to the empire was part of their ethos,
because it was a German-led, liberal empire.

By late April, though, the Auersperg ministry was no more, and Taaffe
was arranging for the German Liberals' political demise. The easy
assumptions underlying the Makart Parade, of an Austrian state led by
a German-liberal 'state people' informed by the rational principles of
Renaissance (Enlightenment) culture were about to be completely undermined and transformed. In 1867 Grillparzer had asked if he was still
German; in reaction to the chauvinist aftermath of the German victory
of 1870, he had claimed he was not German, but rather Austrian. A few
months later, in a response to well-wishers on the occasion of his eightieth
birthday in January 1871, he modulated his identity, describing himself as
'a loyal Austrian (German included)'. By the late 1870s, however, many
were no longer satisfied with this political-cultural, dialectical compromise, but wanted something more definite, stronger, more manly.
Friedjung wrote in 1877 concerning the question of the Compromise:
'Our fatherland will only have fresh life breathed into it by that party
which rules Austria from the [German] national standpoint, makes an
alliance with Germany, keeps the nationalities down and comes to an
arrangement with Hungary, so that both can govern themselves separately and independently from the other – with the proviso that the
stronger part will naturally determine the actions of the other.' After
1879, with the voice of 'Austrian' Germans having been compromised
by their loss of power, the liberalisation since the 1860s had appeared to
have run its course. Liberals had always considered themselves on the

'Left' of Austrian politics, as the heirs of revolution and reform, against the 'Right' of conservatives, clericals and federalists. The Young Liberals, of whom Friedjung was a leading voice, considered themselves even more to the Left than their Old 'Austrian' counterparts, but we would think of their brand of politics as more an ideology of the Right. It was this more nationalist, and less accommodating, more decisive, and selfish brand of politics that was on the ascendant. The nationalisation of the Monarchy had begun.

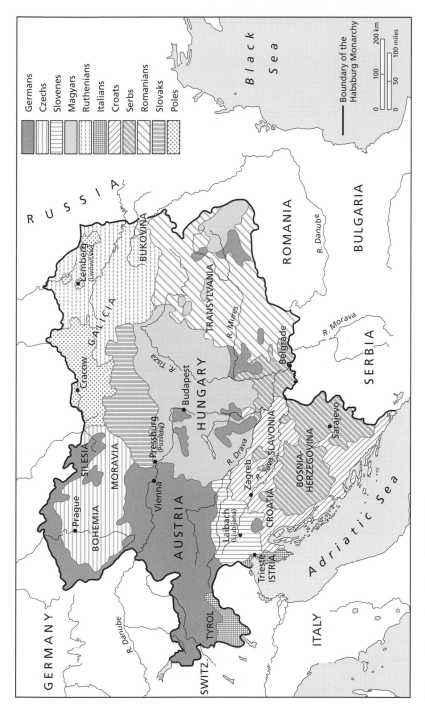

Map 3: The nationalities of the Habsburg Monarchy around 1890.

5   1879–1897: Nationalisation

The end of German Liberal hegemony in the Austrian half of the Monarchy led to a federalist, conservative era that saw the various nationalities within that half gain much more recognition and power. In Hungary, the Magyar Liberal hegemony was strengthened. By 1897, what had been two similar arrangements in both halves looked quite disparate, and were proving politically incompatible. The ongoing crisis set off in 1897 brought the viability of the Monarchy once again into question.

Franz Joseph and conservatives might have thought that by seeing off the German Liberals they could create a new, stable and conservative governmental system in Cisleithania, but new forms of mass politics emerged to complicate and exacerbate the management of the multiethnic and polyglot state. Liberalism was giving way to – or turning into – nationalism as the main form of middle-class politics, but nationalism in turn faced challenges from other mass-political movements: nationalism's radical cousin, racial antisemitism, its culturally conservative rival, Christian Social antisemitism, and the closest heir to liberalism ideologically, Marxian socialism.

By 1897 the developments since 1879 had turned the Monarchy's politics into a witches' brew, and the disparity between both halves added to the crisis. Yet, as with many crises, the Monarchy was also on the cusp of one of its most culturally fruitful eras, partly because political chaos was only part of the Monarchy's life, and partly as an indirect result of the political chaos.

The Iron Ring

When Taaffe took office as prime minister in August 1879, it was not at all certain that he would survive long in his job. When he began, he did not even have an actual majority in the *Reichsrat*, as such, and the Liberals were convinced that they, the natural leaders of Austria, would soon be back in power. Yet Taaffe was able to retain power and ran Cisleithania as

Franz Joseph's *Kaiserminister* (emperor's minister) until 1893. His government, soon known as the Iron Ring, completely changed Austrian politics, both decentralising it on national lines on the one hand, and yet strengthening the imperial state bureaucracy's position on the other.

The election of 1879 took away the Liberals' majority, but did not give Taaffe's coalition a majority either. Liberals and their allies had 174 seats out of 353 in the *Reichsrat*'s House of Deputies, but no more. Taaffe, with a ragtag coalition of conservatives, clericals, federalists, and non-German (usually liberal) nationalists, only controlled 168 seats. (The difference was made up by independents.) Yet he also had the crucial backing of the emperor, and the Liberals were not able to vote him out of office. So he ruled for well over a decade, becoming the longest-serving Cisleithanian prime minister.

Taaffe survived by *Fortwursteln* (muddling through), or, as he preferred to call it *Durchfretten* – eking out a majority. He would reward his supporters with concessions, but never fully, so that they would remain supporters in the hope of more. It was a system of 'well-tempered dissatisfaction'. If members of the coalition became too dissatisfied and obstreperous, he could always threaten them with the alternative: Liberal rule. In the early stages of his administration, Taaffe did indeed rule with moderate Liberals in the cabinet, as long as this was on the emperor's terms. It was also necessary, because there was still a Liberal majority in the *Reichsrat*'s Upper Chamber, the *Herrenhaus*, albeit a very loyal majority; and a two-thirds majority was required for passage of the decennial Defense Bill, so Taaffe needed Liberal votes for that bill's passage, which he obtained with some imperial arm-twisting, in December 1879. However, Liberal intransigence and the emperor's obstinacy meant that after January 1881 Taaffe's cabinet included no German Liberals, and he ruled with members of the Iron Ring alone.

In the *Herrenhaus* Taaffe arranged for a government majority by having Franz Joseph create a whole slew of exclusively conservative peers in 1881, but to keep the Liberals from the door in the Lower House he needed to keep his coalition members, if not happy, at least interested. Predictably, the concessions made to the coalition partners in return for support were made at German Liberal expense. This was, to some extent, following the German Liberals' own playbook, as they had already done this in their dealings with Galicia's Polish nobility, mainly at the expense of the very large Ruthene minority in the province, and at the cost of abandoning the role of the German language there as the bureaucracy's administrative language. Taaffe did not do much more with the Galician leadership than confirm the Polonophile status quo. The area where Taaffe's horse-trading had most effect was in the Bohemian crownlands.

In some respects, this was simply applying the quid pro quo with the Poles to the Czechs. Czech demands for their own university, and the promotion of Czech as a language of administration, could be justified as merely getting what the Poles already had. This was indeed one of the arguments used to justify the founding of a separate Czech university in Prague, leading to the splitting of the ancient (formerly German-speaking) Charles University into German and Czech parts in 1882.

The big difference between Galicia and the Bohemian crownlands was that the main minority was not the relatively powerless and poor Ruthenian peasantry, but rather Germans, and, as luck would have it, the most prosperous and educated part of Austria's German population except for Vienna – the Bohemian crownlands were the heartland of German Liberals.

One could use the practical example of Galicia for promoting Czech as an administrative language, but this came up against the fact that the minority's language in Bohemia was already the established administrative language: German. The relationship between Czech and German was an unequal one, for German had long been the *lingua franca* of education, commerce and administration, whereas Czech, as a modern literary language, was relatively new (the history of Czech culture and language pre-1620 notwithstanding), and certainly still looked down upon by most German-speakers as a language of peasants. Germans were a sizeable minority in Bohemia, at 37 per cent, but their greater wealth meant that they were economically an even larger presence, paying 50 per cent of taxes. It is as though, comparing the Bohemian with the Galician example from a purely intra-provincial perspective, the Germans were the Poles, and the Czechs were the Ruthenes, had the Ruthenes been in the demographic majority. Czechs who wanted to succeed learnt German, but Germans did not, to this point, need to learn Czech to succeed, so most chose not to.

As a concession to the Czechs in the Iron Ring, however, Taaffe and his justice minister, ironically the Liberal and former prime minister, Stremayr, passed an ordinance in April 1880 for Bohemia and Moravia that made Czech an 'external' language of the political (imperial, Vienna-centred) bureaucracy. (The ordinance did not apply to the provincial administration controlled by the provincial assemblies, nor to communal councils.) This meant that Czech-speakers could now conduct business with officials and courts in their own language, while the 'internal' language, for communications within the bureaucracy, remained German. On the face of it this was eminently reasonable, simply facilitating communication between state and public, but the German-Czech language inequality meant that it was seen as threatening to put most official positions with contact with the public in Czech hands. Moreover, even though there were large areas of Bohemia where only German was spoken, the ordinance recognised Czech as a 'locally current' (*landesübliche*) language throughout Bohemia and Moravia, which opened up the possibility that all officials would have to speak Czech should a Czech have business anywhere in Bohemia, even in 'German' Bohemia. Then there was the suspicion among German Liberals that this was just the start, and that the 'internal language' would be next on the concession-block.

The Czech leadership, on the other hand, were frustrated at not having gained more from Taaffe, but other concessions came in due course. There was the symbolically significant splitting of Charles University; then there was the politically highly significant electoral reform of 1882. Along with an expansion of the franchise (see below), the law as it applied to Bohemia made decisive changes to the structure of the Bohemian Diet's landed curia. It did so in such a way that it was clear that it would ensure a Czech majority come the next round of elections in 1885, for a legislative body that up to that point had been firmly under German control.

The German position in Bohemia was being seriously eroded. In 1884, suspecting further linguistic concessions, the German Liberals in the *Reichsrat* tried to get the functional status of German as the 'state language' put into law, approximating how Magyar had become the state language in Hungary, but the *Reichsrat* rejected this. In 1885, the elections led to the loss of the Bohemian Diet; then the German Liberals saw their fears concerning linguistic status realised when in 1886 Alois Pražák, now justice minister, made Czech an *internal* language for the Bohemian and Moravian High Courts in Prague and Brünn. Now definitely on the defensive, the German liberals put forward a proposal in the Bohemian Diet to divide the province into two language-based districts, to protect the jobs of German-only-speaking officials in the German area, but this was voted down as well. In protest, the German Liberals boycotted the Diet, as the Czechs had done before, and Bohemian politics headed for the crisis-ridden years of the 1890s.

Elsewhere there were more concessions to other nationalities. In 1883, Croats in Dalmatia were rewarded by Croatian being allowed as the official language of the province's autonomous administration. Slovenes were allowed a greater use of Slovenian in Carniola's administration as well.

If German interests were sacrificed to reward nationalities, Liberal interests also suffered to reward German Clericals and Conservatives. Clericals were given a provision on teachers in public schools, whereby it was compulsory for the teacher to have 'special competence' in the religion of the majority of their pupils. Given the large Catholic majority among Cisleithanians, this effectively made teaching a Catholic monopoly, or at least a Christian one, with Jews almost entirely excluded. The intent of the law was made clear by the fact that schools in Galicia were exempted, because of the risk of having Jewish or Ruthenian (Orthodox) majorities in the student population. Conservatives were rewarded with qualifications to the eight-year length of compulsory education, but such was the heterogeneous nature of the Iron Ring that other, liberal members, for instance Old Czechs, kept these concessions to a minimum.

The Taaffe government also countered liberal economic and social policy, to satisfy anti-liberal constituencies, such as the peasantry, *Mittelstand* (lower-middle class) and even working class. The changes to the school law concerning length of compulsory education were designed, for instance, to 'allow' peasants' children to leave school at age twelve rather than fourteen so that they could work on the family farm. In 1883 the very laissez-faire Industrial Code of 1859 was reformed, with much more regulation, and proficiency tests for the artisanal trades.

The retreat from 'Manchester' economic liberalism was a European-wide phenomenon, and Austria was no exception. Taaffe followed the lead of Bismarck's Germany in trying to head off socialism in the modernising economy and society by a carrot and stick approach. The stick was very harsh legislation against radical politics, with an emergency Anti-Terror Law passed in 1884, and an Anti-Socialist Law in 1886. The carrot was a set of laws designed by one of Taaffe's closest advisors, the high official Emil Steinbach, to soften the effects of the new industrial economy, and, it was hoped, co-opt the emerging industrial working class. Limits on working hours were introduced, the use of child and female labour in factories and mines limited. Systems of sickness and accident insurance were established for industrial workers, and hence the rudiments of a welfare state were (re-)established.

Taaffe and Steinbach were to some extent pushing against an open door. The trend among the representatives of industry, the Liberals, had been an interventionist one after the 1873 crash, and now there was more of an acknowledgement of the need for further regulation and help for the lower classes. Now in opposition, it was Liberals who saw Taaffe's attacks on socialists as too harsh, and had succeeded in first softening the measures, and then were central to repealing them in 1891. There was, however, a definite political edge to Taaffe's social legislation as well. Urban factory workers were given substantial insurance coverage at the cost largely of their (liberal) employers, but workers in agriculture and forestry (where the employers were more likely to support the Iron Ring) were far less generously provided for.

There was also a decidedly anti-liberal political edge to the electoral reform of 1882. The law's main feature was a lowering of the franchise threshold to payment of five gulden in direct taxes per annum. This opened up the vote to the lower-middle class, which was both more anti-liberal and also more composed of non-German nationalities in the provinces. The change in the franchise, and changes to the composition of the curias, especially the landed curia in Bohemia, adversely affected the German Liberals when elections were held in 1885. Even greater was the impact of electoral pacts between their Iron Ring-linked opponents in Tyrol and Bohemia. The net result was a further shrinking of the German Liberal bloc, which left Taaffe some more room for his wheeling and dealing, but not *too* much. It was the *absence* of a strong majority in the *Reichsrat* that was, according to Steinbach in 1893, what guaranteed the 'crown's full sovereignty' in government. Taaffe's Iron Ring worked because its partners were sufficiently *dis*united to challenge the *Kaiserminister*, Franz Joseph's man, Taaffe.

Hungary Transformed

The reverse solution, in the right hands, also worked in *King* Franz Joseph's favour in Hungary. Instead of breaking the lock of the Liberals and the 'ruling nation' on power, Franz Joseph's Hungarian prime minister, Kálmán Tisza, confirmed it, set it in stone, through the merger of his Left Centre Party and the Deákists to form the Liberal Party in 1875. This was despite the fact that the situation of Magyars and Germans had been demographically quite similar in their respective 'halves', with Germans comprising roughly 37 per cent of Cisleithania's population, and Magyars 40 per cent of Hungary's.

Tisza's rule until 1890 was a crasser version of what might have happened if German Liberals had stayed in power in Vienna's *Reichsrat*. He continued liberal economic and social policies (even if some of these 'liberal' policies resulted in agricultural labourers being returned, effectively, to the control of their employers). Laissez-faire economic policies brought strong growth from the late 1870s, so that twenty years later, by 1900, Hungary had quite a strong industrial sector, from having had virtually none. In religion and education liberal policies also continued. The most striking difference between Hungary and Cisleithania in this area was the approach to the Jewish Question and antisemitism.

In Cisleithania, Taaffe turned a blind eye to the rise of antisemitism in the early 1880s, because the Jewish establishment continued to support his opponents, the Liberals, in other words would not play along with the log-rolling of the Iron Ring. In Hungary, Tisza made sure from the very start, during the Tiszaeszlár Affair of 1882, which revolved around a case of blood libel, an accusation of ritual murder, that Jews were protected and their antisemitic political opponents crushed. One reason was ideological, a liberal belief in civic equality, but there were also more material concerns. Much of Hungary's economic progress was based on a conscious alliance between Magyar gentry politicians, the backbone of the Liberal Party, and the party's financial backers, the urban, capitalist bourgeoisie, which in Hungary was predominantly Jewish. This was especially so in the national capital, where 23 per cent of the total population of Budapest around 1900 was Jewish in any case, and the city's commercial and industrial upper-middle class much more so. Moreover, the Magyar acculturation of Jews was one of the main successes of Magyarisation, and Jews, protected by the political system, reciprocated with often fierce loyalty to the Magyar 'nation-state'.

The acculturated Jewish bourgeoisie also shared the anticlericalism of Tisza (himself a Calvinist), and it was this alliance of anticlerical (often Calvinist) Magyar gentry with the Jewish bourgeoisie that was behind the liberal legislation of late 1894, which made civil marriage compulsory, and declared the equality of religions, effectively disestablishing the Catholic Church – over Franz Joseph's strenuous objections.

Liberal in many respects, Tisza was also a quite oppressive Magyar nationalist, who sharpened the nationalising trend of his predecessors. In Croatia, for instance, the appointment as *ban* of Count Károly Khuen-Héderváry in 1883 began a push to assert much more Magyar control over Croatian affairs than initially envisaged by the creators of the *Nagodba* in 1868. The Education Law of 1879 that had made Magyar a compulsory subject in all schools was tightened up further in laws of 1883 and 1891, with a clearly Magyarising intent. More minority schools were closed, more minority-language publications banned – all to help make the Magyar nation-state a nationally Magyar state as well. This coercive Magyarisation was generally ineffective, and what success it did have in increasing Magyar-speaking numbers was due mainly to the educated urban middle classes, largely Jewish and German, voluntarily integrating into the politically and culturally dominant 'state language', with its rising Magyar culture and society.

The oppressive, even suppressive, approach to the other minority nationalities did help ensure that politics remained wholly within the Magyar national community, with non-Magyar speakers almost entirely excluded from the political discourse. The Magyar political monopoly was also greatly helped by the effectiveness of Tisza's 'management' of the restrictive electoral system and the now centralised governmental system. There was no expansion of the electorate. Instead, Tisza's party agents, the 'Mamelukes', were sent out to operate the machinery of county government (previously decentralised, now very centralised) as a political machine for the Liberal Party. Hungary's own 'electoral geometry' meant that the Liberal Party's strength lay in the small, peripheral constituencies, where the electorate might be Magyar, but the populace usually was not; the small band of Magyar voters in such outlying districts

Figure 11. The Hungarian Parliament Building in Budapest. This deliberately imposing edifice was begun in 1885, inaugurated in 1896 as part of the Millennial Celebrations, and finally completed in 1904. (Published with permission of the Austrian National Library.)

could be more effectively handled by the party machine, whereas the much more populous constituencies in the central plain, which were much more Magyar in population, were more difficult to manage, and often more open to opposition candidates. This system also assured that there were hardly any representatives of the national minorities in the Hungarian Parliament (where the language was, of course, Magyar).

This meant that politics was not one of the 'ruling nation' against the other nationalities, but rather took place generally along a liberal/conservative axis, as seen in the legislation on religion. There was a 'national question' that could cut across this 'normal' political spectrum, but it was one of dualism versus anti-dualism. The Moderate Opposition might take some conservative stands, but when it came to the national question, almost all of the opposition to Tisza's government came from the Left, not the Right, with both the Independence Party and the Moderate Opposition wanting less connection to Austria. Part of Tisza's ability to get Franz Joseph to agree to chauvinist and anticlerical legislation and policy, when the monarch was a conservative Catholic who as Austrian emperor was quite respectful of the rights of nationalities, was the fact that there was no real alternative to Tisza, given the way the system was stitched up, and if there was it would only be more anti-dualist, in other words, worse.

The Magyar leadership therefore had a distinct advantage over its Cisleithanian counterpart: coherence. Even when the Magyar political elite quarrelled, they did so within the ranks of a uniformly militant nationalism. There were very few occasions when Cisleithania, or the Austrian emperor (Franz Joseph), could challenge the Hungarian king (also Franz Joseph) – unless the Hungarian king himself objected, as he did in the late 1880s over the decennial Army Bill.

Tisza held power for fifteen years, but eventually his role of mediator between Magyar chauvinists and the king-emperor over-taxed even his political skills. In 1887 he was able to pass the decennial Economic Compromise in parliament, but the Army Bill, due in early 1889, sparked a fulmination of Magyar nationalism against the 'German' Habsburg oppressor that became a severe crisis. Magyar nationalists viewed the common army as 'alien, dynastic and absolutist' and saw those of its units stationed in Hungary as a form of occupation force. It was not only that the language of command remained German; from a Magyar point of view the fact that soldiers in the ranks from minority nationalities, also those recruited in Hungary, could use their own, non-Magyar language was just as bad – as it countered Magyarisation efforts.

The politics surrounding the army were aggravated in 1886 by the laying of a wreath by an army general on the grave in Budapest of

General Heinrich Hentzi, a loyalist 'martyr' killed by Hungarian revolutionaries in 1849. Politics were made worse by the contents of the decennial Army Bill itself, which had to be passed by both the Hungarian parliament and the *Reichsrat*. This included reform proposals to modernise the military, among other things updating officer training methods, which entailed a rule that would ensure a level of competence for reserve officers by requiring them to sit for an exam in the German language. This was reasonable given that German was the common army's language of command, but it was seen as a German imposition on Magyars and set off demonstrations in Budapest and the provinces, which required military intervention. Instead of hanging tough, prime minister and king decided to compromise. Concessions were made, including allowing reserve officers to take the test in Magyar or Croatian, and the Army Bill was eventually passed in early 1890. It was this crisis which resulted in Tisza's resignation on 13 March.

One of the key concessions that Franz Joseph was forced to make to accommodate Magyar nationalism was a handwritten note of 12 October 1889, in which he agreed that the army and navy be henceforth styled not 'k.k.' as previously, but, as the Magyars had always insisted, 'k.u.k.'. The fervour and extremism of Magyar nationalism, concentrated in one direction as it was, got its way over Cisleithania, and Austria, more often than not.

The Politics of Masses

While Cisleithania and Hungary went their separate ways politically, their economy and societies continued to change dramatically. Calling the period the 'Great Depression' is really only appropriate for the agrarian economy, and does not account for growth in the industrial economy, which was high. Economic growth in this period was high in Cisleithania, and even higher in Hungary, at 2.8 per cent per annum, and this brought increasing industrialisation, and urbanisation, as a large part of the rural population, now redundant after the modernisation of the legal structures and methods of the agrarian economy, flocked to cities. In 1870 Vienna's population was 610,000; by 1900 it was 1,770,000. Budapest's population in 1870 was about 290,000; by 1900 it was 733,000, and the fastest-growing city in Europe. Some former industrial magnets, such as Brünn, had slowed their expansion some (1870: 74,000; 1900: 109,000), but others had taken their place, such as Aussig in northern Bohemia, which grew from 10,000 in 1870 to 40,000 in 1900.

The Monarchy was still, overall, quite agricultural, but in the major metropolises and in certain regions, such as northern Bohemia, a modern industrial society was forming. In Hungary the impact of this politically was muted by the need to maintain a restricted franchise to retain the Magyar political nation's hegemony, but in Cisleithania the political opportunities of the new, mass society were partly opened up by the electoral reform of 1882, and partly seized upon by the nationalist parties and other mass-political movements that took the stage in the 1880s. Politics began to change from one of *Honoratioren*, rather staid, respected members of the community, lawyers, officials and gentry, discussing matters of principle in sedate, formal settings, to one of mass interest politics, in which political success was measured by rousing the masses, organising them in effective, structured political parties and then trading party support for policy favouring your constituency, what in Italian political history came to be called *trasformismo*.

The initial great ideological winner in this modernisation of politics was nationalism. Not only was it the largest gainer from the extension of the franchise to the anti-liberal, more socially oriented lower-middle class, but nationalism was also the main gainer from liberalism's greatest achievement: the spread of education and literacy.

It was through the schools that the question of language became the main form of identity, and division. Literacy was a necessity of the new, industrial and commercial age, but the central question was literacy in which language? It had been through cultural, literary nationalism that national identity had become concrete in the Czech case and many others. Historians had not only told the stories of nations, but had helped create them in the telling. Now it was the source of literacy, schools, that became the main battleground between nationalist groups, fighting for the 'national property' as embodied in the national identity of school children.

The battle was framed by the law's approach to national questions, especially when it came to language and schools. The Austrian bureaucracy in the Taaffe era, and most significantly the independent judiciary, tended to be very accommodating of national rights concerning the schools. One of the more interesting details in this area was the approach to language in the decennial census. In Hungary, the question concerning language went through various versions of which 'mother tongue' one possessed, which on the face of it was a question of origin, although in actuality this was not how it was understood. In Cisleithania, on the other hand, the authorities took a much more neutral, objective line, with the census asking only for one's *Umgangssprache* – 'language of daily use'. This was not your language of descent, or your mother tongue, but merely the language you usually spoke in your daily life, and meant that your identity was not, as such, nationally determined. Nationalists took this, however, as a challenge, for the optional nature of the individual's choice meant that they could try to persuade those individuals to choose to show solidarity with their *real* national community by putting their *national* language as the 'language of daily use'. As the Czech newspaper in Budweis, *Budivoj*, proclaimed in 1890: 'Let our motto be that he who is Czech by descent and origins report as his language of daily use *his mother tongue, Czech!*' Czech politicians in Budweis took a private census in Budweis that year that categorised people by their *real* national identity, not what they said their 'language of daily use' was. That way, they could show how Czech 'national property' was compromised by apostates denying their Czechness. The decennial census thus became the occasion of national, political *campaigns* to get people to fill in the language question 'correctly'.

The census figures could also have a strong influence on the national balance in any area, because of the way in which resources were distributed for schools. In 1884, a ruling of the *Verwaltungsgerichtshof* (Administrative Court) in Vienna mandated that local districts had to provide at public expense schools in a nationality's language, if that nationality could show at least forty school-aged children speaking that language living within two hours walking distance of the local schoolhouse. This was a huge incentive for nationalists. If a nationalist organisation could pay for a school in the area, it could then serve as a magnet for people of that nationality in the area, who previously had not had the option. If enough then responded, the threshold would be reached, and the school could then become a public school, with public funding. This, however, only boosted a competition for the nations' 'kidnapped souls' (children) that had already begun. Both German and Czech liberal nationalists founded organisations, within months of each other in 1880, the Czechs the Central School Foundation, the Germans the German School Association, to further the national cause by privately funding minority schools. These became the strongest nationalist organisations, with large budgets to defend the nation. The competition over schools sharpened the national divide, but it also, almost as a by-product, made an already fairly well-educated populace a very well-educated one.

Galicia offers a stark counter-example to Bohemia when it comes to the relationship between education, nationalism and mass politics. There the Polish political nation, largely still the landed nobility, was already in charge, on a mainly pre-modern basis, as the economy remained largely agrarian and not very dynamic (except for the spectacular exception of the oil industry around Kolomea and Borysław from the 1880s on). Therefore there was little incentive, from the viewpoint of the Polish ruling class, to encourage education, and so the largely autonomous

Sejm (Galician Diet) did not. Less than half of children attended school in 1880, compared to 95 per cent in the rest of Cisleithania, and school attendance was even lower in eastern Galicia, with its mainly Ruthenian population (which the Polish authorities had even less incentive to educate). Ruthenian nationalists, as with their Czech counterparts, sought to obtain funds for schools, but they had a much harder time of it, also with getting parents to support the educational effort. Ruthenian nationalists encouraged education as the way to take advantage of the dynamic modern economy and new technologies: 'the world does not stay in one place, but moves forward, and whoever doesn't move forward with it will fall by the wayside'. The problem was that the nexus between modernisation, education and nationalist mass politics worked against education and nationalism if the economy did not change to merit this claim. This was quite unlike the Bohemian example, to which Ruthenes envyingly appealed.

In Bohemia, obversely, the economic and cultural advance of both Germans and Czechs led to greater, mass-based national conflict. This not only took the form of census campaigns and funding private schools, but also forms of symbolic and actual physical defence, as in the Sokol movement. This organisation was founded in 1862 very much in emulation of the nationalist gymnastics movement in Germany. By 1882 Sokol had become a militant, mass movement, and staged its first mass gymnastics demonstration, the '*slet*' ('flocking of birds') that year. Sokol was instrumental in shifting Czech nationalism from the *Honoratioren* party of the Old Czechs to the more radical, more combative, and more socially oriented, Young Czechs, a parallel in many ways to the 'Young' German Liberals who became German nationalists. Each Czech nationalising institution was matched by one created by Germans in Bohemia, increasing the opportunities and resources for conflict.

In the German camp, the 1880s saw a hollowing out of the German Liberals in favour of a more nationalist approach. A nationalist wing of the German 'Left' had already developed in the late 1870s, as we have seen, but after the crisis of 1879 the nationalists broke away to found their own German Nationalist movement, rallying around a set of policies laid out in the Linz Programme of 1882. This document, in its initial version, was largely written by Friedjung and other members of the largely Jewish Adler group, including Adler himself. Its policies on social issues were to a large part conventionally 'left-wing', as we would understand the term, seeking greater state help for the lower classes, just as it was 'left-wing' in an Austrian-German sense in its radical political German nationalism. This reflected the movement's broad coalition of left-wing Jewish students and nationalist politicians. Soon enough, however, the charismatic former Liberal brought in to lead it, Georg von Schönerer, took the party in a radically, racially antisemitic direction.

Schönerer had been an ally of the radical German nationalist students in Vienna's *Burschenschaften* from the 1870s, and, as we saw, these duelling fraternities had been open to anti-Jewish arguments as early as 1875. In 1882 he got involved in the Reform Association, Vienna's first antisemitic organisation, founded that year to protect Viennese artisans from 'Jewish' 'Manchesterism' (liberal, laissez-faire economics). In 1884–85 he launched a brutally demagogic campaign against the Rothschild 'money Jews' in the Nordbahn Affair, that was radically antisemitic, as was the 'Chinese bill' of 1887 that he proposed against Jewish immigration(named as such because of its imitation of the contemporaneous anti-Chinese laws in the United States). In 1888 Schönerer went too far, even for him, attacking a liberal newspaper's office for a perceived slight to the German emperor, and for this he was imprisoned for several months, and banned from political life for five years. His message, however, in a somewhat more moderate form but still with a racially antisemitic element, was carried forward by other former Liberals such as Karl Hermann Wolf and Otto Steinwender. Steinwender's People's Party was to capture and transform most of what had been the German Liberal camp into nationalists, whose aim was to protect not the Austrian state, but rather German interests within that state. Attempts to found a real, left-liberal, democratic party never got far beyond Vienna, with its heavily Jewish liberal constituency.

To the 'right' of the Liberals emerged another new political movement, Karl Lueger's Christian Social Party. This had many shared origins with Schönerer's movement, such as the Reform Association, and was originally closely allied with the German Nationalists, who were a constituent part of the United Christian Party of 1887. However, what became Vienna's dominant antisemitic party also had clerical and socially conservative support, most notably from the Catholic Social theorist Karl von Vogelsang. Its main support came from a lower-middle class resentful of the new 'Jewish' capitalist economy. This was also Schönerer territory, and Schönerer might have become leader of Viennese antisemitism had he not been imprisoned and banned in 1888. As it was, the movement really only became successful when, in the same year, 1888, Karl Lueger became party leader. Lueger, the master political opportunist of modern Austrian political history, realised that antisemitism was the glue that could hold together a ragtag collection of anti-liberal forces that otherwise opposed each other – such as lower Catholic clergy, anticlerical racial antisemites, conservative aristocrats, Austrian dynastic patriots and German nationalists, as well as quite a few radical democrats, at least

— Herr Doctor Lueger, eine Wählerdeputation ist draußen.

= Sind's Deutsche, Czechen, Juden, Antisemiten? Mir is der Faden ausgegangen, und ich weiß wirklich nicht, soll ich jetzt demokratisch, czechisch, deutsch, jüdisch oder antisemitisch sein.

Figure 12. Cartoon of Karl Lueger, the ultimate political opportunist. From *Der Floh*, 10 May 1885. Informed there is an electoral deputation to see him, Lueger asks: 'Are these Germans, Czechs, Jews or antisemites? I have lost the thread, and I really don't know whether to be democratic, Czech, German, Jewish, or antisemitic.'

initially. Lueger combined the coalition-building skill of Taaffe with the tactics of the 'politics of the new key', with its use of rowdy public meetings and frontal attacks on the integrity and morality of their Jewish or 'Judaised' opponents. The Christian Socials first threatened Liberal hegemony in Vienna in 1891, and then in the municipal elections of April 1895 achieved a majority in the city council. Lueger, famously, was refused the emperor's sanction to be appointed mayor three times, but, as we shall see, eventually received the imperial sanction and became mayor in 1897 – as a quid pro quo for supporting the government in the Badeni Crisis.

Both of the new mass political movements in the German *bürgerlich* camp, German Nationalists and Christian Socials, were antisemitic in their platforms and practice. So were, to varying degrees, most of the other nationalist or clerical parties that emerged among the other nationalities in this new era of mass politics. In the Czech camp, the Young Czechs attacked Jews for being lackeys of the Germans; the Hilsner Affair of 1899, a blood libel case, saw the prominent Czech nationalist politician, Karel Baxa, leader of the Radical State Right Party, as the main legal accuser of Hilsner of the charge of ritual murder. (Baxa was later to be the long-ruling mayor of Prague in independent Czechoslovakia.) In Galicia, the Christian People's Party of Father Ignaz Stojałowski incited riots against Jews in 1898.

The reason why antisemitism was virtually ubiquitous among nationalist and clerical mass parties was not only the usual Catholic prejudice against 'Christ's killers', but also the fact that nationalist mass politics did not allow for the subtleties of minorities being members of the nation, and rejected the liberal idea of the rights of the individual independent of the nation. Nationalists ultimately did not believe in the rights of people, but of peoples, not individuals but the collective nation. Yet the whole Jewish emancipation had been based on the idea that individuals could choose to become members of the greater (national) society, regardless of their religion or origin. Just as Czech nationalists in Budweis rejected the idea that one could legitimately choose to change one's national identity, so radical nationalists ultimately rejected the idea that Jews could become members of the nation. Even when Czech nationalists demanded from Bohemian Jews that they declare themselves Czech speakers, for instance, this did not mean that they accepted them as fully Czech.

Christian Socials shared the same approach, even though it might go against Catholic doctrine concerning conversion. One of the main reasons why they named themselves *Christian* Socials, rather than Catholic Socials, was to avoid the problem that many of their members were former German Nationalists with a racial, quasi-biological understanding of identity, that was quite un-Catholic. Hence the Christian Socials were Christian in the non-religious Austrian, secular sense that they were 'not-Jewish'. In that sense one can argue that the Christian Socials began as a nationalism of negative integration, the national community being 'everyone who was not Jewish'. For nationalist and clerical mass parties, Jews were a ready scapegoat and Other, against which to define one's belonging to the *Volk*, the 'people', the mass.

It should also be said that Jewish liberals were not unsusceptible to German nationalist sentiments. In 1882 Adolf Fischhof, the old '48er, attempted to create a new, pluralistic politics based on the equality of nationalities, with his German People's Party (an ironic name given subsequent events). It never got anywhere. At the meeting to launch the party, Fischhof was heckled by German Nationalists such as Friedjung (also Jewish), and in any case the Jewish establishment in Vienna remained loyal to the increasingly nationalistic German Liberals, who would not accept real equality with the other 'inferior' nationalities. Rabbi Joseph Bloch tried in his *Austrian Weekly* (set up to oppose Friedjung's *German Weekly*) to revive Fischhof's idea of a *civic* Austrian nationalism, whereby Jews, precisely because they had no real nationality (Bloch thought), would be the most Austrian of all groups, but this did not change all that many minds. By 1895, with the Christian Socials in power in Vienna's city council, a formerly assimilationist liberal journalist, Theodor Herzl, decided that the only solution of the 'Jewish Problem' was for Jews too to become nationalists, as Jews, and seek their own state. Jewish nationalism had already been around for some time, but it was the Viennese crisis that set off Herzl's reaction. The Dreyfus Affair might have also had a catalytic effect, perhaps, but it was the 'nationalist' mass politics of Vienna and Cisleithania that was the main context in which Herzl's political Zionism was born.

There was one mass political movement that offered an ostensibly universalist, non-national and non-antisemitic approach: socialism. Re-emerging after decades of suppression, the movement was reunited and re-founded in 1889 as the Austrian Social Democratic Party under the leadership of Victor Adler. This signatory and co-writer of the Linz Programme of 1882 had not changed his left-radical social positions all that radically – and it has been claimed he never fully cured himself of his German nationalism, with the Austrian Social Democrats soon accused of the same Germanocentrism as their Liberal predecessors. Yet the new party of the urban proletariat, with its Marxist revolutionary ideology and rhetoric, was initially just as feared by middle-class liberals and the imperial authorities as the two other new mass parties, if not more so.

Even so, very early on, Jewish liberals in Vienna, including Herzl for a time, saw socialism, universalist and secularist, as a possible answer to the antisemitism of the other parties, and this is what in effect happened. Adler early on decided to stick to the rules of Austrian constitutionalist politics to bring about revolution peacefully, through expansion of the franchise and then through the ballot box, and the party was soon to become the ally of, and refuge to, many liberal and progressive causes, the real successor to liberalism in many respects. With its policy, outlined in the Brünn Programme of 1899, of federalising the Monarchy along national lines, the Social Democrats became a supporter of the continuation of the Monarchy, not splitting it up, and came to be nicknamed the '*k.k. Sozialdemokratie*'. This was something, however, which the non-German sections of the Party were to find increasingly hard to accept in the nationalist atmosphere of the late Monarchy.

Almost all the major developed areas in the Monarchy in the 1880s and 1890s had nationalist politics of one sort or another. Modernity and nationalism appeared to be made for each other, and the more modern an area became, the more radical, mass-political its nationalism. Czech politics was dominated until the late 1880s by the 'Old Czechs', led by Palacký's son-in-law, František Rieger. They were the long-established defenders of the national cause, allied with the conservative federalists, but ideologically moderate liberals, like the German Liberals. They were being challenged by 1889 by the Young Czechs. A splinter group from the Old Czechs' National Party, the Young Czechs were founded in 1874 as the National Liberal Party, but first made a major showing politically in the elections to the Bohemian Diet in 1889. Much as the German nationalists emerged from the student movement and duelling fraternities, the Young Czech leadership started as students or Sokol members, and their political ideology was very similar to that of German nationalists, in terms of more radical social policies and a more democratic approach to politics. They rejected the Old Czechs' alliance with the federalist nobility and were quite anticlerical. There was also a Czech branch of the Social Democrats, but the main force in Czech politics from the late 1880s was the Young Czechs, whose left-liberal, radical approach created a far more strident form of nationalism than that of Rieger's Old Czechs.

Within Slovene ranks as well, 'Young Slovenes' proclaimed the wish for a Slovene province to reflect Slovenian strength, instead of being chopped up between the crownlands of Carniola, Styria, Carinthia and the Littoral. In Galicia, the Christian People's Party and the National Democratic Party practised a similar nationalist mass politics, with a large dose of antisemitism. However, in Galicia radical nationalist politics were usually kept under control (suppressed) by the noble-dominated *Sejm*, much as in Hungary. Lack of development meant the dynamic of mass nationalism did not work as well; the same was true for the more remote, less developed parts of Alpine Austria, such as Tyrol, where conservative, clerical politics dominated.

It is also true that the 'masses' were only nationalist part of the time, when their national identities were either flattered or threatened. There were substantial parts of the population that were comfortable with the a-national or trans-national situation that had obtained earlier. Both German and Czech nationalists were frequently frustrated by the fact that 'their' people on the national border were often content to remain in a bilingual context, not seeing the need to separate from colleagues and neighbours and retreat behind (metaphorical) national walls. Maintaining this inter-national, 'utraquist' comity was not something that nationalists approved of, given their decisive, and exclusive, either/or logic of absolute national identity, and, unfortunately, the census question of 'language of daily use', though designed to be neutral, became a tool in nationalist hands to divide and destroy bilingual communities, as no one could put *both* languages as an answer. Nonetheless, normal life could continue in much of Cisleithania without a constant nationalist emphasis. Nationalist boycotts were vindictive, but usually not very effective and ignored. The superficiality of nationalism in everyday life is something that we should be aware of.

In a sense, however, this non-national quotidian was beside the point when it came to politics, for most of the masses did not have the vote before 1897, and even after that their voice did not count for much, especially in the local communes and provincial assemblies, which retained restrictive franchises to the end of the Monarchy. Among those who did have the vote, usually educated and at least lower-middle-class, nationalism was the political style of the *Bürgertum*, just as the Christian Socials were the party of the *Bürgertum* in more 'Austrian' Vienna. And it only took a cooked-up scandal like the horrendous Hilsner Affair for the 'masses', including the disenfranchised crowd, to respond to nationalist baiting – because this was what, in the moment, validated identity and created a sense of (virtual, imagined) community (and might give vent to an urge to violence, revenge or, in the case of looting, greed).

The Christian Socials, once in power, began to sound like a state-supporting, supra-national, Catholic and dynastic actor on the imperial stage; the Social Democrats also promised, with their universalist rhetoric, a working class that could support supra-national values and policies, and the Habsburg state, even Taaffe, could be attracted to that idea, that the *real* masses would counter the nationalism that was tearing the

Monarchy apart, but if so, even these 'centripetal' forces were going to disappoint.

The Emperor-King and His Peoples (People)

In 1884, Béni Kállay, common finance minister, and hence administrator of Bosnia-Herzegovina, expressed a fear to Alexander Hübner that the future of Europe belonged not to monarchy but to republicanism. Hübner commented: 'Let us face the fact that no one believes in kings anymore, and I do not know whether they believe in themselves. If they believed in themselves, the republics would have no chance.' Yet in the 1880s Franz Joseph had every reason to believe in himself and his monarchy, given that he had secured the rule of two amenable prime ministers, Taaffe and Tisza, in both halves of his empire-kingdom. The foreign policy that he was thus able to pursue on largely his terms also proceeded in a reassuring, fairly low-key manner. Under the emperor's aegis, Andrássy's successors as foreign minister, Baron Heinrich Haymerle (1879–1881), Count Gustav Kálnoky (1881–1895), and Count Agenor Maria Goluchowski (1895–1906), concentrated Habsburg diplomatic efforts in the one sphere of interest remaining to them, the Balkans. This was a less grand game than previously, but just as complex, even more so, given the set of volatile independent or semi-independent states on previously Turkish territory: Serbia, Romania, Montenegro, Bulgaria, Greece, what was left of European Turkey, with the fading Ottoman Empire, and a resurgent Russia, the main rival, as the other main regional players.

Habsburg foreign policy in this era could proceed with some confidence because of the backstop provided by the Dual Alliance with Germany, which Franz Joseph described in 1887 as 'the guiding star of our policy'. Some of that confidence was misplaced, as Germany had its own interests and, while Bismarck was chancellor, was just as interested in remaining friendly with Russia – Austria-Hungary's rival – as with the Monarchy. From 1889 to 1893, the Monarchy had the advantage of a particularly pro-Austro-Hungarian government in Berlin, but then interests again diverged, Germany being more of an economic rival in the Balkans. From 1896 to 1909, there was not even any military co-ordination between the two General Staffs. Despite German unreliability at times, Franz Joseph was happy to be the junior partner to Germany, as it gave him some stability after the momentous events earlier in his reign.

In 1882, Italy joined the Triple Alliance with Germany and Austria-Hungary – against French republicanism – but Italy was always a problematic ally because of its irredentist interest in Southern Tyrol, the Littoral and Istria. As had been the case in 1878, Haymerle initially looked to Britain as the main counterweight to Russia in the Balkans, but British lack of interest and Bismarckian persuasion led to compromise with Russia in the Three Emperors' Alliance of 1881. The Bulgarian Crisis of the mid-1880s led to a collapse of the understanding with Russia, and in 1887 Kálnoky was able to arrange an informal agreement with Britain, the Mediterranean Entente, to counter Russian influence in the Balkans, which lasted until 1897. By then a *rapprochement* had been arranged with the Russians, and so Habsburg diplomacy in the Balkans entered the twentieth century in a fairly stable condition, on the surface anyway. Under the surface, conditions were not so promising. Franz Joseph is recorded as thinking in 1895 that war with Russia would be inevitable, and Austria-Hungary was not particularly well placed in that eventuality. She did have quite good relations with Bulgaria, supposedly a protégé of Russia, but on the other side, her alliance with Serbia (1881) and the secret alliance with Romania (1883) were with monarchs, not peoples, and reliant on those monarchs not being ousted.

Franz Joseph had good relations with the Balkan monarchs in the 1880s and 1890s. The king of Serbia, Milan Obrenovič, even offered to allow the incorporation of his kingdom into the Habsburg Monarchy in 1885. Franz Joseph declined (for the same reasons that had made even the occupation of Bosnia so problematic). Yet public opinion in both Serbia and Romania was strongly nationalist and hence anti-Habsburg. Serbians had felt humiliated by the occupation of 'Serbian' Bosnia, and anti-Romanian policies in Hungary antagonised Romanians. Serbians were alienated by the corruption of the Obrenovič government and looked to their big Orthodox brother, Russia. Both nations, like Italy, looked at the Monarchy's territories and saw 'unredeemed' national lands (irredenta). It was difficult in this context for the Monarchy to be anything but on the defensive.

Yet the full consequences of Balkan nationalism could be downplayed for the two decades up to 1900. Instead, the 1880s could be seen as a 'golden age' for the Monarchy, having at last found a form of moderately conservative equilibrium. The characteristic operetta of the period is Johann Strauss the Younger's hymn to Austro-Hungarian co-operation, *Der Zigeunerbaron* (1885). Strauss's *Emperors' Waltz* dates from 1889, to celebrate the alliance between the *two* emperors, Wilhelm II and Franz Joseph, although it is now only associated with the latter. The Monarchy's complex geographic and ethnographic composition also was celebrated from 1885 on in the *Crown Prince Project*, a massive multi-volume work, sponsored initially by Crown Prince Rudolf, that presented a new(-old) vision of 'unity in diversity' for the Monarchy.

The emperor himself was in a better position in the new political dispensation in Cisleithania, with the governmental structures 'stretched' to allow more decentralised power at the communal and provincial level (in Galicia and Bohemia for instance), less significance for the centralist organ of the parliament, but with the imperial bureaucracy, centred on Vienna, under the 'emperor's minister', Taaffe, being largely in charge. With the 'crown's full sovereignty' secured by the *Reichsrat*'s (manageable) divisions, the monarch and monarchic authority and power were indeed in a good position.

On the other hand, this did open up that imbalance already mentioned where the Magyar tail wagged the Austrian dog, or, to put it more elegantly, 'Hungary governed Austria through the Crown.' The Magyar nationalist elite was united in pressing its advantage against Cisleithania; Kállay, as administrator of Bosnia made sure that new railway routes in the Monarchy's quasi-colony favoured Hungarian interests. In the decennial negotiations, the divided Cisleithanian deputation could not agree upon a united front against the much more cohesive Hungarians, with predictable results. In 1897, Count Gyula Andrássy the Younger (son of the revolutionary/foreign minister) foresaw that the Magyars were destined to be the leading group in the Dual Monarchy, for 'we form a unified state of great antiquity; Austria is a mosaic of nationalities and provinces without an inner unity'. As we have seen, the demographic reality was that both states were mosaics of nationalities, but Andrássy was right about their respective political structures. The net effect was, to reprise Eisenmann, that Hungary paid one-third of the Monarchy's costs, but had significantly over half the say in how the joint concern was run – as well as a veto over any recasting of Cisleithania in its formal structures.

One adverse effect of this strong Magyar position in the Monarchy's governmental structures could be seen in the effect of Magyar nationalism on foreign policy. In the Balkans, diplomats' best-laid plans were often undermined by Magyar mistreatment of Croats or Serbs within the Monarchy, and Hungarian hostility to South Slavs outside the Monarchy undermined economic agreements with the Monarchy's southeastern neighbours, often to Cisleithanian disadvantage. After a particularly egregious stepping out of line of the Magyar leadership, Foreign Minister Kálnoky, himself of Hungarian descent, remarked: 'the gang need watching'.

Another qualification of the 'golden age' was that the extent to which the 'nationalities state' of Cisleithania could realise its multinational logic was limited by the German alliance. The erosion of the German position could only go so far, and the Czechs still saw themselves as oppressed. The German government in Berlin made quite clear that a properly

'Slavicised' Monarchy was not allowable. The German alliance also interacted with the Magyar position within dualism, mutually reinforcing each other as concerned Slavs, but sometimes clashing when it came to other groups and states, such as oppressed Romanians in Hungary and the German ally, Romania. The Triple Alliance also meant that the Italian population in the Monarchy had to be looked after. Frustrated Czechs looked to Russia and France for support for their fully *domestic* issues. Foreign and domestic policy had always been closely interlinked in the Habsburg Monarchy, but now the one impinged on the other even more.

Most worrisome of all for Franz Joseph and the Monarchy in terms of its status in the international power system, the successful neutering of parliamentary control over the military, through the intractable machinery of the Delegations and through the staring down of opposition in both parliaments, meant that there was no one interested in financially supporting it adequately. Franz Joseph gave his most cherished prerogative for safe-keeping over to Archduke Albrecht, as the army's inspector general, and General Friedrich Beck-Rzikowsky, elevated in 1881 to chief of the General Staff. Albrecht and Beck ran the military on very conservative lines, with the constitutional common minister of war effectively their subordinate. Beck was so close to Franz Joseph that he gained the reputation of being a virtual vice-emperor, and after Albrecht's death in 1895, Beck ran the army directly under Franz Joseph, an indication of the lack of any real constitutional control. Franz Joseph was rarely to be seen out of military uniform. The k.u.k. army remained the apple of the emperor's eye, military manoeuvres the main reason for visits outside the capital, and he kept close personal control of it, keeping any meddling politicians away.

As a result, however, of not being given any say much at all in the control of the armed forces, no politicians were enthusiastic to pay for it. Why spend good money on someone else's army? We have already seen the travails of 1889–90 over the Army Bill in Hungary, where Hungarians did not view the dynastically loyal army, with German as the language of command, as *their* army. Yet much the same was true in Cisleithania as well. The German Liberals had never been great supporters of an army they had failed to gain control of, and most other nationalities viewed the army, with its predominantly German-speaking officer corps, as representing German hegemony, and not their army either. Neither was it really nationally German; it was not anyone's army but Franz Joseph's. As a result, neither the Hungarian nor Cisleithanian parliaments – both of whom had to agree jointly to the budget – wanted to pay for it, and so the military budget stagnated, compared to that of other great powers.

By 1890, Austria-Hungary was spending less on its military in absolute terms than Italy, which was a much smaller state in terms of population and economic power. Austria-Hungary could have afforded a larger military; it was doing well economically, and financially, and returned to the gold standard in 1892. Yet its political class had neither the political will, nor cohesion, or even much incentive, to pay for one. Dualism had initially been a means of enhancing the Monarchy's military power, but now its complexities and contradictions were hobbling it.

At the top of the governmental system, it was also the case that Franz Joseph, while even more in control than he could have imagined in the 1870s, was increasingly isolated, socially. Franz Joseph had made a great effort on becoming emperor to restore the 'majesty' to the rather threadbare, informal Imperial Court he inherited from Ferdinand, and in many respects he had succeeded admirably. The imperial family and court aristocracy retained immense social prestige, and the implementation of strict ceremonial associated with such events as the *Hofball*, the Washing of Feet on Maundy Thursday, and the famous Corpus Christi Procession, were most successful exercises in symbolic politics. The narrow exclusivity of the Court (which was tightened under Franz Joseph) raised it majestically above the rest of society. Franz Joseph's twice weekly general audiences, on the other hand, where he condescended to be approached by the least of his subjects, created the image of all-embracing sovereignty that boosted the emperor's image among the public. His spartan domestic life, with his iron bed and daily bureaucratic chores, only added to the effect of his majesty when it came to the pomp and circumstance of hosting dignitaries, imperial tours and the Court's daily ceremonial. The carefully cultivated public image was of a simple man, a 'Christian, humble before God', who nonetheless ruled by divine right.

The exclusivity of the Court had major drawbacks, however. Social and economic change meant that the high aristocracy was no longer the only upper class in the state, but found itself challenged by an increasingly wealthy and influential 'second society' of high bureaucracy and an *haute bourgeoisie* of finance, commerce and industry. In Britain and Germany, Edward VII and Wilhelm II provided some access to the Court for this new wealth and, in return, gained significant leverage over it, but the Habsburg Court under Franz Joseph never did this. Instead it held the line and became increasingly old-fashioned, staid and anachronistic. Moreover, one of the side-effects of the disaster of 1866 was that the Court was full of exiled German princes, the duchess of Cumberland (a *German* aristocrat) being the emperor's consort when Empress Elisabeth was absent, as she almost invariably was. (Franz Joseph did have an *informal* consort, the actress Katharina Schratt, from 1883, but by definition this was nothing to do with the official Court.) There was thus a very large German presence at Court, and not much of any other national nobility. In an age when the state was becoming increasingly multinational, and the economic, cultural and social elite of the 'second society' becoming ever more powerful, the exclusion of newly emerging national and social elites meant that the Court was ceasing to provide a centre of cohesion for the Monarchy's peoples.

Franz Joseph was also becoming personally more isolated. With his Court functionaries, army officers and ministers about him, he had a detailed knowledge of the official version of his empire, but few real opportunities to discuss the actual state of affairs with people from the social and economic elites excluded from Court society. The twice-weekly audiences were spectacle, not much more. His frequent tours to the various provinces of his empire-kingdom were exercises in power-projection, not information-gathering. They transported a set, unvarying version of the Court, Habsburg majesty and state uniformity around the realm, sheltering the emperor from having to deal with too much reality. They almost always involved military manoeuvres and military display, which gratified Franz Joseph, and the tours conveyed an image of a monarch exalted above party and national politics, but it also left the emperor isolated and looking archaic, an old-style monarch in an increasingly modern state.

One of the people who saw the disadvantages of the monarch's distance from social reality the clearest was his own son, Crown Prince Rudolf. Had Rudolf been allowed to play more of a role in government by his father, some of the isolation of the monarch and the anachronism of the Court might have been remedied. Rudolf had the reputation of being liberal, dynamic and forward-thinking, and he and his advisors, including Moritz Szeps, shared the vision of 'unity in diversity' that informed the *Crown Prince Project*. Unfortunately, Franz Joseph isolated his son in turn from any meaningful function in government, for the very dynamism, one suspects, that he showed. It is also the case that Rudolf, frustrated with his talents and efforts being stifled, began to show emotional instability, which made him even less fit in his father's eyes for serious responsibilities. The eventual outcome of Rudolf's worsening state of mind and behaviour was the murder-suicide of Marie Vetsera and himself that he committed at Mayerling on 29 January 1889. This was a massive blow personally for Franz Joseph, who, despite his treatment of him, appears genuinely to have dearly loved his son, but it was also a disaster for the development of the monarchy and dynasty in a more modern direction.

The next in line as heir-apparent, Archduke Franz Ferdinand, was cut from a very different cloth from Rudolf.

The death of Rudolf in early 1889 was a bad omen. For the rest of the year Franz Joseph was faced with the Army Bill crisis, but that was only the start. Soon enough the Bohemian Question had reached yet another critical stage and would soon threaten the foundations of the state itself.

Squaring the Circle IV: Bohemia (Again) and the Badeni Crisis

By 1890, the power structure of the Habsburg Monarchy, already intricate, had become almost unmanageably complex. The asymmetries of Dualism interacted with the unequal geometries of national, social and centre/periphery conflicts in each half, especially in Cisleithania; these in turn were affected by the interference and conflations between domestic and foreign policy. It was within this already unstable context that the Taaffean system, which had once seemed so ideal to the emperor, began to unravel.

The central issue was, once again, the relationship between Czechs and Germans in Bohemia, with an important interlude of German-Slovene relations in southern Styria. The context was the ongoing retreat of German as the administrative language of the Monarchy. It had only a few decades before been the administrative language of the whole Monarchy. By the 1890s, however, it no longer had that status in Hungary, Galicia, Dalmatia or even, in practice, Slovene Carniola, as Vienna had bought off the various national groups and German-speaking urban 'islands' had either assimilated to, or been 'swamped' demographically by, the surrounding and immigrating nationalities. There were still disputes on language use in Tyrol (German and Italian) and Styria (German and Slovenian), but the prosperous Bohemian lands, especially Bohemia itself, remained the most significant contested arena.

For a period in 1890 it looked as though the German-Czech conflict had been settled. The Bohemian Compromise of 1890 had been successfully negotiated between the German Liberals and the Old Czechs and their allies in the Bohemian nobility. Had the agreement stuck, it would have been a great achievement for Franz Joseph and his *Kaiserminister*. It would have preserved many aspects of German hegemony that Franz Joseph actually preferred, such as the use of German as the internal administrative language. While it did not split the province in two as demanded by the Germans, it did divide the crownland into German and Czech administrative and judicial areas, and provide a series of minority protections for the Germans, such as the division of the Diet into national curias with veto powers on nationally sensitive issues. This protected the German interest, but was also an acknowledgement by them that they would never regain their previous dominance either in province or state.

For the very reason that the Compromise could be negotiated, it could not be implemented: the takeover of Czech politics by the left-radical Young Czechs from their more moderate Old Czech rivals. It had been the fear of Young Czech electoral success that had spurred Old Czechs and the emperor to seek an agreement with the Germans before it was too late – but it was too late. Before the Compromise could be implemented, the Young Czechs had run a hugely successful rejectionist campaign in the *Reichsrat* elections of March 1891, reducing the Old Czechs to a mere shadow of their former self, at only twelve *Reichsrat* seats. The Compromise perforce was abandoned, and instead of national peace, Bohemia in the early 1890s was awash in street demonstrations, often violent, and political resistance. In response, Taaffe tried to bring moderate German Liberals into the coalition with promises to implement by decree many of the provisions of the Compromise, especially the redrawing of judicial districts along national lines. The Young Czechs responded to this by obstruction of the Bohemian Diet and a summer of street violence and riots that culminated in 1892 in martial law being imposed on Prague and Moravian Brünn.

By 1893, Taaffe's grasp on Cisleithanian politics was severely weakened. Instead of muddling through, for once he attempted a radical solution. In October 1893, he shocked the *Reichsrat* with a plan, drawn up by Steinbach, for an electoral reform whose plain intent was to cripple the bourgeois national parties. It proposed giving the vote to all literate men over the age of 24 in the rural and urban constituencies. This was not universal or equal suffrage as such, because the new electoral system would have retained curial structures, but it would have meant a dramatic expansion of the electorate, and hence existentially threatened the established parties. Precisely for that reason it could never succeed: the German Liberals and the German Clericals, already under pressure from the more radical German Nationalists and Christian Socials, banded together, though formerly polar opposites on the political spectrum, hashed out a coalition, together with the equally threatened Polish Club, and defeated Taaffe instead. Kálnoky also supported Taaffe's ouster by portraying the reform as a threat to the Triple Alliance.

For the last time, Franz Joseph was forced by parliamentary leaders to dismiss Taaffe and accept the new ministry, an odd fish with a Conservative, Prince Alfred III Windischgrätz as prime minister, and a German Liberal, Ernst von Plener, as finance minister and actual leader of the government. The Clerical-Conservative/Liberal ministry lasted barely two years and was a disaster for both sides, especially the Liberals. Having the responsibility of governing without the real power compromised the Liberals' position with their constituents, for instance, over officials' pay. This meant that they lost ground to the radical nationalist camp, and contributed to the catastrophic defeat of their political allies on the municipal level in Vienna in the historic city council elections in April 1895 that eventually brought Lueger and the Christian Socials to power in the Habsburg capital. Cisleithanian politics were already in crisis, therefore, when the Coalition ministry fell in June 1895 over the attempt to institute a parallel Slovenian class at the *Gymnasium* in Cilli (Celje) in Styria (a repetition in a somewhat more minor key of the Bohemian language conflict).

Cisleithanian politics were now in uproar, and while Franz Joseph appointed Count Eric Kielmannsegg as interim prime minister with a *Beamtenministerium*, he looked for a 'strong man' to cure the political crisis with dynamic action. He might have been satisfied that the Liberals' attempt to return to power had failed, but he was also most concerned at the political radicalisation. He regarded the Pan-German Nationalists and the Young Czechs with contempt, and regarded the Christian Socials at this point as quite unacceptable, not only for their antisemitism, which went far beyond any Catholic anti-Jewish prejudice he might still harbour, but also their radical anti-establishment rhetoric. In mid-September, the crisis worsened, as Lueger's Christian Socials again won an even larger majority on the Vienna city council. The emperor looked around for someone who could form a 'strong non-parliamentary government in which the assembly he despised would find its master', and on 30 September he thought he had found him when he appointed Count Casimir Badeni as Cisleithanian prime minister.

Badeni was appointed on the recommendation of the military high command because of his record as a firm, but effective governor of Galicia. He appears to have been better than his reputation as just an unimaginative 'strong man'. His initial strategy appears to have been to govern with a 'liberal' coalition of German Liberals and Young Czechs. This meant easing up on repressive measures in Bohemia and Moravia, but also looking to the German Liberals, which was a major reason why Badeni recommended to Franz Joseph to refuse sanction of Lueger's election as mayor that October. Yet politics soon began to overtake Badeni. Repeated elections of Lueger as mayor of Vienna led eventually to Badeni striking a deal with him that led to a personal audience with the emperor and an implicit promise of a sanction of the mayoralty, eventually.

The German Liberals were still prepared to support Badeni despite this backsliding, and voted for the electoral reform of May 1896. This was a less radical version of the 1893 proposal. It left the existing curias as they were, with their 353 seats, but added 72 seats to be elected by a fifth curia with universal male suffrage. This appeared relatively moderate, yet it had the effect of making the number of German seats (of all ideological positions) a minority, at 202 out of 425 (in 1873 they had held two-thirds). With gains expected for the Christian Socials and perhaps even Socialists in the new *Reichsrat*, the 'German Left', once Austria's ruling party but now increasingly just another nationalist interest-party, was being backed into a corner.

Badeni continued to negotiate for a German-Czech compromise, despite increasing doubts on both sides. His idea was a trade-off of expanded Czech language rights in the political administration in Bohemia in return for a division of Bohemia, effectively, into two administrative areas, along the lines of the 1890 deal. The problem was that the deal was inherently asymmetrical: the concession to the Czechs could be achieved by ordinance, the restructuring of the province only by action in the Bohemian Diet. Additionally, the German leaders never agreed to it, nor did they make clear the severity of opposition there would be if Badeni tried to force such an agreement through, especially only the first, pro-Czech half, not that they necessarily knew this themselves at the time. Badeni was sensible enough to see that the failure to gain the guaranteed support of any major German group for his government meant his strategy had failed, and so he tendered his resignation long before any language ordinances had been published.

Franz Joseph refused to accept his resignation, and so Badeni was forced to come up with another strategy. The election results of March 1897 on the new franchise made his task that much harder. The socialists made spectacular gains, but the most significant changes for Badeni were the increase in seats for the Christian Socials, Young Czechs and Steinwender's nationalist People's Party. The Liberal element in the German camp was reduced further and the 'Right' had a majority in the new *Reichsrat*. A coalition of German Clericals, Christian Socials, Czechs and Poles now formally constituted itself the majority coalition. This was not at all what Badeni had desired, and initially he resisted the arrangement, vowing in April not to become 'prisoner' of the 'reactionary majority'. When the language ordinances for Bohemia and Moravia were published on 5 April and 22 April respectively, and elicited outraged opposition from the German camp, he was left with little choice but to do exactly what he had vowed not to. He needed a majority in the *Reichsrat* to govern effectively, especially to renew the decennial Compromise with Hungary, and if part of that majority was provided by the Czechs, who demanded applying the language ordinances, so be it.

The language ordinances might appear innocuous today. Their main provision was for all business of the political (imperial) administration in Bohemia and Moravia to be able to be conducted in both German and Czech, a common requirement of bilinguality in many states nowadays. To facilitate this, however, the ordinances also required that all officials in the political administration in the two crownlands have functional knowledge of both languages by 1901. To Bohemian Germans the asymmetry of the two languages (see above), and German reluctance or refusal to learn Czech, meant that the net effect of this proviso would be an administration with hardly any German officials, and a Czech dominance of the bureaucracy, in a society where the bureaucracy remained highly influential. This non-German administrative monopoly might be acceptable in a peripheral province, such as Galicia, but not in German Bohemia, which was the political and industrial heartland of the German middle classes in Cisleithania.

German deputies in the *Reichsrat* reacted to the publication of the ordinances with a flurry of emergency resolutions of nullification, which were all voted down. As an illustration of how much Badeni's policy direction had changed, the abstention by Christian Social deputies in these votes was rewarded by Franz Joseph giving his sanction to Lueger's election as mayor of Vienna. The German camp's response to this failure was to bring the *Reichsrat* to a halt by filibustering. Czech deputies had introduced the tactics of parliamentary obstruction by continuous debate and procedural manoeuvre in the last months of the Windischgrätz government, but the Germans now took it to the extreme. At first, obstruction was just formal, exploiting the 'technical' possibilities afforded by parliamentary procedure, and was confined to the odd pairing of the Progressives (German Bohemian Liberals) and the radical Pan-Germans of Schönerer (now back in politics) and Wolf. As the vehemence of opposition to the ordinances in their constituencies became plain to German deputies, more joined the obstruction, including Steinwender's People's Party. By the summer recess, all of the German Left had joined. Badeni sent the *Reichsrat* home early, to cool off, but the crisis only worsened as constituents protested, positions hardened, and no compromise was reached.

When the deputies came back in the autumn passage of the Compromise legislation became a pressing issue, but obstruction continued. On 25 November, the majority managed to impose new procedures, the 'Lex Falkenhayn', to foil the obstructionists, but this made matters worse, with the *Reichsrat*'s chamber a scene of chaos. With the constitution itself apparently in danger from the strong-arm tactics of Badeni and the Right's majority, the Social Democrats now joined the obstruction. The police were used to remove deputies from the chamber, but this just set off protests in the streets of German towns all over the empire. Bosnian troops fired on a crowd in Graz. Lueger, once an ally of Badeni and now mayor of Vienna, refused to guarantee the safety of the capital's streets. Even German Clericals had joined the obstructionists in the battle for 'national survival'. The *Reichsrat* failed to renew the decennial Compromise with Hungary. There was talk of revolution.

Across the border, the German press ran heated articles about the persecution of fellow Germans, and the German government made quite clear that the attack on the German position in Cisleithania had gone too far, and had to be stopped. The combination of this signal from the indispensable German ally and the serious outbreaks of domestic violence led to Franz Joseph accepting Badeni's resignation on 29 November, but this was just the beginning of months and years of

Die Unruhen in Prag: Räumung des Wenzelsplatzes durch Cavalerie am 30. November.   Nach einer Skizze von R. v. W.

Figure 13. Badeni riots in Prague, 30 November 1897.
(Published with permission of the Austrian National Library.)

trying to regain a semblance of order in Cisleithanian political life. In the case of Czech-German relations in the Bohemian lands, the circle remained very much unsquared. Cisleithanian politics at the end of 1897 was in utter chaos.

Dusk or Dawn?

Joseph Redlich, one of Austria's most articulate chroniclers, wrote of the Badeni Crisis: 'From this moment the Habsburg realm was doomed.' For many decades this remained the conventional assessment, that the controversy over the ordinances effectively blew up Cisleithanian politics and was the first stage of the Monarchy's eventual demise in 1918, which was easy to ascertain looking back in hindsight. Current historiography tends to see things entirely differently. Pieter Judson is the latest historian to point out how the Badeni Crisis was more about mobilisation of new political forces, and in a way demonstrated the effectiveness and elasticity of the system. Unlike 1848, no one really wanted to bring down the regime, they just wanted to have their piece of the pie. The parameters of the Monarchy's political structures were accepted by all sides, and it is the case that after some time a form of order was restored. It was not the same order, and parliamentary government as practised before 1897 never fully returned, but politics went on in other forms and in other venues (behind closed doors), so that the Monarchy continued quite handily almost despite its political system.

There were major problems with the new dispensation that followed, as we shall see, and in some ways Redlich's prophecy did remain true, but the irony is that Cisleithania was about to enter on one of its most productive periods of cultural and intellectual achievement, now famous as 'fin-de-siècle Vienna' or 'Vienna 1900'. Two days before the Badeni ordinances were published, on 3 April, a set of Viennese modern artists and architects, including Gustav Klimt and Josef Hoffmann, had begun the Viennese Secession. On 8 October, Gustav Mahler was formally appointed director of the Court Opera. On 3 July, a miracle of modern technology and popular entertainment, the *Riesenrad* (a giant Ferris wheel) in the Prater, was opened to the public. Meanwhile, in June 1896, Hungary had triumphantly celebrated its Millennium with a massive parade through the new streets and avenues of modern Budapest. This looked back to the glories of Magyar history, but also forward, with great confidence, to a new golden age for Hungary, and, by implication, the Dual Monarchy. In 1897 that Monarchy was in political chaos, but it was also on the cusp of a new, culturally and intellectually creative and innovative, *modern* era.

6   1897–1914: Modernisation

The Monarchy in its final decade and a half of peace presents a conundrum to historians. The assassination of Archduke Franz Ferdinand and his wife, Sophie, at Sarajevo on 28 June 1914, and the World War that followed, loom over everything that happened in the years preceding it. We know what no one knew in 1897, or even the summer of 1914, that the Monarchy was about to disappear from the map only a few years later, leaving chaos, and eventually genocide, in its wake. It is quite understandable why, for the longest time, the Monarchy's history was written from that perspective, to explain why it failed and disappeared. There was also more than enough recognition at the time that the Monarchy was in a severe, existential crisis, due to the failure of its main political institutions. The *Reichsrat* was in seemingly perpetual crisis, there were major financial and organisational problems with the various levels of the domestic administration, and also a seemingly unending controversy over the dualist agreement. The tendency in the traditional historiography to write off the Monarchy as doomed, and to look for reasons for that in its anachronistic nature or its inability as a supra-national dynastic state to handle modern nationalism, appears at first sight quite reasonable.

And yet, we also see now how the Monarchy's populace was in many respects flourishing, that its economy was keeping pace, or even catching up, with Western Europe, that its administration was relatively efficient and not corrupt, especially compared to the situation to its south and east; as an economy and society the Monarchy was modernising quite effectively. We also now see that, culturally and intellectually, the Monarchy was set to be the 'birthplace of the modern world' in a whole range of arts and disciplines. Moreover, even if contemporaries saw the Monarchy as in a state of crisis, very few thought that it would collapse, or were even looking forward to such an event, despite what nationalist hotheads might say to grab attention. They also could not imagine what we now know of the horrors that marked Central European history in the mid-twentieth century, which makes the prewar era seem so relatively benign, in

192

retrospect, almost innocent. Hindsight bathes the last years of the Monarchy in both the darkening gloom of a gathering storm, and the golden, slightly sepia-tinted light of nostalgia, at one and the same time. Hindsight cuts both ways: it is not only the doomsayers who are its potential marks. Those who see the positive aspects of the Monarchy's last years must also examine whether it is not retrospect that has distorted their vision.

Bearing the perils of hindsight in mind, we are still left with the puzzle of a polity and society that was politically in crisis and would, we know, soon collapse, but that had little idea that it would do so, because things seemed, in general, to be going quite well – outside of politics. These two contradictory moods are not, in the end, incompatible. In some respects, it was the political crisis that complemented, and even was a catalyst for, the economic, social and cultural success of the Monarchy, if in often surprising and complex ways. What bracketed the two contradictory impulses was the Monarchy's own special, inclusive, ironic, logic. Fitting then, in an unfitting way, that it was the same Monarchy that destroyed the basis of that logic when it went to war at the end of July 1914.

Many still think of the fateful decision to go to war in 1914 as an atavistic reaction by established elites to the threat of modernity, but others, most notably Modris Eksteins, have asserted that it was modernity itself that was behind the urge to devastating conflict. The whole of the Monarchy's last century was an attempt to deal with modernity in its various forms. Could it be that it was the Monarchy's 'modernisation' itself that was responsible for starting the First World War?

The Everlasting Political Crisis

After Badeni's dismissal, there was a series of *Beamtenministerien*, which attempted to calm things down, but things never did quite return to the previous normality. Badeni's immediate successor was Paul von Gautsch, whose government suspended the language ordinances. This ended German obstruction, but provoked Czech obstruction in its place. Gautsch was replaced in March 1898 by Prince Franz Thun-Hohenstein. Thun was able to get some significant business such as direct tax reform passed, but his proposals on the language question left the German camp unsatisfied, and so he was replaced by Count Manfred Clary-Aldringen in October 1899, prime minister for a few months, during which the ordinances were repealed, and then Heinrich von Wittek held the premiership for a month at the end of the year.

It was not only prime ministers that were casualties of the almost continuous obstruction. The Economic Compromise legislation, which had been a major cause of the initial crisis, could not be passed (either in Cisleithania or Hungary), and the lack of an economic agreement between Cisleithania and Hungary was a major legal and constitutional problem. However, this was got around by annual provisional agreements between the two governments, and, in a very Austrian manner, the complete blockage of the *Reichsrat* was bypassed by the frequent use of the emergency clause in the December Constitution, Article 14.

Cisleithania now entered on an era of post-parliamentary, quasi-absolutist government. There would be times in the next decade or so when the *Reichsrat* functioned reasonably well, but the norm that developed was not parliamentary government. The *Reichsrat* would meet; obstruction would start, blocking the government's legislative programme; the emperor would prorogue parliament; 'emergency decrees' would be passed in its absence to keep government going, and in the period before parliament was scheduled to meet again backroom deals would be made between the ministry and the parliamentary parties, so that when the parliament did meet again the emergency decrees would be approved retrospectively. After a brief lull to get agreed business done, obstruction would start up again, and the process would repeat.

Government was now run by officials of the high bureaucracy, the *Beamtenministerium* being the norm; elected representatives still had a large role, in private negotiations with officials and each other, to hash out deals, but representative government as such was no more. Joseph Redlich called this 'the absolutism of departmental bureaucracy'.

The great master of the new system was Ernest von Koerber. He had come to prominence as general manager of the Austrian State Railways in 1895, and in 1899 had become interior minister. On 19 January 1900, Franz Joseph tapped him as prime minister. Initially Koerber tried to break the deadlock in the *Reichsrat* by holding direct German-Czech negotiations, but his suggested solution to the language question in Bohemia and Moravia was rejected in the *Reichsrat*. In 1901, Koerber tried new elections, but this led to an even more nationalist parliament. Koerber then changed tactics. His very able aide, Rudolf Sieghart, no doubt had some influence, and Koerber's experience with the railways could have contributed; there is also the intriguing fact that Theodor Herzl had suggested to Koerber in a conversation back in May 1900, just after Koerber became prime minister, that he ought to change the subject in Austrian politics by announcing the formation of an 'Economy Party' and stress the economic benefits of political co-operation.

Whatever the cause, Koerber hit his stride by doing just that, changing the subject to economic development.

In a hypertrophic version of Taaffe's log-rolling, Koerber commercialised Austrian politics. He presented an economic recovery programme with many rewards in the form of remunerative works projects, mainly railways and canals, for those on both sides of the parliamentary stand-off, who might now want to reconsider and co-operate instead. It worked – for a while. The *Reichsrat* passed two annual budgets in a row. Behind the parliamentary façade, politicians negotiated in private with officials over which projects could be built where, and competed for favours from the various ministries. It was interest politics at its most naked. Even then, as predicted by the law of diminishing returns, the effect could not last, as those disappointed by the economic goods on offer returned to obstruction to get more. Koerber began running out of economic favours, and so he returned to Taaffe's fare of administrative and educational rewards, but these tended to have the wrong effect. Economic development had regional results, which could bind national rivals to pursue mutual benefit, whereas administrative and educational questions were almost inherently divisive, nationally: instead of focusing on the benefit of more educational institutions, politicians focused on what the language of instruction would be – indeed that was the point of having an *Italian* law faculty, or a *Czech* technical institute.

Koerber recorded several successes. His recovery programme sparked an economic boom, which helped quiet the political and national situation. He also, eventually, was able to negotiate an Economic Compromise agreement with Hungary, increasing the Hungarian quota by 3 per cent to 34.4 per cent. The final deal was reached on New Year's Eve, 1902/1903, after the emperor-king had threatened to abdicate if no agreement was reached (according to Alexander Spitzmüller). Koerber also greatly liberalised the press laws; above all he provided almost five years of respite, during which government ran fairly smoothly. Yet he was still unable to solve the German-Czech problem, or have his proposals for a major overhaul of the administration accepted.

This is not surprising, as Koerber's plan, very much that of a Habsburg official, would, on the one hand, have greatly increased the number of administrative districts (*Bezirke*), bringing the district prefects (*Bezirkshauptmänner*) closer to the public, but on the other hand, it would have greatly curtailed the power of the provincial assemblies in favour, ostensibly, of more local representative assemblies on the district and (renewed) county level. In actuality this would have created an administratively decentralised aspect to the still *centralised* political bureaucracy in Vienna. It would be 'representative government carefully defined and kept in a glass aquarium'. This completely conflicted with the actual political interests in the provinces, and would have made local government the state's pet, not its master; so it was totally rejected, and Koerber resigned on 28 December 1904.

Koerber had succeeded in stabilising Cisleithania's government, run by the 'unpolitical' 'political administration', but Redlich saw a great cost in this: 'the profound demoralisation of Austrian parliamentary representation'. Politics became corrupted, politicians irresponsible, for there was no need to moderate nationalist rhetoric where the serious work of governing was done by the bureaucracy. Nationalists of all stripes and Christian Socials could indulge in Jew-baiting because the Habsburg state would uphold the law, and prevent any (undue) persecution. Hence, in Redlich's opinion, it was Koerber's system that 'paved the way for unbridled demagogy in Austria, both nationalistic and socialistic'.

The turn to interest politics can be seen as a very modern move, and it did have the benefit of bringing the socialists into the political fold, as just another interest group, and former radicals, such as Lueger's Christian Socials, and even some German and Czech nationalists, now became fixtures of the new politics, or were at least domesticated by its sticks and carrots. The biggest gainer of all in this was the imperial bureaucracy itself. It became more arbiter than mediator between the parties, and the focus of power around which the national interests competed for attention.

The new situation did not really encourage compromise between the national groups. Leaving the running of the country to the bureaucracy allowed the nationalists to continue their conflict without the need for giving up (or gaining) anything. There were official compromises in the national question, at the periphery, most substantively the Moravian Compromise of 1905, but even this was not so much a compromise as partition, a separation of Czechs and Germans into separate curias with mutual veto rights over nationally relevant questions, such as education (and with the members of the large landowners' curia not required to have a national identity). As interpreted by the courts, this ended up with the constitutionally guaranteed rights of individuals to enjoy their national expression being turned into a system where nationality was ascribed to the individual, forced on them regardless of the individual's will, where the nation, not the individual, had power, the reverse of the multicultural, complex and diversity-encouraging logic that had typified the Monarchy (and Moravia) to this point.

The real centre of national conflict in Cisleithania, Bohemia, showed no real prospect of solution. The new, hegemonic bureaucracy, with its chief bureaucrat in Franz Joseph, was not necessarily very concerned by this. Bureaucrats benefited the most in terms of power. The emperor himself always expressed hope for a solution of the German/Czech conflict, but privately he was pessimistic of one. He might even have thought such a compromise would be detrimental, because a German-Czech agreement would, as in Hungary, lead to a loss of *his* power.

On the other hand, the new system itself was sapping the Monarchy's, and the monarch's, power in other ways, especially in foreign policy and the military. With its frequent use of Article 14, the system could get legislation passed by decree to keep government going, but there was an 'invisible line' beyond which this 'ex lex' procedure was regarded by political consensus as invalid: when it involved major increases in taxation or the conscription quotas. At a time when increased revenues and more army funding were becoming ever more necessary, they were not available, as this would have been too much for the fragile compromise between government and parties.

The ongoing crisis, and the executive's inability really to rule rather than just administer, had Count Bernhard von Bülow, the German chancellor in Berlin, wondering in 1905 if the Monarchy should not be turned into a neutral 'monarchic, big Switzerland', to be left to sort out her nationalities problems on her own.

Electoral Reform: Austria Is Given Hungary's Medicine

Bülow's views were as much shaped in 1905 by what was happening in Hungary as they were by Cisleithania's impasse. In the 1890s, the Tisza regime had, in effect, continued without Tisza: following liberal economic and social policies, often more liberal than Cisleithania, as shown by the institution of civil marriage in the mid-1890s, and remaining intensely, chauvinistically, nationalist, as much, if not more, against 'Austria' as the minority nationalities. The Army Bill Crisis of 1889–90 had seen the extraction of concessions from the Austrian emperor, and the divisions in Cisleithania saw Magyar nationalist pressure extract more concessions at the end of the 1890s – but they were never enough.

In the wake of the Badeni Crisis, the Hungarian prime minister Baron Deszö Bánnfy was able to procure good terms from a crisis-harried, and hence disadvantaged, Cisleithanian government. As a quid pro quo, partly to avoid such crises in the future, Bánnfy and his counterpart, the Cisleithanian finance minister and Young Czech politician, Josef Kaizl, had agreed on what became known as the Ischl Clause. This would have made the customs union automatically renewable unless voted down by either parliament; because the emperor-king would have veto power over any such abrogation this would have guaranteed the economically very productive customs union. Yet it was precisely such a solidification of the Compromise that Magyar nationalists detested, and so the Compromise legislation was obstructed, leading to the fall of Bánnfy's government. Kálmán Széll's subsequent government refused to accept the Ischl Clause and dragged negotiations on the Compromise up to the final hour, of New Year's Eve 1902/3.

Kaizl's failure to have the Ischl Clause accepted and hence buttress the empire's unity resulted in his falling back on Czech nationalist goals, packing the Finance Ministry in Vienna with Czech officials (a side-effect of the horse-trading between bureaucrats and nationalist politicians). The Magyar animus against any strengthening of the Compromise thus perpetuated the dualist crisis and increased divisive nationalist pressures in Cisleithania.

By 1902, another divisive issue had once again begun to dominate Hungarian politics: the Army Bill. This version modestly raised conscription levels, in line with population growth. Koerber had got it through the *Reichsrat*, but it also needed the Hungarian parliament's approval. Yet again, nationalist criticisms began of the 'imperial' nature of the (now) k.u.k. army, and there was an attempt to 'nationalise' its Hungarian regiments by making them Magyar-speaking, with Magyar and not German the language of command. This was another of those indirect attacks on the status of minority languages in 'Hungarian' non-Magyar ranks, but even more controversially it was a direct assault on the emperor-king's preference to keep German as *the* language of command to preserve *his* army's unity. The language controversy led to obstruction and the replacement of Széll in June 1903 by the former Croatian *ban*, and strongman, Khuen-Héderváry, also an avid Magyar chauvinist, but he could not calm his fellow Magyar politicians either.

The king now drew his line in the sand. On 17 September 1903 Franz Joseph made clear in the Chłopy Order his complete refusal to undermine his prerogative over the army, its unity or 'existing organisation' (including German as the language of command). This set off a crisis to rival the Badeni Crisis, with obstruction and street riots threatening order. Franz Joseph attempted compromise. Khuen-Héderváry was replaced by István Tisza, son of the former prime minister, in November 1903, and relations were patched up with the Magyar parties. In the summer of 1904, the king agreed to the *Honvéd* (Hungary's national militia) gaining its own artillery. Koerber warned that this would undermine the army's cohesion, but Franz Joseph made the concession anyway.

In the autumn, however, the crisis peaked again, with Tisza passing anti-obstruction legislation, much as in the Badeni Crisis with the Lex Falkenhayn, and with similar results: more obstruction and public violence. Tisza responded by holding an election in January 1905, but without the usual 'Mamelukian' rigging, which led to a devastating defeat for the liberals, and left the opposition Coalition, the enemies of the army, in full control. The king invited the opposition leaders, Gyula Andrássy (son of his former foreign minister) and Ferenc Kossuth (son of his nemesis), to form a government, but the terms offered were unacceptable. Eventually, in June, the king appointed a dependable, loyal general, Baron Géza Fejérváry, as prime minister of a Hungarian version of a *Beamtenministerium*, which was by now normal in Cisleithania but not in Hungary. In reaction, the opposition, returning to hallowed pre-dualist traditions, called for passive resistance by the county officials and a tax strike by 'patriots'. Franz Joseph escalated. His Hungarian interior minister, Joseph Kristóffy published a proposal to expand the franchise from 7 per cent to 16 per cent of the population.

From today's perspective, even from the perspective of most Western European states at this time, most of which effectively had universal male suffrage, this was not that radical; but it would have been devastating to the Magyar political nation, for it would have given the vote not only to a large portion of the lower classes, but also to many non-Magyars. At first hesitantly, then after another confrontation in September decisively, Franz Joseph used his ace-in-the-hole, the nationalities card.

As in the Bosnia Crisis, constitutional politics and nationalist politics fused over the question of who 'the people' were, or which of them were going to get the power of the vote.

The Magyar leadership was horrified by the prospect of facing the expanded, multinational electorate, but also at the royal assertion of power, and their initial instinct was to resist, as in 1848 and the 1860s. What had worked then did not work so well now. Partly due to the Magyar elite's own strategy, Hungary was no longer decentralised and undeveloped. The old county autonomy had been reined in by the exigencies of modern local government, leading to reliance on investment and expertise from Budapest, but also by a consciously nationalist, centralising policy that made a safely Magyar parliament the arbiter of the nationally more diverse localities. The executive power that shocked the Magyar leadership was a monster of their own making. The Fejérváry government imposed new local county governors (*föispáns*) and ordered the suspension of subsidies to non-compliant counties and of the salaries of recalcitrant municipal officials. National resistance collapsed.

The government was shunned by the political class, but it had control of the military and police, and the compliance of large swathes of the disenfranchised non-Magyar population and the Magyar lower classes. When parliament was dissolved on 19 February 1906, with the use of troops, the decreeing of radical electoral reform, another revolution from above, looked to be the next inevitable step. At this point, a chastened Magyar leadership, seeing the peril of the situation, offered conditional surrender – and Franz Joseph accepted. The resulting secret agreement met the emperor-king's minimal demands over the army and the acceptance of the dualist settlement. It also committed the Magyar leadership to electoral reform, but on their terms, which meant hardly any reform at all.

In 1871, historians have asserted, Franz Joseph was too optimistic about what he could do to improve fundamentally the structures of the Monarchy. In 1906, he has been accused of being too pessimistic, and cynical, in a situation which was to prove his last realistic opportunity to change the Monarchy's structures and give it a stable basis. In this view, electoral reform was quite feasible and would have led to a less chauvinistic, more interest-based, pliable, multinational politics, similar to Cisleithania after 1879, more suited to remodelling the Monarchy and fairer to and more inclusive of the masses of Hungarian society, Magyar and non-Magyar. This, however, would have required daring and imagination to pull off, and would have risked social revolution. Ultimately, Franz Joseph was more interested in the short-term getting his way concerning the army and his prerogatives, rather than long-term issues of the political development of Hungary; as the old-new Magyar leadership were now prepared to meet his demands on these narrow issues, he traded in the nationalities card: electoral reform. It was for this cynical exploitation and abandonment of electoral reform in Hungary that Oszkár Jászi later condemned Franz Joseph for being a major instigator of the 'final moral disintegration' of the Monarchy.

In the May elections, the opposition Coalition won a large majority, and Sandor Wekerle's new ministry continued a policy of chauvinism in education towards the minority nationalities, as in Apponyi's Education Law of 1907, but adopted a moderate approach towards the Compromise, and a very slow, drawn-out consideration of electoral reform.

Ironically, the Hungarian events had resulted in electoral reform taking wing in Cisleithania. The movement for universal suffrage had been building for years, led by the Social Democrats. It was only when Franz Joseph, in October 1905, followed through on the logic of his own policy in Hungary and officially backed the principle of universal male suffrage that it became feasible, indeed likely. With imperial support, ever larger and more frequent popular demonstrations, and the liberal press ideologically cornered, the *Reichsrat* surrendered to democracy. In the period of over a year in which reform was discussed, nationalism for once took a back seat to a larger question. Even so, much of the negotiation was about national interests. Constituencies were eventually apportioned on a basis that combined demographic with economic considerations. Germans received more seats than their numbers alone justified, but less than their proportion of tax contribution indicated.

It took three ministries to pass the bill, Gautsch (December 1904–May1906) and Prince Conrad von Hohenlohe (May–June 1906) falling before Max Beck, known as the right-hand man to the heir, Franz Ferdinand, was able to pass an electoral reform providing for universal male suffrage for *Reichsrat* elections (and only *Reichsrat* elections – provincial assembly elections remained on the old, restricted curial franchises). This became law on 20 January 1907.

In Hungary Franz Joseph used electoral reform as a bargaining chip, but in Cisleithania he supported it with real dedication. One explanation proffered is that he saw in an expanded franchise, as had Taaffe in 1893, a means to solve the national conflict. The common people – peasants and workers – would be more loyal to the empire than the nationalist middle classes; they would put basic, economic, supra-national interests above national ones. Evidence suggests this is a little too idealistic concerning Franz Joseph. When elections in May 1907 produced a large number of socialist deputies (87 out of 516), reports say that the emperor was not happy. It could be instead that he preferred working with chastened, more amenable, bourgeois nationalist parties, threatened by the mass parties, than with the actual representatives of the lower classes. Even more cynically, he might have supported electoral reform in Cisleithania to keep the Magyars in line *after* the 1906 deal. The emperor's support was, nonetheless, crucial in getting the (male) democratic franchise in Austria in 1907.

The new, democratic *Reichsrat* did not fulfil its initial promise. There was a reduction of the nationalist presence, with two of the biggest losers being the Young Czechs and the radical German Nationalists, and two of the biggest winners being the Christian Socials, now viewed as a Catholic 'imperially-loyal' party (!), and the internationalist Social Democrats. At first Beck was able to rule through a mainly parliamentary ministry, and even gained a favourable Economic Compromise from the (somewhat chastened) Hungarians, with the quota going from 34.4 per cent to 36.4 per cent, at the cost of more concessions in constitutional details. However, there were now thirty (30) parties represented in the *Reichsrat*, which militated against easy collective functioning of the legislature, and the new, nationally based mass parties proved just as liable to nationalist demagoguery as their bourgeois predecessors.

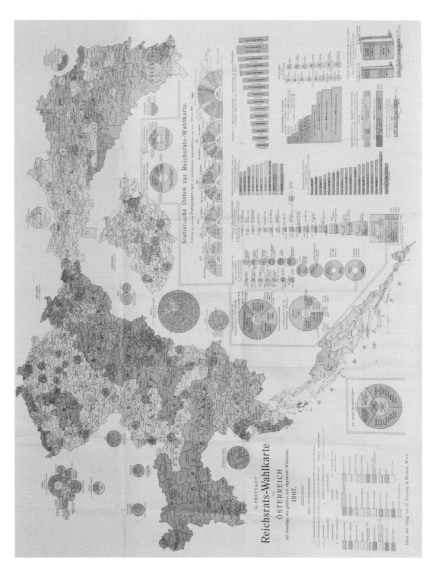

Figure 14. Large-scale wall map of the results of the 1907 *Reichsrat* election, the first general election in Cisleithania with universal male suffrage. Note how the large blank in the middle of the map around which Cisleithania curves (Hungary) is sensibly used for comprehensive statistical representation of the complex, multinational electoral results – and a map of Moravia's Czech electoral districts' results (a consequence of the Moravian Compromise of 1905). (Published courtesy of Oliver Rathkolb.)

In the provinces, the retention of the old curial franchises meant nothing much had changed. Bohemia continued to be an unsolved national conflict: despite occasional hopes that the 'paper-thin' differences could be overcome, they never were. The Young Czech leader Karel Kramář hosted a provocative Neo-Slav Congress in Prague in July 1908. In Galicia, the conflict between Poles and Ruthenes (with Jews somewhere in the crossfire) flared up again. Beck, advised by Rudolf Sieghart, the most influential behind-the-scenes operator in Austrian politics since the Koerber ministry, carried on in increasingly difficult circumstances, with not only national conflicts to mediate but also the Wahrmund Affair, a return to pre-national cultural politics. This saw a clash between German Liberal anticlericals and the German, Catholic Christian Socials over the right to academic freedom of Ludwig Wahrmund, professor of ecclesiastical law at Innsbruck. When the Bosnian Crisis (see below) put Beck in a vulnerable position, the Christian Socials (along with Beck's former patron, Franz Ferdinand) arranged for his defeat in November 1908.

Beck was followed by another official, Baron Richard Bienerth, who had to deal with ever more national conflicts. Violence in Prague led to the imposition of martial law yet again in December 1908. Czech obstruction in the *Reichsrat* led, once more, to the use of Article 14, for the first time for six years. The 1911 elections saw a resurgence of national parties. The German National Alliance, an alliance of 'Liberals' and 'Nationalists' that excluded a number of Jewish Liberal deputies and included racially antisemitic German Nationalist candidates, gained; the Christian Socials and the Polish Club, government parties with ministers in the cabinet, lost seats; and Bienerth resigned as a result. The Social Democrats made more gains, but had also been split on national lines, with the Czech party in Prague declaring its independence in 1910, and formally splitting off as the autonomist Czechoslavic Social Democratic Party in 1911 – taking nine-tenths of the socialists' electoral support among Czechs with it.

The democratically elected parliament was as riven by nationalism as the old. Bienerth was replaced by Gautsch (yet again) in June 1911, and then in November, with Bohemia yet again in turmoil, Karl Stürgkh became prime minister. With the international scene, especially in the Balkans, becoming ever more threatening, Stürgkh was able to get the Military Bill of 1912 passed, which did see a considerable rise in military expenditure and was considered a major legislative achievement, given the fractiousness of parliament.

National conflicts worsened and multiplied in the provincial assemblies. Apart from Bohemia, there was continuing conflict in Galicia; in

Carniola and Styria Slovenes and Germans clashed; in Trieste the Italian patriciate clashed with Slovene immigrants and demanded an Italian university in their city, not in Trent. But it was in Bohemia that things remained unresolved, and were worsening. In July 1913 the German members boycotted the Diet, and Stürgkh used this as an opportunity to dissolve the provincial legislature, suspend its autonomous administration and introduce an imperial administrative commission to govern the province instead. In March 1914, Czech deputies in the *Reichsrat* protested at what was seen as a return to naked absolutism with total obstruction of the parliament, and Stürgkh responded by dissolving that assembly as well. In July 1914, Cisleithania was being ruled more or less as it had been in the 1850s, as a bureaucratic dictatorship.

The political system was not working any better in Hungary. The old antagonisms soon returned after the 1905–1907 crisis. Wekerle resigned in April 1909, and after several months of deadlock, Khuen-Héderváry returned in January 1910, basing his government on the old, pro-dualist Liberals. Tisza (son) now reorganised the Liberals as the 'Party of Work', and in the May elections this time used all the advantages of government, as his father had, to produce a crushing victory: 258 government deputies against 110 for all four Coalition Parties. Khuen remained prime minister, but the real holder of power was Tisza. Khuen's government continued the old Liberal combination of compromise with the monarch and chauvinism towards the minority nationalities. It still was unable to get the Military Bill of 1912 passed, due to obstruction, and another serious political crisis ensued. Khuen was replaced by László Lukács in April 1912, and Tisza became president of the Lower House.

Tisza was now determined to assert order in Hungarian politics, even if this meant the effective end of the independence of the Hungarian Parliament. Tisza countered obstruction by having new, very restrictive Standing Orders passed by his large parliamentary majority, and succeeded in getting the Military Bill passed. Tisza had police eject deputies from the chamber at one point. On 23 May 1912, 'Bloody Thursday', he sent in the army to disperse protesters outside the parliament. Tisza was now virtual dictator of Hungary, managing the country through a 'parliamentary absolutism', an obverse variant of Cisleithania's 'bureaucratic absolutism'. On the last day of 1912, Tisza presented an electoral reform bill, pre-sanctioned by King Franz Joseph, that hardly expanded the franchise at all. The pact between Tisza and the king had been sealed. In June 1913, Lukács resigned, and Tisza became prime minister. From now on, as long as Tisza could provide the votes and monies required, the 'absentee landlord' would tolerate oppressive Magyar hegemony.

In both Cisleithania and Hungary, the executive, the emperor-king, had achieved control over government, but in diametrically opposite ways, and with national and social pressures only uneasily held down on both sides of the Leitha. Things might look calm, even orderly, but the everlasting *domestic* crisis continued. If a foreign crisis occurred, given this fragile situation at home, all bets were off as to how the Monarchy's authorities might respond.

Habsburg State and Society before 1914

That, at least, is how the Monarchy's political trials leading up to 1914 were traditionally narrated for most of the twentieth century. For the last thirty years or so, however, more or less since the beginning of the end of the Cold War in the mid-1980s, a quite different, revisionist approach arose, and this has in turn now become the conventional wisdom among academics (if not the general public). This view asks us to look away from the political shenanigans in Vienna and Budapest, and instead concentrate on what was happening on the local level, and in the economy and society more generally. Once we do this, we see that there is indeed much to be said for the argument that the Habsburg Monarchy was doing much better than the political record would suggest.

This should not be that surprising. Various European countries had major political crises in this period. France at the turn of the century was rent asunder by the Dreyfus Affair; in Germany, the Zabern Affair caused a major crisis in military-civilian relations at the end of 1913; in Britain there was the perpetual Irish Question, which was approaching the boil by 1913, and also the major constitutional crisis of 1909–1911, between the Liberal government and the House of Lords. Tsarist Russia had seen a full-blown revolution in 1905 and was reverting to crisis by 1914, so the Monarchy was not at all alone in having political problems, and it can be argued that these problems could have been overcome, or at least lived with, had not war intervened.

The economy was doing well, growing at a faster rate than the British economy and almost catching up to Western European standards, especially in its more developed regions such as the area around Vienna and Bohemia. The politically inspired economic policy of Koerber had helped spark an economic boom, and one of the Monarchy's major political failures, its inability to provide a large enough military budget, also had its very positive side, because this meant that funds could be used on domestic investments. These might have been politically motivated as well, to buy the support of various nationalist politicians, but many of these measures had positive economic outcomes nonetheless. This was

Figure 15. The ironworks at Vitkovice, Moravia. Developed by the
Rothschilds and Gutmanns from the 1830s, this integrated complex of
coal mines and ironworks became a symbol of the technological and
economic progress, and prosperity, of the Monarchy.
(Published with permission of the Austrian National Library.)

particularly the case in the peripheral regions, such as Galicia, which
might not have received as much economic investment without the
need to placate nationalist political demands; economic historians have
concluded that, while there was still a steep gradient between the developed and more lagging areas, economic development in the Monarchy
overall was more equally distributed than in the United States at the time.

On the local level of everyday life, this was generally an optimistic
era, in which local politicians and leaders, usually nationalists of one
sort or another, invested in a future that assumed the continuation of
the Habsburg state, whether it be investing in new railways, or new
barracks for prospective military units and the spending that came with
them. While politics might be redolent with adversarial, often anti-
imperialist, nationalist rhetoric, the politicians' actions were more
often than not evidence of the ways in which nationalist goals profited
from the Habsburg state context. This was an era of great nationalist
success. Prague, for instance, became a city governed largely by

Czechs for Czechs; Ljubljana one governed by Slovenes for Slovenes. It was also an era in which the incipient client-politics of the Taaffe era came to fruition. In local communal and provincial political life, instead of the minimal-government approach of the German Liberal patriciates, the new, 'modern', nationally oriented mass politics saw politicians elected by lower-middle-class constituents greatly expanding the services that those constituents demanded, in such forms as cultural and educational institutions, transport infrastructure, social welfare and public health. Local, provincial and national politicians might have protested against the oppressive Habsburg state, but they also bought into the bureaucratic gravy train. Initiatives for modernisation often came from the localities, whether this involved peasant co-operatives in Galicia (to bypass Jewish traders), tram systems in middle-sized towns, or prestige cultural projects, to boost civic and national pride, such as the Municipal (Polish National) Theatre in Cracow. There was national development *within* a Habsburg context, and often with the Habsburg bureaucracy's support.

Figure 16. The Municipal Theatre, Cracow, opened in 1893. This theatre functioned as the informal national theatre of Poland.
(Published with permission of the Austrian National Library.)

There was a sense of entering a new, advanced, modern world, where the problems of the past would be swept aside. Karl Kraus put it well, if ironically, when he stated in 1897 that 'Vienna is now being demolished into a big city', and the sense for many citizens (*Bürger*) of the Monarchy was that the future that lay ahead, based on the ruins of the feudal past, would be a national one, within a supra-national or multinational Habsburg context.

The decades-long nationalist confrontation in the political world was also an interaction of those nationalist politicians with the Habsburg bureaucracy, and it is difficult at times to see who co-opted whom. Koerber might have started the 'politics of the bazaar', but it was often the nationalist politicians, also in the localities and provinces, whose logrolling and negotiations influenced where public monies were spent. Local civil society was very active, if usually in nationalist form, but once a nationalist group had secured national dominance of a town council, national issues would then take a back seat to more nuts-and-bolts issues of local governance, which caused political divisions, whether the politicians involved were nationalists or not. As elsewhere in the Western modernising societies of the time, local politics was about giving the public, or at least the people who had voted you in, the services they required.

The Monarchy provided a quite effective context in which this social and economic modernisation could take place. The economic development was greatly helped by the customs union with Hungary. Austria-Hungary was one of the biggest 'single markets' in Europe at the time. It was also helped, as was the Monarchy's social development, by the fact that, overall, the Monarchy provided the rule of law in its extensive realm. Cisleithania had a separation of administrative and judicial systems at all levels, one of the great achievements of Austrian liberalism. This enabled a fully independent judiciary with judicial review, and the records of its two Supreme Courts, the *Reichsgericht* and *Verwaltungsgerichtshof*, were very respectable. Hungary did not have quite the same full separation of the judicial and administrative functions but there was a relatively good legal system there as well. There were abuses of the legal system, especially in Hungary, and the administration in Cisleithania did not always follow the decisions of the two Supreme Courts to the letter either. Perhaps the bureaucracy and legal system did not quite reach the standards of the Prussian system or other Western legal and administrative systems, but in terms of efficiency and honesty in governance, the Monarchy was significantly better than regimes to its south and east. Relatively speaking, and especially compared to what came after, the Monarchy in this era did provide an 'age of security'.

The Habsburg state also protected national rights – in Cisleithania. When it came to education, culture and language use, the two Supreme Courts made an effort to honour the guarantee of national equality in the December Constitution of 1867, and it was the decisions of these courts that were often used by nationalists to further their causes. No side was outwardly satisfied by the state's protection of national rights, but by 1914 Cisleithania did present the picture of a society with many flourishing national cultures, which implicitly suggests considerable success for the protection of national rights. (Hungary was a different story.)

The national 'problem' was also 'solved' in several particular, provincial compromises, resulting from negotiations between the nationalist politicians under the auspices of the officials in the *Beamtenministerien*. The oldest and most significant was the Moravian Compromise of 1905, followed by the Bukovina Compromise of 1910. In these ad hoc settlements, feuding national groups – Germans and Czechs in Moravia; Ruthenes, Romanians, Jews, Germans, Poles and Magyars in Bukovina – ended their disputes by agreeing to divide the political system into national curias, in effect a form of virtual partition. Similar compromises in Galicia (Poles and Ruthenes) and Budweis (Germans and Czechs) were set to be introduced in 1914, but were never implemented.

As noted above, one of the ironies of these compromises, especially the Moravian settlement, was that the consequence was to transform the constitutional rights of individuals to their national culture and expression, as given in the 1867 liberal constitution, to a right of the nation over the individual. The fear of people crossing over to the 'wrong' national group led to national identity being ascribed to individuals by 'objective factors', so that the national curias became as much prisons as fortresses for the members of each nation, and took away the very Habsburg, Central European notion of multiple, inclusive choice when it came to identity and belonging. Compromise in this sense perpetuated division rather than overcoming it.

These compromises also were possible because they were in provinces not central to the Habsburg state, and the central nationality problem in Cisleithania – Bohemia – remained unsolved in 1914, indeed had caused the political and constitutional crisis which was to see the Monarchy go to war without a sitting parliament in Vienna. On the other hand, there were signs of a lessening of the temperature level in Bohemia as well. An article by Heinrich Friedjung, the same Heinrich Friedjung that had been the German nationalist ideologue of the late 1870s, appeared in the *Neue Freie Presse* on 3 October 1913, saying the time of mass violence had passed and compromise in Bohemia was now necessary, citing Adolf Fischhof (whom he had once derided) on the need for Austrians to reach agreement. Even in Hungary, by 1914, there were signs of a readiness to compromise between Tisza's government and the Serbo-Croatian opposition in the Croatian *Sabor*. The national conflict seemed to be losing steam.

Or at least, one can argue, the national question was changing. There was a powerful trend of implicit federalisation in Cisleithania, because of the growth and nationalisation of the communal and provincial bureaucracies that had developed to cope with the new demands of a modernising economy and society. If central representative politics had been substituted by administration as the main forum for nationalist and political negotiation, the emergence of these regional bureaucracies, under the control of the autonomous communes or the provincial

Figure 17. Poster from 1908 for the Austrian Lloyd. Austria's main shipping company had a wide international range. It was particularly well positioned in Trieste for service, through the Suez Canal, to India and beyond.
(Published with permission from the Albertina.)

assemblies, rather than directly under the Vienna-centred Habsburg bureaucracy, could be seen as a natural restructuring, administratively, on federalising lines. Bohemia's provincial, assembly-based bureaucracy (separate from the Habsburg imperial bureaucracy in the province) was almost entirely Czech; Prague had been once a German-speaking town, but by 1914 Germans were a small minority within an overwhelmingly Czech city, as the city population had been boosted by Czech immigration. The Czech-nationalist-led city council ran a mostly Czech-speaking administration, and was angling to make Prague's administration *only* Czech-speaking. Part of Friedjung's moderation concerning the Bohemian conflict was his reading the writing on the wall on the direction of Bohemian governance; this de facto nationalising and federalising of the state had already occurred in Galicia, long ago, and was happening in the Slovene provinces too, to an extent. There was a reason why a Czech nationalist politician such as Karel Kramář, despite his 'neo-Slavism', stated in July 1914 that he was prepared to work *within* the governmental system of the Monarchy, that 'the Czechs lean in no direction outside the empire'. Recent experience had shown that when it came to realising their goal of effectively having Czech-language-based government in Bohemia and the Bohemian capital, Prague, the Czechs were winning. So why would the Czechs have wanted to break up a system that had gained them so much in a relatively short time? The Monarchy was, one can argue, turning itself into a form of multinational federation – at least the national groups were realizing their goals *within* the Monarchy's parameters.

Central Europe 1900

Another major positive move of the pro-Monarchy historiography is to point to the immense cultural achievement of 'Central Europe 1900'. There is not necessarily any contradiction between political crisis and cultural achievement, and indeed the theme of the dialectical contrast between 'decadence and innovation' has been a mainstay of the cultural history of the Monarchy during this period. The idea of a straightforward, direct linkage between political decline and cultural efflorescence is problematic, but there are ways in which the national conflict does appear to have helped raise the cultural and intellectual levels of the Monarchy's society.

Education and culture were, after all, primary fields of national competition, and the conflict resulted in large investments in (national) schools and cultural institutions by all sides; the state also invested in the various national cultures and their institutions, in order to placate the nationalist camps, as well as, at the same time in Cisleithania, trying to encourage an *Austrian* modern culture, which explains the initial support of the 'Austrian' Viennese Secession, and the founding of the 'Modern Gallery' in the Belvedere in 1903 to promote *Austrian* modern art. In Hungary, nationalist ideology meant that large resources were poured into Magyarisation, which meant boosting educational institutions in the non-Magyar periphery (at the cost, ironically, of the Magyar populace in the central plain), as well as into the prestige-leader of the national capital, Budapest. This extra investment in education and culture partly explains the relatively high cultural and intellectual levels in the Monarchy, which served as a foundation of what became the region's cultural prominence.

The cultural diversity of both halves of the Monarchy produced in itself a very creative matrix for a plethora of hybrid, marginocentric cultural forms, which added complexity, but also variety and perspective, to Central European modern culture. Where there was a clearly hegemonic national culture, such as in France or Britain, it is easy to fall into the delusion that there was *one* form of cultural modernism, and to trace the narrative of that singular cultural movement's development, but in the fractured, multinational environment of Habsburg Central Europe, modern cultural developments interacted with the various national, ethnic

Aus dem Café Griensteidl: »Das Lesezimmer«. (Die Schriftsteller-Schwemme.)
Photogr Aufnahme der illustrirten Wochenschrift »Die vornehme Welt«

Figure 18. Reading room of the Café Griensteidl, 1897. The coffeehouse was a central institution of civic and cultural life in the Monarchy.
(Published with permission of the Austrian National Library.)

and religious cultural traditions in a kaleidoscopic manner that makes any attempt to fully categorise 'Central European modernism' virtually impossible. Grossly simplifying, there were approximately four ways in which modern culture developed in Central Europe, in relation to the nationally charged context.

The first and most obvious was a modern, *nationalist* culture, which took the latest cultural developments and put them in the service of the national cause. In Germany, Richard Wagner's music served this national-identity-reinforcing function; for the Czechs, the music of Bedřich Smetana, especially *Ma vlast*, is a classic – Romantic – example. Another example, for Hungary, would be Franz Liszt's *Hungarian Rhapsodies*; as it turned out, however, these were based on gypsy music, rather than ethnically 'authentic' Magyar folk music, as Zoltán Kodály showed in the early 1900s. This brings us to the second way in which modern culture interacted with national culture in the Monarchy. Modernist culture has often been thought to be non-nationalist, even anti-nationalist, but in Central Europe Béla Bartók took the pentatonic scale discovered by Kodály in Magyar folk music (played not only by Magyars but other peasant groups in Hungary and Transylvania) and created a *modern national* music, which then influenced the mainstream of modern music, from a Magyar ethnonational source in the form itself. Depending on the context, therefore, it was quite possible to have an actual *national* aspect to modernist culture.

One of the intentional ironies of Kodály and Bartók's work on Magyar folk music, however, was to show how much different, 'national' ethnic musical traditions had fruitfully interacted to develop their different musical traditions, so 'Magyar' national music also was part of a larger, Central European (and Central Asian) musical universe. There was no such thing as pure, national culture, from this perspective, even if there was a basis for developing a national culture. This provided the third way in which modern culture and national cultures interacted in the Monarchy. The emphasis on the multiplicity and diversity of cultural sources and identities had for a long time been a central component of Habsburg cultural self-understanding, as reflected in the *Crown Prince Project*. Yet this was not just an ideological claim, but reflected the realities of the complex cultural context of the region, also in its modern forms. The most characteristic form of modern mass popular culture of the region, operetta, represented just this sort of multinational, cultural pluralism. On the one hand the *Viennese* operetta came to represent Austrian cultural hegemony in the region; on the other, the themes of operettas were often multinational, as in Strauss's *Zigeunerbaron*, or ironic commentaries on the multinational political and cultural context of the times, as in the greatest of the prewar operettas, Franz Lehár's *The Merry Widow* (based on a French original play), and the musical forms used were almost always multinational by definition, with German waltzes, Czech polkas, and Hungarian csardases and other forms put in the mix. On a higher musical plane, Gustav Mahler's interest in a musical eclecticism, bringing together diverse melodies to produce a greater harmonic whole, presents a similar approach. The significance attached to language, especially the comparative study of language, in Central European intellectual life, can be attributed to this multinational, multicultural, and hence multilinguistic context, where the complex context allowed relativising, pluralist perspectives not so easily available in a monocultural, monolingual environment.

At the same time, there was a fourth form of interaction between modern culture and national culture, or rather a non-interaction. Modern culture could provide precisely that more abstract space that could act as a refuge from the nationalist and antisemitic collectivist

Figure 19. Mahler and friends (from left to right: Max Reinhardt, Gustav Mahler, Carl Moll, Hans Pfitzner, Joseph Hoffmann), Vienna, 1905.
(Published with permission of the Austrian National Library.)

politics that dominated Habsburg society; modernism could therefore also be non-national, and international, a challenge to the nationalist, national, or even multinational, culture of others. At various times, and in various aspects, this non-national, international modernism could be seen in the work of figures such as Adolf Loos, Otto Wagner, Josef Hoffmann and the early philosophy of Ludwig Wittgenstein. The early *Wiener Werkstätte* consciously sought to bring in modern influences from outside the Monarchy, to reattach it to the modern, international world, of French *art nouveau*, and the design of the Glasgow School of Charles Rennie Mackintosh, among others.

It is worth mentioning here that the understandable emphasis on the interaction of the national question with modern culture has sometimes obscured the fact that the Monarchy also had an excellent record in what we might term 'standard' modernity (if there is such a thing). In nationally (even perhaps politically) neutral fields such as medicine and the natural sciences, there were major achievements. In the first half of the century, Gregor Mendel had pioneered genetics, Christian Doppler the understanding of light waves. The Viennese School of Medicine was the most prestigious in nineteenth-century Europe, quite apart from the development of Freudian psychoanalysis. In the second half of the century, scientific dynasties such as the Liebens and Exners, involved in business and government as well as science, helped create a fertile ground for scientific enquiry. Ernst Mach (as in supersonic speed numbers) developed a radically positivist philosophy of science which was to inspire both Albert Einstein's relativity theory and the later logical positivism of the interwar Vienna Circle (whose origins lie in the last decade of the Monarchy). Together with his friendly rival Ludwig Boltzmann, Mach made Vienna a major centre of experimental and theoretical physics. From its founding in 1910, the Institute for Radium Research (the Monarchy being a major source of pitchblende) made major contributions to what became nuclear physics. The greatest breakthroughs in that field were to take place later, and elsewhere; but it is striking how many leading figures in the field came from the Monarchy: Austrians such as Lise Meitner, Erwin Schrödinger and Wolfgang Pauli; Hungarians such as Leo Szilard, Edward Teller, Eugene Wigner and John von Neumann. Many of these scientists were of Jewish descent, and they and other younger émigrés, such as Max Perutz, of necessity fled in the 1930s from a Central Europe taken over by antisemitic fascists, nationalists, and then National Socialists, to seek refuge in the West. Once there, they were to have an immense influence in shaping the natural sciences in the post -Second World War era.

It is ironic, perhaps, that one of the greatest areas of cultural influence of the Monarchy on the English-speaking world, embodied in the *stereotype* of the strangely accented 'mad scientist' from somewhere in Central Europe, is actually so little covered in the historiography of either the Habsburg Monarchy or even 'Central Europe 1900'. Perhaps it is because the natural sciences are a field that appears objective, and hence at first sight not to be a phenomenon linked to nationalism, cultural pluralism or the nature of the Habsburg state. On the other hand, Deborah Coen, in her study of the Exner family, has suggested that what links so many of the Habsburg scientific achievements is their acceptance of uncertainty, and hence their reliance on probability. This does suggest a variant of the Habsburg logic of 'possibilities', and of the Austrian idea.

Certainly, the relationship between modernity, culture and nationalism, or supra-nationalism, in the Monarchy was very complex. Let us use architecture as an illustration: 'Neo-Baroque' was the modern architectural form in this period that was most closely associated with an *Austrian* 'official' identity. Hence it was employed in the *modern* buildings of the new extension of the Hofburg in Vienna (the semicircular building on the Heldenplatz where the National Library now is) and the Ministry of War, both buildings finished in 1913. Yet the architecture of Otto Wagner and Adolf Loos could also be seen as 'Austrian' in their *not* adopting overtly national(ist) forms and instead looking to international influences, especially American and British design. The extent to which 'modern' architecture could straddle the national/international divide is shown by the two Postal Savings Banks in Vienna and Budapest, Wagner's an exercise in an almost de-nationalised, functionalist aesthetic, and Ödön Lechner's an attempt to create a nationalist Magyar *art nouveau*. Both, in their own way, are fine examples of Central European modernist architecture, even though so contradictory, but then it is the multiplicity that is characteristic of the region's modernism.

Added to this is the consideration that the most significant of the cultural and intellectual contributions from the Central European space to modern culture were ones developed against the national and establishment grain. It is no coincidence that Jews had such a large role in this, because if there was an existential crisis caused by the defeat of liberalism by nationalism and antisemitism in Habsburg politics, then it was Habsburg Jewry that was at the heart of it.

There were strong socio-economic factors involved in making Jews so prominent in Central European modern culture. The large Jewish presence in the Monarchy's financial, commercial and also industrial elite was partly a result of Jews, as a scorned religious minority, having been hedged around by various restrictions in the traditional, pre-modern economy, including the exclusion from owning land; partly it was because in the early modern era these very restrictions had resulted in their becoming one of the major entrepreneurial minorities in a largely agrarian region, where entrepreneurial minorities were scarce or looked down on socially. In the modern economy, however, it was precisely such entrepreneurial minorities which benefited from the new freedoms and technologies, and Jewish financiers and entrepreneurs, such as the Rothschilds, were prominent among the winners. This explains partly why so many of modernism's patrons, in Vienna, Budapest, Prague and elsewhere were Jewish or of Jewish descent, whether it be Karl Wittgenstein, the steel magnate of Austria, who financed the Secession Building, Ferdinand Bloch-Bauer, a major sugar industrialist, who paid for Gustav Klimt's portraits of his wife, Adele, or Lajos Hatvany, the son of another sugar baron, who was the major supporter of Budapest's modern literary scene.

The particular nature of Viennese society, with an exclusive court society, and a 'second society' for the members of the higher bureaucracy, academia, liberal professions and a (heavily Jewish) modern-economic elite, also resulted in a prominent social role for Jews. Jewish women, from Fanny von Arnstein, Josephine von Wertheimstein, Berta Zuckerkandl to Eugenia Schwarzwald, played a major role *as salonnières* in providing the connections between artists, writers, and the social elite that might finance or support them. Berta Zuckerkandl, the daughter of one of Vienna's most prominent liberal journalists, Moritz Szeps (once advisor to Crown Prince Rudolf), and married to Emil Zuckerkandl, a leading light in Vienna's School of Medicine, with political, artistic and academic contacts across (mainly second) society, became one of the Secession's main promoters and publicists, and her salon is often seen as at the heart of Viennese modernism.

Furthermore, the prominent position of Jews within the modern 'capitalist' branches of the Monarchy's economy – finance and commerce especially – combined with the equally prominent position of Jews within the advanced secondary schools of the Monarchy's educational system. There is some controversy over why Jewish families were so much more willing or able to send their sons (and daughters) to elite secondary schools in Vienna, Budapest and elsewhere than non-Jews. Social factors certainly played a part, but cannot account for the dramatic differences in attendance rates. Cultural factors – that Jews were more convinced of the benefits of education than most other groups because of their religious tradition and the way that tradition was interpreted in the 'ideology of emancipation' that dominated Jewish integration in the nineteenth

Figure 20. Berta Zuckerkandl, 1908, photographed by Madame d'Ora.
(Published with permission of the Austrian National Library.)

century – appear to me to be an unavoidable part of the explanation.
The net result of the combination of economic, social and cultural factors,
however, is that in Vienna, for example, based on attendance at
Gymnasien (advanced secondary schools), something like two-thirds of
the educated elite of the liberal part of the middle classes, the social

reservoir of modern culture, was Jewish. Jews, therefore, were almost destined to prominence within the modern cultural world in the Monarchy. Yet the political (and social) success of antisemitism and antisemitically tainted nationalism meant that Jews also found themselves in an endangered and adversarial position within Habsburg society. This produced a particularly powerful, and influential, form of Viennese – and Central European – modernism.

It was the Jewish response, as cultural insiders and social and political outsiders, that gave what we now regard as the modern culture of 'Central Europe 1900' its ironic, and critical, edge. There were many different modern cultures in Central Europe around 1900, but it is the modern culture centred on the Jewish experience in, and response to, Central Europe 1900, which has had the most influence on global modern culture, and to which we now pay the most attention, whether this involves Sigmund Freud, Franz Kafka, Ludwig Wittgenstein, Karl Popper, Otto Neurath, Karl Kraus, Gustav Mahler, Arnold Schoenberg or the many other seminal figures who came from this region and shaped our modern world.

Theirs was a variegated, far from uniform response, but a strong 'family resemblance' linking the collective culture was an ironic, 'critical modernism' that had a sense of the limits of modernity and modernisation, and of the truth of language, regardless of which one. The background to this culture was the fact that nationalisation and modernisation, as they happened in the Monarchy, had losers too, including non-nationalised minorities such as acculturated Habsburg Jewry.

Antisemitism did not accompany nationalisation and modernisation in Central Europe by chance, and it was not just the result of an ancient atavism. It was the combination of the traditional place of Jews within pre-modern Central European society and culture, together with the results of modernisation, so that antisemitism was a *modern* phenomenon. Even if in some sense it was a reaction to economic modernisation's effects, it was also, in its exclusory logic, a very modern outgrowth of nationalism itself, the hegemonic form of modernisation, even in the supra-national, dynastic Habsburg Monarchy. Arthur Schnitzler's brilliant analysis of the existential Jewish crisis in this nationalised, antisemitic context, *The Road to the Open*, published in 1908, presented the threat to the situation of Jews from the nationalist, antisemitic logic that would exclude them. It also laid bare the inability of the non-nationalist, Habsburg society, with its non-exclusionary logic, to do anything effectively to counteract this denial of the liberal, individualist basis on which Jewish emancipation, and the Monarchy, had developed since mid-century. It further sketched the many Jewish responses, whether political, social, intellectual, cultural or, ironically, national (in the form of Zionism) that would characterise what we now know as 'Vienna 1900'. In Budapest and Prague, and the other intellectual capitals of Central Europe, there was a similar appreciation of the gap between social and national claims and the realities they masked, a similar ironic criticism of bourgeois verities, but from within.

What this means for our larger discussion is that the best of the achievement of 'Central Europe 1900' was a critique, and adversarial response to, the political and social situation of the Monarchy before 1914. *The Road to the Open*, a contemporary work, was powerful precisely for its analysis not only of the threat of nationalism and antisemitism to Jews, but also its depiction of the lack of a sense of responsibility of the ruling class, as represented in the figure of Georg von Wergenthin. It is not the description of a positive society, but of a dysfunctional one.

A 'Decade of Possibilities': Which Possibilities?

There remain serious problems with the revisionist 'rosy scenario' of the pre-1914 Monarchy. We do not know that the national question would have abated, or if the Monarchy would have solved its nationality problems. Friedjung might have shown some pained optimism, but in an editorial in the *Neue Freie Presse* three days later (6 October 1913), the situation in Bohemia was likened to the situation in Ulster, where loyalists – Ulster's 'English'–had formed the Ulster Volunteer Force and were insisting on separation from the 'Irish'. The editorial spoke of Edward Carson's actions as 'a form of high treason . . . that is the highest form of patriotism'. If German Bohemia was the Monarchy's Ulster, what does this say of the likelihood of a peaceful resolution?

Kramář might speak in public of working within the Monarchy, but Henry Wickham Steed reports Thomas Masaryk, a more moderate figure, as expressing his belief in 1910 that the Monarchy was doomed. In the short term, most nationalist leaders probably did not think outside 'the box' of the Monarchy, but in the long term this is not as clear. In 1908, the Czechs competed as a separate group at the Olympics, under the banner 'Bohème'. The Polish elite in Galicia were undoubtedly most grateful for the refuge offered to Polish national culture and the national cause by the Monarchy, but their goal remained a reunited Polish nation-state, beyond the Habsburg borders. Even among the Ruthenes in 1914 there was a sizeable pro-Russian faction. There were also three other irredentist groups: the Italians in Trentino and even in Trieste could look to Italy; the Romanians in Bukovina and Hungarian Transylvania could look to the nation-state of Romania. Both Italy and

Romania were allies of the Monarchy in 1914, but their national populations within the Monarchy at the very least complicated foreign policy,
especially when the Magyar leadership persecuted Hungarian
Romanians, as it did periodically. In the case of the third irredentist
group, however, that of the South Slavs, as we shall see, there was
a serious and, as it turned out, insuperable problem in the fact that the
external power involved, Serbia, was both expansionist and hostile, and
resembled the Habsburgs' worst nightmare, a South Slav version of
Piedmont.

This had significance because of the relative weakness of the
Monarchy's diplomatic position, which in turn was linked back to the
nationality question. Even if the Monarchy was not being rent asunder by
the nationality conflict, what had happened was that the nationality and
associated constitutional conflicts had greatly weakened the Monarchy in
its primary function, as far as the Habsburg authorities were concerned,
and as far as the emperor-king understood the purpose of his realm, which
was to be a great power. In 1907, Count Franz Conrad von Hötzendorf,
the chief of the k.u.k. General Staff claimed that the Monarchy need not
attend the Second Hague Conference on Disarmament, because the
Monarchy was, effectively, already in a state of permanent disarmament.
By this, he was referring to the fact that the military budget had either
been neglected or blocked for so many years, largely due to the paralysis of
the political system, that the Monarchy was no longer a serious military
force – this at a time when the other great powers had built up their armed
forces. The 1912 Military Bill, as we saw, remedied this somewhat, with
the standing army increased by 22 per cent (from 405,120 to 494,120).
Even then, the joint war minister, General Moritz von Auffenberg, could
not obtain all the budget increases requested to cover the expansion of the
military in the light of the repeated mobilisations triggered by the crisis of
the two Balkan Wars of 1912–13. Some of the increases in the budget
were delayed to take effect in 1914. It was the old problem of politicians
being reluctant to pay for what they regarded as someone else's (Franz
Joseph's) army. The 1912 Bill was still inadequate; the Monarchy's
political impasses had hobbled it externally, relative to the other great
powers.

The Monarchy, domestically, was being run relatively well by the
bureaucracy in both halves, but the administrative system was also in
crisis. The 'dual track' system in Cisleithania, with the central, Habsburg
bureaucracy paralleled by the communal and provincial (assembly-
based) bureaucracies, was not working very well. It was too complicated,
too wasteful and too expensive. Modernisation had great costs, and the
state, as organised, could not afford it. This was true on all levels.

The constitutional settlement of 1867 had left communes and provinces with large responsibilities, which gave them large areas of agency, but without the fiscal instruments to finance them. Larger towns could levy various fees for services and generate income from monopolies, but village communes could not. Provincial assemblies were able to levy surcharges on the state direct tax, and did so at an average of 55 per cent of Cisleithanian direct tax rates (and poorer provinces, such as Galicia levied an average 81.5 per cent surcharge, Bukovina 95 per cent). Yet even at this rate the costs of modern administration and local development mounted, and both communal and provincial budgets went into the red, leading to extremely large debts. Even on the national level, where taxation was somewhat more available, money was getting increasingly short. In 1906, the Monarchy's balance of payments went negative; in 1907, the Monarchy experienced its last budget surplus, all this despite the very low expenditure on the military. Military mobilisation in the crisis of 1908–1909 only made the fiscal situation worse, with large deficits in 1909 and 1910. The bureaucratic solution to the Monarchy's political woes was not working out financially.

One should also not exaggerate the extent to which 'civil society' was gaining in power relative to the officialdom. Modernisation might start with the localities, but the process ultimately led to more complexity, the need for more expertise and more resources, and in the end only the central government could provide this. Despite local initiatives, the dominant form of government remained the étatist bureaucracy. The politicians looked to the bureaucrats for leadership and patronage. Obstruction of parliament became in many instances a way to gain advantage and favour with the officialdom, and positions within it.

In Hungary, the situation was fairly obvious. 'Parliamentary absolutism' had a central, national bureaucracy, under Tisza, rule over the country, and over the subjugated counties. There was a huge expansion of the officialdom (partly to provide jobs to the economically dislocated Magyar gentry). A bureaucracy of 23,000 in 1870 became one of 100,000 by 1902, and by 1918 was at 230,000.

In Cisleithania, the old imperial bureaucracy continued after 1867, shorn of its Hungarian posts. The liberal era reforms had made it somewhat more efficient, but its Josephist tradition remained, and it continued its 'authoritarian state' approach, so that officials did not act as civil servants, but, as Steed put it, believed that 'the people ... is there to be governed'. One can dismiss this as Steed's British bias against state control and over-officiousness. On the other hand, Koerber was one of the best of the officialdom, but his vision of a reformed Austrian administration was precisely of this 'top-down' type, with any representative assemblies to be carefully controlled by the all-wise bureaucracy.

The evidence is that the bureaucracy was indeed not well organised, and slipping back into its old, inefficient ways, which is why a reform commission was instituted in 1911. The history of that commission also suggests that Steed was not entirely wrong when he criticised the bureaucracy's resistance to change, summed up in the expression 'Justament nöt!'. The origin of the commission lay in 1907, in one of the first sessions of the 'democratic' *Reichsrat*, when Joseph Redlich suggested that the main problem with the state's finances was not the tax structure but rather the wastefulness of the administrative inefficiencies of the dual-track system and the imperial bureaucracy. In 1909, he proposed a bill. In 1911, a commission was set up to look into the question, and by 1914 they were still looking into the question. Without the discipline of a functioning parliament, there was no particular call for resolving the issue.

John Deak has described the period of 1904–1914 as 'a decade of possibilities' when it comes to the Habsburg state, but not all possibilities are good ones, or even practical. This sounds all too reminiscent of Robert Musil's description of the world of prewar Vienna in *The Man without Qualities*, where another semi-official body, the Parallel Campaign, spends all its time in talk, and leads nowhere.

The officialdom ballooned as the exigencies of modernisation, such as the nationalised railway system, the ever more sophisticated postal system, new technologies and standards for public health and hygiene systems, required ever more regulation, ever more expert knowledge and ever more paperwork to be processed, and hence ever more bureaucratic positions to be filled. In 1914, the governor of Trieste pleaded for more resources and more official positions to be created, citing the complex tasks that his administration needed to fulfil, concerning military (naval) matters, and Trieste's position as the main shipping hub of the Monarchy, and all in four languages (German, Italian, Slovenian and Croatian), which had led since 1900 to a 'colossal increase in the amount of work'. He complained of not being given enough staff, and one assumes this was a common complaint; even so, there was a vast increase in the number of Habsburg officials, from 80,000 in 1870 to 400,000 by 1910. The cost of the administration had risen from 4 million crowns in 1890 to 18 million crowns by 1911. According to Steed, one-third of public revenues went on administrative expenses. That is why there was a reform commission, which had, however, not found any solution by 1914.

Cisleithania's parliament might have been 'democratised', but the relationship between the state and its citizens was still mainly 'top-down'. Communal and provincial governments had a large degree of autonomy, and they retained their restrictive and curial franchises, which meant that they largely remained in the control of members of the upper and middle classes, with large parts of the public, especially the working class, still unrepresented. The still remote and anonymous state meant that the comfortingly organic concept of the nation could appear a preferable focus of loyalty. Local autonomy did not in itself increase inter-national cooperation, rather there was a tendency to separate out even in bilingual towns, such as Budweis. In rural areas where there had been a tradition of bilingualism, there was a reluctance to give up these inclusive traditions, but there were not that many of these, and it was in the towns, with their nationalised bourgeoisies, that the political trends were set. If a town came under the rule of one nationality, then nationalism could take a back seat to 'normal' politics, but this tended on the communal level to be that of quotidian administration in any case.

The Habsburg bureaucracy prided itself on being the one institution that was keeping the state together, but it also served to allow the peoples' representatives, from the conflicting national camps, to avoid having to cooperate with each other. The suspension of the Bohemian Diet in 1913 brought howls of protests from all sides, but also an unspoken sigh of relief, as it enabled the taxation problems facing the province to be, temporarily, solved, without any need for compromise by either national side. Hierarchical paternalism thus got in the way of lateral national cooperation.

The incipient, informal federalisation outlined above, through the communal and provincial, assembly-based bureaucracies, also had its limits and problems as far as the central, Habsburg bureaucracy was concerned. The effect of modernisation on the relationship between the central administration and the autonomous, local and provincial bureaucracies was mixed, and in many cases the fact that the central government was the only one with the resources to handle the new functions and responsibilities meant that power gravitated back to its local representative, the *Bezirkshauptmann*, and subsequently to Vienna, so that this was in general an era of 'administrative centralism'. Larger towns and cities, and the provincial assembly-based governments had the resources to counter this, and, as we have seen, alternative power centres could be established, embodied in proto-national bureaucracies. However, these had their own financial problems, and needed support from the central bureaucracy, which in turn doubted their loyalty to the larger Cisleithanian state. Were they becoming part of a federalised state, or were they embryonic bureaucracies for new, independent nation-states? Were they harbingers of a break-up rather than federalisation?

Meanwhile back in Vienna, at the heart of the Habsburg bureaucracy, the effects of the politics of nationalisation and modernisation were also resulting in a heterogenisation of the officialdom itself. All the horse-trading in positions and official patronage meant that the central offices of the central bureaucracy were no longer uniformly German. We saw how Kaizl started staffing the Finance Ministry with Czech officials, and this trend was repeated elsewhere, so that national bureaucracies developed within the supra-national bureaucracy, in Vienna. The higher levels of the officialdom were still largely German, but the lower ranks in Vienna were increasingly non-German, with Czechs taking a prominent place. By 1914, almost a quarter of state officials in the Viennese ministries were non-German.

This in itself would not have been necessarily a bad development, had there been a coherent plan for federalisation, but there was no such plan, and this, together with the informal federalisation at local and provincial levels in much of the land, alarmed the representatives of the Austrian German interest, whether politicians or the media, such as the *Neue Freie Presse*, and the higher Habsburg authorities, most notably Franz Joseph, who feared that the Monarchy was slipping out of (their) control.

There were many plans claiming to be solutions of this ad hoc disaggregation of the Monarchy, one of the more persuasive and well-known being the concept of 'personal autonomy' outlined by Karl Renner, the socialist theorist. The ways in which the nationalities were so intricately mixed in the Monarchy, so that few provinces were mono-ethnic in composition, meant that a spatial federation on provincial or national lines would never have been perfect, but some such form of decentralised federation, together with a guarantee of minority national rights, as outlined by such theorists as Fischhof, Jászi, and Aurel Popovici, might have worked, along lines similar to the current European Union. Like that body, the Monarchy could have, hypothetically, developed as a progressive, federal, prosperous, efficient and law-abiding state, where each nation's equal status was protected, and acted as a magnet for the rest of southeastern Europe, becoming a *real* European necessity.

This is only a hypothetical question, however, because there was never a real prospect of such comprehensive reform. This would have required a revision of the Cisleithanian constitution, and the Magyar leadership was always going to use its veto from the dualist settlement on any such federalised Cisleithania that might encourage Hungary's minority nationalities. Moreover the emperor-king was also determined not to test the limits of that settlement ever again, and an eye witness reports that the old emperor simply forbade the mention of the words 'federalism' or 'trialism' (Austria, Hungary, and a third South Slav state carved from the other two) in his presence. Franz Joseph had learnt something in his sixty years on the throne, and he was quite aware in 1904 of how the Monarchy acted as 'a place of refuge, an asylum for all those fragmented nations scattered over central Europe who, if left to their own resources would lead a pitiful existence, becoming the plaything of more powerful neighbours'. Yet he never drew the relevant conclusion, that his Monarchy was better off as a coherently reconstituted 'big Switzerland', because he still regarded it as his dynastic *Hausmacht*. In his dotage, he was still intent on maintaining the Monarchy as he had inherited it, as a great power, and for this he was prepared to make short-term deals that met his minimal foreign policy and military goals. In other words, he had the approach to his Monarchy of a slum landlord, as Jászi put it, or, as Steed put it somewhat more kindly, an 'absentee landlord'.

The main alternative to Franz Joseph before July 1914 was the heir to the throne, Franz Ferdinand, and historians now see him in somewhat more positive light, given his policies of peaceful co-existence with Russia and plans for a federalised empire (which would have likely been impossible given Magyar opposition). His group of advisors in the 'Belvedere Circle' included many of the more 'dynamic' leaders of the late Monarchy, including Baron Lexa von Aehrenthal, Conrad, and Max Beck, but this was not necessarily a good thing, as we shall see with Aehrenthal's foreign policy and Conrad's aggressive approach to 'allies' such as Italy. Also, once his advisors became his uncle's ministers, as in the case of Beck, he often took against them. Franz Ferdinand was seen at the time as being modern in some respects, as in his morganatic marriage to a 'mere' noblewoman, Sophie Chotek, but his version of modernity was anything but that of 'Vienna 1900', being rather one of a 'masculine' federal absolutism.

In any case, Franz Joseph never left him much actual power. Right up to 1914 Franz Joseph remained the emperor-king, the ruler of his Monarchy. He might have recognised his anachronistic status, describing himself to Theodore Roosevelt in 1910, as 'the last monarch of the old school', but he did not regard that as a bad thing, indeed his simply having been emperor for sixty years made him one of the most significant binding agents of his otherwise centrifugal polity. Franz Joseph was still in charge, of his imperial bureaucracy, of his military and of his Monarchy's foreign policy, and that was a problem. Franz Joseph still regarded his Monarchy as an empire, it still needed to be a great power, from his perspective, and his perspective counted. The emperor-king was not an irrelevant epiphenomenon of the Monarchy, but still its ruler, and ultimately he decided its foreign policy. It was foreign policy, diplomacy, that was to let the Monarchy down, however many 'possibilities' remained in the last decade of peace before 1914.

Squaring the Circle V: Bosnia, Again

Even if the Monarchy could have escaped its domestic problems, and even if it could have pursued a foreign policy that avoided serious defeat or dismemberment, because it was seen as a 'European necessity', neither was possible in practice because of the conflation of domestic and foreign policy, an inherent tendency of the Monarchy. Foreign policy is usually extraneous to a state's affairs, but it was 'the essential raison d'être of the Dual Monarchy'. Had the monarch of the Monarchy been different, this might not have been the case, perhaps, but Franz Joseph decided in the end that the prestige of the Monarchy, its honour, could not be impugned by the Serbs, for foreign *and* domestic reasons. It was the *perception* of the South Slav question, seen from the Habsburg imperial perspective, that led to Austria-Hungary declaring war in July 1914, and it was all too tragic that the *casus belli* took place in Franz Joseph's one territorial acquisition: Bosnia-Herzegovina.

Bosnia, Serbia and the South Slav problem revisited the Habsburg problem with Piedmont in the 1850s. The domestic problems of the South Slavs under dualism (split as the South Slav populations were between Cisleithania and Hungary) combined with the position of the Monarchy in the Balkans, its one remaining sphere of foreign policy interest. The link between the two was the irredentist relation of Serbia with not only Serbs but also, as 'Yugoslavs' (South Slavs), Croats and even Slovenes. Serbia came to be seen, quite clearly, as the 'Piedmont of the Balkans'. As such, it was not internal dissension that made Austria-Hungary go to war in 1914, but irredentism.

It nonetheless took a special combination of circumstances to lead to war. From 1897 to 1908, domestic strife and foreign policy were not the combustible mix they later became. Indeed the internal problems of the Monarchy, national and constitutional, probably had a calming effect on foreign policy as a prostrate Austria-Hungary was in no condition to assert itself; fortunately its main competitor in the region, Russia, was more turned towards expansion in the Far East, and was happy to secure its rear by an entente with the Monarchy that maintained the status quo, such as in the Mürzsteg Agreement in 1903 over Macedonia.

Meanwhile the domestic South Slav situation was in crisis. The main cause of contention was the pro-Magyar aggressive tactics within Croatian politics pursued by the regime of the *ban*, Khuen-Héderváry. There was the added complication that Croats also comprised most of the population of two Cisleithanian provinces, Istria and Dalmatia. Traditionally, Croats had prided themselves on their loyalty to the Habsburgs, with Jelačić being the prime national-loyal hero, but there was also a tradition of being disappointed with Habsburg betrayal, as occurred, from a Croat perspective, with Croatia being abandoned to the Hungarians in 1867, for example. It was quite within the traditional approach for a Croat deputation from Istria and Dalmatia to appeal in 1903 to their monarch, Emperor Franz Joseph, for protection for their fellow Croats in Croatia from the Hungarian authorities. Yet Franz Joseph's response also fitted into Croatian tradition: he refused even to see the delegation. He argued that this was a matter for the Hungarian king rather than himself – even though he was *also* the Hungarian king. (He had done the same to a Romanian delegation from Cisleithania appealing for their Transylvanian brethren in 1892.) Given that Hungary was in the middle of a constitutional crisis, and an additional problem was not welcome, perhaps this dismissal of the Cisleithanian Croats was understandable, but it has been viewed as a major political mistake, because it directed Croatian leaders away from thinking of the Habsburg monarch as a possible ally in solving their problems with the Magyar regime.

The Croats' failure to gain Habsburg support, or even a hearing, on the Croatian-Hungarian conflict had consequences. An assembly of Croatian deputies from the diets of both Cisleithanian Dalmatia and 'Hungarian' Croatia at Fiume passed the Fiume Resolution of 2 October 1905, not only supporting a union of Dalmatia and Croatia (across the Cisleithanian/Hungarian border), but also the Magyar opposition to the Hungarian king (Franz Joseph). As if this was not all bad enough, Serbian deputies from the same diets then met at Zara (Zadar) and on 16 October 1905 voted to support the Fiume Resolution. In 1906, in the Croatian *Sabor*, many members of the Croatian Party of Right joined with the Independent Serb Party to form the Croato-Serb Coalition, which gave them a majority (43 out of 84) in the assembly; and the Coalition allied, furthermore, with the Magyar nationalist opponents to Franz Joseph in Budapest. The alliance with the Magyar nationalists quickly broke up, over language questions concerning the railways in Croatia, but the Croato-Serb alliance continued and the resulting political crisis led to what amounted to absolutist rule in 1908, and a high level of alienation of the Croat and Serb political class from both Budapest *and* Vienna.

The situation in occupied Bosnia-Herzegovina, to the south of Croatia and east of Dalmatia, was also the cause of some concern. The Habsburg record in the one Habsburg 'colony' was in some respects quite good. Administered by the Joint Finance Ministry, it had been governed as his virtual fiefdom by the joint finance minister, Kállay, from 1882 until his death in 1903, under the banner of introducing Western civilisation to an oriental territory, as well as guaranteeing cultural and religious equality, in the Habsburg style. There had been some improvement in living standards (despite Hungarian insistence that the occupation pay for itself); and the Kállay regime brought order and peace to the province. Yet there was no serious land reform, in order not to alienate the largely Muslim landowning, ruling class, and this alienated the largely Serb peasant masses, while the Muslim ruling class still looked to its Ottoman overlord. Bosnia might have been an exercise in colonial imperialism in miniature, but it had the same effect of little gratitude to the imperial power and much resentment at their being there in the first place, much like in Northern Italy before 1866.

Just as in that example, anyone who was discontented only had to look across the border, to the new sovereign nation-state of Serbia for inspiration and nationalist hope. Until 1900 this had not been all that much of a problem, as a chaotically ruled, under-developed Serbia did not compare well with relatively civilised Austria-Hungary; and had been in any case a client state of the Monarchy. By 1900 that had changed inasmuch as the Serbian king, Alexander, had switched to Russian patronage. In 1903 a brutal coup replaced the Obrenović with the Karageorgević dynasty, but this did not cause undue concern in Vienna, as Serbia had already been discounted as an ally. The resulting, even closer, relationship between Russia and Serbia was to become a major, if not *the* major, problem of Habsburg foreign policy.

A great Habsburg fear was of Turkey-in-Europe being replaced by a large Slav state under Russian patronage that would then act as a magnet for the Monarchy's South Slav population. The Habsburg foreign minister, Count Agenor Goluchowski, a Pole (and hence Slav) summoned up this nightmare in November 1903, when supporting the idea of an Albanian enclave in Macedonia: 'The Albanian nation after all forms a dam against the flood of the Porte's possessions in the Balkans by the Slav deluge.' Serbia had the potential to be the core of this large Slav state, and this prospect grew in late 1905, when Serbia entered a secret customs union with the other large Slav state in the Balkans, Bulgaria. Bulgaria did not pose any domestic threat to the Monarchy's integrity, but Serbia did, and was seen by Goluchowski as actively agitating for the Serb nationalist cause *within* the Monarchy and Bosnia. In order to counter the perceived threat of a Serbian-Bulgarian union, Austria-Hungary ignored Bulgaria, but launched a campaign against Serbian commercial interests, including the strict enforcement of veterinary regulations on Serbian pig imports, hence the name for the subsequent trade conflict, the 'Pig War' (1906–10). Serbia suffered short-term problems, which it overcame, partly by Germany, the Monarchy's supposed ally, opening its markets to Serbian produce. Austria-Hungary, on the other hand, suffered the long-term effects of losing its stranglehold on the Serbian economy, increasing Serbian animosity towards it, and losing face with the other powers by bullying a smaller power, and losing.

Goluchowski was replaced in October 1906 by Aehrenthal, who was part of a modernising wave of 'new men', including Conrad and Beck (all from Franz Ferdinand's Belvedere Circle), to bring a new forcefulness to Habsburg policy. Aehrenthal had been the long-term ambassador to Russia and supported closer ties with the Monarchy's long-term rival in the Balkans, but he also had ideas about how an assertion of diplomatic independence from Germany could restore Austria-Hungary's status among the great powers. A 'vigorous foreign policy' would increase the Monarchy's self-confidence and hence help improve and stabilise the Monarchy's domestic situation as well. In a February 1907 memorandum, he set down his strategy to use foreign policy to bolster domestic affairs. Bosnia-Herzegovina was to be annexed and integrated into a new South Slav territory amalgamated from Cisleithanian and Hungarian lands. This form of quasi-trialism would be made acceptable to the Hungarians by putting the new territory under the suzerainty of the Hungarian Crown of St Stephen. The Hungarians would be flattered, and the South Slavs would be given their own national territory, domestic problems solved by dynamic foreign policy.

This quite blatant form of 'social imperialism' (solving domestic problems through foreign policy) was recognised at the time by contemporaries, such as the British diplomat, Horace Rumbold, who in an account published in 1909 explained the Bosnian annexation as an attempt to counter the constant national conflicts by resorting to 'a more decided policy in the Near East, in the hope that they may thereby awaken in both halves of the Monarchy a common sense of solidarity and a feeling of devotion to imperial interests, irrespective of nationality, which have long remained dormant in the polyglot empire'. Rumbold's analysis suggests that, after all, the domestic nationalities problem was fatal to the Monarchy, because it led foreign policy makers along the path to the annexation of Bosnia in 1908, which was disastrous for the Monarchy, for the situation in the Balkans and for the European balance of power.

Given constraints on Habsburg interests, the only theatre for more vigour was the Balkans. Hence Aehrenthal's plans for a railway in the Austro-Hungarian-garrisoned Sanjak of Novibazar (the territory between Serbia and Montenegro) to link Habsburg and Ottoman territory. The announcement of this in early 1908 caused consternation in Serbia and Montenegro (both with eyes on the Sanjak), as well as their patron, Russia. The crisis led to talks which by the summer of 1908, in the aftermath of the Young Turk revolution in Constantinople, had turned to extending the Austro-Russian entente, making a deal between Austria-Hungary and Russia over Bosnia and the larger Balkans questions, including the perennial question of the status of the Straits.

The informal agreement reached at Buchlau in September between Aehrenthal and the Russian foreign minister, Alexander Izvolsky, was anything but an aggressive move on the Monarchy's part. Aehrenthal had decided to annex Bosnia-Herzegovina, but as a means of masking the fact that it was retreating from the exposed salient of the Sanjak. There were other good reasons for annexation at this point. Bosnia had been de facto part of the Monarchy since 1878, but its anomalous status would mean, after the Young Turk revolution, that Bosnia would be the only territory in Europe without a constitution. A prospective Turkish parliament also brought up the embarrassing possibility of elections in Bosnia to send deputies to *Constantinople* rather than Vienna or Budapest, as Bosnia-Herzegovina was still Turkish territory, officially. These problems would be solved if Franz Joseph made his first official acquisition of territory and could then grant Bosnia, now under his sovereignty, a constitution. Izvolsky, on the evidence available, appears quite reasonably to have agreed to this Austro-Hungarian *retreat*, in return for vague promises about supporting Russia's position on the Straits question.

It was diplomatic malpractice, by Aehrenthal mainly, but also by Izvolsky and others, that turned a promising agreement into a full-blown and very damaging diplomatic crisis. Aehrenthal announced the annexation on 5 October 1908, without consulting or informing the other great powers beforehand, but he did let Ferdinand of Bulgaria in on the secret, and Ferdinand declared full independence from Turkey two days *before* Bosnian annexation. The other powers suspected an Austro-Bulgarian conspiracy to humiliate the new, constitutional Turkish government. It was in Russia, however, where the impact was worst. The Russian government was angered by Aehrenthal's hasty announcement and the evidence of Austro-Bulgarian collusion, and frustrated when its proposals for a change on the Straits rules got nowhere, but it was also shocked at the reverberations of the annexation in Russian public opinion, of the 'enslavement of Slav brothers in Bosnia' under the Habsburgs. Totally isolated, Izvolsky chose to blame Aehrenthal and deny that he had agreed to anything at Buchlau. Records suggest strongly that he lied to save his job.

The immediate result, unfairly or not, was a diplomatic disaster for Austria-Hungary. Britain and France stood with Russia; Serbia and Montenegro were humiliated and frustrated at the foiling of their own plans for Bosnia; public opinion in the Monarchy's ally Italy talked of Austrian 'imperialism'; even Wilhelm II of Germany spoke of Aehrenthal's 'fearful stupidity'. It also did nothing to improve relations between the authorities and the South Slavs at home. In Bohemia, the protests and riots that engulfed Prague from late October onwards, leading to martial law in December, were at least partially due to pan-Slav resentment at the Bosnian annexation. In Hungary and Croatia, there were also protests, and the Hungarian government tried to counter this by indicting leaders of the Croato-Serb Coalition, including Frano Supilo, for treason. The Zagreb treason trial of 1909 became a major embarrassment for the Monarchy when it became clear that the charges against the South Slav politicians had been based on forgeries. In the same year, Friedjung (the same Friedjung) had published an article accusing the politicians of treason, based on forged documents supplied by the Foreign Ministry. The subsequent Friedjung libel trial later that year had the effect of muddying the Monarchy's reputation as a 'state of law' even more. The defence of Supilo and his fellow indictees became a rallying cause for South Slav nationalists, 'Western' Slav (Czech) leaders such as Thomas Masaryk, and Western liberal Slavophiles such as R.W. Seton-Watson, who spread the image of a corrupt, authoritarian, Slav-oppressing Habsburg system to Western public opinion. The antagonism of South Slav public opinion to the Magyar leadership in Budapest worsened. Even more damagingly, the South Slav leadership's incipient mistrust of Franz Joseph and the imperial authorities that had begun in 1903 gained confirmation.

The intermediate result of the Bosnian Crisis actually saw Habsburg success, because Germany, not liking the prospect of its main ally being humiliated, decided it was necessary to support Austria-Hungary. It recognised the annexation and then resumed high-level military talks with the Austro-Hungarian leadership after years of neglecting the connection. Count Helmut von Moltke promised Conrad on 19 March 1909 that Germany would assist Austria-Hungary militarily in the case of an Austro-Hungarian attack on Serbia leading to a Russian mobilisation. With German support secured, the Monarchy could stand up to Serbia and Montenegro and their Russian patron, and the diplomatic stand-off of March 1909 resulted in Russia backing down and humiliation for Serbia and Montenegro.

Aehrenthal thought his forceful diplomacy had won out. A few months later he opined that the episode had been 'a text-book example of how success is only certain if the strength is there to get one's way ... We are no *quantité négligeable*.' In the somewhat longer term, however, he came to realise that his claims of having restored Austria-Hungary to 'the place that belongs to us among the Powers' were misplaced. Russia, the entente with whom had been a counterweight to German domination, was now again a clear enemy. Britain, also once a traditional partner, was alienated by Aehrenthal's behaviour, and British public opinion disgusted by the revelations about the Zagreb trials. So the Monarchy became ever more dependent on Germany, the reverse of what Aehrenthal had wanted. The Bosnian crisis significantly hardened the front that had begun to emerge in the First Moroccan Crisis of 1906 between Germany and Austria-Hungary on the one hand and the now Triple Entente of Britain, France and Russia on the other. There were other, extra-European reasons for this, but Bosnia did not help the fluidity of the European diplomatic system. Serbia and Montenegro, meanwhile, had been humiliated, but not subdued. And it became clear as well that Austria-Hungary simply could not afford such 'costly adventures' – for the mobilisation made necessary by the crisis had put a large hole in an already worsening fiscal situation.

Aehrenthal recognised this eventually. From 1910, his policy was back to sticking to the status quo in disputes over Albania and Crete, being conciliatory towards both Italy and Britain. Yet the Bosnian genie, once unleashed, was not to be recaptured. Within the Monarchy, the South Slav question remained unsettled. Another Friedjung Trial provided more embarrassment for the government; in Dalmatia in 1909 the government had been forced to allow Croatian to become the *internal* language of the court system. In 1910 the Istrian Diet was dissolved, and did not meet again in peacetime.

In Bosnia-Herzegovina, the newly annexed province was granted a constitution in 1910, but constitutional government remained shaky. There was irony in the fact that the three main national groups, Serbs, Croats and Muslim 'Bosniaks', all spoke more or less the same language, but the curias within the Diet were divided on *religious* rather than linguistic national lines. Bosnia also never gained a recognised legal status *within* the legal and constitutional framework of the Dual Monarchy, because the initial squaring the circle of where to put Bosnia, whether within Cisleithania or Hungary, was never solved.

Figure 21. Franz Joseph on the Old Bridge in Mostar, 3 June 1910.
Note the officials wearing fezzes and the carpets bedecking the bridge.
(Published with permission of the Austrian National Library.)

While the Monarchy's South Slav question festered domestically,
neighbouring Serbia had emerged from the Pig War economically much
more independent of the Monarchy. Even in her backyard Austria-
Hungary was not strong. When the Germans asked for Habsburg help
during the Second Moroccan Crisis in 1911, Aehrenthal was not very
forthcoming: 'What more can I do? We can pursue no *Weltpolitik*.' That
was meant sarcastically, but it was a sad admission for the foreign minister
of the once global Habsburg Monarchy nonetheless.

The Bosnian Crisis had, moreover, set in train a further weakening of
the hold of Turkey on its European and North African possessions.
The Second Moroccan Crisis of the summer of 1911 saw France tighten
its control over Morocco, and this prompted Italy, already looking for
compensation for Austro-Hungarian annexation of Bosnia, to make good
its claims on Libya (from Berlin in 1878) by invading the Ottoman
territory in late September 1911. Aehrenthal was unhappy about this,
but kept to his policy of containment. Conrad, in contrast, wanted
a preventive strike at Italy (ostensibly an ally) while it was vulnerable,
and on 15 November 1911 had an audience with Franz Joseph to press his
case. The emperor made it clear who ran Habsburg foreign policy. 'These
incessant attacks on Aehrenthal, these pinpricks, I forbid them ...

The ever-recurring reproaches regarding Italy and the Balkans are directed at me. Policy – it is I who make it! ... My policy is a policy of peace.'
Soon after Conrad was dismissed, and Aehrenthal's now quietist policy continued. This did not change when he died in February 1912, and was succeeded as foreign minister by Leopold Count Berchtold.

Meanwhile the carving up of the Ottoman Empire proceeded apace, with the main beneficiary being, of all countries, Serbia. The Italian campaign in Libya, which continued up to October 1912, showed the weakness of Turkish forces, which were further hamstrung by revolts in Albania. By the beginning of 1912 a Balkan League was forming, which eventually included Serbia, Bulgaria, Greece and Montenegro, to take advantage of Turkey's exposure. Despite Austro-Hungarian protestations and Russian attempts at restraint, the First Balkan War began on 8 October 1912, with the Italo-Turkish War still not fully over, and resulted in a lightning-fast victory for the League, as the Turkish forces collapsed. Turkey-in-Europe was, to all intents and purposes, no more.

The Habsburg Crown Council had met on 14 September to consider intervention, but there was no money to pay for war, the army was not in a state of readiness and coming to Muslim Turkey's aid against the united Christian states of the Balkans was politically impossible. Therefore the Monarchy was left as a military spectator as its foreign policy was dismantled before its eyes. The Sanjak, the strategic link to Turkey, had been swallowed up by Montenegro and Serbia, who both emerged much stronger from the war. The crisis was so bad that Conrad was recalled as chief of the General Staff on 12 December 1912. In the end, the Monarchy did mobilise troops to back up its attempts to restrict Serbian gains, and forced Serbia and Montenegro's patron, Russia, to back down for a second time – this time over Montenegro's occupation of Scutari. Yet the most the Monarchy could obtain from the Peace of London of 30 May 1913 was to create an independent Albanian state that prevented Serbian access to the sea. Serbia still emerged double its previous size, with no Turkish counterweight at its back, and bitter at Austria-Hungary's denial of its strategic interests.

Serbia had now become the main Habsburg adversary, and the emperor and his foreign policy advisors now became convinced that the Serbian threat might have to be eliminated, even if it meant confrontation with Russia. Yet Serbia was still a poor, backward state, a minnow compared to the Monarchy, so why had the Austro-Hungarian leadership risked war with Russia to deny Serbia a seaport? Because by 1913 Serbia was the centre of South Slav irredentism. There were actually many more South Slavs (Slovenes, Croats, Serbs and Muslim Slavs) living within the

Monarchy (7 million) than in the rest of the Balkans (3 million).[1] Even in 1913, there were almost as many Serbs living in the Monarchy (2.1 million) as in Serbia (2.6 million). The gravitational pull should have been for integration of Serbia in the Monarchy. Writers such as Joseph Baerenreiter saw trialism (Austria, Hungary and a third, South Slav, state) enabling this. One of the reasons why Aehrenthal had proposed the Bosnian annexation was to square the circle by having a quasi-trialist solution, of the South Slav state under Hungarian suzerainty, to counteract, even reverse, Serbian irredentism. Yet this solution had never had a future, given the complete opposition of the Hungarians and Franz Joseph. Instead, Serbia became the feared Piedmont of the South Slavs, with the Habsburg leadership having little if any confidence in the loyalty of its South Slav subjects. Circumstantial evidence from neutral foreign observers suggests that such fears were at least partially grounded: in Dalmatia there were reports of considerable animosity against the 'German' emperor for neglecting the province. Croatia remained a powder keg, with the constitution suspended in 1912, and in Bosnia the new diet had no working majority. Domestic conflict, discontent and disarray among South Slavs meant that an increase of Serbian power and prestige would appear most alarming to the Habsburg leadership.

It is within this context that one can claim that the outcome of the Second Balkan War sealed the Monarchy's fate. Bulgaria and Serbia fell out over dividing the spoils of war, and Bulgaria invaded Serbia in June 1913, but the war ended in August with Bulgaria's total defeat, as Serbia, Greece, Romania – and Turkey – all attacked her. The Treaty of Bucharest of 10 August 1913 left Serbia even larger and with more prestige. The Austro-Hungarian leadership again sat by, surprised by Bulgaria's collapse, and still counting the cost of the previous mobilisation. German support of the anti-Bulgarian coalition furthered the Habsburg sense of helplessness. Austria-Hungary did try to protect Albania, issuing an ultimatum to Serbia on 17 October to withdraw from Albanian territory, and was by now prepared not only to threaten force but use it. This was because Serbia had come to be perceived as a threat both to Habsburg *interests* and to Habsburg *prestige*, in the Balkans *and* within the Monarchy, among its South Slav population. Serbia and its Russian patron backed down a *third* time, but the potential use of force was in the air. Wilhelm II praised the Austrians' successful threat of force and the Habsburg leadership, including Franz Joseph, had concluded that force was all the Serbs understood. The only advocate of a more peaceful approach was by this point Franz Ferdinand.

---

[1] This figure does not include Bulgarians.

Map 4: The Balkans 1912–1914.

By early 1914, the Monarchy saw itself in a desperate position. Serbia and Romania were eyeing their Habsburg irredenta as prospective areas of expansion. Serbia's prime minister, Nikola Pašić, was preparing 'the second round against Austria', and in February received promises from Russia that the next time they would not back down from Habsburg bullying. Romania was a secret ally of the Monarchy, but that did not stop it seeing Transylvania as a future part of Romania. The Entente powers were exploiting Austro-Hungarian diplomatic and financial weakness in the Balkans. Italy was unhappy with Habsburg actions over Albania; Germany was also back to countering Austro-Hungarian economic and diplomatic interests in the Balkans. It was to persuade Germany to be more 'reasonable' that Berchtold had the Matscheko Memorandum drafted in June 1914.

The original memorandum described how Austria-Hungary might improve its poor diplomatic situation. It noted new Russian assertiveness, the Romanian problem, the threat of a new Balkan League under Entente auspices and the threat of a Montenegro-Serbia union that would give Serbia access to the sea and make her so powerful that this was a 'trip wire' for the Monarchy. The memorandum saw a diplomatic offensive as the best way to avoid such lethal contingencies (made worse to scare the Germans, one suspects). It did not originally argue for war. Before it could be sent off, however, news arrived in Vienna that Franz Ferdinand and his wife had been assassinated on 28 June 1914, in Sarajevo, capital of Bosnia-Herzegovina, by a Bosnian Serb student, Gavrilo Princip. A South Slav subject of the emperor had killed the Habsburg heir. Some sort of forceful response was deemed absolutely necessary, given the fear and hatred of Serbia in Habsburg ruling circles and public opinion, as well as the perceived South Slav menace, internal and external, to Habsburg status and prestige. A month was to go by until the logic of the situation worked itself through, but in the end Habsburg imperial pretensions and the turmoil of South Slav nationalism, combined with the tensions of 'world politics' far from the Bosnian backwater, resulted in what appeared to be the only choice. Franz Joseph, the 'peace emperor', was to start a world war.

Swimming in the Afternoon

Franz Kafka noted in his diary: 'August 2, 1914: Germany has declared war on Russia. Went swimming in the afternoon.' This is emblematic of the unreality and disconnectedness that many felt at the start of what was to be a human disaster on an epic scale, the First World War, and it is this sense of how the war just did not fit into the reality of the citizens of the

Figure 22. Czech-language war bonds poster.
(Published with permission of the Austrian National Library.)

monarchy, such as Kafka, that has led to much of the nostalgia concerning the last period of peace in the Monarchy, and the 'if only there had not been a war' argument. We have seen that there are good grounds for thinking that the Monarchy would indeed have survived quite handily without a war, that its modernisation, while with many problems, was proceeding, with significant benefits for most of its population. And yet, that 'everyday empire' was not the only one involved in the Habsburg Monarchy. It was still an empire, a monarchy, with a monarch intent on preserving his dynasty's prestige and power. Given that, given the existing structures by which the Monarchy operated and was ruled, and the functions that it was supposed to fulfil, the arguments from 'if there had not been a war' are pointless, because the ruling class had come to the conclusion that the only way in which *their* version of the Monarchy could survive, decently, was by solving the problem of Serbia and South Slav irredentism. What might appear to us irrational grounds for war were rational, given their values and goals, given the emperor's values and goals. Modernity – Balkan, irredentist South Slav nationalism – was threatening to destroy the entire, rickety edifice of the Monarchy's position, externally and internally. The most 'modern' figures in the Habsburg leadership circles, such as Conrad, were asserting that only a vigorous, dynamic show of force could sweep aside the threat posed by Serbia and South Slav nationalism (and all those other domestic nationalisms) to the Monarchy's existence. Franz Joseph had been a reactionary moderniser in 1848. In a strange way, despite the lessons he had had to learn over sixty or more years, which had made him pursue a 'policy of peace', the emperor came full circle, and ended up conceding the argument to the 'modern' advocates of war. In the end, it was a form of modernisation, a 'reactionary modernism' that echoed the 'virility' of the young emperor of December 1848, which pushed the Monarchy, and Europe, to war.

7   1914–1918: Self-Destruction

The Monarchy went to war in 1914 because the emperor and his advisors feared that not going to war would result in a loss of status and prestige, not only abroad but also at home, especially among irredentist South Slavs, and risked the disintegration and collapse of the Monarchy. The result of going to war was the disintegration and collapse of the Monarchy. Going to war, and then mismanaging it, produced the outcome it was meant to prevent. All those circles that had not been adequately squared, whether Germany, Hungary, Bosnia or Bohemia, to name just the most prominent, coalesced to produce a situation where there were just no circles left to square, where the Monarchy had run out of ad hoc solutions to deep-lying problems, and could no longer escape to fight another time. It was torn apart by its inability to choose between being a supra-national, multinational, polyglot, quasi-federated refuge for the small nations of Central Europe, and being a subordinate part of the great power complex of the greater German Empire. It had always benefited from being able to play both sides of this dichotomy at the same time – that is what made it a 'European necessity' – but the war, with all its distorted modernism, forced the Monarchy to make a choice between *either* supranational pluralism, *or* German (Hungarian) imperialism. It was a false choice, brought on by the war Austria-Hungary started; even so, the false choice was made and not made: the Monarchy threw in its lot with nationalist modernity in the form of the German Empire, ceased to be a 'European necessity', and by the time it once more reversed itself by seeking accommodation with nationalist modernity in the form of a federalisation, it was too late. The result was self-destruction.

The Decision for War

What caused the First World War or, more accurately, who caused the First World War has been for decades one of the most significant and controversial debates in Modern European History. After the war, the Western Allied version of events held that Germany bore the main 'war guilt'. This in turn was challenged in the interwar period by many who saw Germany unfairly blamed for a disaster that had been due to the breakdown of the alliance system and balance of power, where everyone, and no one, was to blame for stumbling into war. Some variant of this survived into the 1960s, when the work of Fritz Fischer and his 'Fischer thesis' returned the main burden of responsibility for starting the war onto Germany. This consensus among Western academic historians that Germany had indeed been the main aggressor in 1914 has recently been challenged in turn with a return to a more open-ended view of how the war came about. The emphasis has indeed changed, most notably in the influential work by Christopher Clark, *The Sleepwalkers*, from 'why' war occurred (with its implicitly moral question of who was to blame) to 'how' it came about (for which there do not have to be any culprits or moral agents, just happenstance).

Germany's role has faded from its previous centrality as scapegoat, and instead other aspects of the war's origins with more contemporary resonance have come to the fore. The role of terrorism in setting off the July Crisis by the assassination in Sarajevo, a terrorism sponsored by a conspiratorial organisation within the intelligence service of a state, has obvious relevance today. The violence of Balkan nationalism, of Bosnian Serbs, and Serbians, before 1914 now has a greater prominence, because, one suspects, the Bosnian Crisis of the 1990s is still so fresh in memory. This is no coincidence: the present makes us look at the past through its perspective.

The global aspect of the war has also received more attention, and the fact that it was not just Germany ready to go to war in 1914, but Russia, France and even Britain. Russia and France especially appear to have had much more aggressive intentions in 1914 than previously thought. It is quite possible that soon it will be Russia who is seen to have been the main aggressor in 1914 (partly because of the way Putin's Russia is acting today). The main problem appears to have been, however, not so much that one country wanted war, but rather that no one was prepared to back down – this time around.

The one power that has remained less prominent in the debate than one might expect, because it had no global ambitions, or even any plans for territorial expansion as war aims, was the one that actually, officially, started it: Austria-Hungary when it declared war on Serbia on 28 July 1914.

It is true that the role of the Monarchy in the origins of the war was on a much more parochial level than the continental or even global considerations dominating the calculations of the truly big powers: France, Britain, Russia and Germany. Nevertheless, it seems mistaken not to pay attention to the Monarchy's role, just as it was for far too long a major oversight to concentrate so much on the history of the war on the western front rather than on the eastern, southeastern and southern fronts, where Austria-Hungary's forces were involved, and where the character of the war was for long stretches quite different from the static trench warfare in Flanders. No matter what the broader, global interests and fears of the other powers were, had the rather limited, regional interest of Austria-Hungary teaching Serbia a lesson not been present, then the chain reaction that led to war would not have happened – not this time anyway, and perhaps never. (We just will never know.)

To understand why the Monarchy went to war is a key part to understanding why, or even how, the war happened. Austria-Hungary did not *have* to go to war in 1914; it chose to do so. Countries can be severely provoked, and no one now or then really doubted that the assassination of Franz Ferdinand, the Habsburg heir, was indeed a severe provocation, but they can decide *not* to go to war as a result. It might lead to a loss of 'credibility' (the modern term for 'prestige and honour'), but that can normally be made up and reversed over time. Going to war is a much more final answer, with not only mortal consequences for individual combatants, but also, sometimes, as in this case, for the combatant states themselves. Why, then, did the Monarchy go to war in 1914?

One explanation, or at least one factor strongly highlighted by some recent accounts, is a variant of the 'social imperialism' school of German history, which saw foreign policy, and the decision for war in 1914, as driven by domestic considerations, with an aggressive foreign policy as a means of diverting the populace from their real economic and political interests and uniting them behind the regime on the platform of expansive nationalism. The Habsburg version of this is to see the Monarchy's aristocratic elite as opting for war to rescue their domestic status. Still prominent in the higher echelons of the military and the diplomatic corps, they had been largely alienated from power elsewhere in the Austrian political structure by the success of the 'political democratisation' that had occurred on various levels of the Cisleithanian system. War was seen by them, it is suggested, as a means to turn the clock back, reassert central power against the nationalities, and restore aristocratic power (in the military, Imperial Court and officialdom) against bourgeois, representative politics, and return to a much more old-fashioned, reactionary, top-down, hierarchical political order. Aehrenthal had tried something (fairly moderate) along these lines, when he had wanted to use the Bosnian annexation to assert Habsburg power externally *and* internally. Now war with Serbia, it is claimed, was seen as an even better opportunity to return the Monarchy to its proper dynastic, aristocratic and authoritarian order.

Conrad is quoted as saying to Redlich: 'It is very difficult to improve the internal situation of the monarchy peacefully.'

Historians have claimed that Cisleithania was already under a form of 'bureaucratic absolutism' before 1914, but, according to this quasi-'social imperialist' interpretation, such a system really was only introduced when war provided the opportunity of overthrowing the constitutional and legal norms that had governed Cisleithania in peacetime. The July Crisis was seized on as a means to restore the elite's power.

There may indeed have been figures in the military and diplomatic circles with this ulterior, domestic motivation. Certainly, political rule became much more bureaucratic and étatist after war began than even beforehand, and the meeting of the *Reichsrat* and the provincial assemblies was put on indefinite hold just *before* war was officially declared. On the other hand, the domestic bureaucracy in Cisleithania, while it clamped down on dissent, managed to resist successfully the military leadership's efforts to put Bohemia under military rule, and it did so with the support of both Stürgkh and, more tellingly, Franz Joseph. If wanting to impose a military dictatorship was a reason for war, it was unsuccessful because two of the leading figures of the conservative elite *resisted* it. In the other half, Hungary's parliament continued to sit throughout the war, under civilian rule (albeit that *was* a form of, albeit representative, aristocracy).

The main reason why the idea of a reactionary counter-revolution through war engineered by the aristocratic elite is dubious is that the actual decision to go to war rested ultimately, as it had since 1848, with Franz Joseph. There is little evidence that he wanted to revise the internal arrangements of the Monarchy; rather he saw war, in the end, as the only way to preserve his patrimony *as it was* (democratisation and all). Eyewitness accounts, such as that of his aide-de-camp, Alexander Margutti, claim that a pacific Franz Joseph was pressured into a war he really did not want, but the evidence suggests that he had decided as early as May 1913 (in the middle of the Balkan Wars) that the Serbian threat had to be dealt with, if necessary, by war.

In the circle around Franz Joseph that influenced Habsburg decision-making, especially in the Crown Council, there had been powerful voices both for and against war before 28 June 1914. Leading the war party was Conrad, who had wanted to wage a preventive war, either against Italy or Serbia, for years. As he later put it, 'in 1909 the war would have been a game with open cards, in 1913 it would still have been a game with chances, in 1914 it had become a game of *va banque*, but there was no other alternative'. In 1911, as we saw, Franz Joseph had vehemently rejected this approach, yet since then he had come round to Conrad's viewpoint, given the ever-growing threat posed by Serbia. There had been, however, significant voices on the side of peace: the foreign minister, Berchtold, had been unenthusiastic about war, and the prime minister of Hungary, Tisza, had also wanted restraint, concerned as he was at how hostilities against Serbia might have an adverse effect not only on the Serbian irredentist problem, but also that between (Hungarian) Transylvania and Romania. The chief voice for peace had been none other than Franz Ferdinand.

In many ways, the Habsburg heir was Tisza's main adversary in the Crown Council, because of his plans to accommodate South Slav (and Romanian) political ambitions at Magyar expense, and his wish to improve relations with the ideologically sympathetic, because authoritarian, Russia. Franz Ferdinand had gone to Bosnia partly to assert Habsburg power and prestige, as the Matscheko Memorandum had recommended, but also to show a benevolent attitude to the South Slav population of the new Habsburg territory. His pro-South Slav policies were probably a major reason why Apis, head of the Serbian intelligence service and leader of the secret terrorist group, the Black Hand, ordered the assassination, to remove a positive, Habsburg alternative to the idea of the integration of Bosnia into Greater Serbia.

Franz Ferdinand's assassination not only created an opportunity for the hawks in the Austro-Hungarian Crown Council to launch their preventive/punitive war against Serbia; it also removed one of the major obstacles to that policy on the Council, the Habsburg heir himself. Previous doves such as Berchtold were now convinced something had to be done against Serbia. The main holdout at the Crown Council meeting of 7 July was now Tisza, whose consent for war was constitutionally necessary (due to dualism). He remained unconvinced that a punitive strike against Serbia would help the Monarchy. He feared its effect on the irredentist problem concerning Romania and Transylvania, and he was dead set against having any more South Slavs in the Monarchy. Hence he insisted, successfully, that Austria-Hungary would go to war with no plans for territorial acquisitions from Serbia. At the meeting on 7 July the Crown Council agreed to his suggestion that an ultimatum should be sent to Serbia first, to put the blame for war on Serbia, should they reject it. He still thought diplomatic humiliation of Serbia, short of war, was preferable. The other council members, however, wanted the ultimatum to be designed to be unacceptable. It took until 14 July, another week, for Tisza to fall in line with this, which was effectively the decision to push for war. Partly this was due to Tisza's becoming convinced that *not* acting against Serbia would unsettle the

Transylvanian situation, but in large measure this was because the emperor had made clear that war was what he wanted.

By then various things had fallen into place. Confessions from the perpetrator, Princip, and his co-conspirators pointed strongly to a Serbian connection. Berchtold's cabinet chief, Alexander Count Hoyos, had been sent to Berlin on 5 July, with a beefed up version of the Matscheko Memorandum, and he had obtained the 'blank cheque' from the German leadership that has traditionally been interpreted as evidence that Germany positively wanted war in 1914. A report from the investigation into the assassination also came back with an interim report on 13 July stating that there was no definite proof that the Serbian government had known of the plot, but it was indisputable that the plot had been prepared in Serbia, and involved Serbian state railway officials. The investigators never did make the link to the Black Hand, and hence that the plot did go very high up in the Serbian government, if not to its elected side. With proof of some form of Serbian involvement, and German backing, the Monarchy then proceeded to prepare to declare war. But it did so far too slowly.

In Berlin, the German 'blank cheque' had been given with the strong suggestion that Austria-Hungary 'exploit the present moment'. The German chancellor, Theobald von Bethmann-Hollweg, had recommended 'immediate intervention', on 6 July, seeing 'the present moment as far more favourable than a later one'. Immediate action, in the aftermath of the trauma of assassination, could have, possibly, occurred while the Entente powers still felt inhibited from action to support the 'guilty' Serbs. The war might have remained localised. Yet Austria-Hungary did not work on that sort of timescale. Not only had Tisza stood in the way of immediate action on 7 July, but even on 14 July the Council had only agreed to draw up an unacceptable ultimatum, the final text of which was agreed on 19 July, and then given to the Serbian government on 23 July. Two more days went by until Serbia gave its qualified acceptance on 25 July, which was deemed insufficient by the Austro-Hungarian leadership, leading to Franz Joseph signing the declaration at Bad Ischl on 27 July, and the official declaration of war following the next day, 28 July: three weeks after the 'blank cheque' had been issued.

This was not just about Tisza and the glacial pace of Habsburg bureaucratic procedure; an immediate strike would never have been possible because there were not enough troops available in any case. The military's policy of giving its rural conscripts leave in the summer to help with the harvest (a policy designed by Conrad) meant that there would not have been an adequate force available for war, even against Serbia, without a recall that would have been severely disruptive of the harvest and would have telegraphed the intent of Austria-Hungary to launch a military strike. Despite what Conrad might have claimed, an immediate military strike was simply not possible, given the practical conditions of the Monarchy's armed forces in the summer of 1914. The longer the decision for war took, however, the more likely it was to end in a continent-wide conflagration.

The members of the Crown Council knew this, sort of. Clark has described the Austro-Hungarian collective decision-making process in the July Crisis as akin to 'hedgehogs scurrying across a highway with their eyes averted from the rushing traffic'. The council members were aware of the strong possibility of a general Russian mobilisation and all that entailed, and discussed it, but they never properly factored this into the calculation of their options. They were intent on solving the Serbian problem, and could think of no alternative. The 'source of the ultimate power of decision' remained Franz Joseph, and he was quite aware on 20 July that the ultimatum would be unacceptable not only to Serbia but also its patron, Russia, which made a European-wide war almost inevitable, given the alliance system (and railway timetables) of the time. He must surely also have been aware that his armed forces would be sorely tested and were not really up to the task of major war. That had, after all, been his experience over six decades, and was the main reason he had become a 'peace emperor'. So why did he decide to go to war, agree to the unacceptable ultimatum and then sign the declaration of war?

Some of the answers can be found in the War Manifesto published on 29 July, justifying to 'my peoples' the declaration of war on Serbia. The war had been forced upon the emperor against his will by Providence, and now had to be fought: to protect the honour of 'my monarchy'; to protect its good name and position among the powers; and to secure its possessions. Later in the manifesto, the emperor justified the use of force as the only way to 'insure tranquillity to my states [plural] within and lasting peace without'. Irredentism's combination of foreign and domestic policy threats thus was a key consideration. The Manifesto ends by listing the three purposes for the sacrifices of 'my peoples': 'the honour, the greatness, and the might of the Fatherland'. The peoples of the Habsburg Monarchy were there to secure the values of honour, greatness and might of 'my monarchy'. It was a starkly old-fashioned, dynastic justification for modern warfare, and this interpretation is confirmed by a later commentary by Berchtold. The emperor's policy had been one of peace, but it had its limits: 'limits of decency and self-respect, but particularly of the concern for the continuation of the patrimonial legacy which he had inherited, with its family of nations entrusted to him'. The family of nations was almost incidental to the need to preserve the patrimony. It was the need to preserve the honour and status of the Monarchy as a great power that was first and foremost in the minds of Franz Joseph and his advisors in July 1914, because that was its purpose. The decision for war might appear irrational today, for its unleashing of untold mayhem and as an act of self-destruction, but on one level the deeper cause of war was 'the very nature of the Monarchy itself', as a creature of foreign policy, a great power.

There was both a sense of fatalism, that this was Providence working, but also there was a sense of a need to assert one's will. If one was a great power, then simply being passive was unacceptable. One had to act, be decisive, to prove one's own worth, even if the result was fated to be one of self-destruction. Franz Joseph's immediate reaction to the news of Franz Ferdinand's assassination had been to talk of 'a higher power' that had restored order that he, Franz Joseph, had been unable to maintain, by allowing Franz Ferdinand's morganatic marriage. Now, he had to assert himself and trust in a 'higher power' because not to do so would lead to a loss of status, as a great power. That status had effectively been lost almost half a century ago, but not formally. Not being able to put Serbia in its place would lead to that loss of face. As Berchtold later wrote, 'For Emperor Franz Joseph it was clear that our role in world history would be over if we feebly allowed fate to do what it willed.'

This was entirely wrong. The only way to keep the Monarchy's fate in its own hands, and to let it continue to be the supranational refuge to the small nations of Central Europe, would have been *not* to go to war. Yet *not* to go to war would have been seen as dishonourable, and appeared to be against the will of the 'higher power'. Franz Joseph said to Alexander von Krobatin on signing the declaration: 'Go, I can do nothing else.' In late July, he had told Conrad: 'If the Monarchy must perish it should at least perish with decency.' It was eerily reminiscent of what the emperor had said in 1866: 'When the whole world is against you and you have no friends, there is little chance of success, but you must go down doing what you can, fulfilling your duty and, in the end, going down with honour.' Franz Joseph went to war, it appears, to defend the honour of his Monarchy as a great power. In doing so he helped destroy it.

Catastrophe

Once Franz Joseph made his 'naked act of decision' to regain control over the Monarchy's destiny, he and Austria-Hungary lost control of events. War by timetables took over. A regional dispute ballooned into world war. The Austro-Hungarian and German leaderships had known full well that it was highly probable that Russia's leadership would decide that – having backed down three times in the last few years – this time they were not going to back down from confronting Austro-Hungarian bullying of Serbia (as Russia saw it). They cannot have been all that surprised, therefore, when Russian general mobilisation was ordered on 30 July. Austro-Hungarian general mobilisation was ordered and German ultimatums sent to Russia and France the next day, because any delay in responding to the Russian mobilisation would make the carefully timed German war plans – to defeat France first and then turn east to Russia – impossible to achieve. Germany declared war on Russia on 1 August, on France on 3 August. Germany's invasion of Belgium enabled the hawks in Britain to effect a British declaration of war on Germany. Almost as afterthoughts, Austria-Hungary declared war on Russia on 6 August, and Britain and France declared war on Austria-Hungary on 12 August. Italy, the other member of the Triple Alliance, predictably declared neutrality on 3 August, arguing that its allies had not informed it of their war plans, and that as it was in a defensive alliance it was not obliged to support allies who had been the aggressors. By mid-August all the other great powers in Europe were at war.

Notoriously, the onset of war saw an outpouring of chauvinistic, martial enthusiasm from the public in all the combatant states, and this included the Monarchy, even in Slav regions. For the moment the national conflicts seemed to be overcome by Habsburg patriotism, the need to teach Serbia a lesson – a popular slogan was 'Serbien muss sterbien!' (Serbia must die!) – and hatred of 'Russian barbarism'. In Hungary, revenge for the Russian occupation of 1849 (to aid the Habsburg emperor) was an additional incentive. The Habsburg army, the target of so many nationalist disputes, remained a much more coherent and disciplined fighting force than some had feared. There were some mutinies and desertions, and when it came to battle some units surrendered suspiciously quickly, yet the degree of dissent in the ranks was much less than had been expected, and the rank and file fought creditably. The direct impact of the nationality conflicts within the army was minimal. The problem was the long-term indirect effect of the laming of the political system by the national and constitutional conflicts over decades.

Even with the Military Bill of 1912, decades of neglect could not be remedied so quickly. The army was badly prepared and poorly provisioned, lacking proper training and equipment. The transportation infrastructure (railways) near the southern and eastern fronts was also poorly developed, and inferior to that on the Russian side, which meant the army at the front could initially only be inadequately supplied and reinforced. It was also very badly led. Control over the military had been one of Franz Joseph's most closely guarded prerogatives, so it is ironic that the beginning of war saw his power over the military, and indeed over the running of the wartime government, effectively cease. He was deemed, at almost eighty-four, too frail to be at the headquarters of the Army High Command in Teschen (in Silesia), and so he remained effectively interned at Schönbrunn, with only a remote, almost passive role in governing (although he would still make some key decisions both in foreign and domestic policy). The official head of the high command was Archduke Friedrich, but the actual leader, and virtual dictator of the Monarchy, was now Conrad. From the start, he made some disastrous decisions that compounded the Monarchy's already weakened position in terms of materiel and personnel. Faced with a two-front war against Serbia and Russia, he vacillated between 'Plan B' (Balkans) and 'Plan R' (Russia), unable to decide which to tackle first and thus bringing about the chaotic mobilisation so wryly depicted in Jaroslav Hašek's *The Good Soldier Švejk*.

The initial invasion of Serbia in August, which was predicted to be an easy win, was almost immediately abandoned because of unexpectedly strong Serbian resistance. Meanwhile, on the eastern front, the Austro-Hungarian forces initially followed Conrad's offensive tactics, but these were costly, and the army was soon in a headlong retreat. The expected, and requested, German support was refused. The Battle of Lemberg in September left the whole of Eastern Galicia, Austria's 'bread basket', in Russian hands by the end of the month, as the Habsburg army retreated all the way to the Carpathian Mountains. It was only in December, at the Battle of Limanowa-Łapanow, that the Habsburg forces managed to hold the Russians back, and then only with German support. By the end of 1914, the front had stabilised, with troops entrenched in the mountains, in horrific, freezing conditions. There were some successes, Czernowitz had been recaptured, but the Habsburg forces had abandoned eastern Galicia and had retreated far into their hinterland. Meanwhile in Serbia, after another failed offensive in September, a third offensive in November succeeded in capturing Belgrade on 2 December, but a Serbian counter-attack meant that by the end of the year the Habsburg forces were back where they had started in August.

The cost to the Monarchy of these disastrous campaigns was horrendous. Four-fifths of the army's trained infantry had been lost, either dead, wounded or taken prisoner, along with half the original officer corps. The campaigns had 'destroyed the Austro-Hungarian army as a first-class fighting force'; the main object of so much political and nationalistic contention had been wiped out in a matter of months.

1915 brought mixed results. There was a major diplomatic disaster. Italy had from the beginning of the war followed a policy of *sacro egoismo* (sacred egotism, or, less euphemistically, ruthless national interest) by demanding 'Italian' territory from Austria-Hungary as compensation for Austro-Hungarian gains in the Balkans (ironically using Aehrenthal's interpretation of article VII of the Triple Alliance) and as reward for at least staying neutral. On 8 August, the Crown Council was already discussing the German suggestion that they cede the Trentino to satisfy the Italians, but the council members decided to reject Italian 'blackmail', and offered only Valona as a symbolic gesture. Franz Joseph heartily approved this stance, forgetting the lessons of 1866. (See Chapter 3.) However, the loss of Italy to the Entente enemy would be a serious blow, and looking increasingly likely without territorial concessions. Berchtold resigned as foreign minister on 11 January 1915 over the emperor's refusal to cede even the Trentino (which was not actually one of the Habsburgs' more ancient territories). His successor, Stefan Count Burián, pressured ever more by the Germans, eventually came round to seeing the need for concessions to Italy, and, despite all the talk of Habsburg honour, an offer of significant Austrian territory was made to Italy in the spring, but by then it was too late. Italy had signed the Treaty of London on 26 April, and declared war on Austria-Hungary on 23 May, an act that a disgusted Franz Joseph regarded as a 'breach of faith'.

The year started no better in military terms. The fortress of Przemyśl, with 120,000 men, surrendered on 22 March, a body blow to Habsburg prestige and manpower. Only a few weeks later, however, the course of the campaign on the eastern front was dramatically changed by the joint Austro-German Gorlice-Tarnow offensive in May, led by the German general, Erich von Falkenhayn. This stunning victory produced the greatest territorial gains of the war, sweeping the Russians entirely out of Poland. Lemberg was retaken in June. In October, another joint Austro-German offensive, under German leadership, and with the support of Bulgaria, ended with the conquest of Serbia, which had been the initial war aim of the Monarchy. The problem for the Habsburg army, however, was that both stellar successes had been won with German assistance, and under German leadership. Austria-Hungary was fast losing its military credibility and independence. In August, Conrad, no friend of the Germans, whom he called 'our underhanded enemy', had attempted to restore this through the 'black-yellow' campaign of Rowno, but this was a humiliating failure. Despite a large advantage in men and materiel, the Austro-Hungarian forces moved only haltingly forward against the Russian line, and then suffered large losses as the Russians counter-attacked. Yet again, the Germans had to intervene and save the Habsburg army. Again that succeeded in halting the Russians, but the price this time was the Austro-Hungarian Fourth Army being put under

German command, a situation likened by an officer on the Habsburg General Staff to an 'autumn pig' (*Herbstsau*) being offered as tribute to the German master. Discussions over the fate of occupied Poland revealed the same master-servant relationship. While the Austrians and Hungarians had quarrelled over some sort of 'Austro-Poland' and an Austro-Magyaro-Polish form of 'trialism', the Germans made clear that the Monarchy's gaining control of Poland would require the effective subjugation of the Monarchy to Germany; as F.R. Bridge puts it, 'by 1915 the control of Austria-Hungary as a satellite had become a German war aim'.

The Austro-Hungarian position worsened markedly in 1916. Determined to assert Habsburg independence, Conrad launched an offensive against Italy from South Tyrol in May, explicitly against the requests of Falkenhayn not to do so. Initially there were significant advances, but the campaign had been delayed by unseasonal weather, the Italians had caught on to Habsburgian plans, and so the offensive began to falter. With Habsburg forces depleted on the Russian front to help in Italy, the Russian general, Alexei Brusilov launched on 4 June a massive offensive on a 300-mile-long front that largely ignored German units, instead concentrating on, and breaking the Austro-Hungarian lines. The Fourth and Seventh Habsburg armies collapsed, and the Russians advanced, again, almost to the Carpathians. The South Tyrol campaign was halted, and reinforcements were rushed to the eastern front, but the Brusilov offensive continued. Romania, a former ally, now entered the war on the Entente's side on 27 August and overran Transylvania. Conrad went to Berlin, cap in hand, for more support. Again, German troops saved the Austro-Hungarian position, halting the Russian advance (of sixty or more miles) on 20 September, and reversing the Romanian offensive, so that General August von Mackensen had captured Bucharest by December.

The Monarchy had been rescued but at a great price. At Pless Palace on 27 July, at the height of the crisis caused by the Brusilov offensive, the German and Habsburg military and civilian leadership had met to discuss future relations, and the result had been a series of Habsburg concessions. On 3 August the Germans had taken over command of virtually the whole eastern front, and on 6 September a Joint High Command, headed by Wilhelm II, Paul von Hindenburg and Erich Ludendorff, all Germans, took control of both German and Habsburg forces, with units now inter-changeable. The Habsburg Monarchy was no longer, militarily, an independent power.

By the autumn of 1916, there was military success but increasing German control. By November, Poland, formerly seen as in the

Habsburg sphere, had become an Austro-German condominium, effectively controlled by Germany. In September, the Salzburg Agreement
had called for greater co-operation between German and Austrian
German parliamentary deputies – with only German(-speaking) deputies
involved. The war to save the Habsburg Monarchy was turning it into
a satellite of the Hohenzollern German Empire.

Trouble on the Home Front(s)

The domestic situation within the Monarchy was also looking increasingly inauspicious. Here too, the military leadership had proven
inadequate to the task at hand. The military had taken over most of
the reins of government at the beginning of mobilisation on 25 July.
Plans that had been formulated secretly in 1906, and amended in
1909 and 1912, were now implemented, leaving the Monarchy under
what was tantamount to a 'military dictatorship'. The Crown Council
ordered the temporary suspension of various constitutional rights,
including the freedom of speech and free association. Instead of
recalling the *Reichsrat* to gain popular consent for the war, Stürgkh
suspended the *Reichsrat* and the provincial assemblies indefinitely.
Article 14, the emergency clause in Cisleithania's constitution, was
now used extensively to pass emergency decrees that imposed a raft of
authoritarian measures to put the country on a war footing. Strict
censorship was introduced; trial by jury was suspended. The War
Production Law militarised several branches of industry, along with
their workforces.

A new army institution, the War Surveillance Office, a vast domestic
security bureaucracy, spying on the public to root out subversive elements, was allowed to operate throughout Cisleithania, even in areas
not in the military zones. Thanks to this institution's diligence, 950
people were arrested in Bohemia for political crimes by the end of 1914,
and 704 handed over to military courts, even though Bohemia was not in
a military zone and the military courts' purview was officially confined
there to military-controlled industrial concerns.

Vast tracts of the Monarchy were designated to be military zones, under
martial law: the whole of Galicia and the Bukovina in the northeast, along
with the eastern parts of Austrian Silesia and Moravia for the eastern
front; Croatia, Dalmatia, southern Hungary, and Bosnia-Herzegovina on
the Serbian front. (When Italy entered the war in 1915, the military zone,
with martial law, was extended accordingly to the adjacent southwest
Austrian crownlands.) The regime in the military zones was under direct
military control and was, perhaps not all that surprisingly, much harsher

than under civilian rule, with summary executions of suspected 'spies' quite common in the war's first months.

The military did not have things all its own way, however. The core Austrian crownlands along the Danube, and Bohemia, the Monarchy's industrial heartland, remained under civilian rule. The military leadership, suspicious of Czech loyalties, had requested that Bohemia be put under martial law on 26 November 1914, but the civilian authorities objected to all Czechs being branded traitors for the sins of a few, and Franz Joseph sided with the civilians. Similarly, in the summer of 1915 the military leadership attempted to have a loyalty test imposed on the civilian officials in Bohemia and then the whole of Austria, with the intent of completely depoliticising the administration. German should also become the state language. Again, the plan got nowhere because of the resistance of the bureaucracy and refusal of the emperor. On 25 September 1915 (at the urging of a number of the emperor's close confidants), Archduke Friedrich, official head of the military, asked the emperor to dismiss Stürgkh because of his inability or unwillingness to stand up to the 'anti-state tendencies' of the Slavic and Italian populations in the Monarchy and radically reform Cisleithania, but Franz Joseph stood by his Cisleithanian prime minister.

Hungary remained under civilian rule throughout the war, under the rule of parliament. It passed its own emergency measures and asserted its continuing domestic independence. It had its own War Surveillance Commission, parallel to the army's War Surveillance Office. Tisza was insistent on limiting the latter's operations in Hungary to a minimum, also in the military zones in Hungarian territory. However, the army was a *joint* institution, with military zones on Hungarian territory, and with Hungarian troops. Civilian Hungarian rule was not necessarily all that less harsh than that of the Habsburg military. The gendarmerie in Hungary had been given wide powers against suspected subversives in a secret 1912 measure, and used it at times ruthlessly, especially against Ruthene and Serb 'suspects'. Early on in the war Tisza warned his subordinates in the counties about the non-Magyar nationalities: 'We must show them our strength.' There were also anti-Serb riots in (Hungarian-controlled) Croatia, and summary executions. Nonetheless, having parliamentary rule in Hungary did tend to a more liberal, less oppressive legal regimen overall, especially when it came to censorship of the press.

Where the army did have full powers, in the designated military zones, its rule has been seen as 'qualitatively more dictatorial than comparable regimes in other belligerent societies'. Its harsh implementation of the new emergency powers signified a radical change from the rule-of-law tradition that had been operating in the Monarchy since the 1860s.

The anti-Slav bias of the military leadership also created hostility where, it has been argued, there was in reality none. The Galician population, overall, was much more anti-Russian than anti-Habsburg, but the military leadership, one eyewitness later claimed, suspected the whole Galician population of disloyalty. In the first months of the war, almost 5,000 Galicians, mostly Ruthenes, were arrested and sentenced to death for 'treasonous activities'. A significant proportion were executed.

The initial enthusiasm to root out subversives led the authorities, both military and civilian, to encourage the public to inform them about any subversive activity, but this led in areas such as Southern Styria and Carinthia, with its mixed Slovene and German population, to an 'uncontrollable orgy of denunciations', as German nationalists took their revenge on Slovenes by accusing them of being 'Serbophiles'. In September, the civilian administration, both in Vienna and in the provinces, tried to ratchet down the crisis by having the gendarmerie not act so swiftly on the denunciations, which were usually baseless, and eventually some calm was restored, but at the cost of deep alienation of the accused (mainly Slovenes) from the Habsburg state, and indeed material damage to their lives, as denunciation had often been followed by arrest and loss of reputation and employment.

Even when there were some grounds to suspect individuals of anti-war sentiment, the heavy-handed approach of the military authorities created needless hostility on the part of the population, for instance with the arrest of the Czech politician Karel Kramář on 21 May 1915, and his subsequent sentencing to death for treason on 3 June 1916. The sentence was commuted to 15 years hard labour, but even so this persecution of a prominent Czech leader was a crass mistake, encouraging Czech resentment against the Habsburg state.

Censorship was extremely strict in the initial phase of the war, and a very tight control of the media was imposed by the army's War Press Office, which exercised a blunt co-option of the media. Most of the German-language press were prepared to play along with the strict control of information, and when the censor expunged words from newspaper articles in the pre-approval process would close up the gaps to make it look as though it had not been censored. Initially, Karl Kraus practised the same legerdemain in the *Fackel*. Later on, he began to realise the terrible consequences of allowing this co-option, and the immense distance it allowed between media reports and the reality they distorted. His post-war masterpiece, *The Last Days of Mankind*, is a magnificent diatribe against the war and the media's role in abetting the 'tragic carnival'. Early on, though, he also co-operated with the censor. The Czech press, on the other hand, had a more adversarial relationship with the military authorities. The War Surveillance Office, suspicious of Czechs from the start, closed down forty-six Czech newspapers in the first months of the war. Those still allowed to publish tended to leave the white spaces of the censor's excisions in their articles. Vendors in Wenceslas Square in Prague are said to have shouted out: 'What is white is the truth – what is black is lies!' The frequent times when official versions of events in the first months of the war were shown to be complete distortions of the truth, as in the back-and-forth reports about the fate of the fortress of Przemyśl, undercut the public's faith in official information and what was allowed to be printed in the press. Rumours and nationalist assertion of conspiracy and skulduggery involving Habsburg officials and war profiteers, an inversion of the phenomenon of denunciation, took over in the information vacuum.

The military authorities in charge of handling information did little effective to counter these negative narratives, as they did not offer any coherent attempt at propaganda, at least in the first years, that would motivate civil society for the war effort. This was because the army was not very interested in such concepts as 'the multinational state'. Their ideal was, instead, a non-national, supranational, absolutist state, much like the army itself. Indeed, all they really wanted the media and their propagandists to do was glorify the army itself. It was the military version of the idea that the people were there to be governed. When the journalist Hugo Ganz complained about the strictness of the censorship in September 1914 he was told 'the people's job in wartime is to shut up and obey'.

There were some efforts by the authorities to build support in the populace, especially from 1916 on. The Interior Ministry published in that year a picture book for children: *Let's Play World War! A Contemporary Picture Book for Our Little Ones* (*Wir spielen Weltkrieg! Ein zeitgemässes Bilderbuch für unsere Kleinen*). In May 1916, an elaborate War Exhibition, replete with trenches, opened in the Prater (on the grounds of an English-owned, hence confiscated, amusement park). Film newsreels became a standard means of lifting the spirits of the populace, and films from the Italian front were particularly popular, probably because of the dramatic mountain scenery. The War Press Office also had an Art Group, where some of Austria's major artists were employed, but the director of it, as a soldier, had no inkling of how to use aesthetics to help morale. At the War Archives, which at various times employed many of Austria's best writers, including Rainer Maria Rilke, a belated attempt was made to come up with more convincing, literary rationales for the state, but almost all of the publications produced were in German, and the propaganda, for instance the journal *Donauland*, was meant mainly for the troops rather than the public.

Even had there been a concerted propaganda effort, it is difficult to see how the ambivalences of Austrian (Austro-Hungarian) identity could have been made coherent, as a convincing message for the public. Hugo von Hofmannsthal attempted just such a message for the more literary part of the populace with his series of publications by Insel of the 'Austrian Library' from 1915 to 1917. Hofmannsthal invited Anton Wildgans, Austria's new patriotic poet, to contribute a poem to sum up 'Austria', which for Hofmannsthal meant an organic synthesis between German and Slavic 'being', the 'beside each other-in each other, … living with each other' ('Nebeneinander-Ineinander, … das Beieinanderhausen')of the Austrian peoples. Wildgans refused, because he had to insist on the 'clear hegemony' of the German people within Austria. He offered Hofmannsthal a poem 'The German Spirit', which Hofmannsthal declined. Instead they agreed on 'Infantry! A poem dedicated to the people-at-arms', with the subject in the first person plural: 'us'. There was no mention of Austria, only of the army. A similar ambivalence was evident in the theatre. The first premiere at the *Burgtheater* after it reopened was of Heinrich von Kleist's *Die Hermannsschlacht*, a classic of German patriotism that could boost the sense of *Nibelungentreue* (total Nibelung loyalty) between the 'German' dynasties of Hohenzollern and Habsburg, except that the 'enemy' in the play was the Roman Empire, of which the Habsburgs still thought of themselves as the direct and spiritual heirs. In any case, the rest of the Monarchy's non-German population seemed irrelevant to this relationship, or on the side of the enemy. So even when German Austrians applied themselves to the 'Austrian idea', the result was often divisive and problematic. The fact that Franz Joseph in October 1915 accepted, after decades of resistance, naming 'the kingdoms and provinces represented in the *Reichsrat*' as 'Austria' was not much consolation.

Morale was a pressing problem from early on in the war. There had been, it is true, the same chauvinistic, jingoistic, emotional release that other countries experienced, at the very beginning of the war, and this is reflected in various chauvinistic and jingoistic works: Hugo Zuckermann's *Song of the Cavalryman* was a great hit. Patriotic waltzes were written by composers such as Franz Lehár. He and Edmund Eysler co-wrote an operetta, *Come, German Brothers!* Emmerich Kálmán wrote a very popular patriotic operetta, *I Gave Gold for Iron!* However, the enthusiasm waned quickly as it became clear, even with censorship, how disastrous the campaigns against Serbia and Russia were going in the autumn of 1914. The mood turned to diffidence, many writers reflected the general public by returning to a Biedermeier-like interiority. Even some of the operettas that on the surface appear gung-ho and chauvinistically patriotic, such as *I Gave Gold for Iron!*, reveal themselves on closer inspection to be not all that martial at all. The moral of the story turns out to be that it is better to listen to your heart than follow the call of duty, a not very convincing argument for martial valour. Another operetta by Eysler, from November 1914, has a promisingly triumphant title, *Frühling am Rhein*, but rather than being about spring on the Rhine, the renaissance of German power, it is about Moritz Frühling, a Jewish merchant who lives in a village on the Rhine. There are some jingoistic digs at the enemy alliance, but no more. Kálmán's *Csardasfürstin*, which premiered in November 1915, has an officer as its rather louche hero, but is not a chauvinistic morale booster. Meanwhile, almost at the same moment, on 6 October 1915, Arthur Schnitzler made an entry in his diary about hearing stories at a dinner party of atrocities committed by Habsburg troops in Serbia: 'Horror upon horror! Injustice upon injustice! Insanity upon insanity!' The bombast of the reports in the newspapers could not convince a worried and sullen populace, which no longer believed what it was reading.

The material state of the home front was just as bad, if not worse. The military took over the logistical task of running the Monarchy's economy and infrastructure, its resources and manpower, to aid the war effort. The First World War was as much a war of logistics as it was one of strategy or tactics, and in this area too the Habsburg military leadership was an abject failure, running the 'warfare state' into the ground. Again, critical mistakes were made at the beginning of the war. Key factory workers were allowed to go to the front to fight, but were not easily replaced, leading to severe economic dislocations as factories had to close down for lack of the properly skilled labour. The War Production Law militarised production in several key industrial branches. Eventually the demand for war goods got many factories going again, converted to armaments production. The lack of manpower was frequently made up for by employing women, but the lack of skilled labour had a lasting drag on production. Central depots (*Zentralen*) were established for the collection of war-related commodities, which created scarcities in the civilian markets. Consumer taxes were raised, but the main way in which the war was paid for was by subscriptions to war bonds, with eight rounds of subscription in Cisleithania; patriotism and other less salubrious and more coercive incentives were used to extract capital from the general public, the financial world and industry.

The Monarchy's infrastructure was also converted to military use; railway rolling stock switched over from supplying goods to civilian markets, especially cities, to supplying the soldiers at the front. The war not only brought economic dislocations on a massive scale, but also human dislocation. The military suspicions of Slav populations in the east and south led to thousands being banished to internal exile in camps in the interior. Then there were non-combatant enemy aliens, who the army thought needed to be interned for the duration of hostilities, and as a result of the catastrophic defeats on the eastern front early in the war, there were many thousands of refugees from Galicia who had to be accommodated, one way or another. Some who had the money were allowed to find their own accommodation, and many Galician Jews with means, or with community help, came to Vienna in late 1914. For those without means, and many refugees from Galicia were peasants whose means (their land) was 'immobile', camps were hastily set up in the Austro-Hungarian interior, for instance at Wanga, to house them. When Galicia was reconquered, many of these refugees returned, whether they wanted to or not, whether their land was arable or not, after the war's devastation. Their place at camps like Wanga was taken up by other refugees, and displaced persons, notably Italians from the Austrian side of the Italian front. There were also many thousands of prisoners of war to deal with, to clothe and to feed, and to employ in menial tasks, often to replace the manpower of those who were at the front. Most of the efforts to accommodate these groups were hastily arranged, poorly organised and inadequately funded, leading to severe distress of the 'guests' in many instances, but they also ate up resources that were badly needed at the front lines, and in civilian society. Even when the military achieved a great victory (with German help) in 1915 and occupied Serbia, Montenegro and Albania, the men and resources needed to maintain an occupation outweighed any benefits from exploiting the resources of the region for the war effort, and supplying the home front.

For far too long, keeping the home front supplied with adequate resources was not a high enough priority for the military leadership. It is understandable that they should try to put all the Monarchy's efforts into winning the war, or at least not losing it, but the relative neglect of the civilian population back home also had severe consequences. Commodities did not get to market, causing economic scarcity and opening up opportunities for the exploitative black market; even more significantly, the supply of basic foodstuffs started to fail.

Some of this was not, as such, the fault of the military's organisation of the 'warfare state', but rather due to other factors. The harvest of 1914 was already poor, and then the loss of eastern Galicia, 'Austria's bread basket', in the first months of the war meant that a large part of Austria's grain supply was blocked (as was the supply of petroleum from the eastern Galician oilfields). The ability of the Entente powers to maintain a blockade of foreign trade to the Monarchy also meant that the loss of Galician supply could not be made up by imports. In 1915, the harvest was very poor, and could not be made up by supplies from conquered territories in Serbia and Russian Poland that year. Although most of eastern Galicia was reconquered, large parts of it had been devastated by the war, and the region was in no condition to start supplying its old markets in western Austria any time soon. The net effect was that the 1915 Austrian harvest of wheat and rye was less than half that of 1914 (which had already been poor); in 1916 it was 44 per cent; 1917, 40 per cent. Substitute grains were found, but not as nutritious or as nice to eat. Hungary fared better, as hardly any of its arable land was directly affected by the war, but it also severely reduced its supplies to the other half of the Monarchy. Before 1914, Hungary supplied 2.1 million tons of grain and flour to Austria. In 1916 the equivalent figure was 100,000 tons. The explanation offered by the Hungarian authorities was that they had to supply the over 3 million men (plus animals) in the Habsburg forces, but this still left the huge gap in food supplies for Austria.

The answer provided by the military was to impose rationing and state control on the market. The 'warfare state' led, logically enough, to the welfare state. In February 1915, a War Grain Control Agency was set up, in November 1916 a Food Office, with Social Democrats included in the supervisory boards of both. In April 1915, ration cards were introduced in both Vienna and Prague. As the war wore on, the rations allotted went ever lower, to levels that were much worse than in Paris or London. The situation in Budapest was not all that much better. The particular problem with the Monarchy's larger cities was not only that there was less food to supply, but also that there were fewer vehicles to transport it, as the railway system could not cope with supplying both the home and war fronts. The result was that even as the official ration allotments became ever more meagre, they often did not reflect what people actually received for food. In Trieste in 1917, an official allotment of 2,400 wagons of potatoes had in practice been only 1,680 wagons, only about two-thirds of what had been promised. This failure to provide an adequate supply of foodstuffs compromised the popular legitimacy of the state. Soldiers were fighting at the front, risking their lives for the Fatherland, but their wives and families were starving at home. Food came to be seen by the populace, of whatever nationality, as a right, part of the social contract. By the summer of 1916, it appears the 'warfare state' was failing to hold up its side of that contract, as reports suggest that even in Bohemia, one of the most prosperous provinces, there was widespread hunger.

There was a wave of labour unrest and strikes in protest at economic conditions, which then made economic conditions worse. The currency started steeply depreciating. The condemnation of Kramář to death for treason riled many Czechs. The refusal of Hungary to increase food supplies to Austria was accompanied by increased political unrest there (where the parliament and representative politics still half-functioned) as the Social Democrats and other opposition parties questioned the rationale of continuing war and protested the economic hardship it caused. On 9 July 1916, a new, breakaway Independence Party was formed with Mihály Károlyi at its head, demanding peace without annexations. Even as the situation had improved militarily by the autumn of 1916, politically the subordination to Germany had only increased, and the socio-economic condition of the home front was deteriorating badly. Austria-Hungary was staring at disaster.

Collapse

The Austro-Hungarian leadership began to look for a way out of the crisis, and to look for peace. Franz Joseph, isolated in Schönbrunn, nonetheless had a sense of doom and demanded that there be peace by the following spring. By October the foreign minister, Count Stefan Burián, was also advocating a quick settlement. The urgency of the moment was heightened when Stürgkh, still the Austrian prime minister, was assassinated by Friedrich Adler (son of the socialist leader Victor Adler) while at luncheon at Meissl und Schadn on 21 October. An increasingly frail Franz Joseph signalled the wish to return to constitutional government by bringing back Ernest Koerber as Austrian prime minister, but his part in the Monarchy's history was now run.

Emperor and king since 2 December 1848, Franz Joseph died a few days short of the sixty-eighth anniversary of his accession, on 21 November. His funeral on 30 November was a great demonstration of Habsburg pomp and Catholic symbolism, but the grandeur of the event seemed to onlookers such as Manès Sperber as strangely hollow, given the existential crisis the Monarchy was already in by that time, made only worse by the loss of the emperor. His longevity had in itself created a form of authority, and the mutton-chop-whiskered image of Franz Joseph that hung in every state institution had become iconic – it had

Figure 23. Karl, accompanied by Zita and Otto, at Franz Joseph's funeral, 30 November 1916.
(Published with permission of the Austrian National Library.).

become *the* image of the Monarchy. The problem was, however, that the authority gained from this identification had been affixed to the person of Franz Joseph alone, not to 'the emperor', and certainly not to his successor, his grandnephew Karl.

The twenty-nine-year-old Karl had none of the authority that came with almost seven decades of familiarity; nor did he have Franz Joseph's experience of the Monarchy's complexities; having a neophyte at the helm was a very risky proposition when the Habsburg Monarchy was in a life-threatening crisis. Karl chose what was probably his most sensible option, which was to make a virtue of his youth (and inexperience), and play the role of the dynamic young leader. By using a new broom to clear out the fusty old system, Karl hoped to rejuvenate the Habsburg cause: achieve peace abroad and radical change at home. His approach had echoes of the previous heir-apparent, Franz Ferdinand, with his peace plans envisaging a return to the Three Emperors League of Germany, Austria-Hungary and Russia, and a sense of the need for radical change of the Monarchy's institutions in a federalising direction. Whereas Franz Ferdinand had tended to a reactionary, absolutist restructuring of the Monarchy, Karl's instinct was towards liberalisation and a return to constitutional rule. This was good in theory, and in many ways has elicited sympathy for his plight from many historians, but in practice it was disastrous. Alexis de Tocqueville had pointed out almost a century before that oppressive regimes collapse not when they are at their harshest but rather when they start easing up, and Karl's record is yet another example of Tocqueville's syndrome, for his policies had Gorbachevian results for the Monarchy.

He soon had changed the chief personnel of the imperial leadership. He himself replaced Archduke Friedrich as Supreme Commander of the Habsburg military on 2 December, and it soon became clear that the era of military dictatorship in the Monarchy was ending. It took a couple of months, but on 27 February Conrad was relieved of his position as chief of the General Staff and replaced by General Arthur Arz von Straussenburg. Karl also had the Army High Command moved from Teschen to Baden bei Wien, much further from the front, but closer to, and hence more convenient for, him. As far as Karl was concerned even the relatively moderate Koerber, expert in compromise, was too much part of the old system, a *Wurschtler* (plodder), as he put it. When Koerber demurred on recalling the *Reichsrat*, Karl immediately accepted his resignation, on 13 December, replacing him with the more ideologically liberal Heinrich Count Clam-Martinic. On 22 December, Karl replaced Burián with Count Ottokar Czernin as foreign minister. (Burián became joint finance minister.)

Under the influence of Czernin and also his wife, Empress Zita, from the dynasty of Bourbon-Parma, Karl attempted to pursue a foreign policy independent from the Germans. Part of this involved developing secret contacts to the French established through Zita's brother, Sixtus, but the desultory negotiations from January to May were without a positive result. On the home front, Karl responded to the increasing unrest in Vienna and the provinces by adopting a more inclusive approach. He agreed to be crowned King of Hungary, which duly took place on 30 December in Budapest with much pomp, partly to show his willingness to follow constitutional norms, and also to reassure the Magyar leadership about his plans for radical reform. (In return, there were also promises from the Hungarians to increase food shipments to Austria.) On the other hand, at a Crown Council meeting of 21 January 1917, he showed himself open to the idea of federalism, which was anathema to the Magyar leadership.

In the summer of 1917, with revolution having broken out in Russia in February, Karl tried further to conciliate dissent in the Monarchy by a wide-ranging amnesty, leading to many political prisoners, including Kramář and Friedrich Adler, being released, much to the disgust of much of Austrian German public opinion. By October the system of war censorship had also been replaced by the far less stringent prewar arrangements. Already on 30 May the *Reichsrat* had met for the first time since March 1914. It was supposed to symbolise the return of constitutional normalcy, and be the start of a great reconciliation of the peoples, with Clam-Martinic seeking a 'cabinet of the peoples' to recreate 'Austria as a federation of autonomous peoples'. This was, from the start, a terrible miscalculation, as the government's vague promises of federalisation were met with calls from the various national groups within the assembly for virtually independent national states.

To what degree the nationalist antagonism to the central state evident in the middle of 1917 reflected prewar attitudes, and whether nationalist antipathy had already undermined the Habsburg war effort, remain contentious issues. The current (revisionist) consensus emphasises just how enthusiastic citizens from all national groups in the Monarchy were to serve their emperor-king in the war, how little disobedience of the authorities there was, and how well military discipline was maintained until virtually the end of the war. From this perspective, it was the needlessly harsh military regime of the first two years of the war, with its unwarranted suspicions of all non-German or non-Magyar national populations, that became a self-fulfilling prophecy, with persecution and incompetence combining to alienate vast sectors of the populace that would otherwise have remained loyal and supportive of the Habsburg state.

Critics of this viewpoint to the still considerable evidence that the 'minority' nationalities in the Monarchy, both in Austria and Hungary, were not as committed to the cause as the Germans and the Magyars. Czech banks, for instance, did not subscribe to war bonds at the same levels as Austro-German ones, and there are instances of Czech bankers advising against this investment in the war effort. The headline cases of whole Czech regiments going over to their Russian Slav brothers might have been fictional, but there is evidence of many Slav units, including Czechs, too easily surrendering to the Russians. The rate of desertion to the enemy has been calculated to have been ten times higher in the Habsburg military than in the German counterpart. The existence of a Czech Legion fighting on the Entente's side was exploited for propaganda purposes, and was largely based on volunteers from PoW camps, but by war's end there were roughly 40,000 in the Legion, which is not inconsiderable. It might have been unwise to arrest Kramář for treason, but there is also good evidence that he was encouraged by the Russian advance in 1914. The claim that in the first part of the war there was no real internal antagonism to the Monarchy's war effort among the minority national groups, that there was no threat of subversion, no dissent, that it was all a figment of the military's imagination, can itself, therefore, be seen as too easy a stance to take.

What is clear, however, is that the experience of two years of ruthless and clumsy military dictatorship had severely exacerbated what hostility to the state and the dominant national groups there had been, and often created such hostility. The *Reichsrat*'s national groups set out demands that went far beyond what the government was prepared to, or even could, meet. The 'Yugoslav Club' demanded in its May Declaration the creation of a South Slav administrative unit for the Monarchy as a whole, regardless of dualist boundaries. The Czech Union similarly called for an autonomous Czech and Slovak state, transgressing dualism. Tisza's Hungarian government was completely against any such change to the Compromise arrangements, and refused to buckle. Tisza also refused to go along with any real electoral reform, and it was on this point that he resigned on 15 June, in effect forced out by Karl. Yet the subsequent Hungarian government of Count Moric Esterházy was no more forth-coming, nor was that of Sándor Wekerle (again) from 18 August. Despite some cosmetic moves in the direction of electoral reform, there really was no major change, and no major concessions to the minority nationalities. Meanwhile, the architect of this attempt at conciliation of the national groups, Clam-Martinic, recognising the failure of his plans, resigned on 23 June, and was replaced as Austrian prime minister by Ernst Seidler von Feuchtenegg.

None of this had much of an effect on the stranglehold that Germany had acquired over Austria-Hungary, militarily, economically and hence politically. In military terms, the war was going well for the Central Powers in 1917, but at the cost of ever-increasing German domination of the junior, Austro-Hungarian partner, and a worsening diplomatic situation. On the eastern front, the February Revolution destroyed the tsarist regime. The new, constitutional Russian regime stayed true to its Western Allies, but Russia's July offensive was a failure. When the Austro-Hungarian and German forces counter-attacked, the Russian war machine started to collapse – for similar logistical and infrastructural reasons that were crippling Austria-Hungary as well. The end result was the October Revolution and the takeover by the Bolsheviks (with Lenin's presence made possible by the German government). The new regime effectively capitulated to the Central Powers at Brest-Litovsk, provision-ally in December 1917, formally in March 1918. Germany and Austria-Hungary, it is worth remembering, won the First World War in the east.

The Central Powers also did well in the south. Yet another Italian offensive on the Isonzo in the summer stalled, and the Austro-Hungarian and German forces then launched their counter-offensive in late October, with the German 14th Army using the latest military technologies, especially a far more sophisticated, and hideously effective, use of poison gas (chemical weapons). The result of the victory of Caporetto was to drive the Italians all the way back to the Piave River, almost to Venice. (The battle experience from the Italian side received its literary memorial in Ernest Hemingway's *A Farewell to Arms*.)

External success was wedded, however, to increasing subordination within the alliance. Habsburg forces were now almost never without German support and direction. The peace arrangements in the eastern theatre were negotiated by the Germans with little regard to Austro-Hungarian concerns. German, not Austro-Hungarian, cities received most of the benefits there were from the 'bread peace'.

Meanwhile, concerned that France and Britain were getting too many supplies from overseas, Germany decided to resume unrestricted submarine warfare on 1 February, which proved a diplomatic disaster of the first order. Initially, the Austro-Hungarian leadership were not in favour of this, given that it was not of immense relevance to them (although there was submarine warfare in the Mediterranean as well as the Atlantic), and that it risked provoking the entry of the United States into the war, but the Crown Council was persuaded to go along. Submarine warfare, combined with the Zimmermann Telegram, led the United States to declare war on Germany on 6 April. It did not declare war on Austria-Hungary, as President Woodrow Wilson still envisaged the possibility of a separate peace with Austria-Hungary. The United States eventually declared war on Austria-Hungary on 7 December.

Having just won in the east, the Central Powers now faced a potentially even stronger adversary from the west. This did not daunt the Germans, who were still convinced of final victory, but on the Habsburg side, Karl and Czernin were less comfortable with their prospects, including their having to operate under German overlordship. They continued secret negotiations with the British and French well into 1918, but these still got nowhere. The Germans, meanwhile, concentrated all their resources on the western front, readying for a March offensive that, *this* time, would gain victory. Unable to make headway in the secret negotiations, and believing German claims of overwhelming advantage, Czernin decided to throw the Monarchy's lot in with the Germans.

In a speech of 2 April 1918 to the Viennese city council, Czernin supported the German ally. Revealing that peace negotiations had indeed occurred with France, he claimed that Austria-Hungary had refused to agree to the return of Alsace-Lorraine as part of any settlement, thus proving Austria-Hungary's loyalty to the German partner. The French prime minister, Georges Clemenceau, incensed by what he saw as a misrepresentation of the talks, then revealed on 12 April Karl's peace offer of March 1917, which had indeed included a *qualified* offer to return Alsace-Lorraine to France. It appeared that someone had lied, and possibly the emperor. In any case, the Austro-Hungarian leadership had clearly gone behind the back of their German ally, betrayed him, one might say. Czernin, 'at his wit's end' ('am Ende meines Lateins'), resigned on 16 April.

The Sixtus Affair, as it is known, completely compromised Austro-Hungarian relations with Germany. The German leadership demanded, and received at the German High Command's headquarters in Spa, Belgium, on 12 May, total Habsburg surrender. Just as Holy Roman Emperor Henry IV had gone to do abject penance before Pope Gregory at Canossa, so now with the 'Austrian Canossa' Karl went to the German emperor and surrendered any remaining Austro-Hungarian independence. Capitulation of Habsburg to Hohenzollern led to the Western Allies giving up on the Monarchy as a 'European necessity', because

Figure 24. Karl and Wilhelm II at Spa, 12 May 1918. Wilhelm in Austro-Hungarian uniform, Karl in German uniform.
(Published with permission of the Austrian National Library.)

now it was only a German puppet state. The Entente had talked of liberating the peoples of the Monarchy from oppressive rule, but that had been little more than talk. It was only now that the Western Allies seriously contemplated breaking up the Monarchy on national lines.

By the time of the Spa meeting, the war's fortunes were also beginning to change. Czernin's bet turned out to be a bad one in any case. Germany's March offensive on the western front made initial gains, but had stalled. In June, the Austro-Hungarian offensive on the Piave began, with hopes of repeating the great gains of the year before. Things had changed. The offensive was ill-conceived, under-resourced, badly led (Conrad was in charge of one of the armies), an unmitigated disaster from the first day – with all Austro-Hungarian reserves soon used up. In August, the Battle of Amiens saw the German front line begin to buckle. In mid-September, the Western Allied forces in the Balkans attacked, leading to the collapse of Bulgaria by the end of the month, and the pull-back of the Central Powers. On the western front, by late summer, the Allied troops, with fresh American reinforcements and new tactics, including the use of tanks, made advances not seen since the war's first days. There, and on the Italian and Balkan fronts as well, the tactical, technological, and logistical superiority of the Western Allies was now evident. By mid-September, Karl had declared his interest in a separate peace, without Germany, but the Allies were not interested in a minor player like Austria-Hungary.

Domestically, by then, Austria-Hungary had already begun to fall apart. The successes at the Italian front of 1917 had played their part in this. The unexpected advances from Caporetto had led to the campaign being extended, which also entailed the extended military deployment of rolling stock, which was therefore unavailable to supply Vienna and other cities with food and fuel. Fleeting military success had resulted in even more severe shortages on the home front. The armaments industry itself was running out of metal from as early as the summer of 1917, and steel production had to be halted in May 1918 because of the lack of coal for the furnaces. Food and fuel were in desperately short supply in the cities. In Vienna, the Court theatres had to curtail their programmes because there was no coal for heating; authors of the Fischer Verlag protested in early 1918, because their books were not being published for lack of paper. More fundamentally, there was popular unrest because women would patiently line up for the bread ration, only to find there was no bread left. Starvation spread.

In such circumstances, the liberalisation of Karl's government did not pacify the populace, but rather allowed the inevitable labour unrest to be better articulated, with a wave of strikes over the winter and spring of

1917/1918. There was a munitions strike in Vienna in January 1918 which spread to Hungary; increasing unrest culminated in a nine-day general strike in Hungary in late June. There was also increasing unrest in the ranks behind the front line: in February there was a mutiny at the naval base of Cattaro, Dalmatia; in May there was a mutiny in Pécs, Hungary.

Government attempts to respond to the material distress of the population also had unintended, disintegrative consequences. In October 1917, a Ministry for Social Welfare was instituted to distribute the funds for widows and orphans to the needy, but this was done in cooperation with the pre-existing, private welfare groups. These welfare organisations were almost all 'national', which is to say not on an *Austrian* basis but on that of the particular nationalities, and it was nationalists who now advised the government, and took responsibility, and credit, for how state funds were distributed to their people: 'nationalist associations had become the state'.

The demands for autonomy for the various nationalities had only been radicalised by events. On 8 January, Wilson had given his Fourteen Points speech, and Paragraph 10 had been of particular interest to Austria-Hungary: 'The people of Austria-Hungary, whose place among the nations we wish to see safeguarded and assured, should be accorded the freest opportunity to autonomous development.' 'Whose' place (the Monarchy's or the people's) should be safeguarded was left excruciatingly ambivalent, but it certainly encouraged talk of federalisation on national lines. The proposal to federalise the Monarchy had, in principle, been on the table since at least January 1917, and had become the major demand of the minority nationalist leaderships at the reconvening of the *Reichsrat* in May, albeit with autonomy *within* a restructured Monarchy. The 'Austrian Canossa' at Spa a year later, in May 1918, had, as part of the capitulation, offered an alternative vision of *Mitteleuropa*, a Central European Customs Union, with the whole of the region now dominated by the German behemoth, a prospect neither the minority nationalists, nor the Western Allies, relished. It was after Spa that the Western Allies recognised the exiled national organisations, the Czechoslovak National Council in Paris in July, also the Romanian and South Slav National Committees. The Polish political leadership decided in September to unite Polish lands, Galicia included, in a Polish nation-state under *German* patronage.

On 27 September, Karl responded to these developments by proposing a far-reaching federalisation, with its final version eventually formulated in the Manifesto published on 16 October. The circle could not be squared, however, for Hungary still objected to any changes in the Compromise.

His efforts had by now been overtaken by events in any case. On 7 October the Regency Council in Warsaw had demanded the union of all Polish territories in a sovereign Polish nation-state. In early October the National Council of Slovenes, Croats and Serbs had convened in Zagreb as the representative body of the Monarchy's South Slavs. On 18 October, Wilson rejected the Austro-Hungarian armistice proposal. On 26 October, Karl withdrew from the alliance with Germany, but this was all far too late, and the emperor's actions irrelevant. On 28 October, the Czechoslovak Republic was declared in Prague. On 29 October, the Croatian *Sabor* in Zagreb declared union with Serbia.

On 11 October, the Hungarian prime minister, Wekerle, had declared that the old Austria, that had agreed the Compromise, was no more, and when Karl's Manifesto was published on 16 October, the Hungarian government concluded that the Compromise was now null and void. Karl was still king, but there would no longer be any link to Austria except through a personal union. Wekerle's government resigned on 23 October, leading to the eventual revolution of 1 November, when the new prime minister, Károlyi, declared Hungary's full independence, and the end of Austria-Hungary.

At the Italian front, desertions increased, troops left to defend *their* homelands, and another Allied offensive on 24 October, with overwhelming superiority in numbers and materiel, drove the depleted Austrian forces back – forcing the Austrians to sign an armistice on 3 November. The Austrians ceased hostilities the same day, but the Italian forces only stopped advancing on 4 November, as the armistice agreement allowed, capturing thousands of Austrian troops, including Ludwig Wittgenstein.

By then the Habsburg Monarchy had, to all intents and purposes, ceased to exist.

Even in what is now Austria the Habsburg monarch was no longer welcome. On 21 October, the Provisional National Assembly of German Austria had been formed from the German deputies of the *Reichsrat* (including deputies from the Bohemian lands). On 30 October, they passed a provisional republican constitution, as part of a future German republic. On 31 October, the last prime minister of Habsburg Austria, Heinrich Lammasch, handed over power to the new German Austrian government, headed by the Social Democrat Karl Renner. The Social Democrats, now clearly the strongest party in the land, demanded the declaration of a real republic on 1 November, supported by mass demonstrations in the streets (the same day as Hungary declared independence, two days before the armistice). On 11 November, Karl renounced his imperial powers. On 12 November the Republic of German Austria was declared. Karl and his family left the new republic on 23 March 1919 for exile in Switzerland.

His restoration attempts in Hungary failed. In 1921 he moved to Madeira for health reasons. The last Habsburg emperor died on that island in the middle of the Atlantic on 1 April 1922.

'The Monarchy melted away through a combination of internal disintegration and external pressure.' It was destroyed from without, but also from within, by its inability, as a dynastic supranational state, to function effectively in an era of ruthless modern warfare, and to maintain its legitimacy in the eyes of its citizens and its troops. This was not only a material failure, to defeat its enemies and feed its populace, but also a spiritual failure, to convince its citizens that they still owed it loyalty and obedience. When troops started leaving the front to defend *their* homelands, the Habsburg Monarchy had ceased to be their home, it had lost its authority over them, and so it disappeared.

Austrians Predict the Future

The Monarchy might have ended on 11 November 1918, but its legacy, often a very troubling legacy, remained. Its administrative structures were inherited by the successor states, as was much of its political culture. It was just that the shoe was on another foot. The war was not really over. Too many resentments remained – social and political relations had been too badly torn – for there to be sustainable peace any time soon.

On 15 November 1918, the *Neue Freie Presse* expressed its dismay at Czech triumphalism and Czech determination not to allow the Germans in German Bohemia to determine their own future and to force them to become part of Czechoslovakia. It predicted terrible consequences: 'The Czech republic, which does not allow for German self-determination, and rouses the Magyars to deadly hatred, will be a "*free-state*" but not a *state which is free*. Surrounded by tensions, the Czechs will always be dependent on foreign help.' On 12 December the newspaper elaborated on the poison that the takeover of German Bohemia, later called the Sudetenland, would create for German-Czech relations, and it warned: 'Times change, and a great people such as the Germans can always reckon on the future.' This was strangely prescient.

Even more prophetic was Karl Kraus's prediction. In the *Last Days of Mankind*, he has the Grumbler (*Nörgler*), comment on the real character of the war: 'It has not taken place on the surface of life, but rather has raged at life's core. The front has spread into the hinterland. It will stay there. And the transformed life, if there still is one, will be teamed up with

Figure 25. Declaration of the Republic of German Austria in Vienna, 12 November 1918. Crowds mass before the Parliament (formerly *Reichsrat*) Building on the *Ringstrasse*.
(Published with permission of the Austrian National Library.)

the old way of thinking. The world will go under, and we will not notice. We will have forgotten everything that happened yesterday; not see what is going on today; and not fear what is coming tomorrow. We will have forgotten that we lost the war, forgotten that we began it, forgotten that we waged it. Therefore it will not stop.'

Conclusion: Central Europe and the Paths Not Taken

It has been well said that the Habsburg Monarchy represented a 'chance for Central Europe', but it was an opportunity that, in the end, was not taken. The various ways in which the Habsburg monarchs and the political leadership attempted to manage their patrimony worked to preserve Habsburg power for over a century after 1815, but they ultimately proved inadequate – partly because the Monarchy was still viewed by them as a patrimony.

It was still a major event when an ancient dynastic empire, which had often been a dominant presence in Central Europe, disappeared, almost overnight, in November 1918. Why the Monarchy failed in the way it did has remained since then a topic for historians to debate and agonise over. Not only the reasons for its disappearance, but also the nature of its legacy, both positive and negative, and further of its 'meaning' for Central Europe, and for Europe more generally, remain live, and often hotly disputed topics. The Monarchy has now been defunct for a century, but the book has not been closed on its nature, its meaning or its demise. Here are some tentative conclusions to further the ongoing discussion.

How an Ancient Empire Disappears

In the Manifesto of 29 July 1914, Franz Joseph claimed that he had 'examined and weighed everything' and came to the conclusion that he must declare war on Serbia. That was not a wise conclusion. If we 'examine and weigh everything' that happened in the Monarchy's last century, as I have attempted to present in abridged form in this book, we can, perhaps, see that some of the explanations given for why the Monarchy eventually disappeared in 1918 are more cogent than others. Older versions of the Monarchy's flaws are not quite as convincing as they used to be.

The once popular idea that the Monarchy remained throughout the period an essentially autocratic state, which never really adjusted to the modern era of representative government, has been shown to have been at best only partly true, and ignored the fact that even in the era of Metternich there was in fact political life, of sorts, in much of the Austrian Empire. After 1867, both Austrian and Hungarian parts of the Monarchy were, more or less, constitutional monarchies with the rule of law and representative governmental institutions. In Cisleithania, at least, there was a form, albeit a rather strange form, of political democratisation in the later decades, which left elected politicians with influence within the bureaucracy, and hence the government. Historians use this 'behind-the-scenes' political bargaining to argue that the Monarchy, in Cisleithania, was not the sort of straightforward 'top-down' power system it was once thought to be. And Hungary had parliamentary government (albeit with a restricted franchise). Autocracy has been seen as a major cause of the Monarchy's demise, but right at the end. In this view, it was the attempt by a reactionary elite to restore properly autocratic (and aristocratic) rule in 1914 that destroyed the otherwise promising developments within Austria-Hungary, and that virtual coup, in 1914, is primarily to blame for the demise of the Monarchy just over four years later.

The other main traditional reason given for the Monarchy's end is its inability to defend itself from 'the thunder of heaven', nationalism. This too is now a far less convincing argument, given recent research and reinterpretations. Nationalism was indeed a very strong force within the Monarchy from the early nineteenth century, but it was not inevitable that the Monarchy would come to be seen mainly in terms of its national groups – that was a consequence of the 'invention', or at least construction, of national identities around which national groups then formed. Moreover, the relationship between the Monarchy and nationalism was never as adversarial as nineteenth-century nationalists, and twentieth-century nationalist historians, would have us believe. The Monarchy was not so much a 'prison of the peoples' as a nursery. In the first period, political nationalism might be frowned upon by the Habsburg authorities, often banned indeed, like all politics, but cultural nationalism was not, it was even encouraged, and later on the *modus vivendi* between the state and the nationalist movements was often an accommodating one, in which the authorities were quite willing to cut a deal to gain support. The very way in which the political leadership came to think of the Monarchy, as above and between the nationalities in its territories, was in itself an ideological triumph of nationalism, because individuals became identified with their nation rather than as independent citizens *sans phrase*. Obversely, most nationalists were quite happy to work for power *within* the Monarchy's parameters. This was not the case for the Italian nationalist leadership of Lombardy-Venetia, but that was the exception. Between 1867 and 1914, most nationalist political parties saw their future *within* the Monarchy rather than outside it. Here again, the current revisionist consensus looks to the decision for war in 1914, and the hostility of the military dictatorship to the minority nationalities thereafter, as the main reason why a promising de facto federalisation on national lines was never allowed to come to maturity.

If it was not liberalism or nationalism, as such, that brought down the absolutist, supra-national dynastic Monarchy, was it just bad luck then? Was it just that the ways chosen to come to terms with the modern world of representative government and national self-determination, of popular sovereignty and the constitutionalist rule of law, were unfortunate, and just did not work out as planned? Was it a case of the paths not taken? The account in the preceding pages should have suggested that there were many points at which, had another person been in charge, Archduke Johann as emperor for instance, had someone else had the power to make decisions, Adolf Fischhof in 1849, Rudolf in the 1880s, Ernest Koerber in 1910, even Franz Ferdinand in 1913, perhaps the course of history might have been better. On the other hand, the preceding account has also shown that at various stages the Monarchy's leadership was faced with performing almost impossible political feats of legerdemain, and if its attempts to square the various circles did not meet with outright success, then that was because those circles were impossible to square in any case, at least without unforeseen consequences and repercussions.

Of all the fateful decisions made before 1914, one of the most significant, and ambivalent, was the decision by Franz Joseph to agree to the Compromise of 1867 that created the Dual Monarchy. On the one hand dualism enabled an accommodation between the Habsburg dynasty and the Magyar leadership that gave the Monarchy a new lease of life, another half century. On the other hand, had there been no special status for Hungary within the Monarchy, then federalisation on approximately national lines would have been much more a possibility, and not always blocked by the Magyar veto. The military dictatorship in Cisleithania after July 1914 might have precipitated the demise of the Monarchy by its crass and ruthless rule alienating the various minority national groups, but Hungary alienated its minority nationalities with its parliamentary government intact, and it was its maintenance of its veto on all major restructuring of Austria that made the last-minute attempt at federalisation a non-starter. It should be recalled that the reason why the Dual Monarchy disappeared was not only that the peripheral groups split off, but also that the Hungarian co-partner terminated the agreement, before the armistice was even signed. Was it dualism then that bought another fifty years of the Monarchy's existence, but at the cost of its future, inevitable demise as the result of an insuperable contractual dispute? Or should we change our perspective and not ask why the Monarchy disappeared, but why it lasted as long as it did, a supra-national, dynastic conglomeration of states in the modern era of the unitary nation-state?

The Monarchy was, despite all the changes and transformations, liberalisation, nationalisation and modernisation, an anachronism, or at least that was true of the monarch who ruled it almost until its end. If the military performed so badly in 1914 because it was starved of resources, and out of date in its organisation and in the thinking of its leadership, then that was at least partially due to the fact that the person who still jealously guarded control of it was an emperor who, in July 1914, was eighty-three years old. Nor had Franz Joseph, as a younger emperor, really moved much with the times. His remark to Theodore Roosevelt in 1910 about being 'the last monarch of the old school' is often quoted in a comfortable way to characterise the ripeness of the Habsburg ruler, but much more telling is his interaction with another American president back in 1878. On the world tour that he undertook with his wife after the end of his presidency, Ulysses S. Grant visited Vienna, 'one of the most beautiful cities in Europe if not the most beautiful'. At a military parade in his honour, Grant remarked to Franz Joseph that he was by now sick of seeing military parades. The idea that a general, one of the most famous generals of the century, would not consider military pomp and circumstance important so astounded the emperor that all he could do was laugh. There was a chasm between Grant's modern view of the military, and the reactionary view of the person who was decades later to start the First World War partly for a value hard to see as modern: to defend *his* Monarchy's *honour*.

Despite all that, despite the decision for dualism, despite the anachronism of Franz Joseph's approach to being a ruler in war and peace, despite the many failures to get ahead of history, whether it was in 1848, 1859, 1866, 1867, 1879, 1897, 1905, or 1907, the Monarchy was still a viable entity in 1914, and it took a catastrophic war to bring down the Habsburg state, so perhaps we should not emphasise the idea of inevitable decline (although the Monarchy was undoubtedly a far less powerful, prominent and influential Great Power in 1914 than it had been in 1815), but rather, as the revisionist consensus now does, that it was the decision for war in 1914, and the appalling handling of the war both on the military and home fronts, that did for the Monarchy in the end. We should also remember that the Habsburg dynasty, as a regime, was not at all alone in losing power because of the war. The Romanovs lost power long before the Habsburgs, and the last Hohenzollern, Wilhelm II, abdicated on 9 November, two days before the last Habsburg, Karl, gave up his powers.

The Ottoman Empire was dismembered, and any remaining dynastic role officially abolished in 1922. Among the victors there were also severe consequences from the war. There was an especially detrimental effect in Italy, where the constitutional monarchy was soon to be usurped by Mussolini's fascism. Therefore, the demise of the Habsburg dynastic *regime* was not at all unusual as a consequence of the war, and can largely be explained by military inadequacy, and the inability of the warfare state to fulfill its social contract with the populace. Almost everywhere in Europe, as a result of the war's deprivations, the established political regimes were overturned by revolutions of one sort or another, supported by mass demonstrations of people revolting against hunger and exhaustion for a regime they no longer respected, or obeyed. To paraphrase a famous Viennese saying: no food, no political legitimacy.

On the other hand those other polities did not disappear. The closest parallel was the Ottoman Empire, whose partition was indeed analogous to that of the Habsburg Monarchy, with the creation of states such as Iraq, Syria and Palestine, yet there was still a considerable Turkish state straddling the Bosporus and with the large territory of Asia Minor. Germany was much reduced, but still a large nation-state after the Peace of Versailles. The Bolshevik Soviet Union lost large territories on the Baltic littoral and in eastern Europe, but remained a huge, continent-spanning state. In contrast, there seemed nothing left of the Monarchy at all. It disappeared from the map.

The Monarchy was carved up as part of the Versailles settlement, more specifically two treaties: the Treaty of St Germain, between the Allied Powers and German Austria, of 10 September 1919; and the Treaty of Trianon, between the Allied Powers and Hungary, of 4 June 1920. Hungary, reduced to a third of its previous area, was now much more homogeneously Magyar. The new state of Czechoslovakia was formed from the historic Bohemian crownlands, plus the ethnically Slovak areas of what had been Upper Hungary (plus Sub-Carpatho-Ruthenia which no other state much wanted), all previously territories of the Monarchy. Other large tranches of territory were given over to new or existing 'nation-states'. Galicia and small parts of Silesia and Bukovina became part of the restored Poland; most of Bukovina, including Czernowitz, and most of Transylvania, were handed over to Romania; Croatia-Slavonia, Dalmatia, plus the areas in the southern part of Hungary and in southern Austria (Carniola, southern Styria and southern Carinthia) with majority South Slav populations, became part of the new Kingdom of Serbs, Croats and Slovenes, otherwise known as Yugoslavia. Trieste, Istria and the Adriatic littoral, plus South Tyrol all the way to the Brenner Pass,

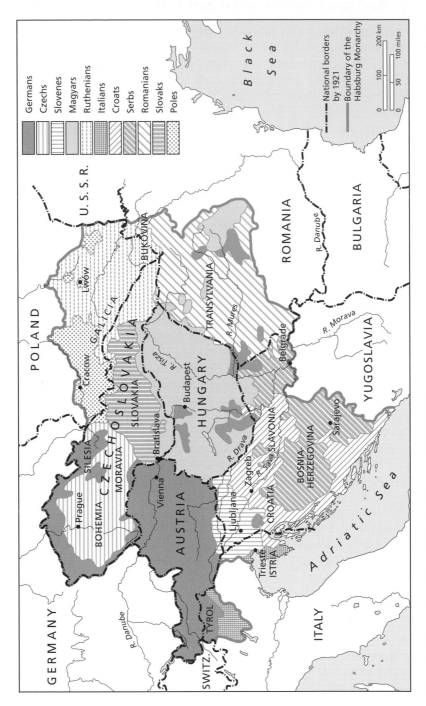

Map 5: The nationalising of Central Europe, 1918–1921.

were 'redeemed' by Italy as Italian territory, despite the fact that the northern part of South Tyrol was almost entirely German-speaking. '*Ce qui reste*', as Clemenceau put it, was German Austria, which came to be regarded as the main successor to the Habsburg Monarchy. Most Habsburg officials who did not feel welcome in the new states came back to 'German Austria' and its capital, Vienna. The new leadership of German Austria would have liked to complete the disappearance of the Monarchy by becoming part of the new Weimar Republic of Germany, but that was denied them by the victorious Allies. As part of the Treaty of St Germain, German Austria was forced to retain its independence and change its name to the more anonymous Republic of Austria. There were territorial disputes between the successor states, some of them leading to violence, and Hungary never accepted the demise of the Kingdom of St Stephen. Many Hungarians still have not. The Monarchy, however, had disappeared, and was, initially not much mourned by anyone except the strictest monarchists.

How could a 'European necessity' have vanished so completely? The short answer has already been given: the Monarchy's ceding of effective sovereignty to Germany in 1918 meant it no longer would have performed its necessary function of a multinational buffer and counterweight, had it survived the war. The last thing the Western Allies wanted was a stronger Germany as a result of the war, and so they gave up on the Monarchy and listened to the various national councils in exile instead. By the summer of 1918, therefore, a new template, following, approximately, Wilsonian notions of national self-determination and autonomy, was adopted. It saw Central European plurality better managed as a set of small to medium-sized 'nation-states', linked to the Western allies by treaties, and, it was to be hoped, to each other in some form of Danubian Federation or trade area. This had been already present *in utero* in the plans for the autonomous national state units advocated by nationalist politicians *within* the Monarchy both before and during the war (after January 1917). That, plus irredentism, meant that the transition from advocating for autonomous units within the Monarchy, to independent nation-states without the Monarchy *at all*, was almost a seamless process over the course of the summer and autumn of 1918. The exit of Czechs, Slovaks, Poles, Romanians, Italians, and South Slavs would have still left a fairly substantial Austro-Hungarian core. It was only after the two 'ruling' groups, German Austrians and Magyars, had split because of Hungarian rejection of the plans for federation, that any trace of the Monarchy vanished. Imagine if France left the European Union.

Legacies: Presence and Absence

Then again, in so many ways, the Monarchy really did not disappear at all, and is still strangely present in its former territories, even as a painfully felt absence.

In the main successor states, there was a remarkable amount of administrative continuity, and even the political culture did not change as much as one might have thought, or was claimed at the time. The first law of the Czech National Committee in October 1918 was one confirming the validity of all existing (imperial and provincial) laws and regulations. Alois Rašín, a member of the committee, later justified this acceptance of the Habsburg legal order as a way to avoid anarchy, 'so that our whole state administration would remain and continue on October 29 as if there had been no revolution at all'. This was not a revolution against the existing order; it was a taking over of the existing order which was seen as 'our' order in any case, a fair description, given the extent to which, as we saw previously, Czechs had already become predominant in the administrative personnel of the Bohemian lands. Even such laws as those concerning when a school needed to be made available to a minority nationality followed Habsburg law almost to the letter. The only difference was that in Czechoslovakia the state-people, the ruling nation, was Czech, and Germans were now the minority. Czechoslovakia was a republic, and it lauded its democratic traditions, but it was strangely reminiscent that the rather elderly Thomas Masaryk, sixty-eight when he became president at the end of 1918, became effectively president-for-life, sitting in the Hradschin, the royal palace where Franz Joseph *would* have been crowned King of Bohemia.

Even more reminiscent of the Monarchy was the fact that Czechoslovakia was anything but a nation-state, rather a multinational empire, of Czechs, Slovaks, Germans, Magyars, Ruthenes, Jews and Roma. Czechs were not even a majority of the populace. None of the nation-states that were formed out of the Monarchy were actually properly nation-states: they were all little 'empires', with considerable populations of minority nationalities. Poland had Ruthenes, Germans and Jews in its formerly 'Austrian' lands; Romania took over a sizeable Magyar and Sekler population in Transylvania, along with German-speaking 'Saxons' and Jews; Yugoslavia was already a multinational state, although it was run like Greater Serbia in many respects. Italy had Slovenes and Croats in its new Adriatic territories, and Germans in the northern part of South Tyrol. These multinational situations might have been manageable had the Cisleithanian, 'imperial', pluralist approach that arose after 1880 been taken, but the Magyar approach, itself based on the French model, of treating a multinational state as a nation-state was the preferred policy, which explains much of the conflict that East Central Europe experienced in the interwar period and beyond. Even the Czechoslovak Republic, which was the most liberal and responsible of the new states, was still, at its core a Czech nation-state, and as a result never could succeed in squaring the circle of the Sudetenland question – of how to include the German Bohemians.

Hungary as well kept many links to the Habsburg past. Initially, Károlyi's left-liberal regime was overwhelmed by first the 'red' Bolshevik revolution of Bela Kun, and they in turn by the 'white' counter-revolution of Admiral Miklós Horthy. Horthy returned Hungary to a royal regime, acting under the constitution as 'regent' for the Habsburg monarch. Both times that the actual Habsburg monarch, Karl, tried to return to claim his throne in 1921, Horthy rebuffed him, because the retention of the traditional forms of government by his reactionary, authoritarian regime did not go so far as to accept the legitimate sovereign. The Magyar nationalism that had characterised Hungarian politics before 1914 was as strong, if not stronger, after 1918, but now in a state which was almost all Magyar, the ruling class looked inward for enemies; it no longer needed to be inclusive of the one remaining ethnic minority, Jews, and so Hungary became the first country in Central Europe to introduce a quota for Jews in higher education.

In the Austrian Republic, many tried to distance themselves from the Habsburg heritage, most notably in the attempt to become fully part of Germany, rebuffed by the Allies though it was. Nonetheless, Austria too adopted almost the entire legal framework of the Monarchy, and even the new constitution echoed the Habsburg arrangements in key ways, such as with the emergency laws. Not all of this juridical inheritance was positive. Partly because of the legal interpretations of national identity from before 1914, especially of the Moravian Compromise, Austrian courts in the interwar period deemed that Austrian citizens from Galicia of Jewish descent were Jewish, not German, and hence not entitled to (German) Austrian citizenship. The racial definition of Jews in the interwar period was thus a development of Habsburg jurisprudence. The whole polarising dynamic between 'Red Vienna' and the 'black' (conservative Catholic) provinces that was to hobble and then destroy the Austrian Republic was also already implicit in the last years of the Monarchy. Perhaps the most poisonous legacy of all was the continuing inability of Austrian Germans to decide if they were Germans or something different: Austrians; the only legacy of the Monarchy more evil than that, and closely associated, was the antisemitism of both conservative Catholics and 'liberal' German nationalists in the republic (where the word 'national' in politics referred to a German identification, not an Austrian one). Adolf Hitler had grown up in Habsburg Austria, after all.

A common heritage of the successor states, which had its good and bad sides, was the reliance on the bureaucratic state. In interwar Poland, much of the administration was staffed by Galicians, because that was the one group of Poles that had been given much administrative responsibility and training in pre-1914 Polish lands. On the other hand, the top-down authoritarian character of too much of the Habsburg bureaucracy, despite some 'democratisation' trends before 1914, also carried over to the interwar states, and beyond. Under the reactionary and conservative regimes of the 1920s, the authoritarian and fascist regimes of the 1930s, the Nazi or Nazi-allied regimes of the 1940s and then the communist regimes of the 1950s, the bureaucratic mentality continued largely unaffected. The 'big brother' communist states of the second half of the twentieth century did not appear all that out of place given that authoritarian experience and bureaucratic tradition. Of course, there was also a sly, ironic cultural response to this, but the fact that Hašek's Schwejk could easily have had a role in Milos Forman's *Firemen's Ball* is indicative of cultural continuities. That it was so easy for the communist regimes to co-opt nationalism as part of their legitimacy also suggests a dialectical inheritance from the nationalist experience of the Monarchy and the interwar nationalist political cultures.

As the last paragraph indicates, the liberal democratic promise of national self-determination or even the socialist dreams of truly democratic people's republics, for which the Monarchy was traded in in 1918, soon foundered in the harsh realities of interwar Central Europe. The economic situation would have been dire even had the Monarchy's economic free trade area been retained, but it was made exponentially worse by the division of the region not only into 'nation-states' but also into mutually hostile economic units. Vienna and the Austrian Republic suffered particularly, as before 1914 it had received much of its food from Galicia or Hungary, and its fuel (mostly coal) from the Bohemian lands; in the immediate post-war period all of this was cut off, some of it deliberately. But, as was well understood by many at the time, all countries suffered from the economic dislocations of the new borders, even the relatively prosperous Czechoslovakia. The political unrest caused by the generally weak economic performances of the region congealed with the still sore national resentments, especially in a revanchist Hungary, intent on restoring the *full* territory of the lands of St Stephen, to produce first mostly conservative governments in the 1920s, then in the 1930s increasingly authoritarian and fascist regimes, and finally, in the late 1930s and early 1940s, collaborator-regimes with the Nazis, in those countries not already conquered by Germany. Czechoslovakia was the one major exception, until Munich in September 1938 and the Nazi takeover (with Slovak and Hungarian co-operation) in early 1939. After 1945, there was the descent of most of the region under Soviet-induced communist rule, which was only fully shaken off in 1989 (or even 1991). In Yugoslavia, developments were a little different after 1945, but there was also a sense of liberation for many when that communist state broke up after 1990.

It is hardly surprising, given this appalling track record for the former Habsburg region, that a strong nostalgia began to develop for the Monarchy, and even the monarch, starting some time in the 1930s. The literature of the Habsburg myth – the novels of Joseph Roth, Franz Werfel, and even Robert Musil – reflects the understanding that, for all its problems, something important was lost, for the region, and also for Europe more generally, by the absence of the Monarchy. Ever since then, this idea that the Monarchy was some sort of 'European necessity' after all, and that it was a tragic mistake to discard it in 1918, has grown in popularity and persuasiveness. For all its many flaws and faults, it did fulfill the function not only of being a 'refuge' for the small nations, in international political terms, but also as an economic space that allowed a much more productive exchange of goods than the small, isolated economies of the interwar period. It also provided a hugely productive cultural space, of great diversity and plurality, where, despite the national divisions, or almost because of them, through and against the national, ethnic and religious differences (to channel Hofmannsthal temporarily), the 'beside each other' and 'in each other', 'living with each other' of the Austrian peoples, created a remarkably fecund, complex and inclusive, marginocentric cultural matrix that produced many of the most foremost thinkers and writers of twentieth-century modernity. The inclusive logic and pluralist thinking of so many 'Austrian' thinkers, with its emphasis on *un*certainty (probability) rather than certainty, shared by figures as disparate as Sigmund Freud, Karl Popper, Ludwig Wittgenstein, Otto Neurath and Erwin Schrödinger, is the actual basis of our modern world, perhaps the Monarchy's most ironic legacy. It is more than coincidence that the political liberation of Central Europe in the 1980s took place at just the same time that the former power of the culture of the region had come to be given global recognition.

Nor is it coincidence that the new refuge of the countries of Central Europe, or the former Habsburg lands, was soon seen to be inclusion in the European Union, for that was the spiritual political heir of the Habsburg Monarchy, as a supra-national, multi-national polity, only this time with the virtue of being composed of democratic states sharing their sovereignty, rather than a dynastic collection of possessions under central dominion. The centrality of Brussels and the Eurocracy in nationalist rhetoric about the European Union does suggest, however, that from a negative perspective the Union and the Monarchy look all too similar. Just as the absence of the Monarchy proved its absolute necessity, however, so we should be more aware than we are of how poorly off contemporary Europe would be without the European Union, for all its flaws.

How Can a 'European Necessity' Fail?

If the Monarchy really was such a necessity, regionally, economically and culturally, even spiritually in some sense, that its function has had to be restored through a European Union to overcome the shortcomings and bad effects of the simpler, decisive but limited and inadequate nation-state, why did it really fail in 1918? One fairly sophisticated reason for the inability of the Monarchy to maintain its authority, and hence its power, was given by Berthold Molden, a journalist with links to Franz Ferdinand's Belvedere Circle. On 6 July 1914, at the onset of the July Crisis, when Germany had already given its blank cheque, Molden addressed the question of how to improve relations with the Monarchy's Serbs. He reached back to a previous episode of Habsburg history: 'the Venetians, in their time, used to say that they did not wish for Austria to govern them well – it should not govern them at all'. In an era when modernity meant allowing societies to govern themselves, when modernisation went hand in hand with Kantian self-determination, the old Habsburg role of being the imperial power, of governing people well, whether they accepted your legitimate authority as their ruler or not, would no longer work.

In the past, the role of empire as umpire had suited the Habsburgs well, as Holy Roman Emperors and then Austrian emperors. They had acted as arbitrators, sometimes as mediators, between the political interests in their multi-faceted empires, who had accepted the external rule, because it was better than the chaos of infighting and conflict that such a power above the fray prevented. Modernisation demanded the acceptance of popular sovereignty, but the Habsburg leadership, specifically Franz I, Metternich and Franz Joseph, never did accept that principle. Even the December Constitution of 1867 was given by the grace of the emperor, not based on the people's sovereignty. It never adequately adapted to the logic of constitutional, representative government, along federalised, or some sort of pluralised, lines.

It made major adjustments, as we have seen, but some of these, such as the Compromise of 1867, may have made matters worse.

The Monarchy's leadership, especially Franz Joseph, could never give up the dynastic approach that saw the Monarchy as the Habsburgs' patrimony, its main goal to preserve dynastic power and status. No matter how much the Austrian bureaucracy tried honestly to mediate the national conflicts, one of the main obstacles was that it, the bureaucracy, was there to begin with, above and between the protagonists, not of them.

Looking at Molden's statement, it is not that the Habsburg regime was wrong to want to govern well, it was that it was not seen as part of the group being governed. Had Venetians (or Serbs for that matter) thought of themselves as Austrians, as Habsburgians, the problematic dichotomy would never arise.

The problem was that the Monarchy, as a political enterprise, was unable to create in modern form the authority and legitimacy that it had possessed before the modern age. It could not finesse national loyalties with an effective supra-ethnic, supra-national, 'Austrian' loyalty and identity, at least not enough to tide it over when the storm of 1914 broke over it. There was some such identity, and while the 'old emperor' was alive there was a strong dynastic and even personal loyalty to him among most of the Monarchy's populace, in his last decades at least. Yet it attached to him, not to his heir, nor, to anything like the same degree, to the larger Austrian state, let alone Austria-Hungary. When he was gone, and his heir proved unable to emulate him, ending up being cast aside by history and his peoples (or at least their representatives), and the dynasty with him, there was nothing left strong enough to keep the bonds between the various parts from breaking asunder.

On 1 October 1918, in a review of a performance of Grillparzer's *King Ottokar's Fortune and End*, Egon Friedell wrote: 'Grillparzer's patriotism is, as with Austrian patriotism in general, a problem. For the German this emotion is summed up in the words "Deutschland über alles!", for the Frenchman in the sentence "Vive la France!" These are simple formulae, incapable of misinterpretation. But the Austrian views his fatherland with a sort of Strindbergian love-hate, in which the word "fatherland" itself appears to him as something ridiculous, which he cannot utter without a slightly sarcastic tone creeping in.' There is a terrible irony here that it was precisely the complexity and, yes, irony involved in Austria self-understanding, and the distance between self and 'fatherland' that made the cultural and intellectual achievement of the Monarchy's peoples so noteworthy, but Friedell's point still stands. The Monarchy, at least the set of people who ruled it, was never able to produce a strong enough identification between its citizens and itself to counteract the centrifugal, divisive forces of nationalist particularism. It did not need to be a 'simple formula' – 'Vive la France!' has its own inherent complexities – but it did need to be strong enough, and heartfelt enough, and it never was, until, perhaps, it was too late. The Habsburg leadership was never able to square the circle that could turn a dynastic conglomerate of possessions into an all-embracing home for all its people, as well as peoples. It could never come up with a way to convert necessity into a coherent identity. The 'Austrian Idea' never achieved cogent meaning. That is why the Habsburg Monarchy collapsed in the crisis of 1918.

One final, counter-factual thought: perhaps it was bound to disappear in any case, given its anachronistic structures and style. If so, the problem was that it failed in its vocation of giving life to a set of collaborative, self-governing states, perhaps nation-states, underneath an umbrella of co-operation of some kind, such as the British Commonwealth, or to a more unified polity, such as a Danubian Federation with or without a (purely formal) Habsburg head of state, a prototype of the European Union. The tragedy was that such a transition was never given the time it needed, that the logic of the Monarchy as a dynastic power, set in a sea of irredentist nationalism, led to war and catastrophe in 1914. Nothing sustainable or positive could come from such a conflict. It was not the disappearance of the Monarchy that was so disastrous, therefore, as the way of its departure. This would bring a special meaning to Czernin's oft-quoted adage: 'We were bound to die. We were at liberty to choose the manner of our death, and we chose the most terrible.'

Bibliography

The following is not comprehensive but is rather intended as a guide to further reading. Publications are included in three languages: English, German and French. This reflects my own language competence, but also encompasses the three languages most likely to be read by English-speaking students and readers interested in Central European history. English titles are given preference, but the ideas and themes presented in this book are incomprehensible without some grasp of foreign-language publications, especially those in German. Please note: frequently-quoted journals and reference works are quoted by abbreviation in square brackets, e.g., *Austrian History Yearbook* = [*AHY*].

Periodicals

Those interested in tracing the most recent research results and trends, and historiographical questions related to the Monarchy's last century, are strongly advised to consult the leading periodicals in the field. In English, this should start with the *Austrian History Yearbook* (Minneapolis, MN, 1965–) [*AHY*]. *Austrian Studies* (Edinburgh, 1990–) [*AS*], *Journal of Austrian Studies* (Lincoln, NE,–) (formerly *Modern Austrian Literature*), and *Central Europe* (London, 2003–) [*CE*] have a more cultural and literary emphasis but should also be consulted. *Central European History* (Atlanta, GA, 1968–) [*CEH*] is useful for more Germanocentric aspects. *Contemporary Austrian Studies* (New Orleans, LA, 1990–) [*CAS*] can be useful for the later period of the subject.

Books

General

There has been a major revision of interpretation of the Monarchy's last century, but many standard works are still worth reading, if only to see the change in approach currently. Oscar Jászi, *The Dissolution of the Habsburg Monarchy* (Chicago, IL, 1929) remains a seminal text for the subject. Among British historians, A.J.P. Taylor, *The Habsburg Monarchy 1809–1918*

(Harmondsworth, 1948, 1964); and C.A. Macartney, *The Habsburg Empire, 1790–1918* (London, 1969) provide the traditional narratives; with C.A. Macartney, *The House of Austria: The Later Phase 1790–1918* (Edinburgh, 1978) providing a more concise version of the latter. Even more concise is John W. Mason, *The Dissolution of the Austro-Hungarian Empire, 1867–1918* (Harlow, 1985). Two American historians of the older generation worth reading are Arthur J. May, *The Habsburg Monarchy 1867–1914* (Cambridge, MA, 1965); and the Austrian émigré Robert A. Kann, *A History of the Habsburg Empire 1526–1918* (Berkeley, CA, 1977). An intriguing example of how approaches can change is illustrated by Henry Wickham Steed, *The Habsburg Monarchy* (New York, NY, 1969), repr. of 1914, Second edn.; and Steed's later, much darker work, *The Doom of the Habsburgs* (London, 1937). A sophisticated reworking of the traditional approach, with more of a socio-economic perspective, is provided in Robin Okey, *The Habsburg Monarchy: From Enlightenment to Eclipse* (New York, NY, 2001). F.R. Bridge, *The Habsburg Monarchy among the Great Powers, 1815–1918* (Oxford, 1990) is an excellent account of the interaction of foreign and domestic policy, so central to the Monarchy's history.

A classic revisionist text is François Fejtö, *Requiem pour un empire défunt: histoire de la destruction de l'Autriche-Hongrie* (Paris, 1988); the pioneering revisionist work in English is Alan Sked, *The Decline and Fall of the Habsburg Empire, 1815–1918* (London, 1989). (Do not be fooled by the title.) A very influential essay on the topic is Gary B. Cohen, 'Neither Absolutism nor Anarchy: New Narratives on Society and Government in Late Imperial Austria', in *AHY*, 29 (1998), pt. 1, pp. 37–61. The most recent major statement of the revisionist position is the highly recommended Pieter M. Judson, *The Habsburg Empire: A New History* (Cambridge, MA, 2016). In the relevant sections of Steven Beller, *A Concise History of Austria* (Cambridge, 2006), I discussed the points raised by Sked and others, as my current work similarly responds to Judson's work.

Two standard works by Austrian historians on the general subject are the magisterial and indispensable Helmut Rumpler, *Eine Chance für Mitteleuropa: bürgerliche Emanzipation und Staatsverfall in der Habsburgermonarchie 1804–1914* (Vienna, 1997); and the overlapping, equally impressive Ernst Hanisch, *Der lange Schatten des Staates: Österreichische Gesellschaftsgeschichte im 20. Jahrhundert 1890–1990* (Vienna, 1994). A large-scale work that serves as a reference work for modern Habsburg history, but also includes excellent essays, is A. Wandruszka, P. Urbanitsch, eds. *Die Habsburgermonarchie 1848–1918*, 11 vols. (Vienna, 1973–).

Other Perspectives

James J. Sheehan, *German History 1770–1866* (Oxford, 1989); and Christopher Clark, *The Iron Kingdom: The Rise and Downfall of Prussia 1600–1947* (London, 2006), provide a German perspective; for a specific analysis of German-Habsburg relations see J. Kořalka, 'Deutschland und die Habsburgermonarchie', in *Die Habsburgermonarchie*, 1993, vol. 6, pt. 2,

Aussenpolitik. For broader perspectives I suggest Brendan Simms, *Europe: The Struggle for Supremacy, from 1453 to the Present* (London, 2013); and Lonnie Johnson, *Central Europe: Enemies, Neighbours, Friends* (Oxford, 1996).

Suggestions for various topics and themes extending over the whole period are given later; here are more specialised accounts according to chronological period.

Pre-1815 Monarchy

This book is the "sequel" to Charles W. Ingrao, *The Habsburg Monarchy 1618–1815.* Second edn. (Cambridge, 2000), which offers an excellent summary of the history up to 1815, as well as an extensive bibliography for the pre-1815 period. I would nonetheless urge the reading of the seminal R.J.W. Evans, *The Making of the Habsburg Monarchy, 1550–1700: An Interpretation* (Oxford, 1979). On the Habsburgs, Andrew Wheatcroft, *The Habsburgs: Embodying Empire* (London, 1995), is interesting. On the crucial figure of Joseph II, Derek Beales, *Joseph II*, 2 vols. (Cambridge, 1987, 2009) is definitive; T.C.W. Blanning, *Joseph II* (London, 1994) is cogent and concise.

1815–1852

On the diplomacy that established the Vienna system after 1815, a standard work is Henry A. Kissinger, *A World Restored: Metternich, Castlereagh and the Problems of Peace, 1812–1822* (Boston, 1957). More recent works are Mark Jarrett, *The Congress of Vienna and Its Legacy: War and Great Power Diplomacy after Napoleon* (London, 2013); and Brian E. Vick, *The Congress of Vienna: Power and Politics after Napoleon* (Cambridge, MA, 2014); also Thierry Lentz, *1815: Der Wiener Kongress und die Neugründung Europas* (Munich, 2014). On the central figure of Metternich: Clemens von Metternich, *The Autobiography, 1773–1815* (Welwyn Garden City, 2004); and especially Alan Sked, *Metternich and Austria: An Evaluation* (Basingstoke, 2008), which continues the revisionist discussion of his earlier general history.

C.A. Macartney, 'The Austrian Monarchy, 1792–1847', in C.W. Crawley, ed., *The New Cambridge Modern History*, vol. 9: *War and Peace in an Age of Upheaval 1793–1830* (Cambridge, 1960), pp. 395–411, still provides a useful political narrative. On the classic era in music: Alice M. Hanson, *Musical Life in Biedermeier Vienna* (Cambridge, 1985).

The revolutionary events of 1848 are covered with great insight by Jonathan Sperber, *The European Revolutions 1848–1851* (Cambridge, 1994); there is also Peter N. Stearns, *1848: The Revolutionary Tide in Europe* (New York, NY, 1974). On Vienna specifically: R.J. Rath, *The Viennese Revolution* (New York, NY, 1969); and Hungary: István Deák, *The Lawful Revolution: Louis Kossuth and the Hungarians, 1848–1849* (New York, NY, 1979). On other aspects: Alan Sked, *The Survival of the Habsburg Empire: Radetzky, the Imperial Army and the Class War 1848* (London, 1979); and H.H. Brandt, 'The Revolution of 1848 and the Problem of Central European Nationalities', in H. Schulze, ed., *Nation-Building in Central Europe* (Leamington Spa, 1987), pp. 107–134.

1852–1897

C.A. Macartney, 'The Austrian Empire and Its Problems, 1848–1867', in J.P.T. Bury, ed. *The New Cambridge Modern History*, vol. 10: *The Zenith of European Power 1830–1870* (Cambridge, 1960), pp. 522–551, is still a good narrative account of a complex era. On the diplomatic and military disasters: David M. Goldfrank, *The Origins of the Crimean War* (Harlow, 1994); and Geoffrey Wawro, *The Austro-Prussian War: Austria's War with Prussia and Italy in 1866* (Cambridge, 1996).

For the establishment of the Dual Monarchy: Louis Eisenmann, *Le Compromis Austro-Hongrois de 1867: étude sur le dualism* (Hattiesburg, MS, 1971 (1904)). The debates surrounding this are available in H. Rumpler, W. Heindl, eds., *Die Protokolle des österreichischen Ministerrates 1848–1867* (Vienna, 1973–) and I. Diószegi and E. Somogyi, eds., *Die Protokolle des gemeinsamen Ministerrates der österreichisch-ungarischen Monarchie, 1867–1918* (Budapest, 1991–).

On the era of the Iron Ring: W.A. Jenks, *Austria under the Iron Ring, 1879–1893* (Charlottesville, VA, 1965). The changes in (Austrian) German attitudes is brilliantly outlined in Lothar Höbelt, *Kornblume und Kaiseradler: die deutschfrei-heitlichen Parteien Altösterreichs 1882–1918* (Munich, 1993). William J. McGrath, *Dionysian Art and Populist Politics in Austria* (New Haven, CT, 1974) is an insightful study into a key group of political and cultural figures, including many Jews, who came from a Wagnerian, German nationalist background. David Brodbeck, *Defining Deutschtum Political Ideology, German Identity, and Music-Critical Discourse in Liberal Vienna* (Oxford, 2014) provides a parallel account of national/cultural debates in the musical world. For a recent account of the German nationalist leader: Steven Beller, 'Hitler's Hero: Georg von Schönerer and the Origins of Nazism', in R. Haynes, M. Rady, eds., *In the Shadow of Hitler: Personalities of the Right in Central and Eastern Europe* (London, 2011), pp. 38–54.

Joseph S. Bloch, *Erinnerungen aus meinem Leben* (Vienna, 1922) provides a Jewish perspective on the rise of nationalism and antisemitism in Vienna. John W. Boyer, *Political Radicalism in Late Imperial Vienna: Origins of the Christian Social Movement 1848–1897* (Chicago, IL, 1981) provides a seminal account of the rise of the party in the Monarchy that most success-fully exploited antisemitic prejudice.

1897–1918

On political events, John W. Boyer, *Culture and Political Crisis in Vienna: Christian Socialism in Power 1897–1918* (Chicago, IL, 1995) is a magisterial guide from a Christian Social perspective, although another suggested per-spective is Richard S. Geehr, *Karl Lueger, Mayor of Fin-de-Siècle Vienna* (Detroit, MI, 1990). Höbelt, *Kornblume und Kaiseradler* is an excellent guide to this period as well for German liberal and nationalist politics. Personal accounts of note: Alexander Spitzmüller, *Memoirs* (Boulder, CO, 1987); Joseph Redlich, *Schicksalsjahre Österreichs: das politische Tagebuch Joseph Redlichs*, ed. F. Fellner, 2 vols. (Vienna, 1953).

On the central figure of Aehrenthal: Solomon Wank, *In the Twilight of Empire: Count Alois Lexa von Aehrenthal (1854–1912)*, vol. 1 (Vienna, 2009); Solomon Wank, ed. *Aus dem Nachlass Aehrenthal*, 2 vols. (Graz, 1994).

On the coming of the First World War, the standard guide for the Monarchy is now Samuel R. Williamson, Jr., *Austria-Hungary and the Origins of the First World War* (London, 1991). Also recommended are Mark Cornwall, ed., *The Last Years of Austria-Hungary: A Multi-National Experiment in Early Twentieth-Century Europe*, rev. ed. (Exeter, 2002) (also for aspects of the war itself); R.J.W. Evans, 'The Habsburg Monarchy and the Coming of War', in R.J.W. Evans and H. Pogge von Strandmann, eds., *The Coming of the First World War* (Oxford, 1988), pp. 33–55; and, especially for the South Slav question, Hugh and Christopher Seton-Watson, *The Making of a New Europe: R.W. Seton-Watson and the Last Years of Austria-Hungary* (Seattle, WA, 1981).

The role of modern culture in promoting war is covered in Modris Eksteins, *Rites of Spring: The Great War and the Birth of the Modern Age* (New York, NY, 1989), although it is as well to read Florian Illies, *1913: The Year before the Storm* (London, 2013) for another perspective.

On *how* war began, see Christopher Clark, *The Sleepwalkers: How Europe Went to War in 1914* (London, 2012). On specifically Austro-Hungarian causes, see, apart from Williamson: William D. Godsey, Jr., *Aristocratic Redoubt: The Austro-Hungarian Foreign Office on the Eve of the First World War* (West Lafayette, IN, 1999); and Geoffrey Wawro, *A Mad Catastrophe: The Outbreak of World War I and the Collapse of the Habsburg Empire* (New York, NY, 2014).

On the war itself: Lawrence Sondhaus, *Franz Conrad von Hötzendorf: Architect of the Apocalypse* (Boston, MA, 2000); Lawrence Sondhaus, *World War One: The Global Revolution* (Cambridge, 2011); and the pioneering Norman Stone, *The Eastern Front, 1914–1917* (London, 1975). The standard text in German is Manfred Rauchensteiner, *Der Tod des Doppeladlers: Österreich-Ungarn und der erste Weltkrieg* (Graz, 1993). A condensed version is provided by Manfred Rauchensteiner and Josef Broukal, *Der erste Weltkrieg und das Ende der Habsburgermonarchie – in aller Kürze* (Vienna, 2015).

Maureen Healy, *Vienna and the Fall of the Habsburg Empire: Total War and Everyday Life in World War I* (Cambridge, 2004) provides a generally convincing account of how the war was lost on the domestic front. Joseph Redlich, *Österreichische Regierung und Verwaltung im Weltkriege* (Vienna, 1925) is also an important text on how the Habsburg state went wrong in wartime. For the role of culture during the war: Steven Beller, 'The Tragic Carnival: Austrian Culture in the First World War', in A. Roshwald and R. Stites, eds., *European Culture in the Great War: The Arts, Entertainment and Propaganda, 1914–1918* (Cambridge, 1999), pp. 127–161. Key literary texts are Karl Kraus, *The Last Days of Mankind: The Complete Text*, trans. F. Bridgham and E. Timms (New Haven, CT, 2015); Jaroslav Hašek, *The Good Soldier Švejk* (London, 2016, 1973); and Manès Sperber, *God's Water Carriers* (New York, NY, 1987), especially for Sperber's account of Franz Joseph's funeral procession.

Franz Joseph and the Dynasty

Recent biographies of Franz Joseph in English include Jean-Paul Bled, *Franz Joseph* (Oxford, 1992); and Alan Palmer, *Twilight of the Habsburgs: The Life and Times of Emperor Francis Joseph* (London, 1994). My own account, Steven Beller, *Francis Joseph* (Harlow, 1996), concentrates more on his political career in the larger context. An older text in English, Joseph Redlich, *Emperor Francis Joseph of Austria: A Biography* (New York, NY, 1929), is still very much worth reading, as is, in German, the exhaustive E.C. Corti, *Franz Joseph I.*, 3 vols.: *Vom Kind zu Kaiser* (Graz, 1950); *Mensch und Herrscher* (Graz, 1952); with H. Sokol, *Der alte Kaiser* (Graz, 1955). On other aspects of the emperor-king's life: Alexander Margutti, *The Emperor Francis Joseph and His Times* (London, 1921); Robert A. Kann, *Dynasty, Politics and Culture: Selected Essays* (Boulder, CO, 1991); Horace Rumbold, *Recollections of a Diplomatist*, 2 vols. (London, 1902); and Ernst von Steinitz, ed., *Erinnerungen an Franz Joseph I* (Berlin, 1991). Horace Rumbold, *The Austrian Court in the Nineteenth Century* (London, 1909) is also of note, if only for its early description of 'social imperialism'.

On other members of the dynasty: Hans Magenschab, *Erzherzog Johann: Habsburgs grüner Rebell* (Graz, 1995); Brigitte Hamann, ed., Kronprinz Rudolf, *Majestät, ich warne Sie: geheime und private Schriften* (Vienna, 1979); Katrin Unterreiner, *Sisi: Mythos und Wahrheit* (Vienna, 2015).

Military

The standard work remains Gunther E. Rothenberg, *The Army of Francis Joseph* (West Lafayette, IN, 1976), but see also Wawro's books on 1866 and the First World War in this bibliography. Other aspects of the military culture are treated in Laurence Cole, *Military Culture and Popular Patriotism in Late Imperial Austria* (Oxford, 2014); and István Deák, *Beyond Nationalism: A Social and Political History of the Habsburg Officer Corps 1848–1918* (Oxford, 1990). For the navy, see Lawrence Sondhaus, *Habsburg Empire and Sea: Austrian Naval Policy, 1797–1866* (West Lafayette, IN, 1989).

Bureaucracy

John Deak, *Forging a Multinational State: State Making in Imperial Austria from the Enlightenment to the First World War* (Palo Alto, 2015), now provides an excellent introduction in English to the development of the bureaucratic state. The standard work on the subject of the bureaucracy remains Waltraud Heindl, *Gehorsame Rebellen: Bürokratie und Beamte in Österreich 1780 bis 1848* (Vienna, 1991); and Waltraud Heindl, *Josephinische Mandarine: Bürokratie und Beamte in Österreich 1848–1914* (Vienna, 2013). Also see the classic work: Joseph Redlich, *Das österreichische Staats- und Reichsproblem*, 2 vols. (Leipzig, 1920). The essays on the Cisleithanian and Hungarian bureaucracies, by Walter Goldinger, Jiři Klabouch, Ernst C. Hellbling and George Barany in A. Wandruszka, P. Urbanitsch, eds. *Die Habsburgermonarchie*, vol. 2: *Verwaltung und Rechtswesen* (Vienna, 1975) are very useful.

Nationalities

The role of the various nationalities is one of the main sources of controversy in the Monarchy's history. Much of the general literature on nationalism, especially the classic work by Ernest Gellner, *Nations and Nationalism* (Oxford, 1983, 2006) can be seen as a response to the Monarchy's experience of nationalism. That said, there are several useful works specific to the Monarchy. Robert A. Kann, *The Multinational Empire: Nationalism and National Reform in the Habsburg Monarchy, 1848–1918*, 2 vols. (New York, NY, 1977) is quite old, but worth consulting, as are these stimulating essay collections: R.L. Rudolph and D.F. Good, eds., *Nationalism and Empire* (New York, NY, 1992); P.M. Judson and M. Rozenblit, eds., *Constructing Nationalities in East Central Europe* (Oxford, 2005); and N.M. Wingfield, ed., *Creating the Other: Ethnic Conflict and Nationalism in Habsburg Central Europe* (Oxford, 2003). How the historiographic debate developed can be gauged by comparing two articles: Solomon Wank, 'Foreign Policy and the Nationality Problem in Austria-Hungary 1867–1914', in *AHY 3* (1967); and Solomon Wank, 'The Nationalities Question in the Habsburg Monarchy: Reflections on the Historical Record', *Working Papers in Austrian Studies* 93, 3 (1993). The Austrian legal system's response to national questions has been brilliantly treated by Gerald Stourzh in a number of essays, especially Gerald Stourzh, 'Die Gleichberechtigung der Volksstämme als Verfassungsprinzip 1848–1918', in *Die Habsburgermonarchie*, vol. 3, pt. 2, *Die Völker des Reiches* (Vienna, 1980). Several of Stourzh's essays are available in English in Part II of his highly recommended anthology, *From Vienna to Chicago and Back* (Chicago, IL, 2007). Stourzh's important essay 'Ethnic Attribution in Late Imperial Austria: Good Intentions, Evil Consequences', is also available in R. Robertson, E. Timms, eds., *The Habsburg Legacy: National Identity in Historical Perspective*, *AS* 5 (Edinburgh, 1994), which offers essays on the relations of many of the national groups to the Monarchy. Tara Zahra, 'Imagined Noncommunities: National Indifference as a Category of Analysis', in *Slavic Review* 69, 1 (Spring 2010), pp. 93–119, provides a contrasting context in which to assess the debate on nationalism.

A. Wandruszka, P. Urbanitsch, eds. *Die Habsburgermonarchie*, vol. 3: *Die Völker des Reiches* (Vienna, 1980) provides a comprehensive approach to the individual national groups. On developments within the Monarchy's German(-speaking) population, see Steven Beller, 'Germans and Jews as Central European and "mitteleuropäisch" élites', in P. Stirk, ed. *Mitteleuropa* (Edinburgh, 1994), pp. 61–85; Andrew G. Whiteside, 'The Germans as an Integrative Force in Imperial Austria: The Dilemma of Dominance', *AHY* 3, 1 (1967); and Gary B. Cohen, *The Politics of Ethnic Survival: Germans in Prague, 1861–1914* (Princeton, 1981). The national/language conflict between Germans and other groups, especially Czechs is the subject of much stimulating research, including: Pieter M. Judson, *Guardians of the Nation: Activists on the Language Frontiers of Imperial Austria* (Cambridge, MA, 2006); Jeremy King, *Budweisers into Czechs and Germans: A Local History of Bohemian Politics, 1848–1948* (Princeton, NJ, 2002); and Tara Zahra, *Kidnapped Souls: National Indifference and the Battle for Children in the Bohemian Lands 1900–1948* (Ithaca, NY, 2008). The nationalist extremism that resulted from these conflicts, including National Socialism, is detailed in

Michael Wladika, *Hitlers Vätergeneration: die Ursprünge des Nationalsozialismus in der k. u. k. Monarchie* (Vienna, 2005).

The Czech perspective is well presented in: Derek Sayer, *The Coasts of Bohemia: A Czech History* (Princeton, NJ, 1998); and Hugh Agnew, *The Czechs and the Lands of the Bohemian Crown* (Stanford, CA, 2004). There is also John F. Bradley, *Czech Nationalism in the Nineteenth Century* (New York, NY, 1984). Andrei S. Markovits, 'Empire and Province', in A.S. Markovits and F.E. Sysyn, *Nationbuilding and the Politics of Nationalism: Essays on Austrian Galicia* (Cambridge, MA, 1982) is of interest on Galicia. On Bosnia: Noel Malcolm, *Bosnia: A Short History* (London, 1994). John Erickson, *Panslavism* (London, 1964) is also worth consulting.

On Hungary, Miklós Molnár, *A Concise History of Hungary* (Cambridge, 2001); and Jörg K. Hoensch, *A History of Modern Hungary 1867–1986* (Harlow, 1988) provide good introductions. R.J.W. Evans, *Austria, Hungary and the Habsburgs: Central Europe c. 1683–1867* (Oxford, 2006); and László Péter, *Hungary's Long Nineteenth Century: Constitutional and Democratic Traditions in a European Perspective* (Leiden, 2012), esp. 'The Dualist Character of the 1867 Hungarian Settlement', pp. 213–280, provide important insights. Alice Freifeld, *Nationalism and the Crowd in Liberal Hungary, 1848–1914* (Baltimore, MD, 2000); and Robert Nemes, *Another Hungary: The Nineteenth Century Provinces in Eight Lives* (Stanford, 2016) offer stimulating new perspectives on the Hungarian experience.

Economic, Social and Cultural History

The standard work on the Monarchy's economy is David F. Good, *The Economic Rise of the Habsburg Empire, 1750–1914* (Berkeley, CA, 1984). Nachum T. Gross, 'The Habsburg Monarchy', in C.M. Cipolla, ed., *The Fontana Economic History of Europe*, 5 vols. (Glasgow, 1973) vol. 4, pt. 1 is also useful. Although ostensibly a work of economic history, Alison Fleig Frank, *Oil Empire: Visions of Prosperity in Austrian Galicia* (Cambridge, MA, 2005) is a brilliant account that touches on many interlocking aspects of Galician and Habsburg history.

The peculiarities, and particularities, of the Habsburg middle classes, the *Bürgertum*, is well illustrated in E. Bruckmüller, U. Döcker, H. Stekl and P. Urbanitsch, eds., *Bürgertum in der Habsburgermonarchie* (Vienna, 1990). The role of education in the Monarchy is expertly treated in Gary B. Cohen, *Education and Middle-Class Society in Imperial Austria 1848–1918* (West Lafayette, IN, 1996). The social history of Vienna's (and hence the Monarchy's) moneyed elite is the subject of Roman Sandgruber, *Traumzeit für Millionäre: die 929 reichsten Wienerinnen und Wiener im Jahr 1910* (Vienna, 2013). A contemporary description of that elite is provided in Paul Vasili, *Die Wiener Gesellschaft* (Leipzig, 1885). Developments over time in the aristocracy and the middle classes are discussed in Hannes Stekl, *Adel und Bürgertum in der Habsburgermonarchie 18. Bis 20. Jahrhundert* (Vienna, 2004). The role of the aristocracy in Habsburg politics and society is discussed in Solomon Wank, 'Aristocrats and Politics in Austria 1867–1914: A Case of Historiographical Neglect', *East European Quarterly* 26, 2 (1992), pp. 133–148. More general perspectives on the aristocracy can be found in Dominic Lieven, *The Aristocracy in Europe, 1815–1914* (New York, NY, 1992).

Quite how strong the aristocratic role still was in the Monarchy, and Europe generally, is controversial, but Arno J. Mayer, *The Persistence of the Old Régime: Europe to the Great War* (New York, NY, 1981) is still worth considering.

On women's history, see Harriet Anderson, *Utopian Feminism: Women's Movements in Fin-de-Siècle Vienna* (New Haven, CT, 1992); and D.F. Good, M. Grandner and M.J. Maynes, eds., *Austrian Women in the Nineteenth and Twentieth Centuries: Cross-Disciplinary Perspectives* (Oxford, 1996).

Political Ideology and Religion

On liberalism, see E. Brix, W. Mantl, eds., *Liberalismus: Interpretationen und Perspektiven* (Vienna, 1996); and Pieter M. Judson, *Exclusive Revolutionaries: Liberal Politics, Social Experience, and National Identity in the Austrian Empire, 1848–1914* (Ann Arbor, MI, 1996), which points out how much liberalism and nationalism were linked. The conservative, pro-dynastic forces in society have also received more attention of late, especially concerning symbolic politics: M. Bucur and N.M. Wingfield, eds., *Staging the Past: The Politics of Commemoration in Habsburg Central Europe, 1848 to the Present* (West Lafayette, IN, 2001); Daniel L. Unowsky, *The Pomp and Politics of Patriotism: Imperial Celebrations in Habsburg Austria, 1848–1916* (West Lafayette, IN, 2005); L. Cole and D. Unowsky, eds., *The Limits of Loyalty: Imperial Symbolism, Popular Allegiances, and State Patriotism in the Late Habsburg Monarchy* (Oxford, 2007). John Boyer's work on the Christian Socials (see above) is highly recommended. Peter Pulzer, *The Rise of Political Anti-Semitism in Germany and Austria*, rev. edn. (London, 1988) is still an excellent introduction to the role of antisemitism in the Monarchy's politics.

William D. Bowman, *Priest and Parish in Vienna, 1780–1880* (Boston, MA, 1999); and Rupert Klieber, *Jüdische, christliche, muslimische Lebenswelten der Donaumonarchie 1848–1918* (Vienna, 2010), provide important insights into the religious life of the Monarchy.

Vienna 1900/Central Europe 1900

Good introductory texts by two products of Vienna 1900 are: Ilsa Barea, *Vienna: Legend and Reality* (New York, NY, 1966); and Hilde Spiel, *Vienna's Golden Autumn, 1866–1938* (London, 1987). As an academic discipline, Vienna 1900 is founded on three books: Carl E. Schorske, *Fin-de-Siècle Vienna: Politics and Culture* (London, 1980); Allan Janik and Stephen Toulmin, *Wittgenstein's Vienna*, rev. edn. (Chicago, 1996); and William M. Johnston, *The Austrian Mind: An Intellectual and Social History 1848–1938* (Berkeley, CA, 1972). Schorske's interpretation has been extremely influential, but has not gone uncontested. See James Shedel, *Art and Society: The New Art Movement in Vienna, 1897–1914* (Palo Alto, CA, 1981); Malachi Hacohen, *Karl Popper: The Formative Years, 1902–1945* (Cambridge, 2002); and Steven Beller, ed., *Rethinking Vienna 1900* (Oxford, 2001), which has contributions from many of the leading scholars in the field. Robert Musil, *The Man without Qualities*, 2 vols. (New York, NY, 1995) is highly recommended as a literary introduction to the subject, and for interpretation of Musil: David S. Luft, *Robert Musil and the Crisis of European Culture, 1880–1942* (Berkeley, CA, 1980); and David S. Luft, *Eros and Inwardness in Vienna: Weininger, Musil, Doderer* (Chicago, IL, 2003).

The central role played in Viennese modern culture by Jews is outlined in Steven Beller, *Vienna and the Jews, 1867–1938: A Cultural History* (Cambridge, 1989); Robert S. Wistrich, *The Jews of Vienna in the Age of Franz Joseph* (Oxford, 1989); and I. Oxaal, M. Pollak and G. Botz, eds., *Jews, Antisemitism and Culture in Vienna* (London, 1987). A contemporary account is Arthur Schnitzler, *The Road to the Open* (Evanston, IL, 1991). A more recent, most interesting commentary is Peter Singer, *Pushing Time Away: My Grandfather and the Tragedy of Jewish Vienna* (New York, NY, 2003). On the culture of critical modernism, apart from *Wittgenstein's Vienna*, there is, on Karl Kraus: Frank Field, *The Last Days of Mankind: Karl Kraus and His Vienna* (London, 1967); and especially Edward Timms, *Karl Kraus, Apocalyptic Satirist: Culture and Catastrophe in Habsburg Vienna* (New Haven, CT, 1986). On Wittgenstein: Ray Monk, *Ludwig Wittgenstein: The Duty of Genius* (London, 1990); Brian McGuinness, *Wittgenstein: A Life: Young Ludwig, 1889–1921* (London, 1988); and a key text, Paul Engelmann, *Letters from Wittgenstein, with a Memoir* (Oxford, 1967). Also see Marjorie Perloff, *Edge of Irony: Modernism in the Shadow of the Habsburg Empire* (Chicago, IL, 2016).

On the social context of this culture: C. Ashby, T. Gronberg and S. Shaw-Miller, eds., *The Viennese Café and Fin-de-Siècle culture* (Oxford, 2013); and Elisabeth Röhrlich, ed., *Migration und Innovation um 1900: Perspektiven auf das Wien der Jahrhundertwende* (Vienna, 2016). On the Social context, see Berta Zuckerkandl, *Österreich intim* (Vienna, 1981/2013). On the relatively neglected scientific achievement, see Deborah R. Coen, *Vienna in the Age of Uncertainty: Science, Liberalism and Private Life* (Chicago, IL, 2007); R. Werner Soukup, ed., *Die wissenschaftliche Welt von gestern* (Vienna, 2004); and Robert W. Rosner, ed., *Chemie in Österreich 1740–1914: Lehre – Forschung – Industrie* (Vienna, 2004). For a view of the other side to Vienna 1900: Brigitte Hamann, *Hitler's Vienna: A Dictator's Apprenticeship* (Oxford, 2000).

For the larger context of Central Europe 1900, see Robert Pynsent, ed., *Decadence and Innovation: Austro-Hungarian Life and Art at the Turn of the Century* (London, 1989), esp. 'Conclusory Essay', pp. 111–248; M. Gee, T. Kirk and J. Steward, *The City in Central Europe: Culture and Society from 1800 to the Present* (Aldershot, 1999); and William M. Johnston, *Zur Kulturgeschichte Österreichs und Ungarns 1890–1938: Auf der Suche nach verborgenen Gemeinsamkeiten* (Vienna, 2015). There are also important studies of other major cultural centres. On Prague: Peter Demetz, *Prague in Black and Gold: The History of a City* (London, 1997); Derek Sayer, *Prague: Capital of the Twentieth Century* (Princeton, NJ, 2013); and J.P. Stern, ed., *The World of Franz Kafka* (London, 1980). On Budapest: John Lukacs, *Budapest 1900: A Historical Portrait of a City and Its Culture* (London, 1989); Mary Gluck, *Georg Lukács and His Generation 1900–1918* (Cambridge, MA, 1985); William O. McCagg, Jr., *Jewish Nobles and Geniuses in Modern Hungary* (New York, NY, 1972); and Mary Gluck, *The Invisible Jewish Budapest: Metropolitan Culture at the Fin de Siècle* (Madison, WI, 2016). On Trieste: Claudio Magris and Angelo Ara,

Triest: eine literarische Hauptstadt in Mitteleuropa (Munich, 1993); and Jan Morris, *Trieste and the Meaning of Nowhere* (London, 2001).

The Austrian Idea

For discussion of the 'meaning' of the Monarchy in hindsight through the slightly more neutral concept of Central Europe, see Emil Brix and Erhard Busek, *Projekt Mitteleuropa* (Vienna, 1986); Peter Stirk, *Mitteleuropa: History and prospects* (Edinburgh, 1994); and the brilliant Claudio Magris, *Danube: A Sentimental Journey from the Source to the Black Sea* (London, 1989). Magris also wrote the standard introduction to the literary works evoking the Habsburg myth, *Das habsburgische Mythos in der modernen österreichischen Literatur* (Vienna, 2013 (1966)). Leading examples of the genre are Stefan Zweig, *The World of Yesterday* (New York, NY, 1943); Joseph Roth, *The Radetzky March* (London, 2013); and Franz Werfel, *The Pure in Heart* (New York, NY, 1931) [trans. of *Barbara, oder Die Frömmigkeit*]. An ironic counterpoint, from Trieste, originally published in 1923, is provided by Italo Svevo, *Confessions of Zeno* (London, 1964)

On contemporary attempts to understand or reimagine the Monarchy's purpose, see T. Bottomore and P. Goode, eds., *Austromarxism* (Oxford, 1978); Ian Reifowitz, *Imagining In Austrian Nation: Joseph Samuel Bloch and the Search for a Supraethnic Austrian Identity, 1848–1918* (New York, NY, 2003); and Amy Ng, *Nationalism and Political Liberty: Redlich, Namier and the Crisis of Empire* (Oxford, 2004). R. Robertson and E. Timms, eds., *The Habsburg Legacy: National Identity in Historical Perspective*, *AS* 5 (Edinburgh, 1994) also has relevant contributions, as does J. Feichtinger and G. B. Cohen, eds. *Understanding Multiculturalism: The Habsburg Central European Experience* (Oxford, 2014). Gerald Stieg, *Sein oder Schein: die Österreich-Idee von Maria Theresia bis zum Anschluss* (Vienna, 2016) offers a leading Austrian literary scholar's critique of the concept of the Austrian idea.

Aviel Roshwald, *Ethnic Nationalism and the Fall of Empires: Central Europe, the Middle East and Russia, 1914–23* (Abingdon, 2000) points to why the Monarchy's passing came to be so regretted. Solomon Wank, 'Desperate Counsel in Vienna in July 1914: Berthold Molden's Unpublished Memorandum', *CEH* 26, 3 (1993), pp. 281 310, points to why, in all likelihood, it could not have survived.

Index